Web-Safe Colors

A 24-bit, true color monitor can display more than 16 million colors. A 16-bit monitor can display more than 65,000 colors. Older 8-bit monitors can display only 256 colors, 216 of which are considered Web-safe. To display additional colors, the monitor must mix or dither colors, which can lead to unexpected results. When coloring text or backgrounds, consider using these 216 Web-safe colors.

#000000	#339900	#990000	#CC9900
#000033	#339933	#990033	#CC9933
#000066	#339966	#990066	#CC9966
#000099	#339999	#990099	#CC9999
#0000CC	#3399CC	#9900CC	#CC99CC
#0000FF	#3399FF	#9900FF	#CC99FF
#003300	#33CC00	#993300	#CCCC00
#003333	#33CC33	#993333	#CCCC33
#003366	#33CC66	#993366	#CCCC66
#003399	#33CC99	#993399	#CCCC99
#0033CC	#33CCCC	#9933CC	#CCCCCC
#0033FF	#33CCFF	#9933FF	#CCCCFF
#006600	#33FF00	#996600	#CCFF00
#006633	#33FF33	#996633	#CCFF33
#006666	#33FF66	#996666	#CCFF66
#006699	#33FF99	#996699	#CCFF99
#0066CC	#33FFCC	#9966CC	#CCFFCC
#0066FF	#33FFFF	#9966FF	#CCFFFF
#009900	#660000	#999900	#FF0000
#009933	#660033	#999933	#FF0033
#009966	#660066	#999966	#FF0066
#009999	#660099	#999999	#FF0099
#0099CC	#6600CC	#9999CC	#FF00CC
#0099FF	#6600FF	#9999FF	#FF00FF
#00CC00	#663300	#99CC00	#FF3300
#00CC33	#663333	#99CC33	#FF3333
#00CC66	#663366	#99CC66	#FF3366
#00CC99	#663399	#99CC99	#FF3399
#00CCCC	#6633CC	#99CCCC	#FF33CC
#00CCFF	#6633FF	#99CCFF	#FF33FF
#00FF00	#666600	#99FF00	#FF6600
#00FF33	#666633	#99FF33	#FF6633
#00FF66	#666666	#99FF66	#FF6666
#00FF99	#666699	#99FF99	#FF6699
#00FFCC	#6666CC	#99FFCC	#FF66CC
#00FFFF	#6666FF	#99FFFF	#FF66FF
#330000	#669900	#CC0000	#FF9900
#330033	#669933	#CC0033	#FF9933
#330066	#669966	#CC0066	#FF9966
#330099	#669999	#CC0099	#FF9999
#3300CC	#6699CC	#CC00CC	#FF99CC
#3300FF	#6699FF	#CC00FF	#FF99FF
#333300	#66CC00	#CC3300	#FFCC00
#333333	#66CC33	#CC3333	#FFCC33
#333366	#66CC66	#CC3366	#FFCC66
#333399	#66CC99	#CC3399	#FFCC99
#3333CC	#66CCCC	#CC33CC	#FFCCCC
#3333FF	#66CCFF	#CC33FF	#FFCCFF
#336600	#66FF00	#CC6600	#FFFF00
#336633	#66FF33	#CC6633	#FFFF33
#336666	#66FF66	#CC6666	#FFFF66
#336699	#66FF99	#CC6699	#FFFF99
#3366CC	#66FFCC	#CC66CC	#FFFFCC
#3366FF	#66FFFF	#CC66FF	#FFFFFF

P9-DDR-490

HTML Tags Reference

Basic HTML Tags

Tag/Attribute	Description
\<a\>	Defines an anchor, which usually converts text or an image into a link or marks a location in a document that points to another link
href	Specifies the URL of the page to which the link connects
\<b\>	Bolds text
\<body\>	Identifies the main content of a Web page
\<br\>	Starts a new line
\<h1\> to **\<h6\>**	Creates headings in different font sizes and styles, usually bold
\<head\>	Identifies heading information for a Web page
\<hr\>	Inserts a horizontal rule
\<html\>	Identifies the beginning of an HTML document
\</html\>	Identifies the end of an HTML document
\<i\>	Italicizes text
\<img\>	Inserts an image
href	Specifies the location of the image file
\<object\>	Inserts an embedded object, such as an audio or video clip
\<p\>	Identifies a paragraph
\<style\>	Defines a style
\<title\>	Creates a title in the Web browser title bar for a Web page

Lists

Tag/Attribute	Description
\<dd\>	Identifies a definition in a list
\<dl\>	Creates a list of terms with definitions
\<dt\>	Identifies a term in a list
\<li\>	Identifies an item in an ordered or unordered list
\<ol\>	Creates an ordered list
\<ul\>	Creates an unordered list

Tables

Tag/Attribute	Description
\<table\>	Creates a table
border	Adds a border to a table
cellpadding	Changes the amount of space around the contents of cells
cellspacing	Changes the amount of space between cells
\<td\>	Creates a data cell in a table
colspan	Combines two or more data cells across columns
rowspan	Combines two or more cells down rows
\<th\>	Creates a table header cell, which usually displays bold text
\<tr\>	Creates a row in a table

Teach Yourself VISUALLY™

HTML, 2nd Edition

Visual™

Sherry Willard Kinkoph

WILEY

Wiley Publishing, Inc.

Teach Yourself VISUALLY™ HTML, 2nd Edition

Published by
Wiley Publishing, Inc.
111 River Street
Hoboken, NJ 07030-5774

Published simultaneously in Canada

Copyright © 2005 by Wiley Publishing, Inc., Indianapolis, Indiana

No part of this publication may be reproduced, stored in a retrieval system or transmitted in any form or by any means, electronic, mechanical, photocopying, recording, scanning or otherwise, except as permitted under Sections 107 or 108 of the 1976 United States Copyright Act, without either the prior written permission of the Publisher, or authorization through payment of the appropriate per-copy fee to the Copyright Clearance Center, 222 Rosewood Drive, Danvers, MA 01923, (978) 750-8400, fax (978) 646-8600. Requests to the Publisher for permission should be addressed to the Legal Department, Wiley Publishing, Inc., 10475 Crosspoint Blvd., Indianapolis, IN 46256, (317) 572-3447, fax (317) 572-4355, online: www.wiley.com/go/permisssions.

Library of Congress Control Number: 2005923204

ISBN-13: 978-0-7645-7984-4
ISBN-10: 0-7645-7984-3

Manufactured in the United States of America

10 9 8 7 6 5 4 3 2

Trademark Acknowledgments

Wiley, the Wiley Publishing logo, Visual, the Visual logo, Teach Yourself VISUALLY, Read Less - Learn More and related trade dress are trademarks or registered trademarks of John Wiley & Sons, Inc. and/or its affiliates. All other trademarks are the property of their respective owners. Wiley Publishing, Inc. is not associated with any product or vendor mentioned in this book.

Contact Us

For general information on our other products and services please contact our Customer Care Department within the U.S. at 800-762-2974, outside the U.S. at 317-572-3993 or fax 317-572-4002.

For technical support please visit www.wiley.com/techsupport.

LIMIT OF LIABILITY/DISCLAIMER OF WARRANTY: THE PUBLISHER AND THE AUTHOR MAKE NO REPRESENTATIONS OR WARRANTIES WITH RESPECT TO THE ACCURACY OR COMPLETENESS OF THE CONTENTS OF THIS WORK AND SPECIFICALLY DISCLAIM ALL WARRANTIES, INCLUDING WITHOUT LIMITATION WARRANTIES OF FITNESS FOR A PARTICULAR PURPOSE. NO WARRANTY MAY BE CREATED OR EXTENDED BY SALES OR PROMOTIONAL MATERIALS. THE ADVICE AND STRATEGIES CONTAINED HEREIN MAY NOT BE SUITABLE FOR EVERY SITUATION. THIS WORK IS SOLD WITH THE UNDERSTANDING THAT THE PUBLISHER IS NOT ENGAGED IN RENDERING LEGAL, ACCOUNTING, OR OTHER PROFESSIONAL SERVICES. IF PROFESSIONAL ASSISTANCE IS REQUIRED, THE SERVICES OF A COMPETENT PROFESSIONAL PERSON SHOULD BE SOUGHT. NEITHER THE PUBLISHER NOR THE AUTHOR SHALL BE LIABLE FOR DAMAGES ARISING HEREFROM. THE FACT THAT AN ORGANIZATION OR WEBSITE IS REFERRED TO IN THIS WORK AS A CITATION AND/OR A POTENTIAL SOURCE OF FURTHER INFORMATION DOES NOT MEAN THAT THE AUTHOR OR THE PUBLISHER ENDORSES THE INFORMATION THE ORGANIZATION OR WEBSITE MAY PROVIDE OR RECOMMENDATIONS IT MAY MAKE. FURTHER, READERS SHOULD BE AWARE THAT INTERNET WEBSITES LISTED IN THIS WORK MAY HAVE CHANGED OR DISAPPEARED BETWEEN WHEN THIS WORK WAS WRITTEN AND WHEN IT IS READ.

FOR PURPOSES OF ILLUSTRATING THE CONCEPTS AND TECHNIQUES DESCRIBED IN THIS BOOK, THE AUTHOR HAS CREATED VARIOUS NAMES, COMPANY NAMES, MAILING, E-MAIL AND INTERNET ADDRESSES, PHONE AND FAX NUMBERS AND SIMILAR INFORMATION, ALL OF WHICH ARE FICTITIOUS. ANY RESEMBLANCE OF THESE FICTITIOUS NAMES, ADDRESSES, PHONE AND FAX NUMBERS AND SIMILAR INFORMATION TO ANY ACTUAL PERSON, COMPANY AND/OR ORGANIZATION IS UNINTENTIONAL AND PURELY COINCIDENTAL.

WILEY

Wiley Publishing, Inc.

Sales
Contact Wiley at (800) 762-2974 or fax (317) 572-4002.

Praise for Visual Books

"Like a lot of other people, I understand things best when I see them visually. Your books really make learning easy and life more fun."

John T. Frey (Cadillac, MI)

"I have quite a few of your Visual books and have been very pleased with all of them. I love the way the lessons are presented!"

Mary Jane Newman (Yorba Linda, CA)

"I just purchased my third Visual book (my first two are dog-eared now!), and, once again, your product has surpassed my expectations.

Tracey Moore (Memphis, TN)

"I am an avid fan of your Visual books. If I need to learn anything, I just buy one of your books and learn the topic in no time. Wonders! I have even trained my friends to give me Visual books as gifts."

Illona Bergstrom (Aventura, FL)

"Thank you for making it so clear. I appreciate it. I will buy many more Visual books."

J.P. Sangdong (North York, Ontario, Canada)

"I have several books from the Visual series and have always found them to be valuable resources."

Stephen P. Miller (Ballston Spa, NY)

"Thank you for the wonderful books you produce. It wasn't until I was an adult that I discovered how I learn – visually. Nothing compares to Visual books. I love the simple layout. I can just grab a book and use it at my computer, lesson by lesson. And I understand the material! You really know the way I think and learn. Thanks so much!"

Stacey Han (Avondale, AZ)

"I absolutely admire your company's work. Your books are terrific. The format is perfect, especially for visual learners like me. Keep them coming!"

Frederick A. Taylor, Jr. (New Port Richey, FL)

"I have several of your Visual books and they are the best I have ever used."

Stanley Clark (Crawfordville, FL)

"I bought my first Teach Yourself VISUALLY book last month. Wow. Now I want to learn everything in this easy format!"

Tom Vial (New York, NY)

"Thank you, thank you, thank you...for making it so easy for me to break into this high-tech world. I now own four of your books. I recommend them to anyone who is a beginner like myself."

Gay O'Donnell (Calgary, Alberta, Canada)

"I write to extend my thanks and appreciation for your books. They are clear, easy to follow, and straight to the point. Keep up the good work! I bought several of your books and they are just right! No regrets! I will always buy your books because they are the best."

Seward Kollie (Dakar, Senegal)

"Compliments to the chef!! Your books are extraordinary! Or, simply put, extra-ordinary, meaning way above the rest! THANKYOU THANKYOU THANKYOU! I buy them for friends, family, and colleagues."

Christine J. Manfrin (Castle Rock, CO)

"What fantastic teaching books you have produced! Congratulations to you and your staff. You deserve the Nobel Prize in Education in the Software category. Thanks for helping me understand computers."

Bruno Tonon (Melbourne, Australia)

"Over time, I have bought a number of your 'Read Less - Learn More' books. For me, they are THE way to learn anything easily. I learn easiest using your method of teaching."

José A. Mazón (Cuba, NY)

"I am an avid purchaser and reader of the Visual series, and they are the greatest computer books I've seen. The Visual books are perfect for people like myself who enjoy the computer, but want to know how to use it more efficiently. Your books have definitely given me a greater understanding of my computer, and have taught me to use it more effectively. Thank you very much for the hard work, effort, and dedication that you put into this series."

Alex Diaz (Las Vegas, NV)

Credits

Project Editors
Tim Borek
Maureen Spears

Acquisitions Editor
Jody Lefevere

Product Development Manager
Lindsay Sandman

Copy Editor
Nancy Rappaport

Technical Editor
Allen Wyatt

Editorial Manager
Robyn Siesky

Manufacturing
Allan Conley
Linda Cook
Paul Gilchrist
Jennifer Guynn

Illustrators
Steve Amory
Matt Bell
Ronda David-Burroughs
Cheryl Grubbs
Jake Mansfield
Rita Marley
Tyler Roloff

Book Design
Kathie Rickard

Production Coordinator
Maridee Ennis

Layout
Jennifer Heleine
LeAndra Hosier
Amanda Spagnuolo

Screen Artist
Jill A. Proll

Proofreader
Vicki Broyles

Quality Control
Laura Albert

Indexer
Joan Griffitts

Special Help
Kim Heusel
Adrienne Porter
Scott Tullis

Vice President and Executive Group Publisher
Richard Swadley

Vice President and Publisher
Barry Pruett

Composition Director
Debbie Stailey

About the Author

Sherry Willard Kinkoph has written and edited over 60 books over the past 10 years covering a variety of computer topics ranging from hardware to software, from Microsoft Office programs to the Internet. Her recent titles include *Master VISUALLY Dreamwever MX and Flash MX*, *Teach Yourself VISUALLY Restortation and Retouching with Photoshop Elements 2.0*, and *Top 100 Simplified Tips and Tricks Office 2003*. Sherry's ongoing quest is to help users of all levels master the ever-changing computer technologies. No matter how many times they — the software manufacturers and hardware conglomerates — throw out a new version or upgrade, Sherry vows to be there to make sense of it all and help computer users get the most out of their machines.

Author's Acknowledgments

Special thanks go out to publisher Barry Pruett and to acquisitions editor Jody Lefevere, for allowing me to tackle this project; to project editors Tim Borek and Maureen Spears, for their dedication and guidance in guiding this project from start to finish; to copy editor Nancy Rappaport, for ensuring that all the I's were dotted and t's were crossed; to technical editor Allen Wyatt, for skillfully checking each step and offering valuable input along the way; and finally, very special thanks to the entire production team at Wiley, for all of their efforts in producing such a visual learning guide.

Table of Contents

 **chapter 1   HTML and Web Page Basics**

Internet Basics 4

An Introduction to HTML 6

Explore Web Browsers 8

Explore HTML Editors 9

Understanding HTML Syntax and Rules 10

View HTML Code in a Browser 12

Plan a Web Site 14

 **chapter 2   Creating Your First HTML Page**

Understanding HTML Document Structure 18

Start an HTML Document 20

Save an HTML Document 24

View an HTML Page 26

Add a Document Declaration 28

Add Metadata 30

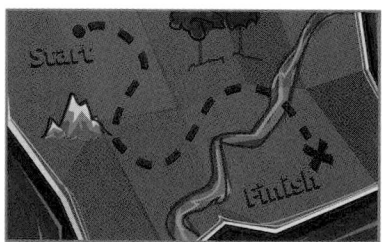

 **chapter 3   Adding Text**

Create a New Paragraph 34

Change Paragraph Alignment 35

Add a Line Break 36

Insert a Blank Space 37

Insert Preformatted Text 38

Insert a Heading 39

Add Block Quotes 40

Insert a Comment 41

Create a Numbered List 42

Create a Bulleted List 44

Create a Nested List 46

Create a Definition List 47

Insert Special Characters 48

Special Characters 49

chapter 4   **Formatting Text**

Make Text Bold 52

Italicize Text 53

Add Underlining to Text 54

Change Fonts 55

Change Font Size 56

Change the Text Color 58

Adjust Margins 60

Set a Page Background Color 61

Add a Horizontal Line 62

chapter 5   **Creating Style Sheets**

Understanding Style Sheets 66

Create an External Style Sheet 68

Link to a Style Sheet 70

Add Comments to a Style Sheet 71

Create an Internal Style Sheet 72

Create a Class 74

Apply a Style with the DIV Tag 76

Apply a Style Locally 78

Apply a Style Using the ID Attribute 79

Table of Contents

chapter 6   Formatting Text with Style Sheets

Add Bold to Text 82

Italicize Text 83

Indent Text 84

Change the Font Size 85

Change the Font 86

Change the Text Case 88

Change Text Alignment 89

Control Line Spacing 90

Control Letter Spacing 91

Set Margins 92

Add Padding 93

Add Color to Text 94

Change the Text Background Color 95

Add a Border 96

Control Element Position 98

Wrap Text around Elements 100

Change Vertical Alignment 101

Set Width and Height for an Element 102

Add a Background Color to an Element 103

Add a Background Image to an Element 104

Change Link Colors 106

Change Bullet or Number Styles 108

chapter 7   Adding Images

Understanding Web Page Images 112

Prepare Your Images for the Web 114

Insert an Image 116

Specify an Image Size 118
Add Alternative Text 120
Create an Image Label 121
Add Copyright Text to Images 122
Align an Image Horizontally 123
Align an Image Vertically 124
Center an Image 125
Wrap Text between Images 126
Stop Text Wrap 127
Set an Image Border 128
Add Space around an Image 129
Add a Background Image 130
Create an Image Banner 131

chapter 8 Adding Links

Understanding Links 134
Understanding URLs 136
Insert a Link to Another Page 138
Insert a Link to a New Window 140
Insert a Link to an Area on the Same Page 142
Link to Another File Type 144
Link to an E-mail Address 146
Change Link Colors 148

chapter 9 Working with Tables

Understanding Table Structure 152
Add a Table 154
Assign a Table Border 156

Table of Contents

Adjust Cell Padding and Spacing 158

Adjust Cell Width and Height 160

Add Column Labels 162

Create Newspaper-Style Columns 163

Add a Table Header 164

Add a Table Caption 165

Control Which Borders to Display 166

Adjust the Table Size 168

Change Cell Alignment 170

Span Cells across Columns and Rows 172

Create Column and Row Groups 174

Add Background Color to Cells 178

Add a Background Color to a Table 179

Insert an Image in a Cell 180

Insert a Table Background Image 181

Change Table Alignment 182

Control Text Wrapping in Cells 184

Nest a Table within a Table 185

chapter 10 Working with Frames

Understanding Frames 188

Create Frames 190

Customize Frame Borders 192

Control Frame Margins 194

Add Alternative Text 195

Prevent Frame Resizing 196

Hide or Display Frame Scroll Bars 197

Target a Link 198

Create a Nesting Frameset 200

Create an Inline Frame 201

chapter 11 Creating Forms

Understanding Forms 204

Types of Form Elements 206

Gather Form Data 208

Create a Form 210

Send Form Data to an E-mail Address 211

Add a Text Box 212

Add a Large Text Area 214

Add Check Boxes 216

Add Radio Buttons 218

Add a Menu List 220

Add a Submit Button 222

Add a Reset Button 223

Add Active Labels 224

Change the Tab Order 225

Add a File Upload Element 226

Group Form Elements 228

chapter 12 Adding Sounds and Videos

Understanding Multimedia Elements 232

Understanding Plug-ins and Players 234

Link to Audio or Video Files 236

Embed an Audio File 238

Embed a Video File 240

Embed a Flash Movie 242

Set Up Background Audio 243

Table of Contents

chapter 13   Working with JavaScript

Understanding JavaScript 246

Understanding Script Events and Handlers 248

Add JavaScript to a Web Page 250

Create a JavaScript File 251

Hide JavaScript 252

Add Alternative Text 253

Insert the Current Date and Time 254

Display an Alert Message Box 255

Display a Pop-Up Window 256

Customize the Status Bar Message for a Link 257

Create an Image Rollover Effect 258

Validate Form Data 260

chapter 14   Adding Extra Touches

Insert Text over an Image 264

Add ToolTips to Web Page Elements 266

Add a Java Applet 267

Add a Scrolling Marquee 268

Create an Image Map 270

Create Thumbnail Images 274

Automatically Load Another Web Page 276

chapter 15 Publishing Your Web Pages

Understanding Web Page Publishing 280
Transfer Files to a Web Server with WS_FTP 284
Troubleshoot Your Web Pages 288
Promote Your Web Site 290

Appendix HTML Tags

Basic Tags/Attributes 292
Text Formatting Tags/Attributes 292
List Tags/Attributes 293
Table Tags/Attributes 294
Image Tags/Attributes 295
Links Tags/Attributes 296
Image Map Tags/Attributes 296
Multimedia Tags/Attributes 296
Java and JavaScript Tags/Attributes 297
Frame Tags/Attributes 298
Form Tags/Attributes 298
Style Sheet Tags/Attributes 299
Style Sheet Characteristics 300
Style Sheet Syntax 301
Sixteen Named Colors 301

CHAPTER 1

HTML and Web Page Basics

Are you interested in building your own Web pages? This chapter introduces you to basic HTML concepts and methods for creating your own Web content.

Internet Basics 4

An Introduction to HTML 6

Explore Web Browsers 8

Explore HTML Editors 9

Understanding HTML Syntax and Rules 10

View HTML Code in a Browser 12

Plan a Web Site 14

Internet Basics

The Internet has grown from a military research project in the late 1960s to a global network of computers today. The number of Internet users around the globe is expected to reach over 1 billion by the year 2005.

Offering everything from e-mail to information to commerce, the Internet brings users an unprecedented way to communicate and exchange data. Constructed of thousands of networks and computers around the world, the Internet connects organizations, governments, businesses, and individuals.

Types of Connections

Users connect to the Internet through a variety of sources. Individuals can connect through a modem and a phone line, cable, or satellite. If you use a modem to connect to the Internet, you typically utilize an *Internet service provider*, also called an ISP, or a commercial service, such as America Online. You can also use cable TV companies to connect to the Internet through a cable modem, or you can connect through digital phone lines, such as ISDN (Integrated Services Digital Network) and DSL (Digital Subscriber Line).

Connection Speeds

Connection speeds play an important part in a user's Internet experience. Slower connections result in slower file transfers and Web page viewing. Modem connections offer the slowest connection speeds to the Internet, up to 56 Kbps (Kilobits per second), followed by ISDN connections at 64–128 Kbps. Cable modems can achieve connection speeds up to 1.5 Mbps, while DSL offers speeds of 1,000–9,000 Kbps.

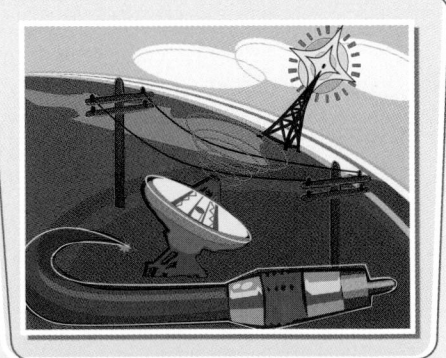

TCP/IP

Internet connection relies on a collection of protocols that govern how computers and networks talk to each other. *Transmission Control Protocol/Internet Protocol*, or TCP/IP for short, is simply a set of rules that control how information flows between computers and allows for individual computers to communicate with the Internet as if they are directly connected.

URLS and Links

Every page on the Web has a unique address, called a *URL*, short for Uniform Resource Locator. If you know a page's URL, you can view it over the Internet. You can also view pages using links. Hyperlinks, or *links*, connect pages through embedded URLs presented as text or images on a page. Users can jump from one page to another by clicking links. The activity of viewing Web pages is casually called *Web surfing*.

The World Wide Web

The World Wide Web is a giant collection of documents, or pages, stored on computers around the globe. Commonly called *the Web*, this collection of pages houses a wealth of text, images, audio, video, and more. Web pages are stored on *servers*, which are computers designed for holding and transferring data. When you place a document on a server, it is accessible for other users to view. Typically, companies, government agencies, organizations, and individuals maintain Web pages.

Browsers

To view Web pages, you must use a *Web browser*. Browsers are specialized programs that retrieve Web pages from servers and display them on a user's computer. Microsoft Internet Explorer and Netscape Navigator are the two most popular browsers used today. Other browsers are available, including Apple's *Safari*, Mozilla's *Firefox*, and Opera. Each program has evolved through a myriad of versions, each improving over the last. As you write HTML code, just remember that not all users have the most recent version of a particular browser.

Web pages are built using HTML, short for *HyperText Markup Language*. HTML documents are comprised of text and coding that instruct a Web browser how to display the data. HTML documents are identified by their .html or .htm file extension. Because any Web browser can read an HTML document, you do not need a special platform, such as Windows, UNIX, or Mac, to view the information.

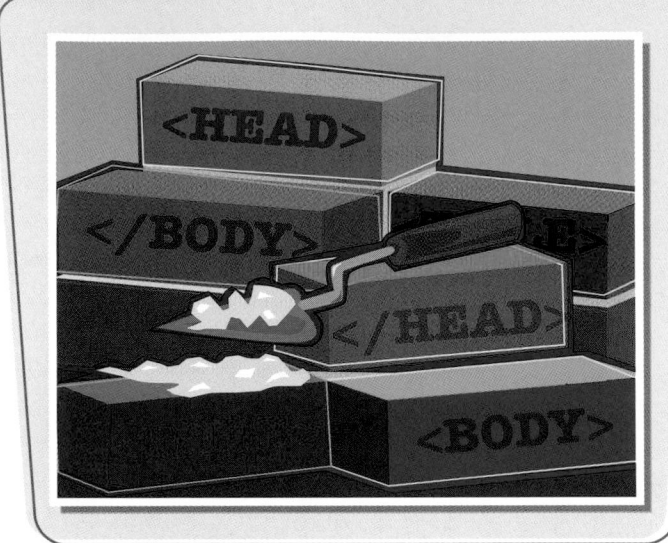

HTML Coding

HTML coding consists of tags. Tags are individual instructions to the browser and are surrounded by brackets, < >. Many tags include an opening tag and a closing tag. When writing tags, you can use upper- or lowercase letters. To make the coding easy to read, most users type it in uppercase to distinguish the coding from regular text data on the page. Tags can also include attributes you can define, such as color values or measurements.

HTML Standards

The World Wide Web Consortium, or W3C for short, sets HTML standards. This international group consists of the Web's founders and industry leaders, including companies such as Microsoft and Netscape. Web developers look to the W3C to establish standards and introduce new Web technologies. The W3C is responsible for maintaining and guiding HTML standards.

HTML Versions

The most recent version of HTML is version 4. Version 4 allows for separate formatting instructions, called cascading style sheets (CSS) and other presentation controls. By moving all the formatting controls to style sheets, HTML 4 frees up the Web developer to assign formatting to not only paragraphs of text, but also to the entire page or every page on the Web site. Moving formatting to a separate style sheet makes it easier to maintain other coding on the HTML document.

XHTML

Although XHTML is technically an XML application, it closely copies much of HTML 4 — so much so, that many view XHTML as a stricter version of HTML. With XHTML, you cannot leave off tags, and the order of tags is strictly enforced. Tags are closed in the reverse order in which they were opened. You must also write XHTML coding in lowercase letters, and all attributes must be enclosed in quotes. These are just a few examples of code-writing details users must follow to create XHTML documents.

HTML Evolution

Seeing a need for additional structure for HTML documents, the W3C next introduced XML (*Extensible Markup Language*). XML is a meta-markup language for creating other languages; however, it is not as lenient as HTML, so the W3C rewrote HTML in XML and called it XHTML. XHTML has all the features of HTML but gains XML's power and flexibility.

HTML versus XHTML

Version 4 is the last version of HTML the W3C will introduce. The future of Web page development lies in XHTML. However, billions of Web pages are already written in HTML, and browser support is more common for HTML, so HTML documents are not likely go away for quite some time. If you learn HTML, the transition to XHTML is an easy one, requiring only a dedication to detail when writing well-formed code.

Web browsers are designed to read HTML instructions and display the content on your screen. You can use a browser to display HTML files you save on your computer, called *local pages*, or HTML pages transferred through a Web server. You can also use a browser to test your HTML pages.

Browser Discrepancies

There are many different Web browsers around today, and numerous versions of each. Each browser interprets HTML code in its own way, which means Web pages do not always appear the same from one browser to another. HTML standardization helps alleviate some of the discrepancies, but not all. For this reason, you need to write clean, well-formed HTML code and be sure to test your pages in different browsers to see the varying results.

Finding Browsers

Microsoft Internet Explorer (www.microsoft.com/ie) and Netscape Navigator (www.netscape.com) are the two most popular browsers available today. You should also test your pages in a few of the lesser-known browsers, such as Opera (www.opera.com) and Amaya (www.w3.org/Amaya/). For a complete list of browsers, visit http://dir.yahoo.com/Computers_and_Internet/Software/Internet/World_Wide_Web/Browsers.

In the early days of Web development, plain old text editors were the application of choice. Today, you can use a variety of programs to write your HTML code.

Simple Text Editors

Simple text editors, also called plain-text editors, are easy to find. Most computers come with one, such as Windows Notepad. You can also find shareware and freeware versions on the Internet, such as TextPad, EditPad Lite, and UltraEdit. Simple text editors offer no-frills word processing and are often the best choice for writing HTML code.

Word Processing Programs

You can also use word processing programs, such as Microsoft Word, to write HTML. Use caution, however, because commercial word processors can store extraneous information with your files, some of which interferes with HTML.

HTML Editors

HTML editors are dedicated programs for writing HTML code. Microsoft FrontPage and Macromedia Dreamweaver are examples of HTML editors. HTML editors can shield you from learning HTML code in detail by offering a graphical environment for building Web pages. However, most also allow you to switch to text-based editing as well.

Understanding HTML Syntax and Rules

The HTML language is a simple language for describing Web page content. HTML rules, called *syntax*, govern the way in which code is written. Learning the right way to write your code can save you confusion and errors later.

Writing HTML

The instructions you write in HTML are called *tags*. Tags are surrounded by angle brackets, < >. You can write tags in upper- or lowercase letters. Many users prefer to write their tags in uppercase to make them easier to identify on the document page. If you create a page in XHTML, a stricter variation of HTML, you need to use lowercase letters for your tags.

Elements

Elements identify the different parts of your HTML document. For example, <BODY> and </BODY> are tags defining the body text element on a page. The browser reads any text between the two tags as part of the body element. Many elements use tag pairs, an opening and closing tag, such as <P> and </P>, while others, such as the Image tag (<IMG>) do not. Closing tags must always include a slash (/).

Attributes and Values

Each element has unique attributes you can assign. Many attributes require that you set a value, such as a measurement or specification. For example, you can set a paragraph's alignment on the page using the ALIGN attribute, and set a value for the alignment by specifying the value as left, right, or center. For example, the code might read:

```
<P ALIGN="center">My paragraph text.</P>
```

Values are always enclosed in quotation marks and appear within the element's start tag.

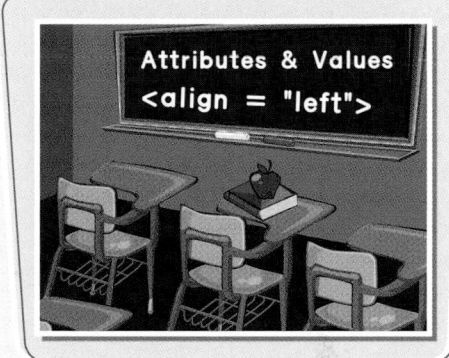

Entities

Any special characters you add to a page, such as a copyright symbol or a fraction, are called *entities*. HTML uses entities to represent characters not readily available on the keyboard. All entities are preceded with an ampersand (&) and ended with a semicolon (;). For example, to add a copyright symbol to your page, the code looks like this:

```
&copy;
```

Avoid Syntax Errors

To avoid HTML errors, always take time to proofread your code. Make sure you have brackets on your tags and that your closing tags include a slash. You must surround any values you define for attributes with quotation marks. It also helps to write your closing tags in reverse order of the opening tags. For example:

```
<P ALIGN="center"><B>My text.</B></P>
```

To help make your HTML readable, consider using new lines to enter code instead of running everything together on one long line. Using white space can also help, without increasing the file size.

View HTML Code in a Browser

You can view the HTML code for any Web page using your browser window. Viewing other Web developers' code is a good way to learn how to write your own code, and it can help you generate new ideas for your own pages. You can also save a Web page to study later.

If you generate HTML code using a program, such as Microsoft FrontPage or Macromedia Dreamweaver, the code can appear overwhelmingly complex.

View HTML Code in a Browser

VIEW THE SOURCE CODE

① Open your browser window to the page you want to view.

② Click **View**.

③ Click **Source** (Internet Explorer) or **Page Source** (Navigator).

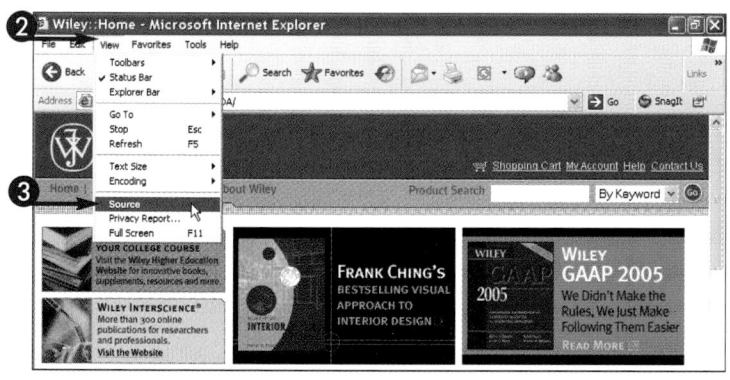

A window appears displaying the HTML source code for the page.

④ Click the **Close** button (⊠) when finished.

The window closes.

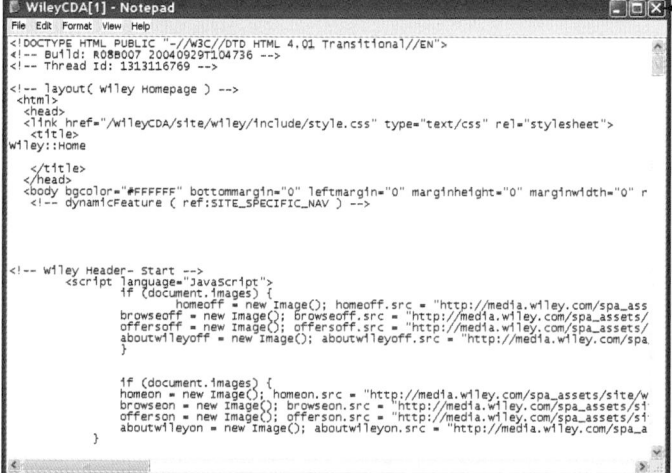

SAVE AN HTML DOCUMENT

1. With the source code window open, click **File**.

2. Click **Save As** (Internet Explorer) or **Save Page As** (Navigator).

The Save As dialog box appears.

3. Navigate to the folder where you want to store the page.

4. Type a name for the page.

5. Click **Save**.

The page is saved.

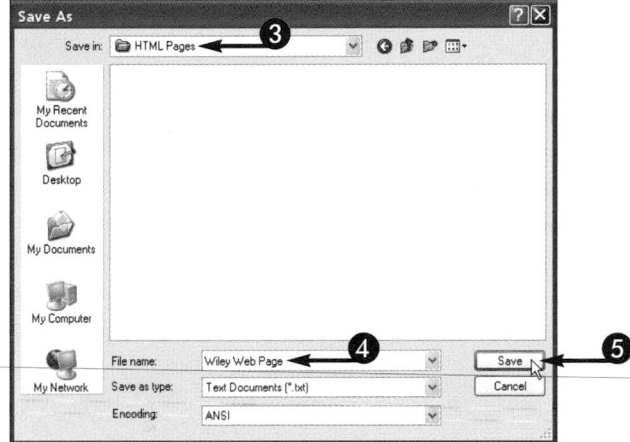

 TIPS

Can I copy the source code from another page?

You can copy HTML code you see on other pages; however, you should always obtain permission to reuse it yourself. Most Web page authors are happy to share their code with others, especially something complex and innovative, but make sure it is okay before attempting to do so.

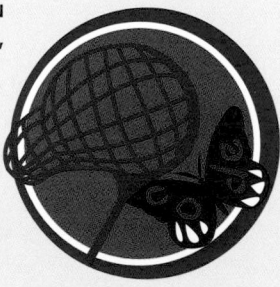

How do I print the HTML code from the viewer window?

You can print the code from the text viewer window by clicking **File** and clicking **Print**. This opens the Print dialog box, where you can choose a printer or click **Print** to print your code. This technique works in both Internet Explorer and Navigator.

Planning is essential for creating a Web site, whether your site consists of one page or many. Start by deciding what your goal is for the site and the type of information you want to convey. Next, gather all the necessary information you need to build your pages, including text, images, multimedia files, and other pertinent data. Choose a text editor in which to write your HTML code and you are ready to begin.

A Home Page

Most Web sites start with a home page, the main page of the site. A home page includes an introduction to the site as well as links to other pages on the site. The home page is usually the first page users see when they visit your Web site, and it often uses index.html or index.htm as the filename.

Design Options

When designing your site, you need to decide how you want your pages organized in terms of flow. For example, do you want the user to start with a home page and progress to each page on the site, or do you want to allow the user to jump to different pages radiating off the home page? Take time to sketch out the flow of your site and how each page is connected, starting with the main page.

Linear

A linear site layout moves the user through your pages in a linear fashion. Linear layouts are good for presenting a series of steps or graduated information. Linear layouts usually link the user to the next or previous page, allowing your visitor to move forward and backward in the site.

Spider Web

A Web layout flows out from the home page much like a spider web. Users can link to different pages without progressing from page to page in a certain order. With a Web layout, pages include links to other pages on the site, which allow the user to move freely from topic to topic.

Hierarchical

A hierarchical layout resembles a pyramid, with the home page at the top and other pages linking out from the top page. Hierarchical layouts are good for introducing brief topics on the top page in the layout and presenting greater topic details in subsequent pages.

Study Other Web Sites

Research can really help you determine how you want your site to flow and help you gather ideas for page design. Visit your favorite Web sites and study how the Web developer lays out the content. Take note of the design details that make some Web sites more user-friendly and appealing than others, and try to emulate those same principles in your own pages.

Creating Your First HTML Page

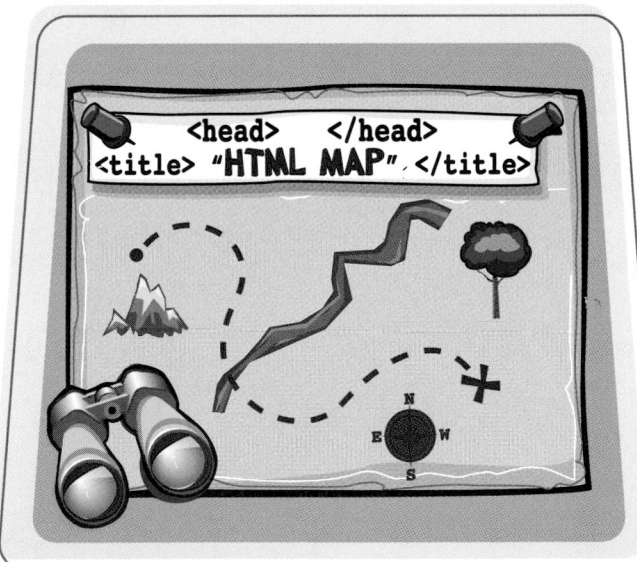

Are you ready to start creating a Web page? This chapter shows you how to get started with a basic HTML document.

Understanding HTML Document Structure....18

Start an HTML Document 20

Save an HTML Document 24

View an HTML Page 26

Add a Document Declaration 28

Add Metadata..30

Understanding HTML Document Structure

All HTML documents are built on key elements that define a page's structure. Although every HTML page differs in content and layout, the underlying structure remains the same. Understanding the basic structure of a document can help you understand how to build and improve your own HTML pages.

HTML Element

The `<HTML>` and `</HTML>` tags are the main tags used to identify an HTML document. When a browser encounters these tags, it knows that anything within the two tags is part of an HTML document. With the latest version of HTML and newer versions of Web browsers, the tags are not always necessary, but adding them is always good form. Older Web browsers expect to see the HTML element tags.

Document Type Declaration

You can add a `DOCTYPE` declaration to specify the version of HTML upon which the page is based. There are three types of HTML you can declare: HTML 4.0 Transitional, HTML 4.0 Strict, and HTML 4.0 Frameset. The transitional version is the most inclusive, incorporating both structural and presentation elements. The strict version is more pared-down and excludes presentation elements. The frameset version is the same as the transitional version but includes all the elements necessary to make frames on a page.

Document Header

You can use the document header to add basic information about your page. The document header tags, <HEAD> and </HEAD>, follow the <HTML> opening tag. You can use the document header to include title information, metadata, and base and script elements. Learn more about scripts in Chapter 13.

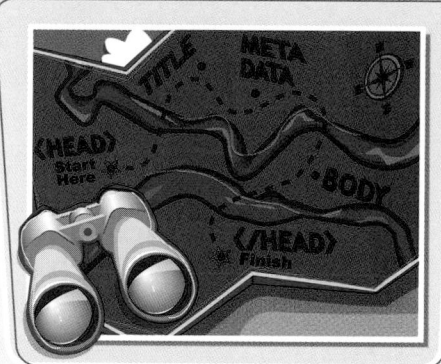

Metadata

Metadata is data that describes the material on your page, such as author information, any programs you used to create the page, a description of the page, and keywords for search engines. You can use the metadata tags to add author and copyright information, too. You can place metadata between your document header tags.

Title

You can add a title to your document header to help others identify your page. For example, if you are building a Web page for a business, your company name is a good page title. Web browsers display the title in the browser window's title bar. You can use the <TITLE> and </TITLE> tags to define a page title. For best results, keep the title brief and to the point.

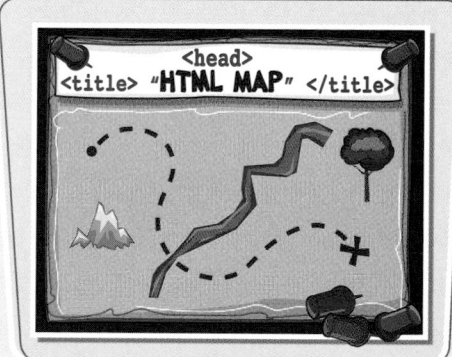

Body

The content of your page, including paragraphs, lists, and images, appears within the body of your HTML document. The body of the document is identified by the <BODY> and </BODY> tags. Anything you place between these tags appears on the document and in the browser window. The body of the document includes blocks of text, headings, lists, tables, and forms. You learn more about working with body text in Chapter 3.

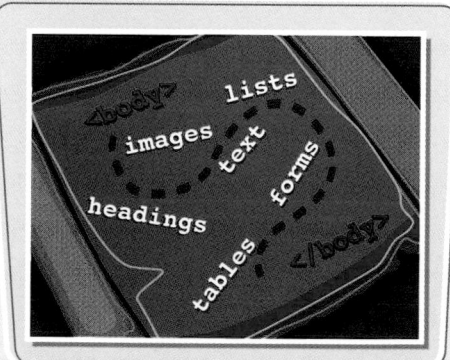

Start an HTML Document

You can start an HTML document using a text editor or word processing program. You can use sets of HTML tags to define the basic structure of your page.

The <HTML>, <HEAD>, and <TITLE> tags are basic to Web pages. The <HEAD> and <TITLE> information does not appear on the Web page itself; however, the text you include between these tags declares the type of document and briefly describes the page. The text you place between these tags appears in the browser window's title bar.

Start an HMTL Document

① Open the text editor or word processing program you want to use.

Note: See Chapter 1 to learn more about text editors.

② Type **<HTML>**.

This tag declares the document is an HTML document.

③ Press **Enter**.

Note: See Chapter 1 to learn more about HTML tag sets.

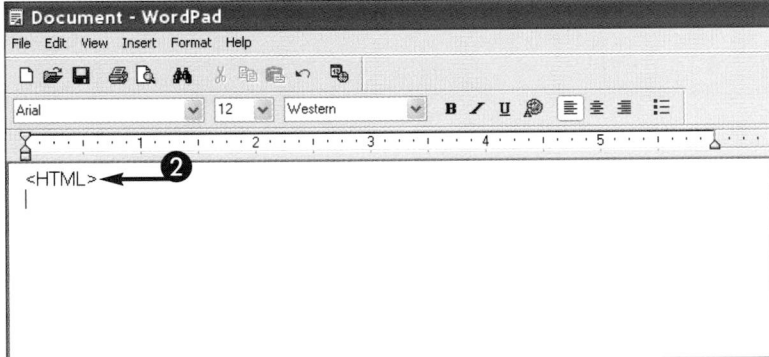

④ Type **<HEAD>**.

This tag starts the information describing the page, including any title text.

⑤ Press **Enter**.

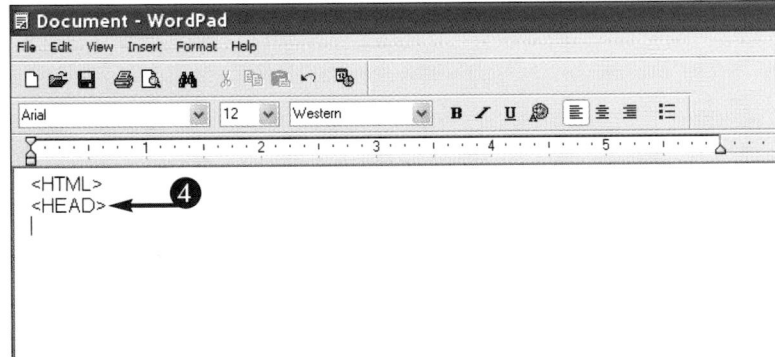

6 Type **<TITLE>**.

7 Type title text for your page.

Title text describes the contents of the page and appears in the title bar of the Web browser.

8 Type **</TITLE>**.

9 Press Enter.

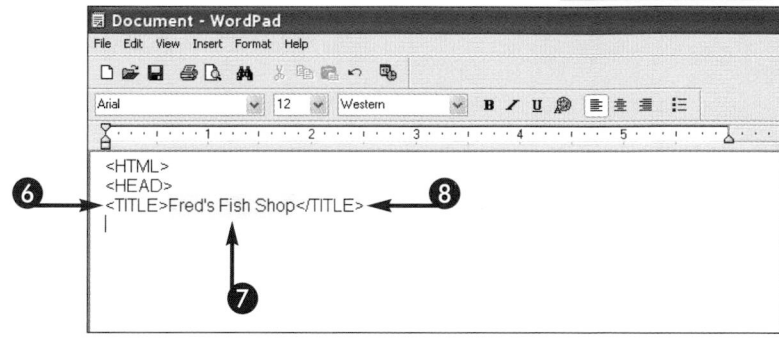

10 Type **</HEAD>**.

This tag completes the document heading information for the page.

11 Press Enter.

Note: You do not need to press Enter each time you start a new tag or add a close tag. However, placing tags on their own lines in the code can help you more easily identify your page structure.

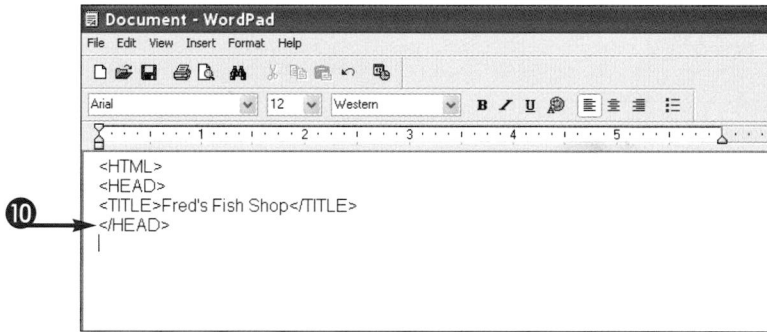

 TIPS

Which is faster – typing the content first and then adding tags, or typing everything as I go?

Either method works fine; however, if you are just getting started, you may want to define your tags first and then add the content. This allows you to easily see the insertion of both start and close tags before you add more text to the document. The more text you type, the more difficult it becomes to locate tag errors later.

Does it matter if I type upper- and lowercase letters or all caps for my tags?

No. However, it helps to be consistent with your tags, particularly if you run across an error later. For example, typing tags in all uppercase letters can make it easier to identify the tags on the page.

continued

Start an HTML Document *(continued)*

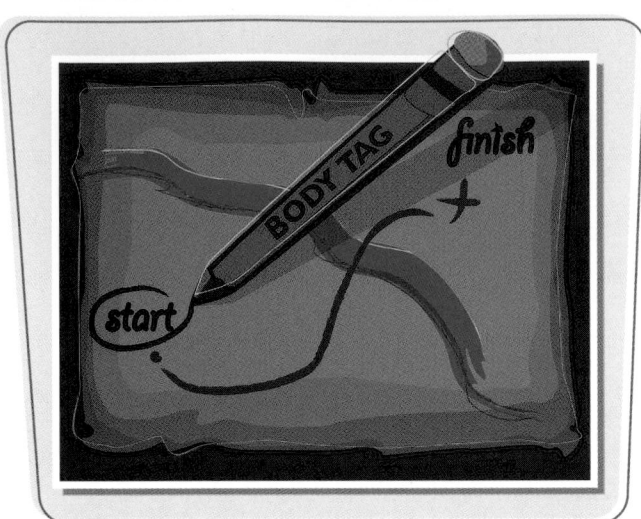

You can use the body tags, `<BODY>` and `</BODY>`, to add content to your page. Page content can include lines of text, paragraphs, bulleted and numbered lists, and more.

Start an HTML Document *(continued)*

⑫ Type **<BODY>**.

This tag starts the actual content of your Web page.

⑬ Press **Enter**.

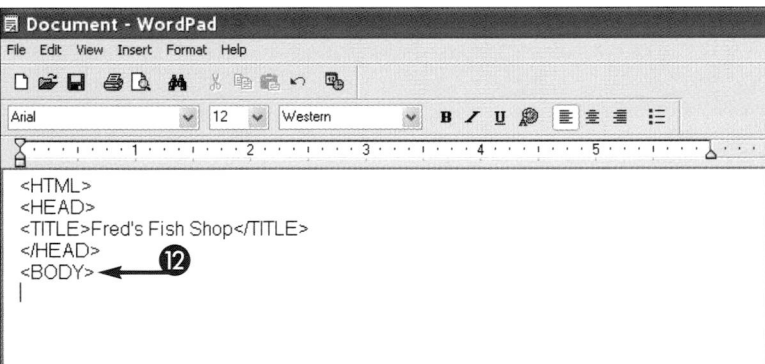

⑭ Type the body text you want to appear on the page.

Body text is the content of your page, including lines of text, paragraphs, lists, and more.

For practice, consider typing a simple paragraph for the body text.

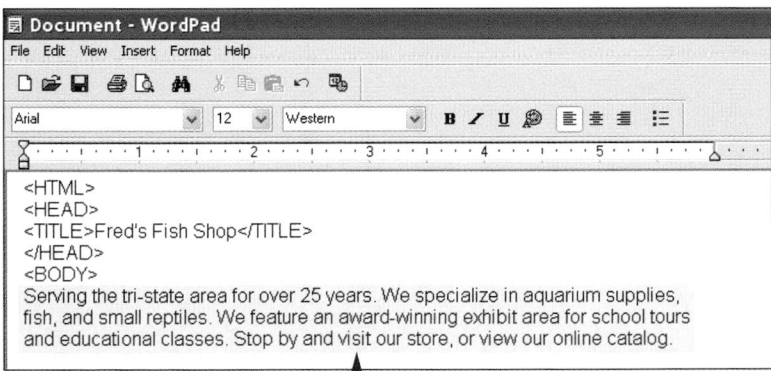

⑮ Press **Enter**.

⑯ Type **</BODY>**.

This tag closes the body portion of the page.

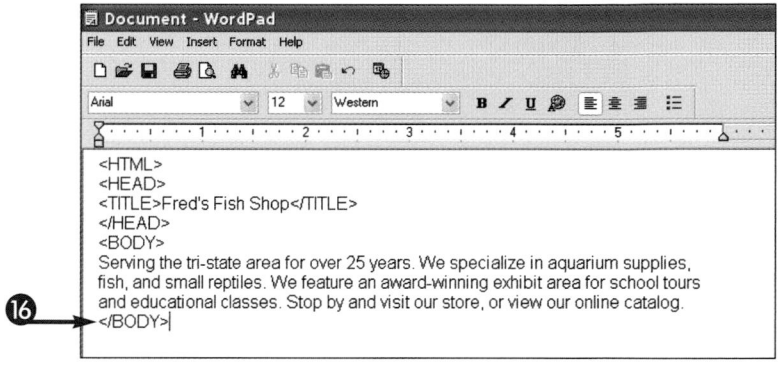

⑰ Press **Enter**.

⑱ Type **</HTML>**.

This tag closes the HTML declaration.

You can now save and view your page in a Web browser.

Note: See the section "Save an HTML Document" to learn how to save a file. See the section "View an HTML Page" to learn how to view the results of your HTML coding.

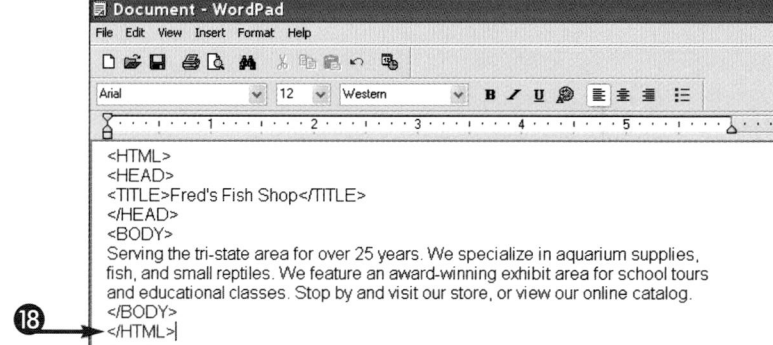

TIP

How do I turn off WordPad's text wrapping?

If the text you type in WordPad scrolls off the screen, the text wrapping feature is turned off. You can turn on the text wrapping feature to keep the text in view at all times.

❶ Click **View**.

❷ Click **Options**.

This opens the Options dialog box.

❸ On the **Text** tab, click the **Wrap to window** option (◯ changes to ◉).

❹ Click **OK**.

Text wrapping is now activated.

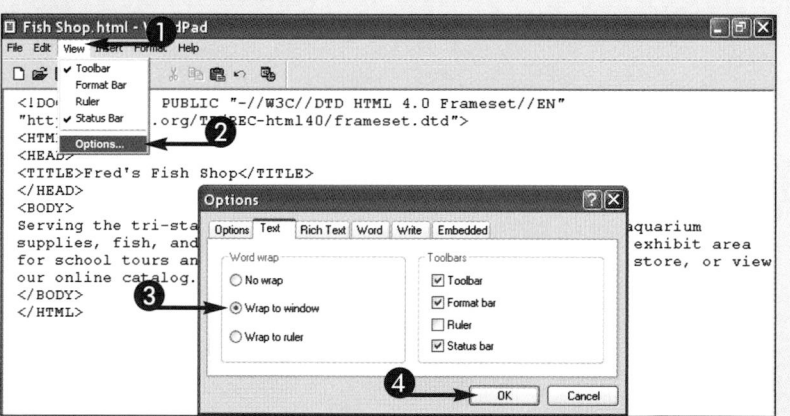

Save an HTML Document

You can save your Web page as an HTML file type so that users can view it in a Web browser. When saving a Web page, you can use the HTML or HTM file extension.

When naming a Web page, do not use spaces, and keep your filenames to letters and numbers. If you are creating a main page for a Web site, it is common to name the page index.html or default.htm.

Save an Html Document

1 Click **File**.

Note: Your text editor may have a different command name for saving files. See your program's documentation for more information.

2 Click **Save**.

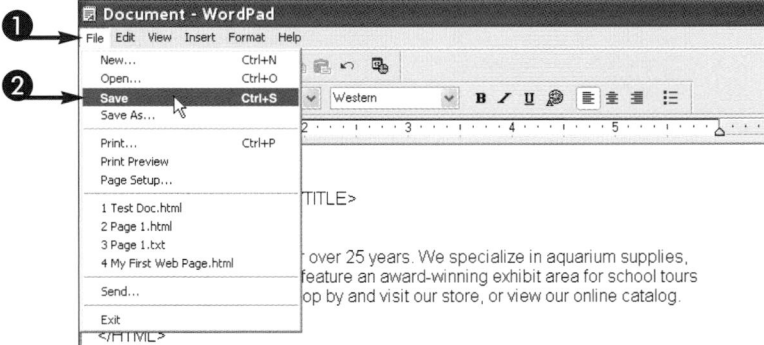

3 Navigate to the folder or drive where you want to store the file.

● You can click here and select a different folder or drive.

4 Click here and select **Text Document**.

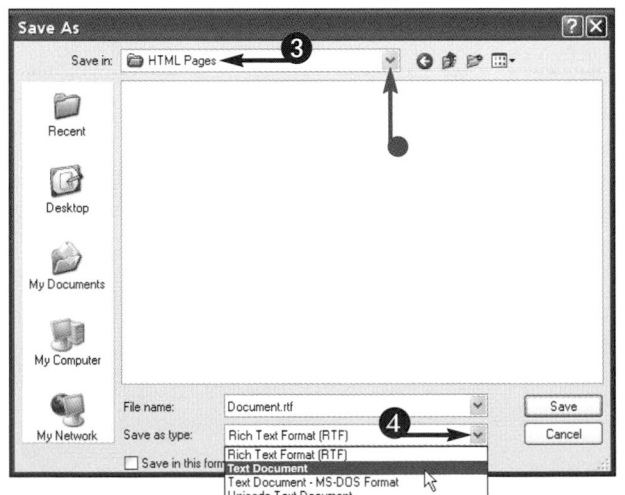

⑤ Type a name for the file, followed by **.html** or **.htm**.

⑥ Click **Save**.

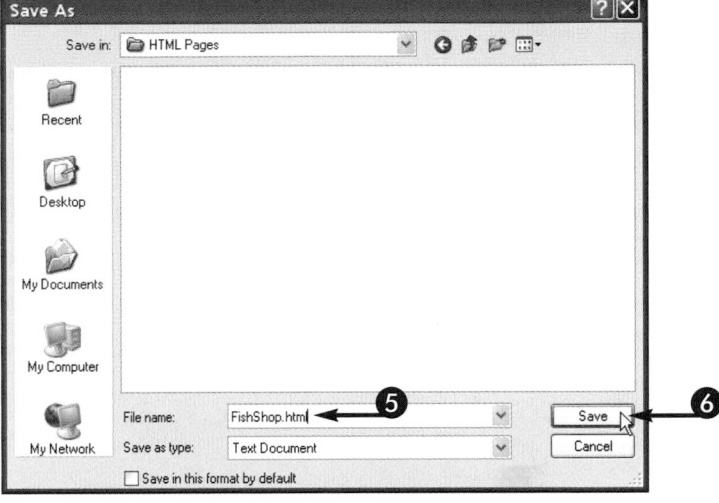

A dialog box may appear prompting you that all the formatting will be removed.

⑦ Click **Yes**.

The file is saved.

TIPS

What is the difference between the .html and .htm suffix?

The shorter suffix, also called a file extension, .htm, is left over from the days of DOS when filenames could utilize only a three-character file extension. Microsoft Windows-based systems still default to the .htm extension. If you use a Microsoft program, such as FrontPage, to create an HTML file, it automatically assigns the .htm extension. Today's computers can handle much longer filenames and extensions, so the three-character limitation is no longer an issue. Web browsers and servers can read either extension; however, for consistency you might want to stick with .html. The .html extension is more universally used with various hosting systems.

What makes a good filename for a Web page?

Any time you name a file, you need to keep the name simple enough so that you can remember it and locate it again later. In addition, because filenames are important when used as hyperlinks and page titles, it is best to utilize a name that makes sense to the type of page you are designing. For example, if you are creating a company Web site, your filenames might use your company name. It is also a good idea to keep your Web page files in one folder and give the folder a name that clearly identifies the content, such as My Web Pages.

View an HTML Page

After you create and save an HTML document, you can view it in your Web browser.

View an Html Page

1 Open your Web browser.

2 Click **File**.

3 Click **Open**.

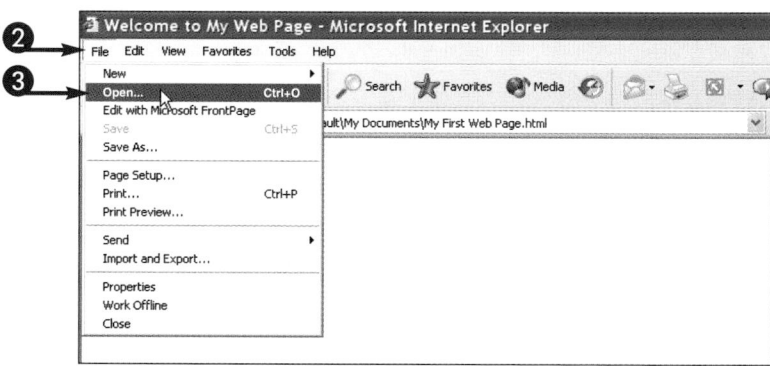

The Open dialog box appears.

4 Click **Browse**.

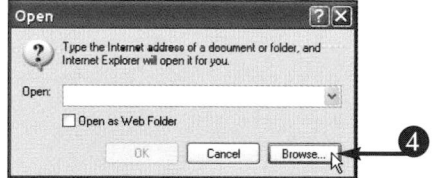

⑤ Navigate to the folder or drive in which your HTML document is stored.

⑥ Click the filename.

⑦ Click **Open**.

● The Open dialog box displays the path and name of the file.

⑧ Click **OK**.

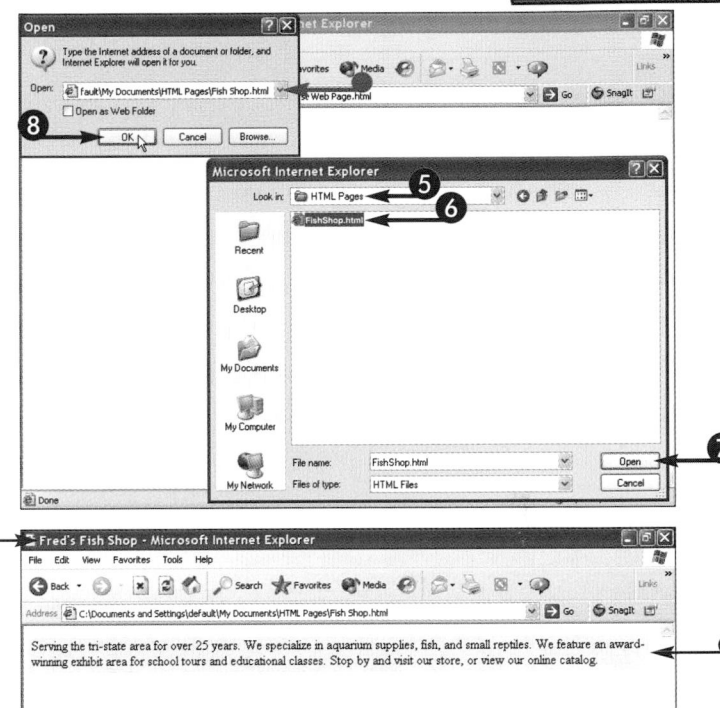

The Web browser displays the page.

● The title information appears here.

● The body information appears here.

Note: You cannot see metadata information on the browser page.

TIPS

Does it matter whether I view a page with Microsoft Internet Explorer or Netscape Navigator?

No. Both browsers are set up to view pages offline as well as online. If you use a browser other than the two mentioned, you may need to follow a different set of steps to open an offline HTML document. Be sure to consult your browser's documentation for more information.

What happens if I cannot view my page?

If you do not see any content for your page, you need to double-check your HTML coding for errors. Make sure your document uses correctly paired start and end tags, and proofread your HTML codes to make sure everything is correct.

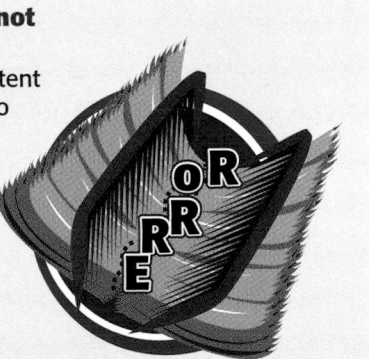

Add a Document Declaration

You can use a document declaration at the top of your Web page to declare which version of HTML you are using to create the page. You can utilize three types of HTML: HTML 4.0 Transitional, HTML 4.0 Strict, and HTML 4.0 Frameset. The document declaration tags contain a statement declaring the version.

The transitional version of HTML is the most inclusive version you can use. It includes all the standard structural elements as well as presentation elements. The strict version is a streamlined version of the transitional version. The frameset version is the transitional version along with all the necessary frame elements to display frames on a Web page.

Add a Document Declaration

① Open the HTML document you want to edit.

② Insert a new line before the `<HTML>` tag.

You can press **Enter** to create a new line.

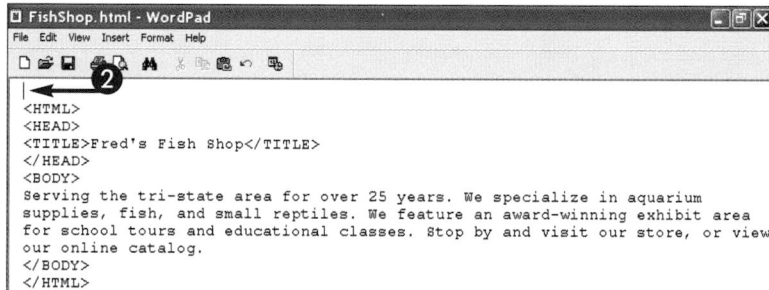

③ Type the DOCTYPE declaration.

● To specify HTML 4.0 Transitional, type:

<!DOCTYPE HTML PUBLIC "-//W3C// DTD HTML 4.0 Transitional//EN""http:// www.w3.org/TR/REC-html40/loose.dtd">

You may need to press **Enter** to continue the coding to a new line.

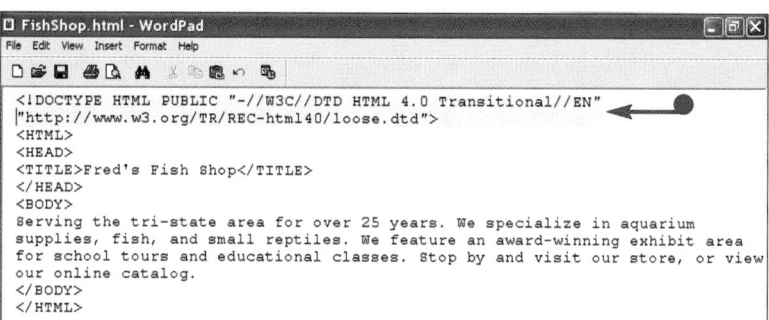

● To specify HTML 4.0 Strict, type:

<!DOCTYPE HTML PUBLIC "-//W3C// DTD HTML 4.0 Strict//EN""http:// www.w3.org/TR/REC-html40/ strict.dtd">

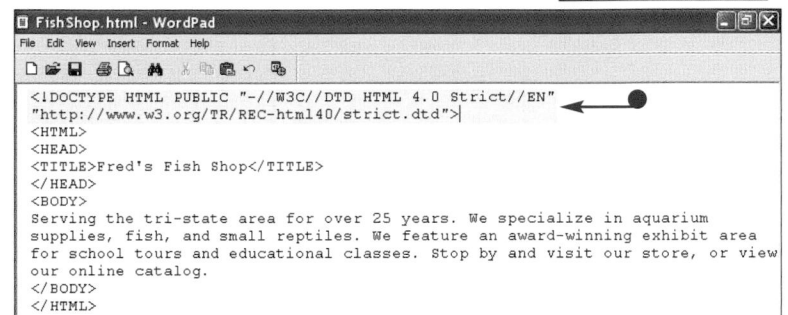

```
<!DOCTYPE HTML PUBLIC "-//W3C//DTD HTML 4.0 Strict//EN"
"http://www.w3.org/TR/REC-html40/strict.dtd">
<HTML>
<HEAD>
<TITLE>Fred's Fish Shop</TITLE>
</HEAD>
<BODY>
Serving the tri-state area for over 25 years. We specialize in aquarium
supplies, fish, and small reptiles. We feature an award-winning exhibit area
for school tours and educational classes. Stop by and visit our store, or view
our online catalog.
</BODY>
</HTML>
```

● To specify HTML 4.0 Frameset, type:

<!DOCTYPE HTML PUBLIC "-//W3C// DTD HTML 4.0 Frameset//EN""http:// www.w3.org/TR/REC-html40/ frameset.dtd">

The declaration statement is complete.

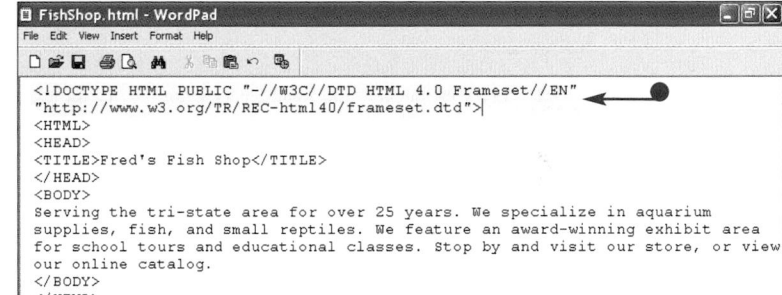

```
<!DOCTYPE HTML PUBLIC "-//W3C//DTD HTML 4.0 Frameset//EN"
"http://www.w3.org/TR/REC-html40/frameset.dtd">
<HTML>
<HEAD>
<TITLE>Fred's Fish Shop</TITLE>
</HEAD>
<BODY>
Serving the tri-state area for over 25 years. We specialize in aquarium
supplies, fish, and small reptiles. We feature an award-winning exhibit area
for school tours and educational classes. Stop by and visit our store, or view
our online catalog.
</BODY>
</HTML>
```

Do I have to declare an HTML version?

No. Most browsers can display your page without a DOCTYPE declaration, but some browsers do not. To make sure your page is viewable by all Web users, it is a good idea to include a DOCTYPE declaration. You may want to add such a declaration as you become more familiar with designing Web pages.

Which version of HTML should I use?

All Web browsers support HTML Transitional. However, developers are moving more toward HTML Strict and using it with CSS (cascading style sheets) to control page formatting. CSS offers greater flexibility with formatting yet does not necessarily work well with all browsers. If your page uses frames, then you use HTML Frameset because it allows you to add frames to a page. Deciding which version to use really depends on what Web page elements you plan to use.

Add Metadata

You can use metadata to give more details about your page, such as a page description, authoring information, copyrights, keywords, and more. Although metadata does not appear on the Web page itself, the information you insert in the metadata tags is useful with search engines that glean information about your page.

Keywords and page descriptions are the most common data Web developers enter into the metadata tags. However, metadata is also a great source for other Web page developers, enabling them to see who you are and what sort of notes or techniques you applied to create your page.

Add Metadata

ADD AN AUTHOR NAME

1 Click between the `<HEAD>` and `</HEAD>` tags to start a new line.

In this example, the metadata appears below the `<TITLE>` tags.

2 Type **<META NAME="author"** and a blank space.

3 Type **CONTENT="*My Name*">**, replacing *My Name* with your name.

4 Press Enter.

ADD A PAGE DESCRIPTION

5 Type **<META NAME="description"** and a blank space.

6 Type **CONTENT="*Page Description*">**, replacing *Page Description* with your own page description.

7 Press Enter.

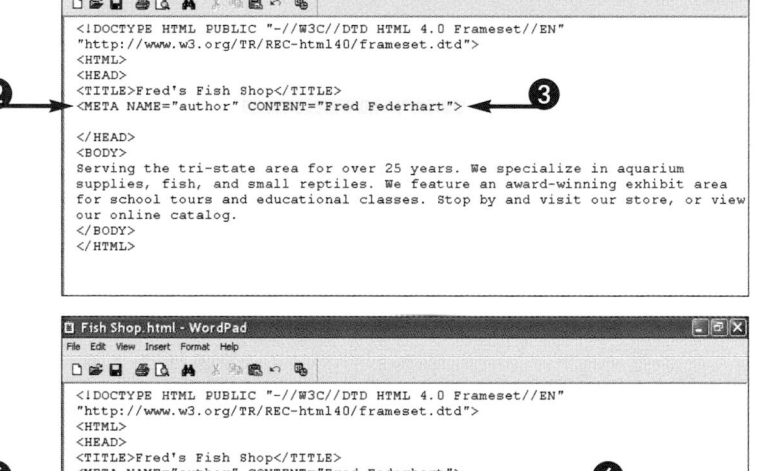

SPECIFY KEYWORDS

8 Type **<META NAME="keywords"** and a blank space.

9 Type **CONTENT="*My Keywords*">**, replacing *My Keywords* with a keyword.

For multiple keywords, use a space and commas to separate each keyword.

10 Press Enter .

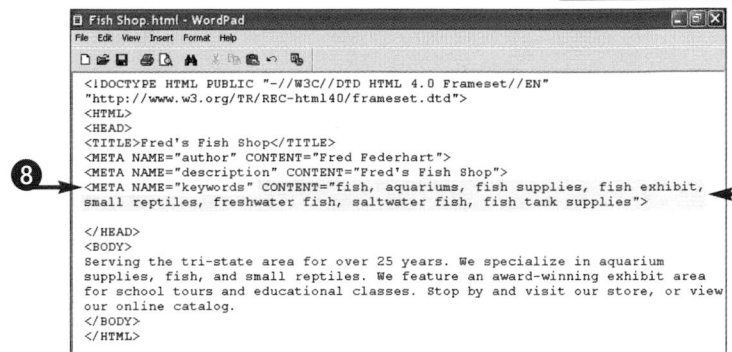

ADD A COPYRIGHT

11 Type **<META NAME="copyright"** and a blank space.

12 Type **CONTENT="*2004*">**, replacing *2004* with your own numbers or copyright information.

13 Press Enter .

The copyright statement is now a part of the document.

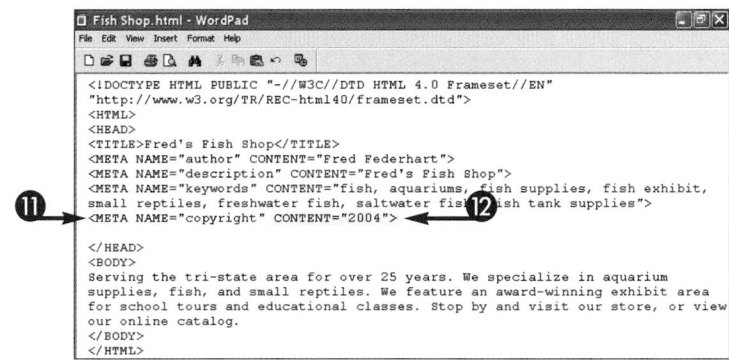

 TIPS

How do I add the name of the program I used to design my page to the metadata information?

To specify an authoring program, type **<META NAME= "generator" CONTENT= "*Program Name*">**. Substitute your own program name for the text "*Program Name*".

Who can view my metadata?

The only time users can see your metadata information is if they view the HTML code for the page. To view the HTML coding of any page in your browser window, click **View** and then click **Source**. This opens your text editor window and you can see the HTML used to create the page. Any metadata assigned to the document appears at the top, within the <HEAD> and </HEAD> tags.

CHAPTER 3

Adding Text

Are you ready to begin entering text to build your Web page content? This chapter shows you how to add different types of text elements to a document.

Create a New Paragraph 34

Change Paragraph Alignment 35

Add a Line Break 36

Insert a Blank Space 37

Insert Preformatted Text 38

Insert a Heading 39

Add Block Quotes 40

Insert a Comment 41

Create a Numbered List 42

Create a Bulleted List 44

Create a Nested List 46

Create a Definition List 47

Insert Special Characters 48

Special Characters 49

Create a New Paragraph

You can use paragraph tags to start new paragraphs in an HTML document. In a word processing program, you press the Enter or Return key to start a new line. Web browsers do not read these line breaks. Instead, you must insert a <P> tag any time you want to start a new paragraph in your Web page.

Paragraphs are left-aligned by default, but you can use the align tags to change the horizontal alignment of text. See the section "Change Paragraph Alignment" to learn more.

Create a New Paragraph

① Type **<P>** in front of the text you want to create as a new paragraph.

② Type **</P>** at the end of the paragraph.

When displayed in a Web browser, the text appears as a paragraph with extra space before and after the block of text.

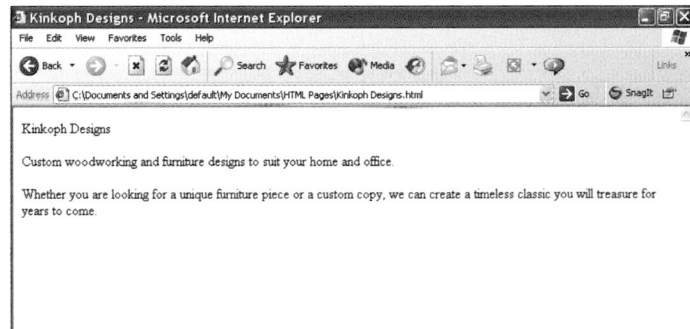

Change Paragraph Alignment

You can control the horizontal positioning, or alignment, of your paragraphs using the align tags. You can choose to align a paragraph to the left, right, center, or justify the text to create both a left and right alignment with the margins. Paragraphs are left-aligned by default unless you specify another alignment.

You can use the ALIGN **attribute within numerous tag elements, including headings, lists, and more. For example, you can center a heading or right-align a bulleted list.**

Change Paragraph Alignment

① Click inside the **<P>** tag in which you want to change alignment.

② Type **ALIGN="?"**, replacing the *?* with **Left**, **Center**, **Right**, or **Justify**.

Note: *You can type HTML commands in upper- and lowercase letters, or a mixture of both.*

When displayed in a Web browser, the text aligns as specified.

● In this example, the line of text is centered on the page.

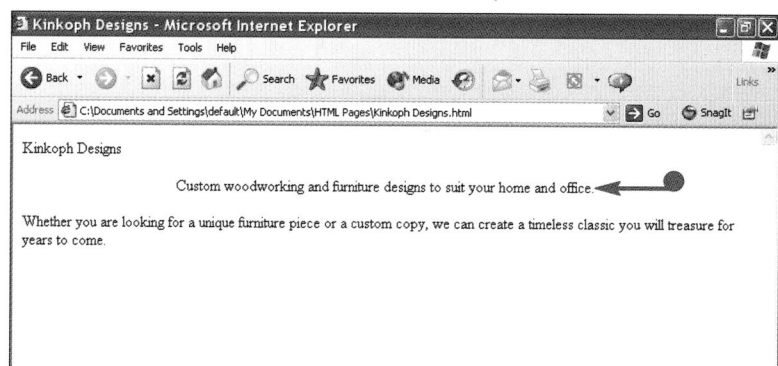

Add a Line Break

You can use the break tag, <BR>, to create a line break to start a new line of text. Ordinarily, Web browsers wrap text automatically so it continues to the next line when the current line reaches the right side of the browser window. You can insert a line break to instruct the browser to break the text to a new line. Line breaks give you control over where the text breaks.

You can also use the
 tag to add extra blank lines between paragraphs. This is useful if you want to add extra space above or below a block of text or heading.

Add a Line Break

1 Type **
** in front or at the end of each line of text that you want to appear as a new line.

Note: You do not need a close tag for the
 tag.

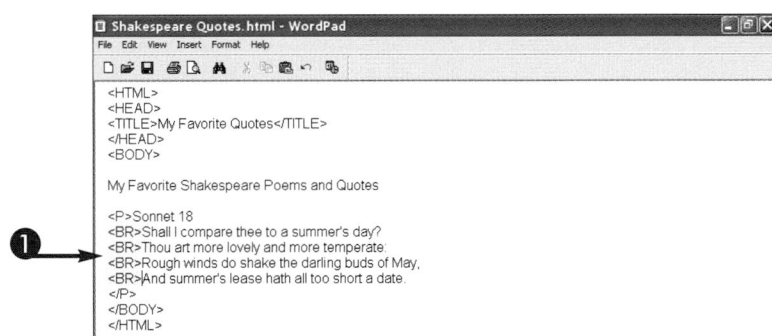

● When displayed in a Web browser, each instance of the tag creates a new text line.

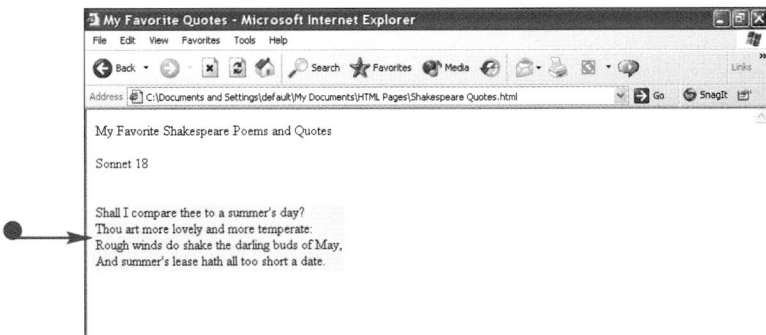

Insert a Blank Space

You can insert blank spaces within a line of text to create indents or add emphasis to the text. You can also use blank spaces to help position elements on a Web page, such as a graphic or photo.

Insert a Blank Space

1 Type ** ** in the line where you want to add a blank space.

To add multiple spaces, type the code multiple times.

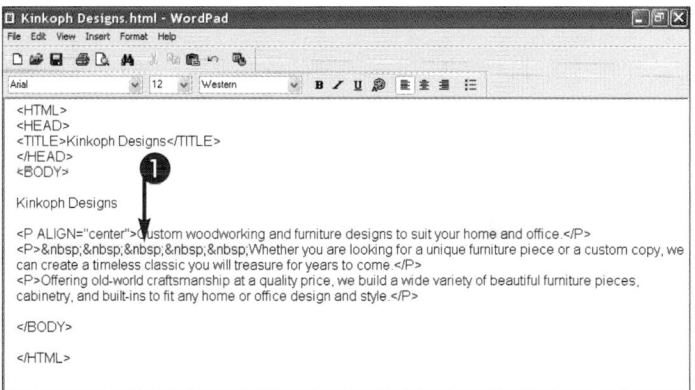

The browser displays blank spaces in the line.

● In this example, the blank spaces create an indent for a paragraph.

Insert Preformatted Text

You can use the preformatted tags, `<PRE>` and `</PRE>`, to keep the line breaks and spaces you enter for a paragraph or block of text. Web browsers ignore hard returns, line breaks, or extra spaces between words unless you insert the preformatted text element tags. If you type a paragraph with spacing just the way you want it, you can assign the preformatted tags to keep the spacing in place.

Insert Preformatted Text

① Type **`<PRE>`** above the text you want to keep intact.

② Type **`</PRE>`** below the text.

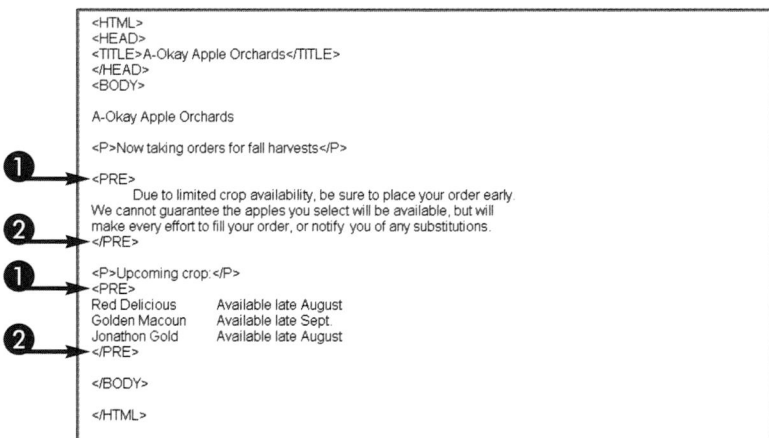

```
<HTML>
<HEAD>
<TITLE>A-Okay Apple Orchards</TITLE>
</HEAD>
<BODY>

A-Okay Apple Orchards

<P>Now taking orders for fall harvests</P>

<PRE>
        Due to limited crop availability, be sure to place your order early.
We cannot guarantee the apples you select will be available, but will
make every effort to fill your order, or notify you of any substitutions.
</PRE>

<P>Upcoming crop:</P>
<PRE>
Red Delicious      Available late August
Golden Macoun      Available late Sept.
Jonathon Gold      Available late August
</PRE>

</BODY>

</HTML>
```

● When displayed in a Web browser, the text retains all the white space you originally added to the text.

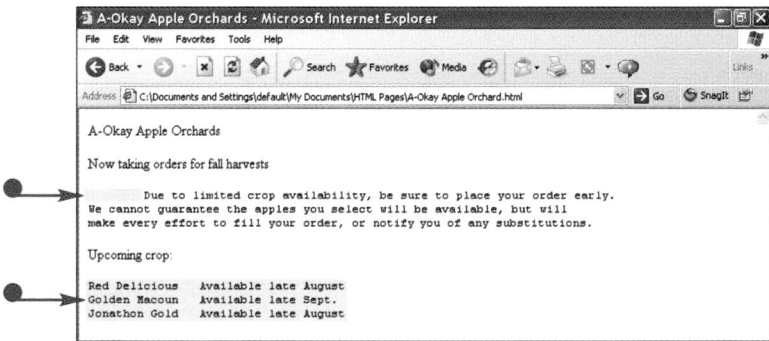

You can use headings to help clarify information on a page, organize text, and create visual structure. You can choose from six different heading levels for a document, ranging from heading level 1 (<H1>), the largest, to heading level 6 (<H6>), the smallest. Headings appear as bold type on a Web page.

You can use the ALIGN **element to change the horizontal alignment of a heading, such as** <H1 ALIGN="right">. **See the section "Change Paragraph Alignment" to learn more about inserting alignment controls with your text.**

Insert a Heading

① Type **<H?>** in front of the text you want to turn into a heading, replacing the *?* with the heading level number you want to assign.

You can set a heading level from 1 to 6.

② Type **</H?>** at the end of the heading text, replacing the *?* with the corresponding heading level you assign.

```
<HTML>
<HEAD>
<TITLE>A-Okay Apple Orchards</TITLE>
</HEAD>
<BODY>

<H1>A-Okay Apple Orchards</H1>

<H2>Growing Apples, Pears, and Pumpkins</H2>

<H3>Now taking orders for fall harvests</H3>

<H4>Featuring Jonathon Gold, Red Delicious, Golden Delicious, Fuji, Macoun, and Honey Crisp apples</H4>

<H5>Due to limited crop availability, be sure to place your order early. We cannot gaurantee the apples you select
will be available, but will make every effort to fill your order, or notify you of any substitutions.</H5>

<H6>Located in lovely lower Wisconsin</H6>

</BODY>

</HTML>
```

● The heading appears in bold text in the Web browser.

This figure shows an example of each heading size in descending order.

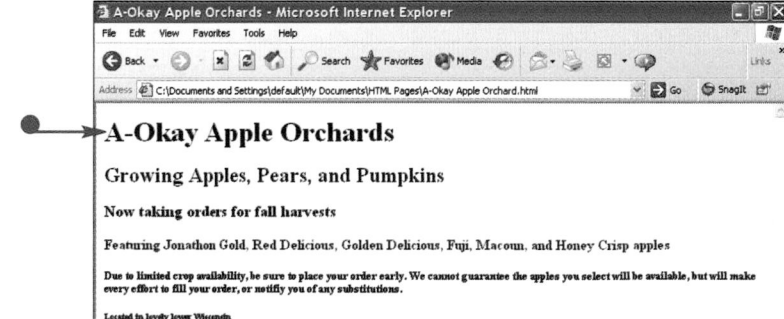

You can use block quotes to set off a paragraph from the rest of the document page. Block quotes are commonly used with quoted text or excerpts from other sources.

Add Block Quotes

① Type **<BLOCKQUOTE>** in front of the text you want to turn into a block quote.

② Type **</BLOCKQUOTE>** at the end of the text.

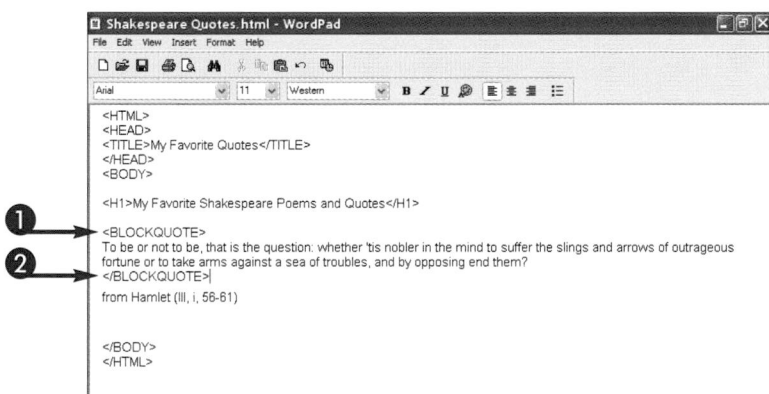

● The Web browser displays the block quote as inset text on the document page.

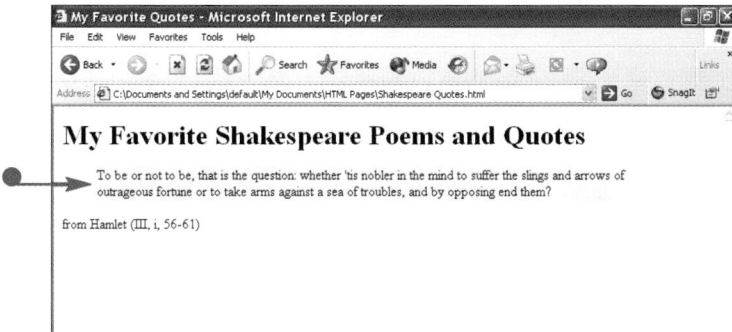

Insert a Comment

You can use comments to write notes to yourself within an HTML document. Comments do not appear on the actual Web page. For example, you might leave a comment about a future editing task, or leave a note to other Web developers viewing your HTML source code.

Insert a Comment

① Type **<!-->** where you want to place a comment.

② Type the comment text.

③ Type **-->**.

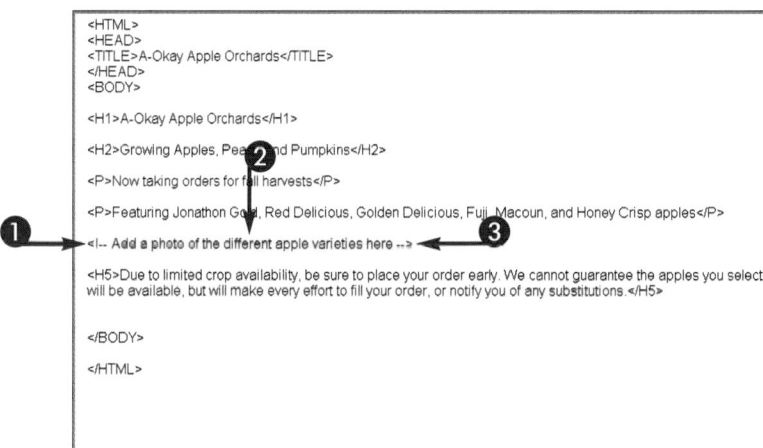

```
<HTML>
<HEAD>
<TITLE>A-Okay Apple Orchards</TITLE>
</HEAD>
<BODY>

<H1>A-Okay Apple Orchards</H1>

<H2>Growing Apples, Pears and Pumpkins</H2>

<P>Now taking orders for fall harvests</P>

<P>Featuring Jonathon Gold, Red Delicious, Golden Delicious, Fuji, Macoun, and Honey Crisp apples</P>

<!-- Add a photo of the different apple varieties here -->

<H5>Due to limited crop availability, be sure to place your order early. We cannot guarantee the apples you select
will be available, but will make every effort to fill your order, or notify you of any substitutions.</H5>

</BODY>

</HTML>
```

The comment does not appear on the page when viewed in a Web browser.

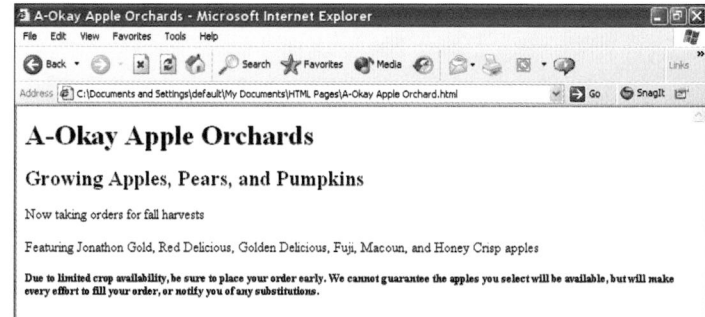

A-Okay Apple Orchards - Microsoft Internet Explorer

File   Edit   View   Favorites   Tools   Help

Address C:\Documents and Settings\default\My Documents\HTML Pages\A-Okay Apple Orchard.html

A-Okay Apple Orchards

Growing Apples, Pears, and Pumpkins

Now taking orders for fall harvests

Featuring Jonathon Gold, Red Delicious, Golden Delicious, Fuji, Macoun, and Honey Crisp apples

Due to limited crop availability, be sure to place your order early. We cannot guarantee the apples you select will be available, but will make every effort to fill your order, or notify you of any substitutions.

You can use numbered lists in your Web page to display all kinds of ordered lists. For example, you can use numbered lists to show steps or prioritize items.

Create a Numbered List

PLACE TEXT IN A NUMBERED LIST

1 Type **<OL>** above the text you want to turn into a numbered list.

2 Type **<LI>** in front of each item in the list.

3 Type **</LI>** after each list item.

4 Type **</OL>** after the list text.

```
<HTML>
<HEAD>
<TITLE>A-Okay Apple Orchards</TITLE>
</HEAD>
<BODY>

<H1>A-Okay Apple Orchards</H1>

<H2>Growing Apples, Pears, and Pumpkins</H2>

<P>Now taking orders for fall harvests</P>

<P>Featuring Jonathon Gold, Red Delicious, Golden Delicious, Fuji, Macoun, and Honey Crisp apples</P>

<!-- Add a photo of the different apple varieties here -->

<P>How to Order:</P>
<OL>
<LI>Specify an apple variety, pear variety, or pumpkin type and size.</LI>
<LI>Fill out your shipping information.</LI>
<LI>Select a payment method.</LI>
<LI>Submit your order.</LI>
<LI>Receive a confirmation e-mail.</LI>
</OL>

<H5>Due to limited crop availability, be sure to place your order early. We cannot guarantee the apples you
select will be available, but will make every effort to fill your order, or notify you of any substitutions.</H5>
```

● The text appears as a numbered list on the Web page.

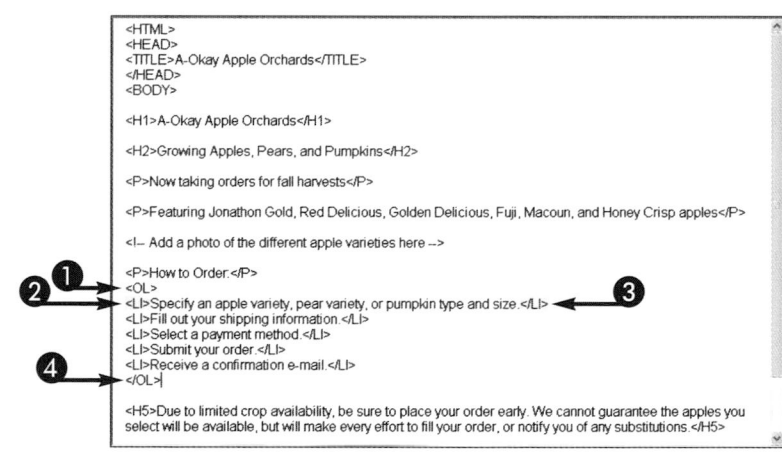

A-Okay Apple Orchards

Growing Apples, Pears, and Pumpkins

Now taking orders for fall harvests

Featuring Jonathon Gold, Red Delicious, Golden Delicious, Fuji, Macoun, and Honey Crisp apples

How to Order:

1. Specify an apple variety, pear variety, or pumpkin type and size.
2. Fill out your shipping information.
3. Select a payment method.
4. Submit your order.
5. Receive a confirmation e-mail.

Due to limited crop availability, be sure to place your order early. We cannot guarantee the apples you select will be available, but will make every effort to fill your order, or notify you of any substitutions.

SET A NUMBER STYLE

1 Type **TYPE="?"** within the <OL> tag, replacing the *?* with a number style code:

A: A, B, C

a: a, b, c

I: I, II, III

I: i, ii, iii

1: 1, 2, 3

```
<HTML>
<HEAD>
<TITLE>A-Okay Apple Orchards</TITLE>
</HEAD>
<BODY> 1

<H1>Kinkoph Designs</H1>

<H2>Table of Contents</H2>
<OL TYPE="A">
<LI>Welcome</LI>
<LI>Company History</LI>
<LI>Mission Statement</LI>
<LI>Goals</LI>
<LI>Manufacturing Process</LI>
<LI>Product Descriptions</LI>
<LI>Contact and Ordering Information</LI>
</OL>


</BODY>

</HTML>
```

The numbered list displays the style you selected.

● In this example, the list is numbered by letters rather than numbers.

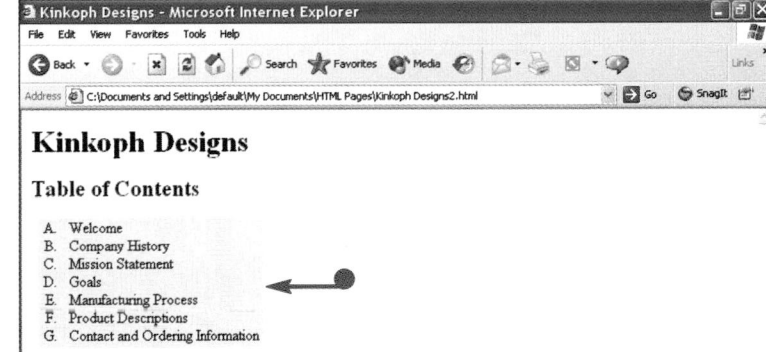

Kinkoph Designs

Table of Contents

- A. Welcome
- B. Company History
- C. Mission Statement
- D. Goals
- E. Manufacturing Process
- F. Product Descriptions
- G. Contact and Ordering Information

TIPS

How do I add another item to my numbered list?

Simply insert the text where you want it to appear in the list and add the <LI> and </LI> tags before and after the text. The Web browser displays the new list order the next time you view the page.

How do I start my numbered list with a different numbering than the default numbering?

By default, a Web browser reads your numbered list coding and starts with the number 1. To start with a different number, you must add a START attribute to the <OL> tag. For example, to start the numbering at 5, the coding would read <OL START="5" TYPE="1">.

Create a Bulleted List

You can add a bulleted list to your document to set apart a list of items from the rest of the page of text. Also called an unordered list, you can use a bulleted list when you do not need to show the items in a particular order.

By default, bulleted lists appear with solid bullets on a Web page. If you want to utilize another bullet style, you must add an attribute to the <UL> tag.

Create a Bulleted List

PLACE TEXT IN A BULLETED LIST

① Type **<UL>** above the text you want to turn into a numbered list.

② Type **<LI>** in front of each item in the list.

③ Type **</LI>** after each list item.

④ Type **</UL>** after the list text.

The text appears as a bulleted list on the Web page.

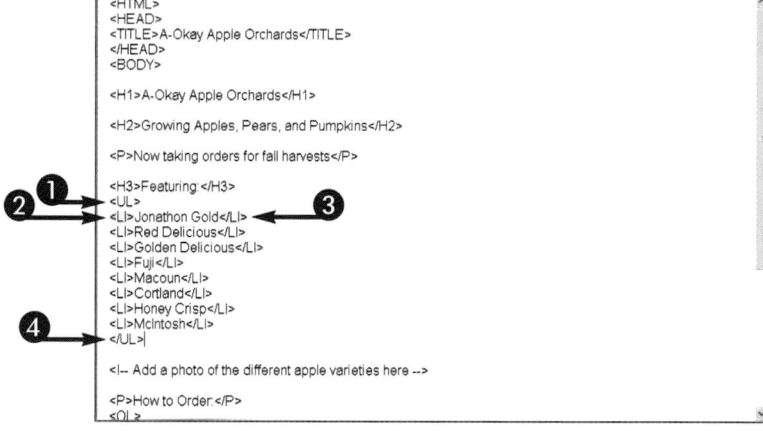

SET A BULLET STYLE

① Type **TYPE="*?*"** within the `<UL>` tag, replacing the *?* with a bullet style code:

circle: ○

disc: ●

square: ■

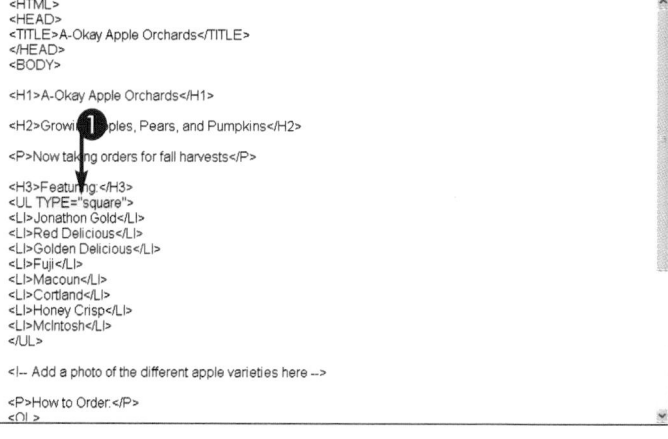

```
<HTML>
<HEAD>
<TITLE>A-Okay Apple Orchards</TITLE>
</HEAD>
<BODY>

<H1>A-Okay Apple Orchards</H1>

<H2>Growing Apples, Pears, and Pumpkins</H2>

<P>Now taking orders for fall harvests</P>

<H3>Featuring:</H3>
<UL TYPE="square">
<LI>Jonathon Gold</LI>
<LI>Red Delicious</LI>
<LI>Golden Delicious</LI>
<LI>Fuji</LI>
<LI>Macoun</LI>
<LI>Cortland</LI>
<LI>Honey Crisp</LI>
<LI>McIntosh</LI>
</UL>

<!-- Add a photo of the different apple varieties here -->

<P>How to Order:</P>
<OL>
```

The bulleted list displays the style you selected.

 In this example, the bulleted list uses square bullets.

A-Okay Apple Orchards

Growing Apples, Pears, and Pumpkins

Now taking orders for fall harvests

Featuring:

- Jonathon Gold
- Red Delicious
- Golden Delicious
- Fuji
- Macoun
- Cortland
- Honey Crisp
- McIntosh

How to Order:

1. Specify an apple variety, pear variety, or pumpkin type and size.
2. Fill out your shipping information.
3. Select a payment method.

TIP

Can I stop a bulleted list for one line of text, and continue the bullets again for the next line?

Yes. If you leave off the `<LI>` and `</LI>` tags for a line of text within the list, a Web browser reads the line as regular text. However, you can insert a line break (`<BR>`) or use the paragraph or heading tags before the non-bulleted text line so that it appears as a separate line in the list. For example:

```
<UL>
<LI>Dogs</LI>
<LI>Cats</LI>
<BR>Birds
<LI>Reptiles</LI>
</UL>
```

Create a Nested List

You can use a nested list to add a list within a list on your Web page. Nested lists allow you to display listed text at different levels within the list hierarchy. You can use both numbered and bulleted lists within an existing list.

Create a Nested List

1. Click where you want to insert a nested list, or add a new line within the existing list and type **<OL>** for a numbered list or **<UL>** for an unordered list.

   In this example, the <UL> tag includes an attribute for changing the bullet style.

   Note: See the section "Create a Numbered List" to create a numbered list, or the section "Create a Bulleted List" to create a bulleted list.

2. Type the new list text including **<LI>** and **</LI>** tags using the same technique used to create the existing list.

3. Type **</OL>** or **</UL>** at the end of the nested list.

● The text appears as a nested list within a list on the Web page.

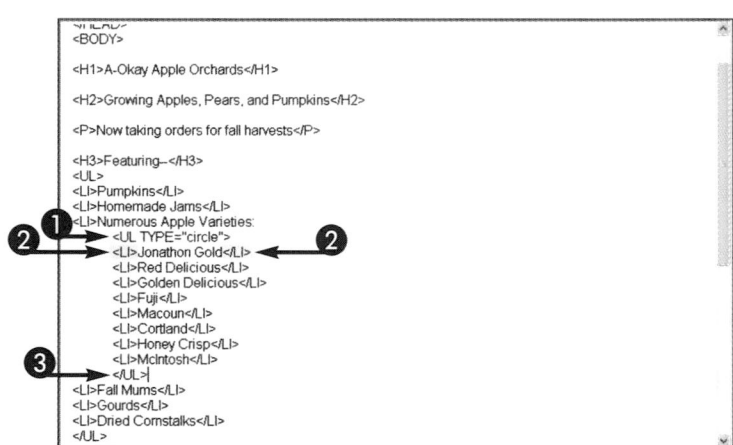

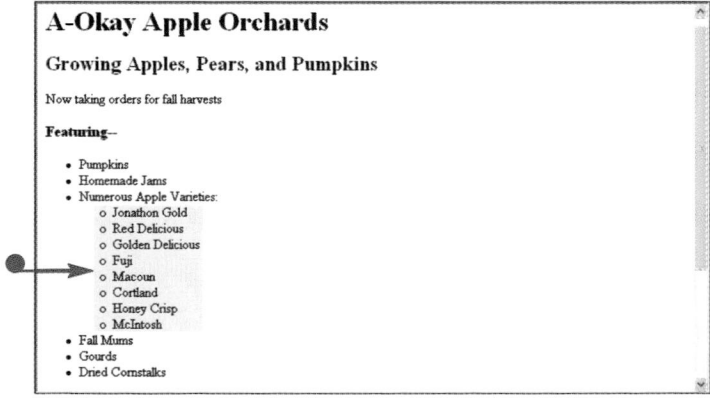

A-Okay Apple Orchards

Growing Apples, Pears, and Pumpkins

Now taking orders for fall harvests

Featuring--

- Pumpkins
- Homemade Jams
- Numerous Apple Varieties:
  - Jonathon Gold
  - Red Delicious
  - Golden Delicious
  - Fuji
  - Macoun
  - Cortland
  - Honey Crisp
  - McIntosh
- Fall Mums
- Gourds
- Dried Cornstalks

You can use a definition list in your document to set apart text in the format of a glossary or dictionary.

Create a Definition List

① Type **<DL>** above the text you want to set as a definition list.

② Type **<DT>** in front of each term and **</DT>** after each term.

③ Type **<DD>** in front of each definition and **</DD>** after each definition.

④ Type **</DL>** after the definition list text.

```
<HTML>
<HEAD>
<TITLE>A-Okay Apple Orchards</TITLE>
</HEAD>
<BODY>

<H1 ALIGN="center">A-Okay Apple Orchards</H1>

<H3 ALIGN="center">Growing Apples, Pears, and Pumpkins</H3>
<BR>
<BR>
<BR>

<H2>Want to know more about our various apple varieties?</H2>

<DL>
<DT>Honey Crisp</DT>
<DD>Developed from a 1960 cross of Macoun and Honeygold apples, the goal in creating this apple was to
develop a variety that could withstand difficult winters without losing fruit quality. Skin is mostly red with a yellow
background, while the surface has shallow dimples and dots; sweet, crunchy, and crisp, the flavor ranges from
mild to strongly aromatic, depending on degree of maturity; flesh is cream-colored and coarse.</DD>
<DT>Cortland</DT>
<DD>Sweet, juicy, and just a hint of tartness, this apple is known for its tender snow white flesh. Good for eating
and baking.</DD>
</DL>

</BODY>
```

The text appears as a definition list on the Web page.

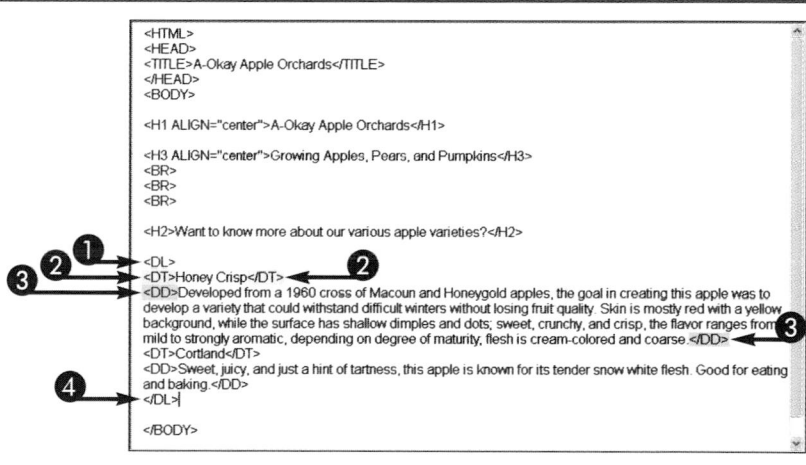

Insert Special Characters

You can use HTML code to insert special characters into your Web page text. Special characters are characters that do not appear on your keyboard.

Special characters use number or name codes preceded by an ampersand and ending with a semicolon, such as `&frac13;` for the fraction ⅓ or `&para;` for a paragraph symbol.

Insert Special Characters

① Click where you want to insert a special character.

② Type the number or name code for the character, with an ampersand (**&**) before the code and a semicolon (**;**) following the code.

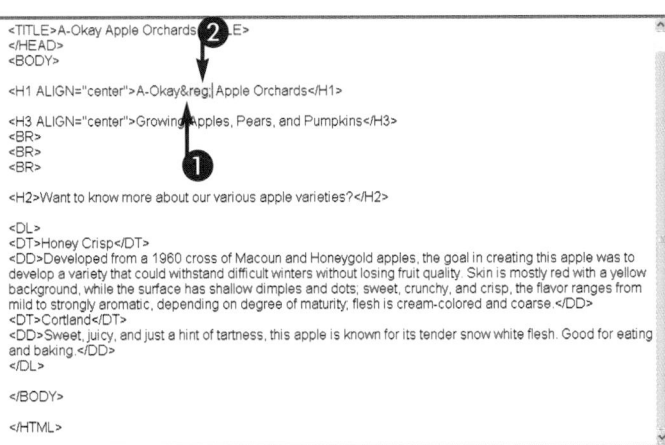

● The Web browser displays the designated character in the text.

To properly insert a character into your Web page text, you need to know the code. The following table gives a list of the common special characters you can insert. For more on inserting these special characters, see the section "Insert Special Characters."

Description	Special Character	Code
copyright	©	&#169;
registered trademark	®	&#174;
trademark	™	&#8482;
paragraph mark	¶	&#182;
quotation mark	"	&#34;
left angle quote	«	&#171;
right angle quote	»	&#187;
ampersand	&	&#38;
inverted exclamation	¡	&#161;
inverted question mark	¿	&#191;
broken vertical bar	¦	&#166;
section sign	§	&#167;
not sign	¬	&#172;
umlaut	¨	&#168;
acute accent	´	&#180;
cedilla	¸	&#184;
bullet	•	&#8226;
capital N, tilde	Ñ	&#209;
small n, tilde	ñ	&#241;
capital A, tilde	Ã	&#195;
small a, tilde	ã	&#227;
capital A, grave accent	À	&#192;
small a, grave accent	à	&#224;
capital O, slash	Ø	&#216;

Description	Special Character	Code
small o, slash	ø	&#248;
em dash	—	&#8212;
en dash	–	&#8211;
micro sign	µ	&#181;
macron	¯	&#175;
superscript one	¹	&#185;
superscript two	²	&#178;
superscript three	³	&#179;
one-half fraction	½	&#189;
one-fourth fraction	¼	&#188;
three-fourths fraction	¾	&#190;
degree sign	°	&#186;
multiply sign	×	&#215;
division sign	÷	&#247;
plus or minus sign	±	&#177;
less-than sign	<	&#60;
greater-than sign	>	&#62;
dagger	†	&#8224;
double-dagger	‡	&#8225;
cent sign	¢	&#162;
pound sterling	£	&#163;
euro	€	&#8363;
yen sign	¥	&#165;
general currency	¤	&#164;

CHAPTER 4

Formatting Text

You can apply numerous formatting tags to control the appearance of text on your Web page. This chapter shows you how to utilize attributes and tags to make your text look its best.

Make Text Bold 52

Italicize Text 53

Add Underlining to Text..............................54

Change Fonts 55

Change Font Size..56

Change the Text Color 58

Adjust Margins..60

Set a Page Background Color 61

Add a Horizontal Line 62

Make Text Bold

You can add bold formatting to your text to give it more emphasis or make your page more visually appealing. For example, you might make a company name bold in a paragraph or add bold to a list of items.

Make Text Bold

1 Type **<B>** in front of the text you want to make bold.

2 Type **</B>** at the end of the text.

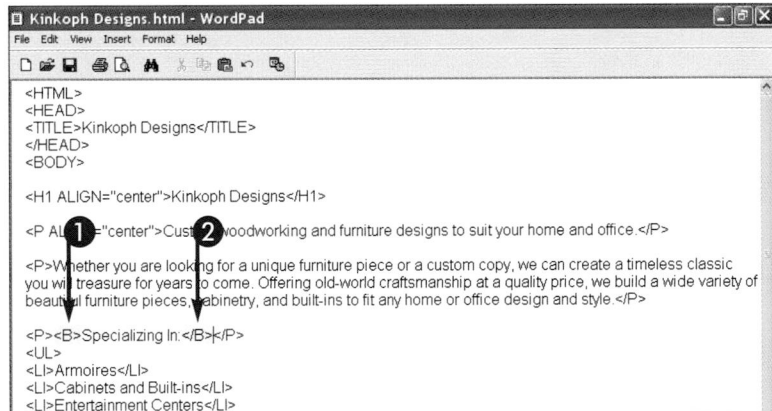

● When displayed in a Web browser, the text appears as bold.

You can add italics to your text to give it more emphasis or make your page more visually appealing. For example, you might make a description under a heading italic to distinguish it from the rest of the page.

Common uses for italicized text include emphasizing a new term or setting apart the title of a literary work.

Italicize Text

1 Type **<I>** in front of the text you want to italicize.

2 Type **</I>** at the end of the text.

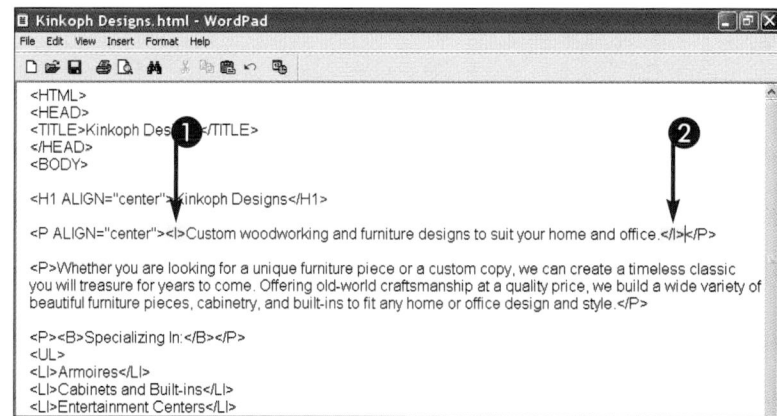

● When displayed in a Web browser, the text appears in italics.

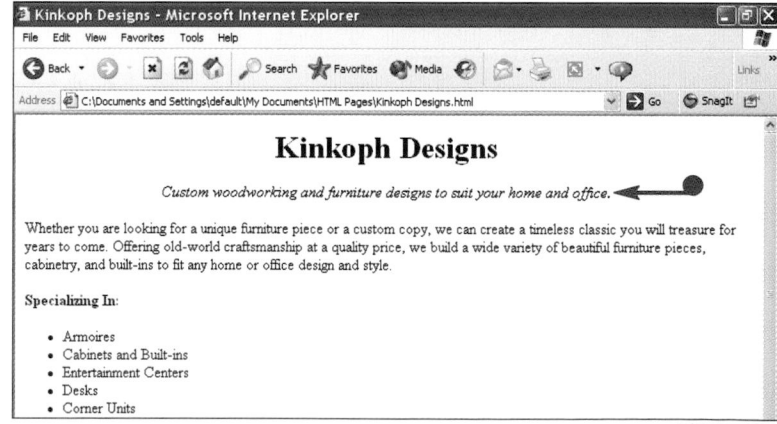

Add Underlining to Text

You can add underlining to your text for added emphasis. For example, you might underline a term or an important name.

Use caution when applying underlining to Web pages, however, as some users will mistake the underlined text for a hyperlink. See Chapter 6 to learn more about using links in Web pages.

Add Underlining to Text

① Type **\<U\>** in front of the text you want to underline.

② Type **\</U\>** at the end of the text.

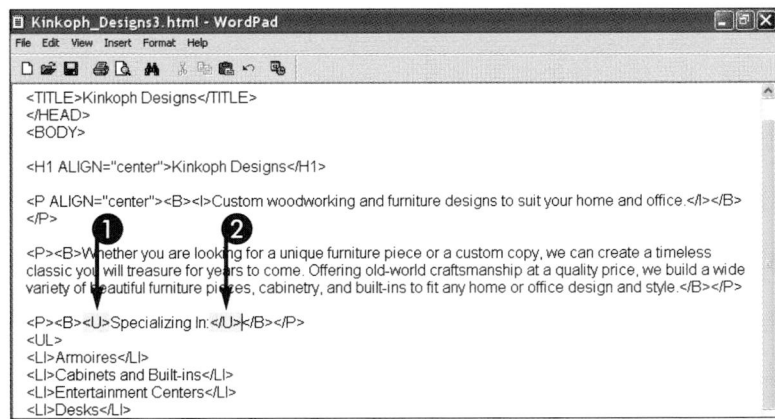

● The text appears underlined on the Web page.

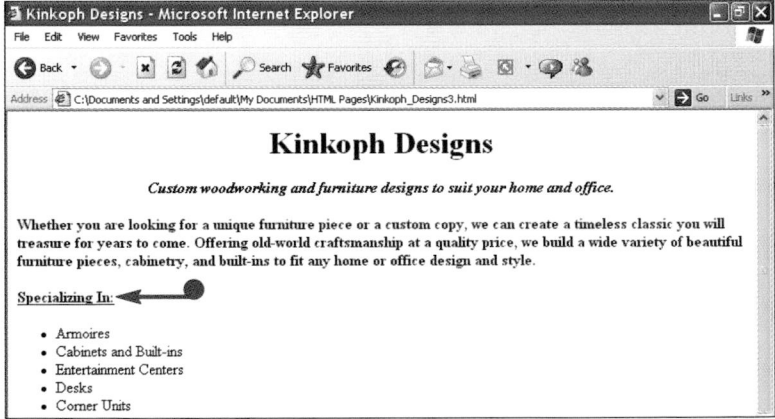

You can change the font of your text using the Font tags, <FONT> and </FONT>, along with the FACE attribute. You can use the attribute to specify a font by name.

Not all Web browsers can display a variety of fonts. It is best to assign common fonts typically found on computers, such as Times New Roman and Arial. It is also a good idea to list more than one font name in the FACE attribute, in case the first font is not available on the viewer's computer.

Change Fonts

1 Type **<FONT FACE="Arial, Times New Roman">** in front of the text you want to change.

You can substitute different font names for those listed in quotes.

In case the first font you list is not available on the user's computer, list a second font as an alternative.

2 Type **</FONT>** at the end of the text.

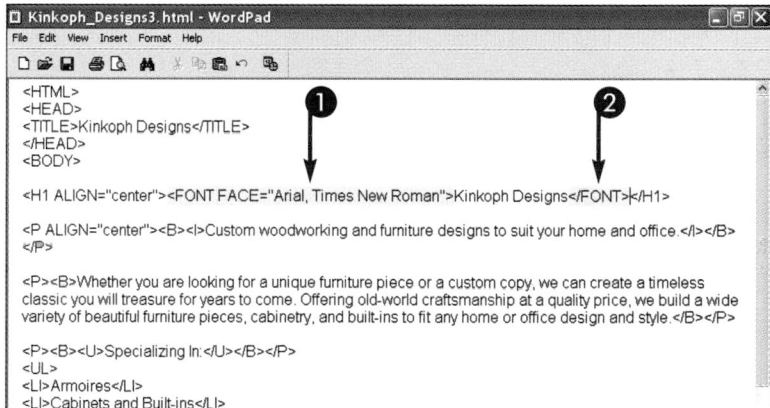

● The text appears with a font change on the Web page.

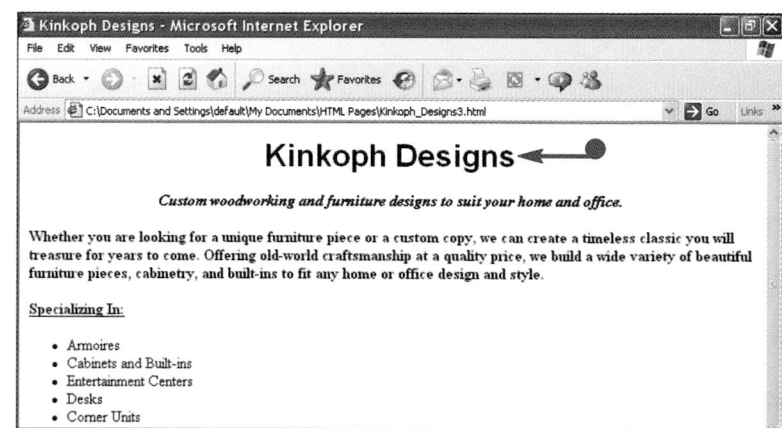

Change Font Size

You can change the font size for your Web page text using the SIZE attribute. HTML coding categorizes fonts into seven different sizes for Web pages. Font Size 1, the smallest, sets your text to 8-point, while Font Size 7, the largest, sets your text to 36-point. The exact point size may vary between browsers, but the size variations are consistent — Font Size 1 is always the smallest text, while Font Size 7 is always the largest.

You can use the SIZE attribute to set a new size for a section of text or you can use the <BASEFONT> tag to change the font size for the entire page. Keep in mind that the font size you specify may not always display properly in all Web browsers.

Change Font Size

CHANGE A SECTION OF TEXT

1️⃣ Type **<FONT SIZE="?">** in front of the text you want to change, replacing *?* with the size you want to specify, ranging from **1** to **7**.

2️⃣ Type **</FONT>** at the end of the text.

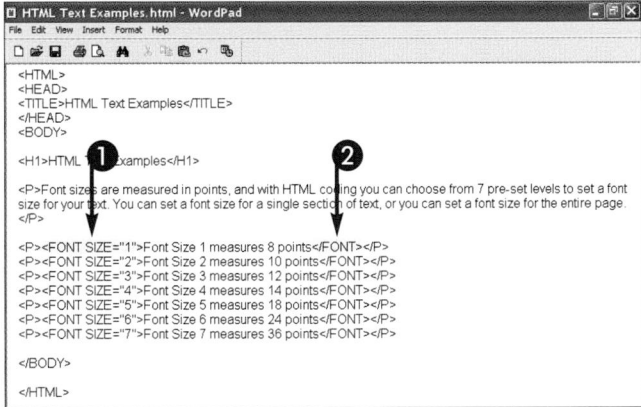

● The text appears with the designated font size on the Web page.

This figure shows samples of all seven font size levels.

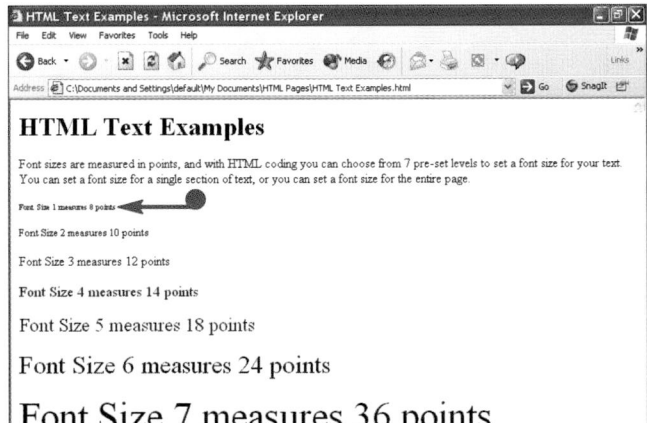

CHANGE ALL THE TEXT

1 Type **<BASEFONT SIZE="?">** at the top of your Web page text, replacing *?* with the size you want to specify, ranging from **1** to **7**.

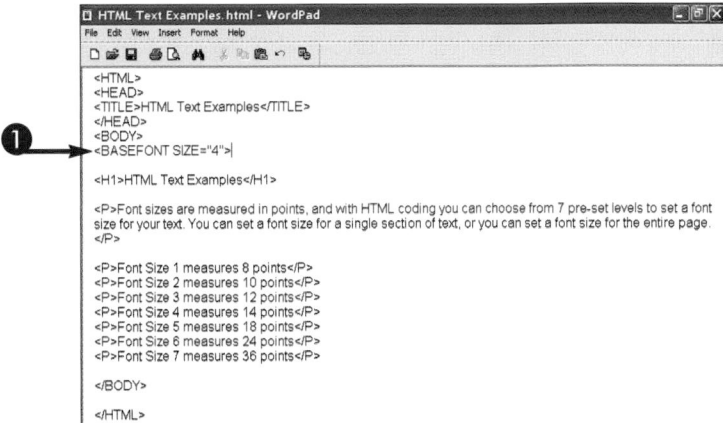

All the text appears using the new size in the Web browser.

Note: *The <BASEFONT> tag does not affect the size of any headings (<H1>) within your Web page text.*

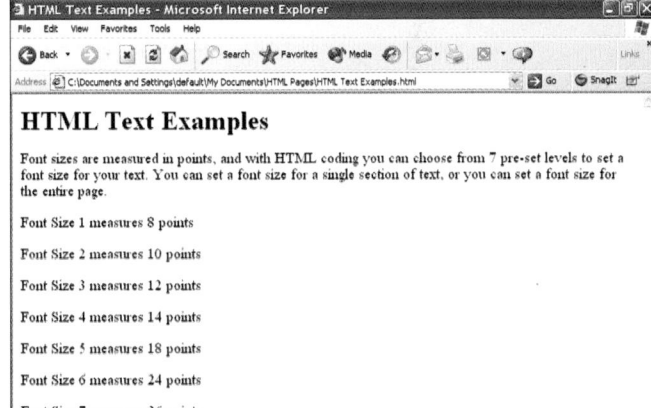

TIPS

What font sizes can I apply with the SIZE attribute?

HTML coding sets a range of acceptable font sizes, called *absolute font sizes.* These are sizes with proven legibility in most computers and browsers. Not all browsers apply the same exact point sizes, but the sizing variations still hold true—Font Size 1 displays the smallest size to Font Size 7 which displays the largest size.

SIZE Attribute	Font Size
Font Size 1	8 points
Font Size 2	10 points
Font Size 3	12 points
Font Size 4	14 points
Font Size 5	18 points
Font Size 6	24 points
Font Size 7	36 points

Can I set a size other than the recommended size levels?

Yes. You can use relative font sizes to make variations to the set size groups. If you type a plus (+) or minus (-) sign before the size level number, the browser displays a size relative to the surrounding text. For example, if you type <FONT SIZE="+2">, the browser displays the text as two sizes larger than the surrounding text. If you type <FONT SIZE="-2">, the browser displays the text two times smaller than the surrounding text.

Change the Text Color

You can enhance your text by adding color. The COLOR attribute works along with the <FONT> and </FONT> tags to change the color of text on a page. HTML color is based on hexadecimal values. You can choose from 16 colors.

Legibility is always a concern when applying color attributes to text. Be sure to choose a color that is easy to read on a Web page. Use caution when applying color text to a color background. Always test your page to make sure the colors do not clash and your message text remains legible.

Change the Text Color

CHANGE A SECTION OF TEXT

① Type **<FONT COLOR="?">** in front of the text you want to change, replacing *?* with the color you want to specify.

You can type the color name or hexadecimal value.

This example shows the hexadecimal value for green. Always precede a hexadecimal value with a # sign.

② Type **</FONT>** at the end of the text.

● The text appears with the designated color on the Web page.

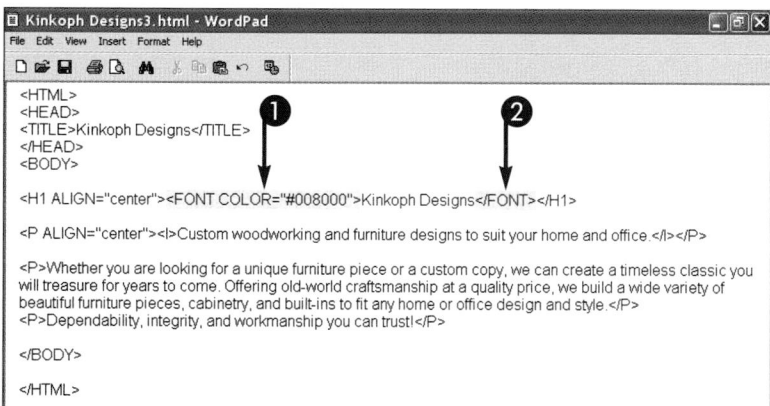

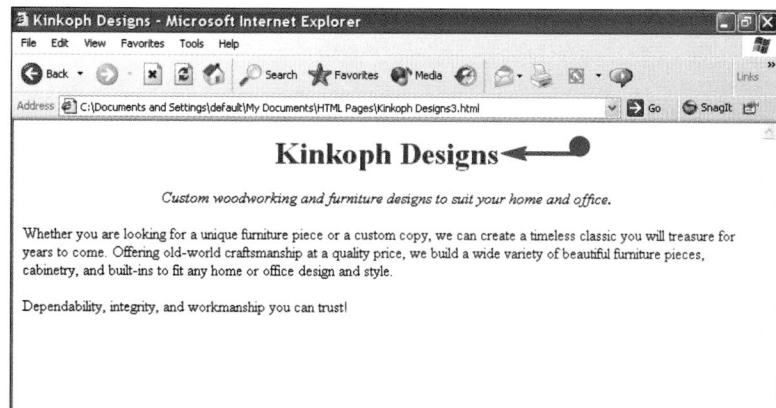

CHANGE ALL THE TEXT

① Within the <BODY> tag, type **TEXT="?"**, replacing *?* with the color you want to specify.

You can type the color name or hexadecimal value.

This example uses a color name instead of the hexadecimal value.

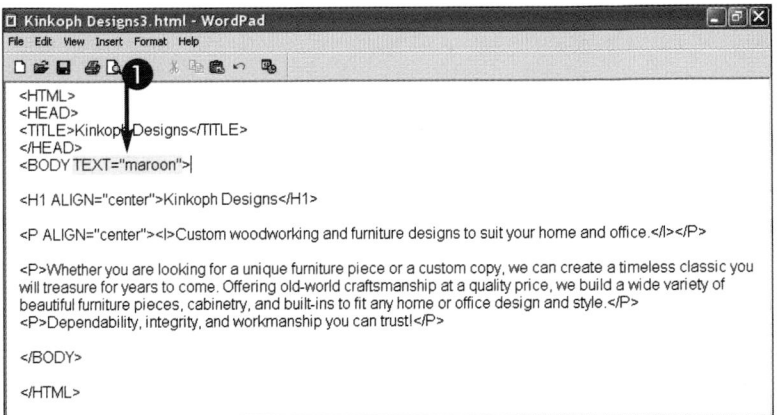

All the text appears with the new color in the Web browser.

Note: The TEXT attribute tag does not affect the link color. To learn more about links, see Chapter 6.

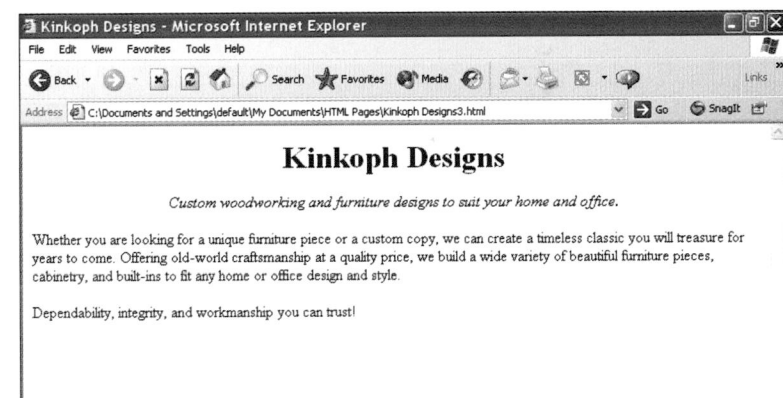

What colors can I set for my Web page text?

HTML coding uses hexadecimal values for colors, preceded by a number sign (#) followed by a six-digit value, as shown in this table. Browsers can also read some basic colors, including black, white, gray, silver, maroon, red, purple, fuchsia, green, lime, olive, yellow, navy, blue, teal, and aqua. Rather than type a number value, you can type a text value for the color.

Color	Hexadecimal value		Color	Hexadecimal value
Black	#000000		Silver	#C0C0C0
White	#FFFFFF		Navy	#000080
Blue	#0000FF		Fuchsia	#FF00FF
Red	#FF0000		Lime	#00FF00
Yellow	#FFFF00		Maroon	#800000
Green	#008000		Olive	#808000
Purple	#800080		Teal	#008080
Gray	#808080			

Adjust Margins

You can adjust the margins of your Web page to change the amount of space that appears at the top, bottom, left, or right edges of the page. By default, the HTML margins are set at approximately 10 pixels. You can adjust the settings to suit the design needs of your page.

You can use the margin attributes to control page margins; however, these attributes vary in coding between Internet Explorer and Netscape Navigator. Internet Explorer recognizes the `LEFTMARGIN`, `RIGHTMARGIN`, `TOPMARGIN`, **and** `BOTTOMMARGIN` **attributes. Netscape Navigator recognizes** `MARGINWIDTH` **and** `MARGINHEIGHT`. **Be sure to enter both browser types so your page is viewable by all users.**

Adjust Margins

① Within the `<BODY>` tag, type **_MARGIN_="?"**.

Substitute _MARGIN_ with the margin attribute you want to change: **LEFTMARGIN**, **RIGHTMARGIN**, **TOPMARGIN**, **BOTTOMMARGIN**, **MARGINWIDTH**, or **MARGINHEIGHT**.

Substitute the _?_ with the amount of indentation you want to create, measured in pixels.

You can set the margin for one side of the page, or all four sides, all within the `<BODY>` tag.

The Web browser displays your page with the specified margins.

Note: See Chapter 3 to learn how to change the alignment of text on a page.

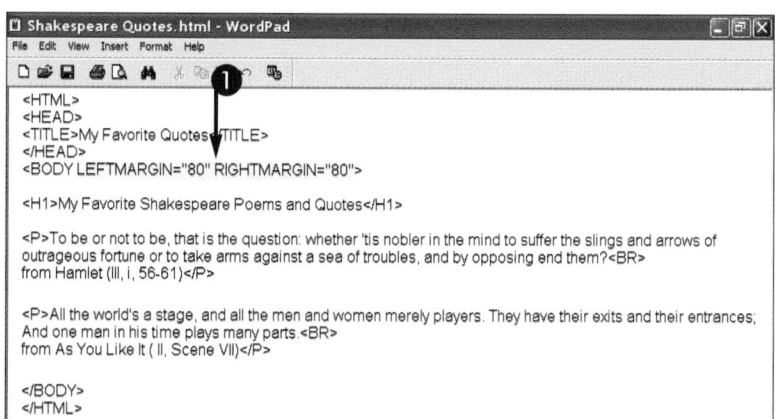

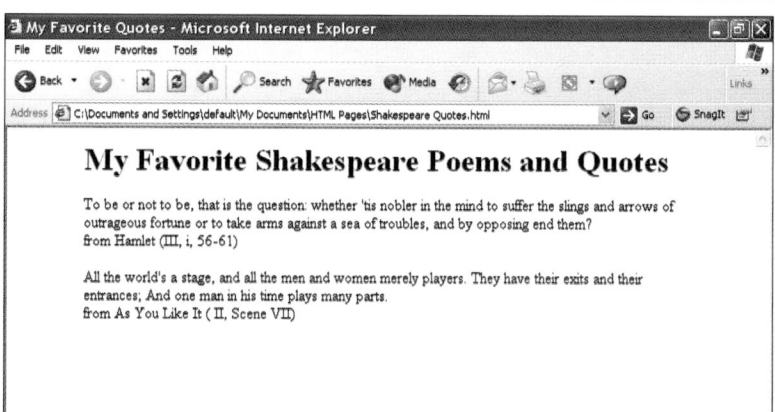

Set a Page Background Color

You can add color to the background of the page using the BGCOLOR attribute. Always choose a background color that complements your text.

Set a Page Background Color

1 Within the `<BODY>` tag, type **BGCOLOR="?"**.

Substitute *?* with a color value for the color you want to use, such as **#808000** for olive.

You can also type a color name instead of the hexadecimal value.

Note: *See the section "Change the Text Color" for a table of 15 color codes you can apply.*

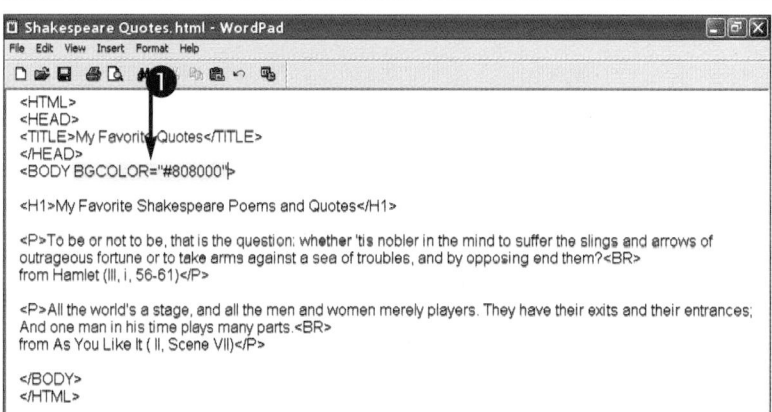

The page appears in the Web browser with a background color assigned.

You can add a solid horizontal line, or *rule*, across your page to give the page visual interest or break up blocks of information. Horizontal rules must occupy a line by themselves and cannot appear within a paragraph.

You can define the thickness and length of a horizontal line using the SIZE **and** WIDTH **attributes. For example, you can make the line extend across half the page.**

Add a Horizontal Line

ADD A SIMPLE LINE

1 Type **<HR>** where you want to insert a horizontal rule.

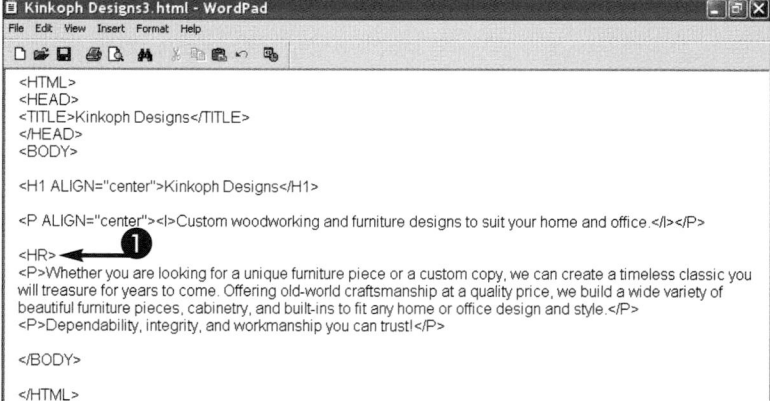

The browser displays the line across the page.

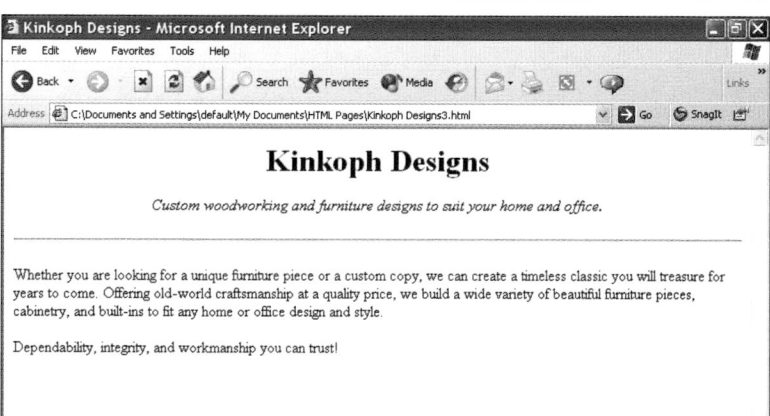

SET A LINE THICKNESS AND WIDTH

1 Within the `<HR>` tag, type **SIZE="?"**, replacing *?* with the thickness you want to assign, measured in pixels.

2 Within the `<HR>` tag, type **WIDTH="?%"**, replacing *?* with the percentage of the page you want to set the rule across.

The browser displays the line across the page.

TIPS

How do I make my line appear more solid?

By default, the browser displays horizontal rules with shading, giving the lines a three-dimensional effect. To remove the shading, add the NOSHADE attribute to your `<HR>` tag, such as `<HR NOSHADE>`.

Can I add color to a horizontal line?

Yes. You can insert the COLOR attribute and assign a color value to a line. For example, if you type **`<HR COLOR= "#0000FF">`**, the browser displays the line as blue. See the back of this book for a full color chart you can use to assign colors to Web pages.

Creating Style Sheets

Looking for an easier way to format your Web pages? This chapter shows you how to use style sheets to assign formatting properties and values to your HTML documents.

Understanding Style Sheets 66

Create an External Style Sheet.......................68

Link to a Style Sheet...70

Add Comments to a Style Sheet 71

Create an Internal Style Sheet 72

Create a Class 74

Apply a Style with the DIV Tag........................76

Apply a Style Locally..78

Apply a Style Using the ID Attribute..............79

Understanding Style Sheets

You can use *cascading style sheets*, or CSS, to exercise precise control over the appearance of your HTML documents. Style sheets can help you maintain a consistent look and feel throughout your Web site. By regulating formatting controls to another sheet, you can free up your HTML documents of repetitive coding to concentrate on the main elements that make up your pages.

Defining Style Sheets

A style sheet is simply a separate text file with the .css file extension. Style sheets can also be internal, residing within an HTML document. A style sheet holds formatting codes that control your Web page's appearance. You can use style sheets to change the look of any Web page element, such as paragraphs, lists, backgrounds, and more. Any time you want to apply the formatting to an HTML document, you attach — or *link* — the style sheet to the page.

Style Sheets Can Control Multiple Pages

You can link every page in your Web site to a single style sheet. Any changes you make to the style sheet formatting are reflected in every HTML document linking to the sheet. By storing all the formatting information in one convenient spot, you can easily update the appearance of your site's pages in one fell swoop. This can be a real time-saver if your site consists of lots of pages.

Style Sheet Syntax

Style sheets are made up of rules, and each rule has two distinct parts: selectors and declarations. A *selector* specifies the element to which you want to apply a style rule. The *declaration* specifies the formatting for the selector. For example, in the style rule H2 {color: silver}, H2 is the selector and the declaration sets the color property to silver. Declarations can include a property and a value. If you attach a page to the rule H2 {color: silver}, all level 2 headings on the page will appear in silver.

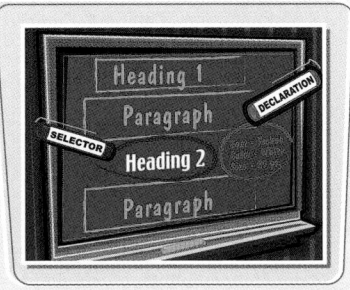

Writing Style Syntax

When writing style sheet syntax, always start with the selector — the element to which you want to apply the rule, followed by the declaration in curly brackets, {}. The declaration consists of a property and a value, and if you use more than one declaration, you must separate each with a semicolon. If you forget to include a semicolon, the browser ignores the rule. To help keep your style sheets readable, consider typing rules and declarations on separate lines. Learn more about writing style rules in Chapter 6.

Inheritance

Elements you add within other elements inherit the first element's formatting, unless otherwise specified. For example, if you define a style for the <BODY> element, any elements you nest within the <BODY> element inherit the same formatting. HTML inheritance makes it easy to keep the formatting intact as you add new items within an element.

Style Classes

For times in which you want to apply formatting only to a particular instance of an element, you can use a class attribute. You can assign a distinct name to a class and add a style rule that applies only to that class. For example, perhaps you want to add select formatting to a paragraph. You define the style rule on your style sheet, and then refer to the class name in your HTML document.

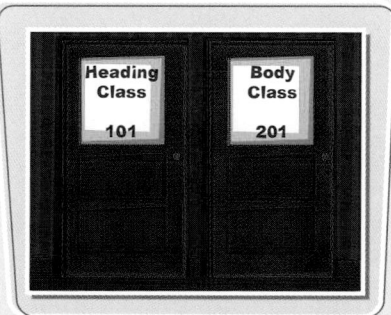

External and Internal Style Sheets

You can connect an HTML document to an external style sheet or an internal style sheet. *Internal style sheets* exist within an existing HTML page, while *external style sheets* are separate files. External style sheets are used more often because you can link them to more than one HTML document. You might use an internal style sheet if your site consists of a single page.

Create an External Style Sheet

You can use an external style sheet to define formatting and layout instructions as well as to link the page to your HTML documents. You can save the style sheet as a text file and assign the .css file extension to identify the file as a cascading style sheet.

For more on style sheets and how they work, see the section "Understanding Style Sheets."

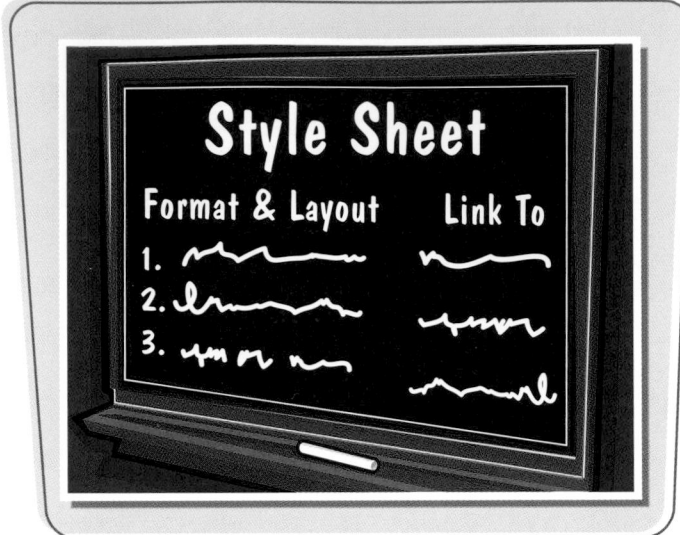

Create an External Style Sheet

1 Create a new document in your text editor.

Note: *See Chapter 2 to learn how to start and save HTML documents.*

2 To create a style rule, type the element tag for which you want to define formatting properties.

This example shows the beginnings of a style rule for defining level 2 headings.

3 Type a space.

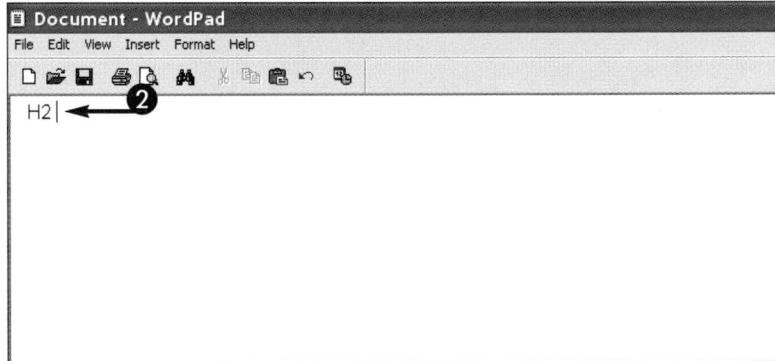

4 Type **{**.

5 Type the properties and values for the rule.

Be sure to separate declarations with a semicolon.

In this example, the rule includes setting a font and a font style.

Note: *See Chapter 6 to learn more about writing formatting style rules.*

6 Type **}** to end the rule.

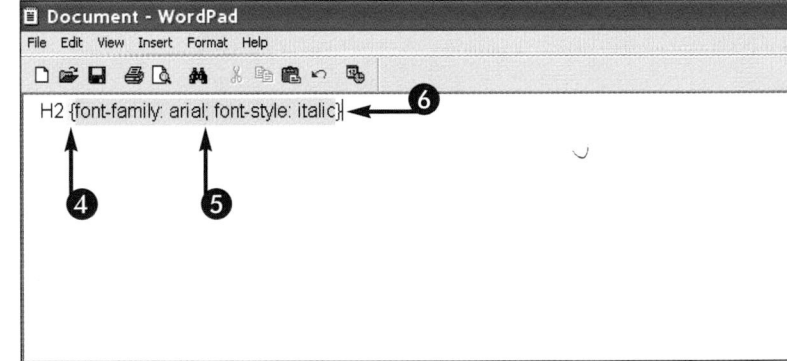

⑦ Repeat steps **2** to **6** to continue adding style rules to your style sheet.

⑧ Click **File**.

⑨ Click **Save**.

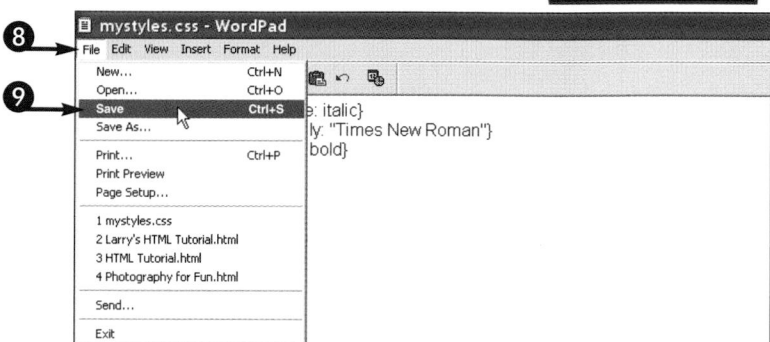

The Save As dialog box appears.

⑩ Navigate to the folder storing your HTML pages.

⑪ Type a unique filename for your style sheet and the **.css** extension.

⑫ Click **Save**.

The new style sheet is saved.

Note: See the section "Link to a Style Sheet" to learn how to apply a style sheet to your HTML documents.

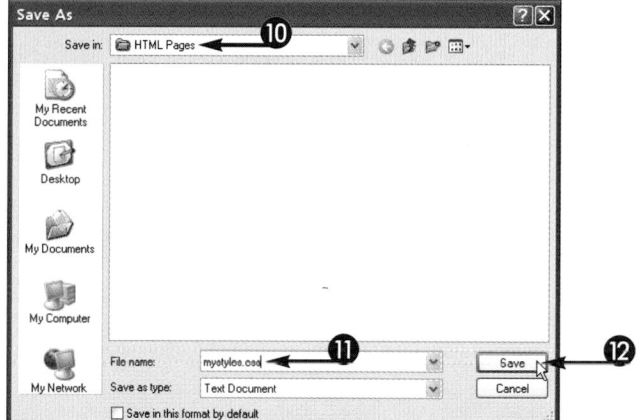

TIPS

Can I use more than one style sheet with my HTML page?

Yes. You can import a style sheet and use the `<STYLE>` tags within the `<HEAD>` tags to reference the sheet. You can import more than one sheet. For example, you can use the code to import two sheets:

```
<STYLE>
@IMPORT URL("?");
@IMPORT URL("?");
</STYLE>
```

Replace the *?* with the location and name of the style sheet. Keep in mind that not all browsers support the `@IMPORT` command.

What is XSL?

XSL, short for *extensible style language*, is a newer style sheet language used with XHTML documents. Because XHTML is a newer markup language version than HTML, XSL is not as widely supported yet as CSS. If you are building your Web pages in XHTML and prefer to use XSL as your style sheet language, be sure to save the text file as an XSL file instead of an CSS file.

You can link to a style sheet to assign the preset formatting to your HTML document. You can link multiple documents to the same style sheet to give all the pages in your site a consistent look and feel.

See the previous section, "Create an External Style Sheet," to learn how to create and save a style sheet.

Link to a Style Sheet

1 Open the HTML document you want to link to a style sheet.

Note: *See the previous section, "Create an External Style Sheet," to learn how to create a style sheet.*

2 Click within the `<HEAD>` and `</HEAD>` tags and add a new line.

3 Type **<LINK REL="stylesheet" TYPE="text/css"**.

4 Type a blank space and **HREF="?">**, replacing the *?* with the name of the style sheet.

The style sheet is now linked with the page.

You can test your page in a browser to see the style sheet results.

Note: *See Chapter 2 to learn more.*

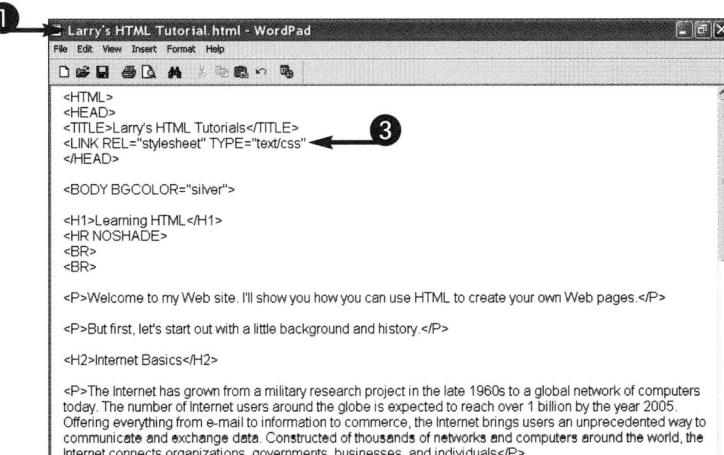

Add Comments to a Style Sheet

You can add comments — or notes — to your style sheet to help you identify your style rules. For example, you might add a comment describing the results of the rule when applied to text. Your Web browser does not read comments.

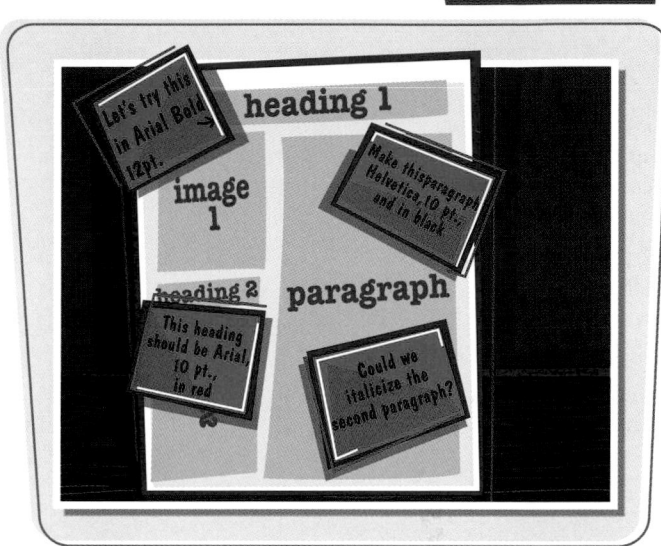

Add Comments to a Style Sheet

1 In your style sheet document, type **/*** to begin your comment.

Note: See the section, "Create an External Style Sheet," to learn how to create a style sheet.

2 Type your comment text.

3 Type ***/** to end the comment.

When you display your style sheet in a Web browser, the comments do not appear.

Create an Internal Style Sheet

You can create an internal style sheet that resides within your HTML document. Internal style sheets are handy if your Web site consists of a single page because this allows you to change both style rules and page markup from the same page.

Create an Internal Style Sheet

① Within the `<HEAD>` and `</HEAD>` tags, add a new line and type **`<STYLE>`**.

② Add a new line and type the element tag for which you want to create a style rule.

In this example, a new style rule is created for the H2 element.

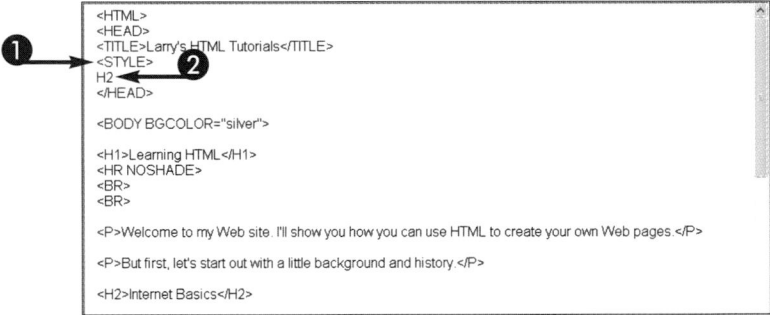

③ Type **{**.

④ Type the properties and values for the rule.

If you intend to add more than one declaration to the rule, be sure to separate declarations with a semicolon.

⑤ Type **}** to end the rule.

Note: *See Chapter 6 to learn more about writing formatting style rules.*

6 Repeat steps **2** to **5** to continue adding style rules to your internal style sheet.

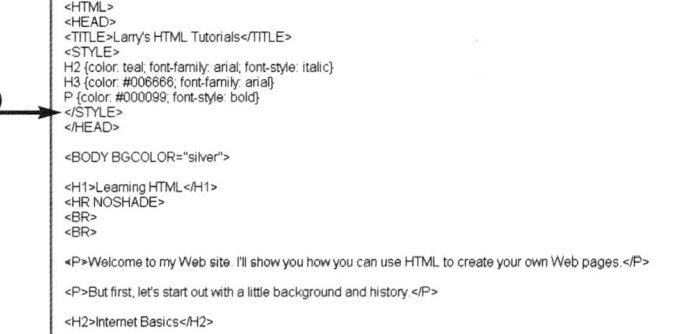

```
<HTML>
<HEAD>
<TITLE>Larry's HTML Tutorials</TITLE>
<STYLE>
H2 {color: teal; font-family: arial; font-style: italic}
H3 {color: #006666; font-family: arial}          6
P {color: #000099; font-style: bold}
</HEAD>

<BODY BGCOLOR="silver">

<H1>Learning HTML</H1>
<HR NOSHADE>
<BR>
<BR>

<P>Welcome to my Web site. I'll show you how you can use HTML to create your own Web pages.</P>

<P>But first, let's start out with a little background and history.</P>

<H2>Internet Basics</H2>

<P>The Internet has grown from a military research project in the late 1960s to a global network of computers today. The number of Internet users around the globe is expected to reach over 1 billion by the year 2005. Offering everything from e-mail to information to commerce, the Internet brings users an unprecedented way to communicate and exchange data. Constructed of thousands of networks and computers around the world, the Internet connects organizations, governments, businesses, and individuals</P>
```

7 Add a new line and type **</STYLE>**.

The closing tag completes the style sheet.

You can test your page in a browser to see the style sheet results.

Note: *See Chapter 2 to learn more about viewing HTML documents in a browser.*

```
<HTML>
<HEAD>
<TITLE>Larry's HTML Tutorials</TITLE>
<STYLE>
H2 {color: teal; font-family: arial; font-style: italic}
H3 {color: #006666; font-family: arial}
P {color: #000099; font-style: bold}      7
</STYLE>
</HEAD>

<BODY BGCOLOR="silver">

<H1>Learning HTML</H1>
<HR NOSHADE>
<BR>
<BR>

<P>Welcome to my Web site. I'll show you how you can use HTML to create your own Web pages.</P>

<P>But first, let's start out with a little background and history.</P>

<H2>Internet Basics</H2>

<P>The Internet has grown from a military research project in the late 1960s to a global network of computers today. The number of Internet users around the globe is expected to reach over 1 billion by the year 2005. Offering everything from e-mail to information to commerce, the Internet brings users an unprecedented way to communicate and exchange data. Constructed of thousands of networks and computers around the world, the Internet connects organizations, governments, businesses, and individuals</P>
```

TIPS

Do older browsers recognize internal style sheets?

Older browsers do not support styles, so they ignore the <STYLE> tags. However, the content of the <STYLE> tag is displayed in older browsers, so any coding you type in between the <STYLE> tags appears on the page. You can prevent an older browser from displaying style tag coding by typing <!-- and --> before and after the style tag details, such as :

<STYLE TYPE="text/css">

<!--

HR {color: red}

P {margin-left: 20px}

-->

</STYLE>

Can I link another Web page to my internal style sheet?

No. In order for multiple Web pages to take advantage of a style sheet, you must use an external style sheet and link the pages to the sheet. An internal style sheet is useful only for a one-page HTML document. See the section "Create an External Style Sheet" to learn more.

Create a Class

You can create a class to apply a style rule to certain tags throughout your Web page. For example, if you want all the introductory paragraphs formatted differently than all the regular paragraphs, you can create a class specifically for the introductory paragraphs. Once you create the class, the browser applies it to all the paragraphs to which the class is assigned.

You can set up a class in your external or internal style sheet, and then use the CLASS attribute in your document to assign the properties and values. To learn more about creating external or internal style sheets, see the sections "Create an External Style Sheet" and "Create an Internal Style Sheet."

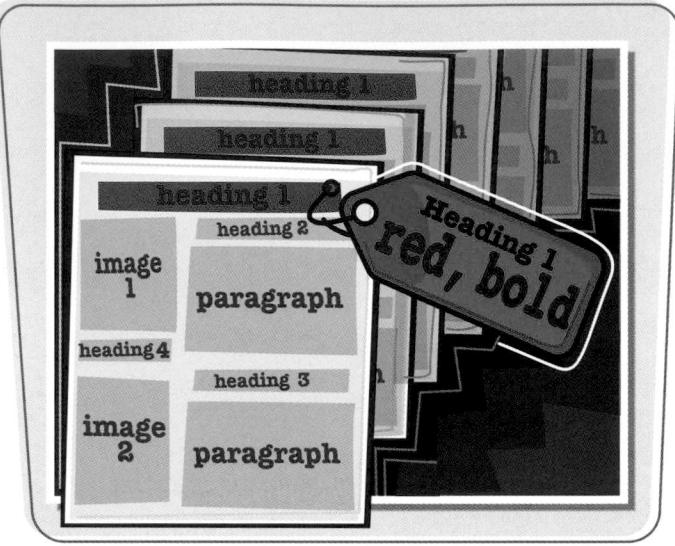

Create a Class

DEFINE A CLASS

① In your external or internal style sheet, type the tag for which you want to create a class.

Note: See the section "Create an External Style Sheet" to learn more about building style sheets.

② Type a period.

③ Type a name for the class.

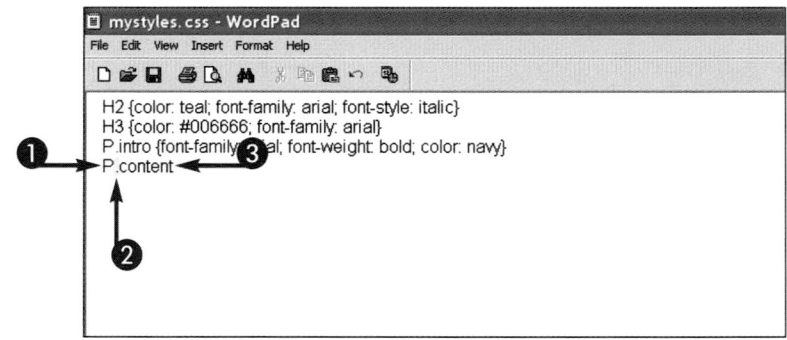

④ Type {.

⑤ Type the properties and values for the class.

If you intend to add more than one declaration to the rule, be sure to separate declarations with a semicolon.

Note: See Chapter 6 to learn more about writing formatting style rules.

⑥ Type } to end the style rule.

Your class is now defined.

If you are editing an external style sheet, save the sheet.

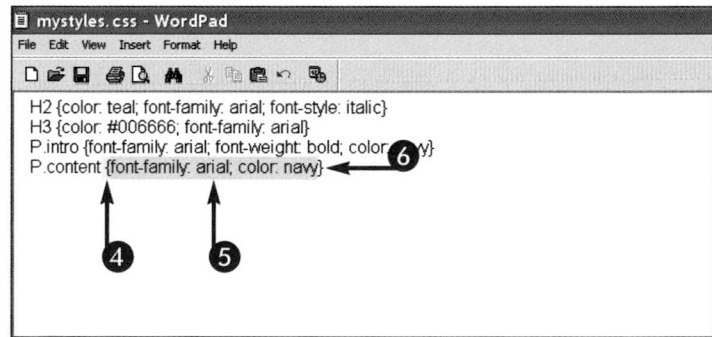

ASSIGN A CLASS

1 Open the HTML document and click in the tag to which you want to assign a class.

2 Type **CLASS="?"**, replacing the *?* with the class name.

The Web browser reads the instructions for the formatting and displays the properties you specified for the class.

```
<H1>Learning HTML</H1>
<HR NOSHADE>
<BR>
<BR>

<P>Welcome to my Web site. I'll show you how you can use HTML to create your own Web pages.</P>

<P>But first, let's start out with a little background and history.</P>
<HR NOSHADE>

<H2>Internet Basics</H2>

<P CLASS="intro">The Internet has grown from a military research project in the late 1960s to a global
network of computers today. The number of Internet users around the globe is expected to reach over 1 billion
by the year 2005. Offering everything from e-mail to information to commerce, the Internet brings users an
unprecedented way to communicate and exchange data. Constructed of thousands of networks and computers
around the world, the Internet connects organizations, governments, businesses, and individuals</P>

<H3>Types of Connections</H3>

<P CLASS="content">Users connect to the Internet through a variety of sources. Individuals can connect
through a modem and a phone line, cable, or satellite. If you use a modem to connect to the Internet, you
typically use a dial-up service, called an Internet Service Provider, or a commercial service, such as America
Online. You can also use cable TV companies to connect to the Internet through a cable modem, or you can
connect through digital phone lines, such as ISDN (Integrated Services Digital Network) and DSL (Digital
Subscriber Line).</P>
```

Welcome to my Web site. I'll show you how you can use HTML to create your own Web pages.

But first, let's start out with a little background and history.

Internet Basics

The Internet has grown from a military research project in the late 1960s to a global network of computers today. The number of Internet users around the globe is expected to reach over 1 billion by the year 2005. Offering everything from e-mail to information to commerce, the Internet brings users an unprecedented way to communicate and exchange data. Constructed of thousands of networks and computers around the world, the Internet connects organizations, governments, businesses, and individuals

Types of Connections

Users connect to the Internet through a variety of sources. Individuals can connect through a modem and a phone line, cable, or satellite. If you use a modem to connect to the Internet, you typically use a dial-up service, called an Internet Service Provider, or a commercial service, such as America Online. You can also use cable TV companies to connect to the Internet through a cable modem, or you can connect through digital phone lines, such as ISDN (Integrated Services Digital Network) and DSL (Digital Subscriber Line).

TIPS

What is a generic class?

You can use a generic class to format two or more different elements. For example, you might use a generic class to format both paragraphs and headings in a document, even though both elements use different tags. When defining a generic class, simply type a period followed by the class name, such as `.mytext`. When applying the class, use the class name, such as `<P CLASS="mytext">` or `<H2 CLASS="mytext">`.

How does inheritance work with classes?

When you apply a class, it inherits all the formatting that the class does not specifically override. For example, perhaps your HTML document contains three types of paragraphs. An introduction paragraph, a content paragraph, and a summary paragraph, and you want each to exhibit a slightly different appearance, yet all use the same font and size. You can use style rules to differentiate the changes in each, yet leave the font and size the same as defined in the `<P>` tag. Each class inherits the formatting of the `<P>` tag, but includes any overriding formatting, such as a change in bold or italics, or color.

Apply a Style with the DIV Tag

You can apply styles to different areas, or sections, of your Web page using the `<DIV>` tag. You can set up the `<DIV>` tag in your external or internal style sheet, and then apply it in your HTML document. When you apply styles with the `<DIV>` tag, the browser overrides the existing formatting for that particular section and replaces it with the style you specify.

You can use the `<DIV>` tag to group block-level elements, such as paragraphs and headings. When you apply the `<DIV>` tag, the Web browser inserts a blank line between the sections.

Apply a Style with the DIV Tag

SET UP THE DIV STYLE

① In your external or internal style sheet, type **DIV.?**, replacing the *?* with the name you want to assign the DIV style.

② Type **{**.

③ Type the properties and values for the DIV style.

If you intend to type more than one property, use a semicolon to separate properties.

Note: *See Chapter 6 to learn more about writing formatting style rules.*

④ Type **}**.

The style rule is complete.

If you are editing an external style sheet, save the sheet.

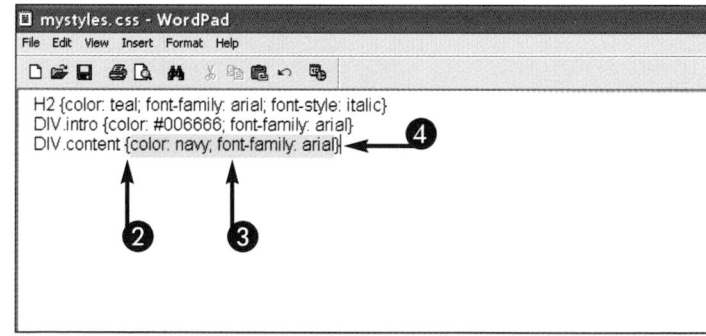

APPLY THE DIV TAG

1 In the HTML document, click in front of the section to which you want to assign a DIV tag and add a line.

2 Type **<DIV CLASS="?">**, replacing the *?* with the DIV style name.

3 Type **</DIV>** at the end of the section.

```
<HR NOSHADE>

<DIV CLASS="intro">
<H2>Internet Basics</H2>

<P>The Internet has grown from a military research project in the late 1960s to a global network of computers
today. The number of Internet users around the globe is expected to reach over 1 billion by the year 2005.
Offering everything from e-mail to information to commerce, the Internet brings users an unprecedented way to
communicate and exchange data. Constructed of thousands of networks and computers around the world, the
Internet connects organizations, governments, businesses, and individuals</P>
</DIV>

<DIV CLASS="content">
<H3>Types of Connections</H3>

<P>Users connect to the Internet through a variety of sources. Individuals can connect through a modem and a
phone line, cable, or satellite. If you use a modem to connect to the Internet, you typically use a dial-up service,
called an Internet Service Provider, or a commercial service, such as America Online. You can also use cable
TV companies to connect to the Internet through a cable modem, or you can connect through digital phone lines,
such as ISDN (Integrated Services Digital Network) and DSL (Digital Subscriber Line).</P>

<H3>Connection Speeds</H3>
<P>Connection speeds play an important part in a user's Internet experience. Slower connections result in
slower file transfers and Web page viewing. Modem connections offer the slowest connection speeds to the
Internet, up to 56 Kbps (Kilobits per second), followed by ISDN connections at 64-128 Kbps. Cable modems
can achieve connection speeds of 3000 Kbps and more, while DSL offers speeds of 1000-9000 Kbps.</P>
</DIV>
```

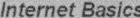

● The Web browser displays the properties you specified for that particular area of the page.

Note: *Be sure to save your HTML document before attempting to view the page in a browser window. You can click the Refresh button in your browser to see updated changes you make to your HTML document.*

Internet Basics

The Internet has grown from a military research project in the late 1960s to a global network of computers today. The number of Internet users around the globe is expected to reach over 1 billion by the year 2005. Offering everything from e-mail to information to commerce, the Internet brings users an unprecedented way to communicate and exchange data. Constructed of thousands of networks and computers around the world, the Internet connects organizations, governments, businesses, and individuals

Types of Connections

Users connect to the Internet through a variety of sources. Individuals can connect through a modem and a phone line, cable, or satellite. If you use a modem to connect to the Internet, you typically use a dial-up service, called an Internet Service Provider, or a commercial service, such as America Online. You can also use cable TV companies to connect to the Internet through a cable modem, or you can connect through digital phone lines, such as ISDN (Integrated Services Digital Network) and DSL (Digital Subscriber Line).

Connection Speeds

Connection speeds play an important part in a user's Internet experience. Slower connections result in slower file transfers and Web page viewing. Modem connections offer the slowest connection speeds to the Internet, up to 56 Kbps (Kilobits per second), followed by ISDN connections at 64-128 Kbps. Cable modems can achieve connection speeds of 3000 Kbps and more, while DSL offers speeds of 1000-9000 Kbps.

TIP

How do I format part of a paragraph or other element?

You can use the `<SPAN>` tag to apply formatting to a portion of text in your HTML document. Unlike the `<DIV>` tag, the `<SPAN>` tag is an inline tag, which means it does not add blank lines in between elements. To apply a style using the `<SPAN>` tag, first define the class you want to assign:

```
<STYLE>
SPAN.companyname  {FONT: bold "Helvetica"}
</STYLE>
```

When you want to apply the style rule, your coding might look like this:

```
<P><SPAN CLASS="companyname">
```

Apply a Style Locally

You can apply a style to a single instance of a tag in your document. For example, perhaps you want to make one of your level 2 headings stand out differently on the page than the rest of the level 2 headings. The STYLE attribute allows you to apply formatting like a style sheet without having to create an actual style sheet yourself.

When you apply a style locally, it overrides any styles found on external or internal style sheets for the same tag. Applying styles locally works best for one-time changes. You should use regular style sheets to control formatting and layouts on your pages.

Apply a Style Locally

1 Click in the tag for the element you want to change and type **STYLE="?"**, replacing the *?* with the properties and values you want to assign.

If you intend to assign more than one property, separate the properties with a semicolon.

Note: *See Chapter 6 to learn more about writing formatting style rules.*

```
<HTML>
<HEAD>
<TITLE>Larry's HTML Tutorials</TITLE>
<LINK REL="stylesheet" TYPE="text/css" HREF="mystyles.css">
</HEAD>

<BODY BGCOLOR="silver">

<H1 STYLE="font-family: arial; color: navy">Learning HTML</H1>
<HR NOSHADE>
<BR>
<BR>

<P>Welcome to my W    te. I'll show you how you can use HTML to create your own Web pages.</P>

<P>But first, let's start out with a little background and history.</P>
<HR NOSHADE>

<H2>Internet Basics</H2>

<P>The Internet has grown from a military research project in the late 1960s to a global network of computers today. The number of Internet users around the globe is expected to reach over 1 billion by the year 2005. Offering everything from e-mail to information to commerce, the Internet brings users an unprecedented way to communicate and exchange data. Constructed of thousands of networks and computers around the world, the Internet connects organizations, governments, businesses, and individuals</P>

<H3>Types of Connections</H3>
```

● The Web browser displays the element with the formatting you specified.

Learning HTML

Welcome to my Web site. I'll show you how you can use HTML to create your own Web pages.

But first, let's start out with a little background and history.

Internet Basics

The Internet has grown from a military research project in the late 1960s to a global network of computers today. The number of Internet users around the globe is expected to reach over 1 billion by the year 2005. Offering everything from e-mail to information to commerce, the Internet brings users an unprecedented way to communicate and exchange data. Constructed of thousands of networks and computers around the world, the Internet connects organizations, governments, businesses, and individuals

Types of Connections

Users connect to the Internet through a variety of sources. Individuals can connect through a modem and a phone line, cable,

You can use the ID attribute to assign a style rule to an individual Web page element. Instead of creating a style sheet first, then applying the styles to your document, you can use the ID attribute to assign a style name to a tag first and then define the rule in the style sheet.

IDs are like classes, except they are not associated with specific elements. If you want to assign a style rule to more than one element of the same tag, create a class instead. See the section, "Create a Class," to learn more.

Apply a Style Using the ID Attribute

1 In the tag element for which you want to create a style rule, type **ID="?"**, replacing the *?* with a unique name for the element.

```
<HTML>
<HEAD>
<TITLE>Larry's HTML Tutorials</TITLE>
<STYLE>
H1 {color: teal}
H2 {font-family: arial; color: teal; font-style: italic}
H3 {font-family: arial; color: teal}
P {color: navy}
</STYLE>
</HEAD>

<BODY BGCOLOR="silver">

<H1>Learning HTML</H1>
<HR NOSHADE>
<BR>
<BR>

<P>Welcome to my Web site. I'll show you how you can use HTML to create your own Web pages.</P>

<P>But, let's start out with a little background and history.</P>
<HR NOSHADE>

<H2>Internet Basics</H2>

<P ID="intro">The Internet has grown from a military research project in the late 1960s to a global network of
computers today. The number of Internet users around the globe is expected to reach over 1 billion by the year
2005. Offering everything from e-mail to information to commerce, the Internet brings users an unprecedented
```

2 Open your external style sheet, or scroll to your internal style sheet.

3 Type the tag to which you assigned an ID.

4 Type **#?**, replacing the *?* with the ID name.

5 Type a blank space and define the style rule.

The style is complete.

Note: *See the section "Understanding Style Sheets" to learn more about syntax rules.*

```
<HTML>
<HEAD>
<TITLE>Larry's HTML Tutorials</TITLE>
<STYLE>
H1 {color: teal}
H2 {font-family: arial; color: teal; font-style: italic}
H3 {font-family: arial; color: teal}
P {color: navy}
P#intro {color: teal; font-weight: bold}
</STYLE>
</HEAD>

<BODY BGCOLOR="silver">

<H1>Learning HTML</H1>
<HR NOSHADE>
<BR>
<BR>

<P>Welcome to my Web site. I'll show you how you can use HTML to create your own Web pages.</P>

<P>But first, let's start out with a little background and history.</P>
<HR NOSHADE>

<H2>Internet Basics</H2>

<P ID="intro">The Internet has grown from a military research project in the late 1960s to a global network of
computers today. The number of Internet users around the globe is expected to reach over 1 billion by the year
```

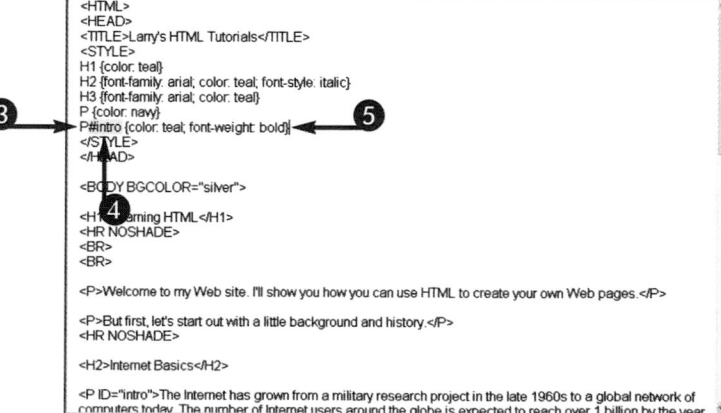

CHAPTER 6

Formatting Text with Style Sheets

Ready to start formatting your Web page with style sheets? This chapter shows you how to apply formatting to your HTML elements using style sheet properties.

Add Bold to Text 82

Italicize Text 83

Indent Text..84

Change the Font Size 85

Change the Font..86

Change the Text Case 88

Change Text Alignment 89

Control Line Spacing..................................90

Control Letter Spacing 91

Set Margins..92

Add Padding 93

Add Color to Text......................................94

Change the Text Background Color................95

Add a Border..96

Control Element Position..............................98

Wrap Text around Elements 100

Change Vertical Alignment 101

Set Width and Height for an Element 102

Add a Background Color to an Element 103

Add a Background Image to an Element 104

Change Link Colors 106

Change Bullet or Number Styles 108

You can make Web page text bold using the `font-weight` property in a style rule. The bold value allows you to control the amount of boldness, ranging from a lighter value to a darker value. You can also specify the level of boldness using a multiple of 100, with 100 as the lightest and 900 as the darkest value.

Add Bold to Text

① Click inside the tag declaration and type **font-weight:**.

Note: To learn more about writing style sheets and rules, see Chapter 5.

② Type a space.

③ Type **bold**.

You can also specify a number value using a multiple of 100 to control the boldness level.

The Web browser bolds all the text to which the tag is applied.

● In this example, all the paragraph text is now bold.

Note: To learn more about how to link a style sheet to all the pages on your Web site, see Chapter 5.

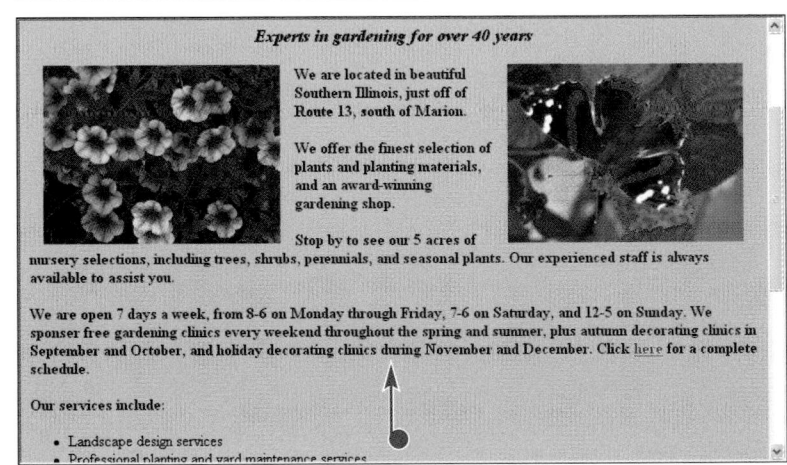

You can use the `font-style` property to italicize Web page text. Italics is an easy way to add emphasis to text. You can choose from three values when italicizing text in a style sheet: `italic`, `oblique`, and `normal`.

The `italic` value assigns an italic version of the font. If no italic version exists, `oblique` is the computer's attempt to turn the existing font into a slanted version to create italics. You can use the `normal` value to remove italics that may be inherited from previous paragraph elements.

Italicize Text

❶ Click inside the tag declaration and type **font-style:**.

Note: To learn more about writing style sheets and rules, see Chapter 5.

❷ Type a space.

❸ Type an italics value (**italic**, **oblique**, or **normal**).

The Web browser italicizes all the text to which the tag is applied.

● In this example, the unordered list text is italicized.

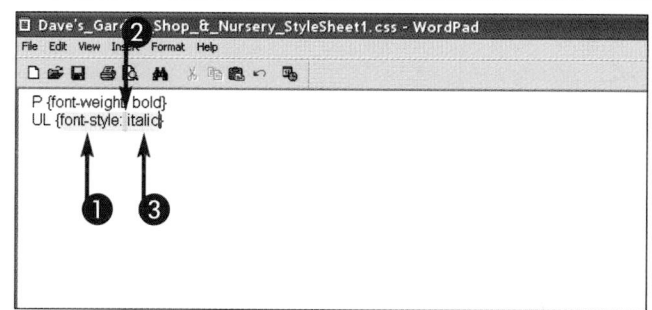

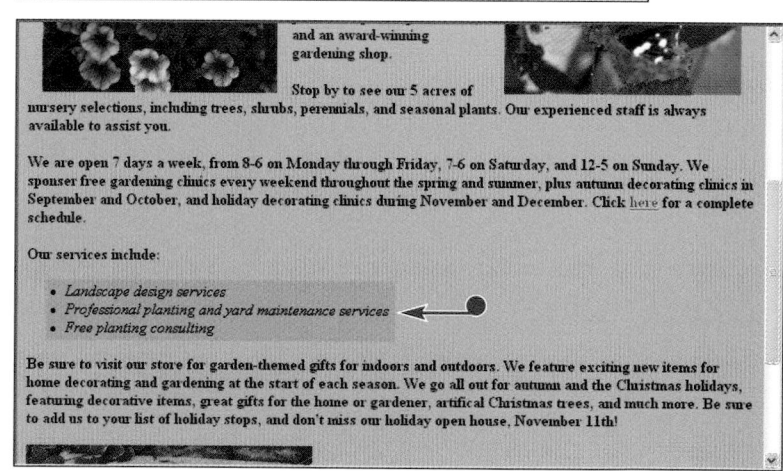

You can indent the first line in a paragraph using the `text-indent` property in a style rule. By default, the amount of indent is measured in pixels unless you specify another measurement.

You can also define a first line indent in millimeters (mm), centimeters (cm), inches (in), points (pt), picas (pc), x-height (ex), or em. You can also set the indent as a percentage of the overall text block width.

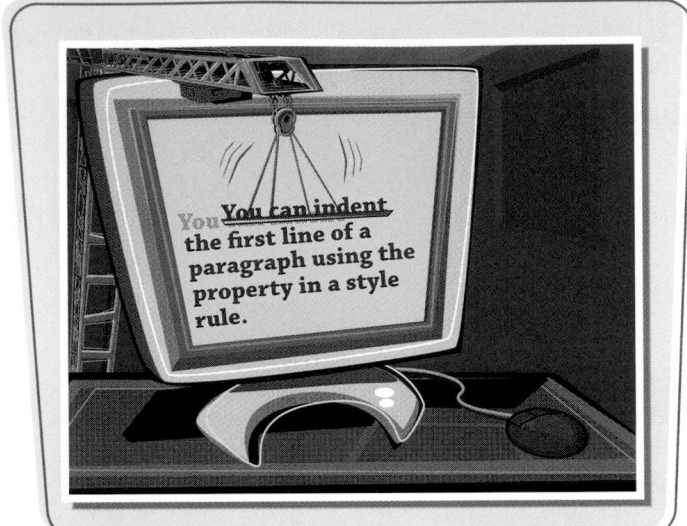

Indent Text

① Click inside the tag declaration and type **text-indent: ?**, replacing *?* with the amount of space you want to indent, measured in pixels.

You can also set an indent size as a percentage of the text block width, or set a size measurement in millimeters (mm), centimeters (cm), inches (in), points (pt), picas (pc), x-height (ex), or em.

The Web browser indents the first line of all the text to which the tag is applied.

● In this example, all the `<P>` tags are indented.

Note: To indent text with margins, see the section "Set Margins" later in this chapter.

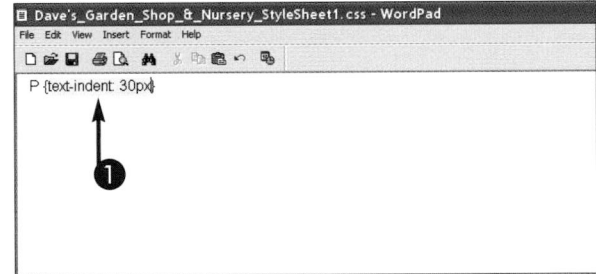

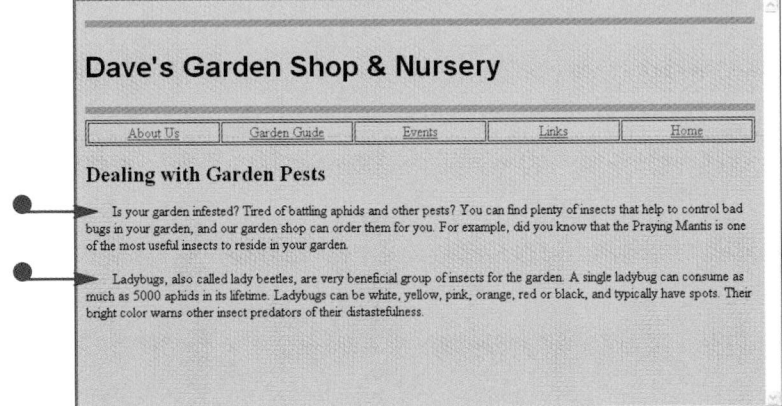

Change the Font Size

You can use the `font-size` property to change the font size for a document's text. Rather than going through your document and changing each instance of a tag, you can use the style sheet rule to change the font size for all uses of the tag in your document.

The `font-size` property allows you to set a font size using several different measurements. You can set the size in points, pixels, millimeters, centimeters, inches, picas, x-height (the height of the lowercase *x*), or em (the height of the current font). You can also specify the size as descriptive or relative. Descriptive includes the small, medium, or large values. Use the relative value to set a size percentage based on surrounding text.

Change the Font Size

① Click inside the tag declaration and type **font-size:** and a space.

② Type a font size in points (pt), pixels (px), millimeters (mm), centimeters (cm), inches (in), picas (pc), x-height (ex), or em.

You can also type a descriptive (**xx-small**, **x-small**, **small**, **medium**, **large**, **x-large**, or **xx-large**) font size.

The Web browser uses the assigned font size for any text to which the tag is applied.

● In this example, all the table text reflects a larger font size assignment.

Note: *Learn how to create tables in Chapter 9.*

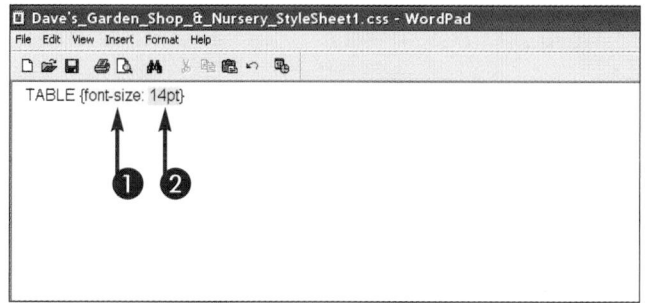

Change the Font

To change the font for your HTML text, you can use the `font-family` property. You can specify a font by name. Because not all fonts are available on all computers, you can designate a second or third font choice. This way, if the computer does not have the first choice installed, the browser tries to display the next choice instead.

For best results, try to stick with the more commonly used fonts, such as Arial, Verdana, Courier, and Times New Roman. You might also target other popular Windows fonts, including Impact and Comic Sans MS.

Change the Font

① Click inside the tag declaration and type **font-family:**.

Note: To learn more about writing style sheets and rules, see Chapter 5.

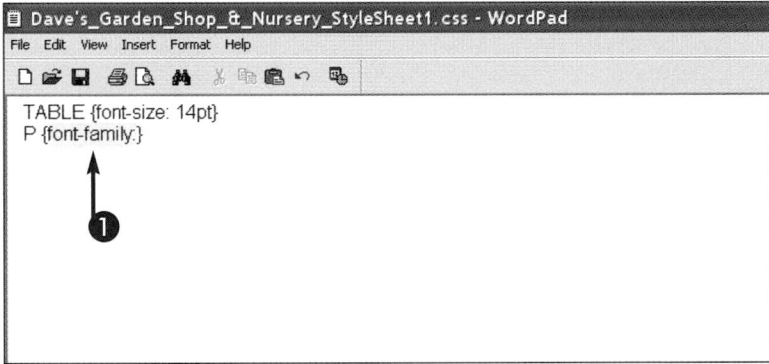

② Type a space and type **"?"**, replacing *?* with the name of the font you want to use.

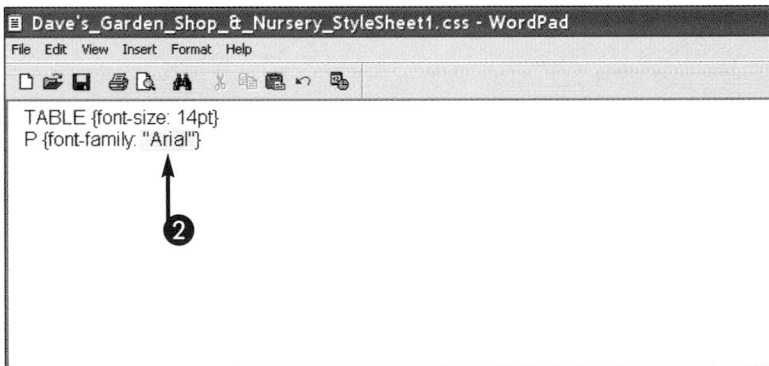

3 To designate a second font choice, type a comma, a space, and the second font name.

Be sure to enclose font names in double quotes.

You can repeat step **3** to assign additional fonts.

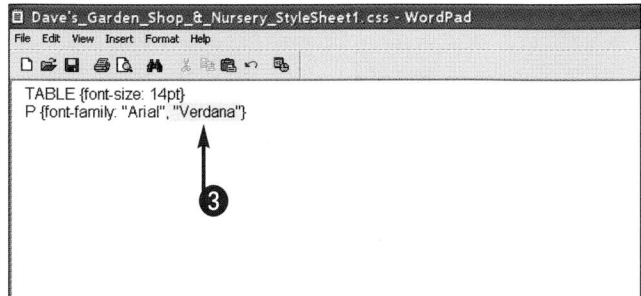

```
TABLE {font-size: 14pt}
P {font-family: "Arial", "Verdana"}
```

The Web browser uses the assigned font for any text to which the tag is applied.

● In this example, all the <P> tags reflect a new font assignment.

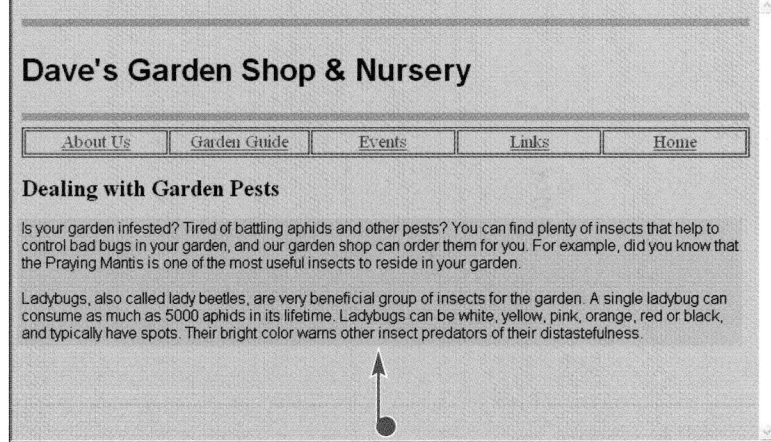

Dave's Garden Shop & Nursery

| About Us | Garden Guide | Events | Links | Home |

Dealing with Garden Pests

Is your garden infested? Tired of battling aphids and other pests? You can find plenty of insects that help to control bad bugs in your garden, and our garden shop can order them for you. For example, did you know that the Praying Mantis is one of the most useful insects to reside in your garden.

Ladybugs, also called lady beetles, are very beneficial group of insects for the garden. A single ladybug can consume as much as 5000 aphids in its lifetime. Ladybugs can be white, yellow, pink, orange, red or black, and typically have spots. Their bright color warns other insect predators of their distastefulness.

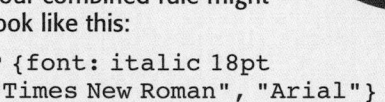

Can I change multiple font settings at the same time?

Yes. You can write a style rule that combines several font settings in one fell swoop using the `font` property. For example, you can designate the font, font size, and font style for a particular tag rather than write three different rules for the tag. Your combined rule might look like this:

```
P {font: italic 18pt
"Times New Roman", "Arial"}
```

Some browsers may require you to enter the properties in a particular order, such as font style before font size.

Is there a way to include a font with my page so users can see it even if they do not have the font installed?

Yes. You can embed the font in your Web page. If you embed the font, you must store it on the Web server, and it must use the EOT format, a requirement in Internet Explorer. You can use a special program, called WEFT, to convert an installed font into the EOT format. Visit www.microsoft.com/typography/web/embedding/weft/ to learn more. To embed the font in a style rule, follow this example:

```
@font-face {font-family: "Sunnyside";
src:url(?.eot)}
```

Replace *?* with the name of the embedded font.

You can use the `text-transform` property to change the text case for a tag. For example, you may want all `<H1>` text to appear in all capital letters. With the `text-transform` property, you can control how the browser displays the text regardless of how it was typed.

You can choose from four case values: `capitalize`, `uppercase`, `lowercase`, **and** `none`. **Use the** `capitalize` **value if you want the first character of each word to appear capitalized. Use the** `none` **value to leave text as is. The** `none` **value cancels any case values the text may have inherited.**

Change the Text Case

① Click inside the tag declaration and type **text-transform:** and a space.

② Type a text case value (**capitalize**, **uppercase**, **lowercase**, or **none**).

Note: To learn more about writing style sheets and rules, see Chapter 5.

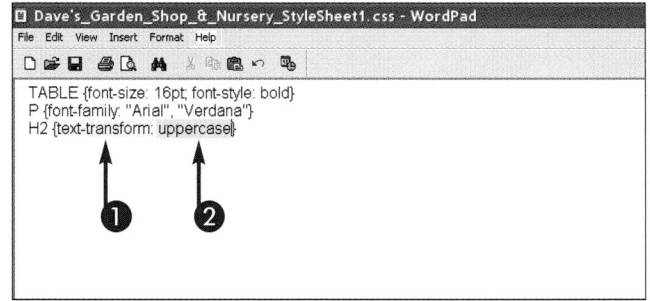

The Web browser uses the assigned text case for any text to which the tag is applied.

● In this example, the `<H2>` tag is now displayed in uppercase letters.

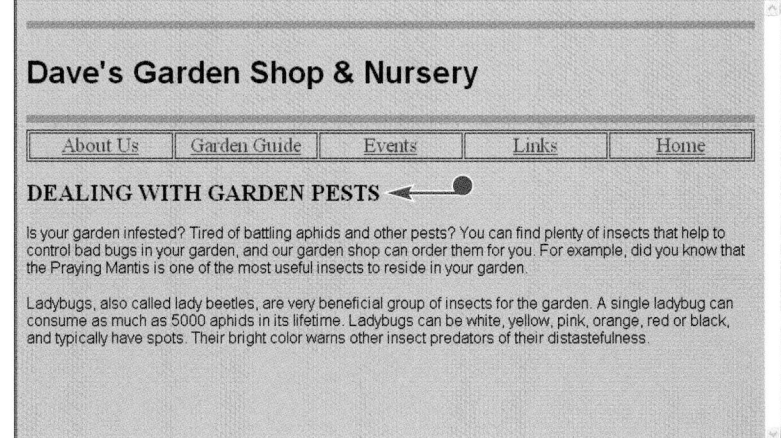

You can control the horizontal positioning of block-level text in your page using the `text-align` property. Block-level text includes paragraphs, tables, and other elements that display a blank line before and after the element on the page. You can align text to the left or right, center the text, or create justified text. By default, most browsers align text to the left unless instructed otherwise.

Change Text Alignment

① Click inside the tag declaration and type **text-align:** and a space.

② Type an alignment (**left**, **center**, **right**, or **justify**).

Note: *To learn more about writing style sheets and rules, see Chapter 5.*

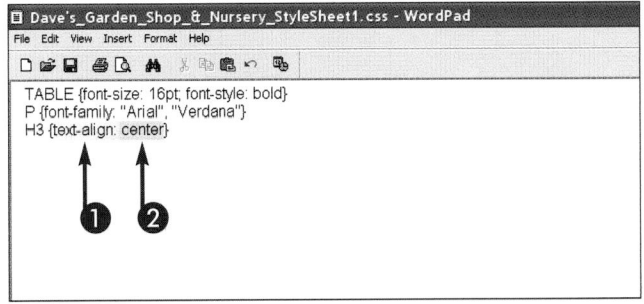

The Web browser uses the assigned alignment for any text to which the tag is applied.

● In this example, the `<H3>` tags are centered.

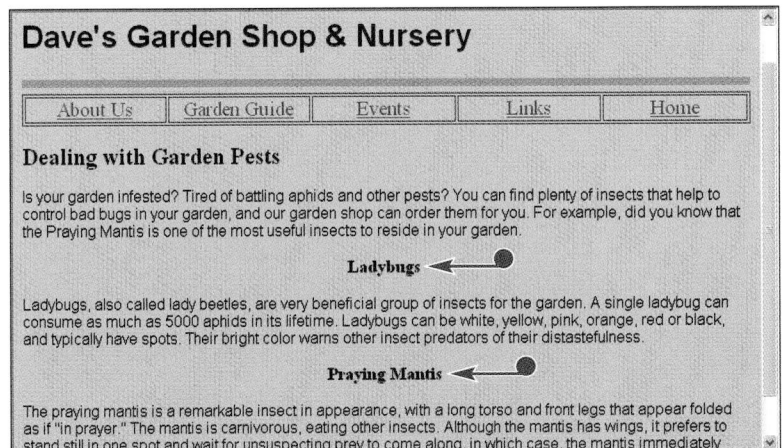

Control Line Spacing

You can use the `line-height` property to adjust the spacing between lines of text. Also called leading, line spacing can make your Web page text easier to read. The line spacing value is specified as a multiple of the height of the element's font. For example, a line height value of 2.0 multiplies the current font height by 2.

You can also set the line spacing using a percentage of the font size, such as 50%, or an absolute value measured in pixels (px), points (pt), or another measurement.

Control Line Spacing

① Click inside the tag declaration and type **line-height:** and a space.

② Type a value for the spacing.

For example, you can type **2.0** to multiply the spacing two times the current font height.

You can also set a percentage or an absolute value for the spacing.

Note: *To learn more about writing style sheets and rules, see Chapter 5.*

The Web browser uses the assigned spacing for any text to which the tag is applied.

In this example, the <P> tags all display extra line spacing.

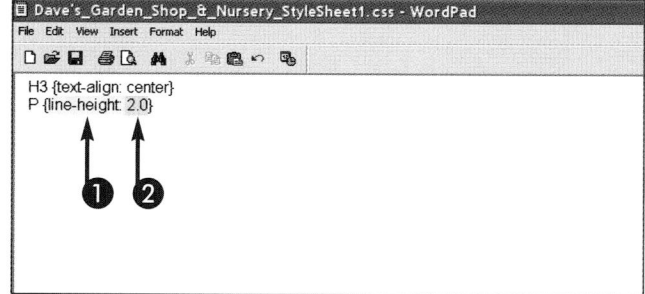

Dealing with Garden Pests

Is your garden infested? Tired of battling aphids and other pests? You can find plenty of insects that help to control bad bugs in your garden, and our garden shop can order them for you. For example, did you know that the Praying Mantis is one of the most useful insects to reside in your garden.

Ladybugs

Ladybugs, also called lady beetles, are very beneficial group of insects for the garden. A single ladybug can consume as much as 5000 aphids in its lifetime. Ladybugs can be white, yellow, pink, orange, red or black, and typically have spots. Their bright color warns other insect predators of their distastefulness.

Praying Mantis

The praying mantis is a remarkable insect in appearance, with a long torso and front legs that appear folded as if "in prayer." The mantis is carnivorous, eating other insects. Although the mantis has wings, it prefers to stand still in one spot and wait for unsuspecting prey to come along, in which case, the mantis immediately springs to action. The mantis is one of few insects fast

You can control the spacing between characters using the `letter-spacing` property. Called *kerning*, letter spacing changes the appearance of your text by spacing it out or condensing it.

You can specify letter spacing in points (pt), pixels (px), millimeters (mm), centimeters (cm), inches (in), picas (pc), x-height (ex), or em.

Control Letter Spacing

1 Click inside the tag declaration and type **letter-spacing:** and a space.

2 Type a value for the spacing.

Note: *To learn more about writing style sheets and rules, see Chapter 5.*

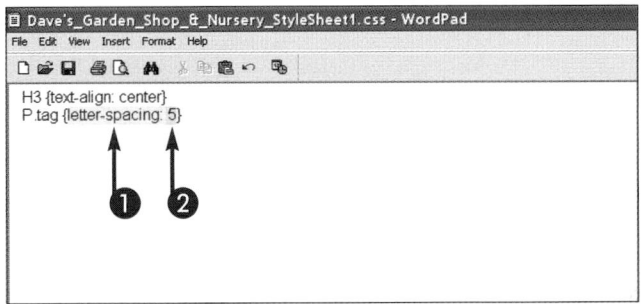

The Web browser uses the assigned letter spacing for any text to which the tag is applied.

● In this example, letter spacing is applied to a paragraph class.

Note: *See Chapter 5 to learn more about creating classes in your style sheets.*

Set Margins

You can control the margins of your Web page elements using the margin properties. You can set margin values for the top, bottom, left, and right margins around a Web page element.

You can set margin sizing using points (pt), pixels (px), millimeters (mm), centimeters (cm), inches (in), picas (pc), x-height (ex), or em.

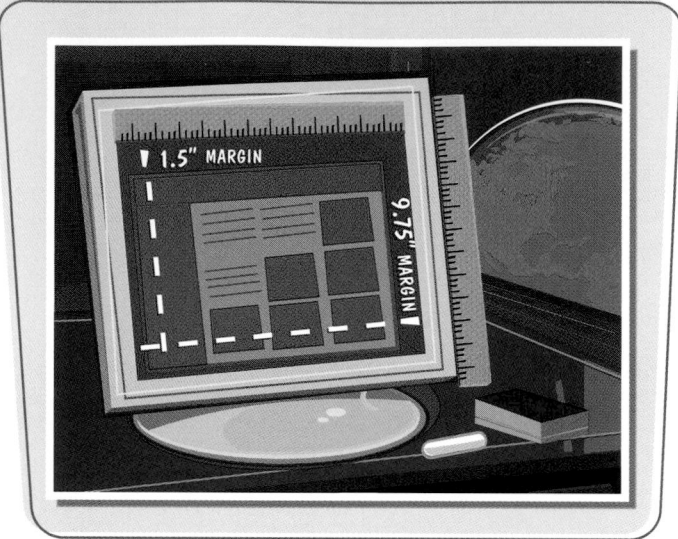

Set Margins

1 Click inside the tag declaration and type **margin-?:** and a space, replacing *?* with the margin you want to adjust (**top**, **bottom**, **left**, or **right**).

2 Type a value for the margin spacing.

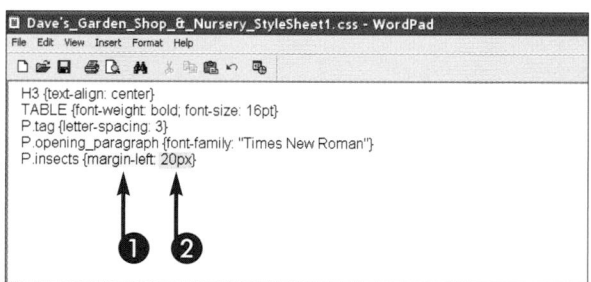

The Web browser uses the assigned margins for the Web page element.

● In this example, margins are assigned to a paragraph class.

Note: *See Chapter 5 to learn more about creating classes in your style sheets.*

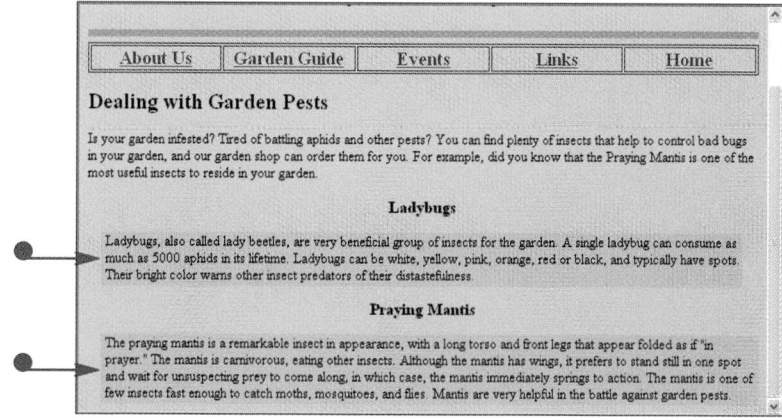

You can use the `padding` property to add space around a Web page element. For example, you might add padding around an image, a table, or a heading.

You can specify padding in points (pt), pixels (px), millimeters (mm), centimeters (cm), inches (in), picas (pc), x-height (ex), or em.

Add Padding

① Click inside the tag declaration and type **padding:** and a space.

② Type a value for the spacing.

Note: To learn more about writing style sheets and rules, see Chapter 5.

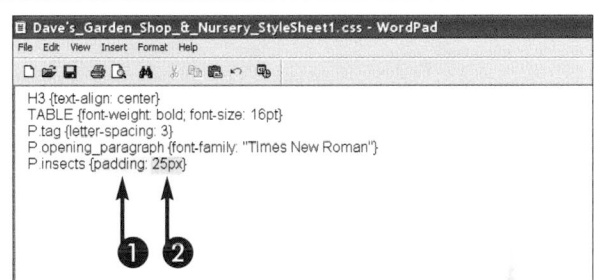

The Web browser uses the assigned padding for the element to which the tag is applied.

● In this example, padding is added to a paragraph class.

Note: See Chapter 5 to learn more about creating classes in your style sheets.

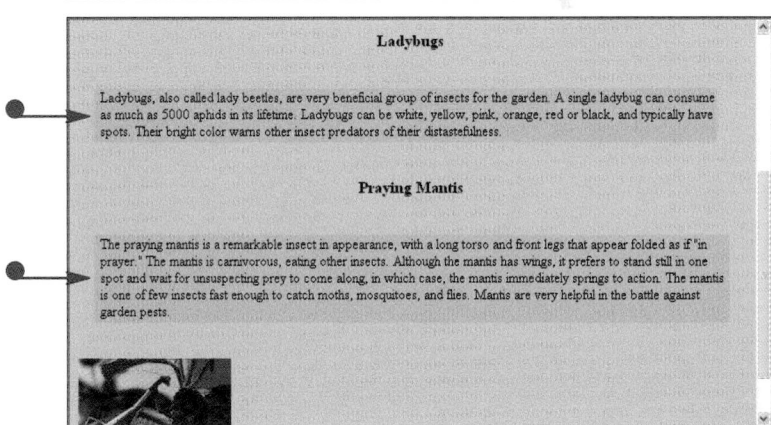

You can use the `color` property to change the color of text in your Web page. You can specify a color name from the 16 predefined colors or specify a color from the hexadecimal color palette.

You can also use the `color` property to change other Web page elements, such as tables, borders, and horizontal rules. To see a full list of color values, see the Appendix at the back of this book.

Add Color to Text

① Click inside the tag declaration and type **color:** and a space.

② Type a color name or hexadecimal value for the color you want to assign.

Note: See the Appendix for a color chart of HTML color values.

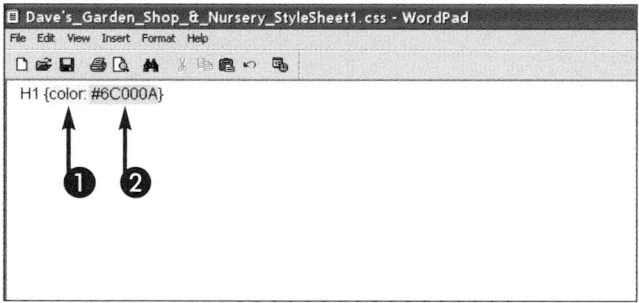

The Web browser uses the assigned color for the text to which the tag is applied.

● In this example, color is assigned to the `<H1>` tags.

Change the Text Background Color

You can use the background property to change the color that appears behind your text without changing the entire page's background. You might use this property to make your text stand out or to make sure it is legible in a busy background image.

Change the Text Background Color

① Click inside the tag declaration and type **background:** and a space.

If adding more than one property to a tag, separate properties with a semicolon (;).

② Type a color name or hexadecimal value for the color you want to assign.

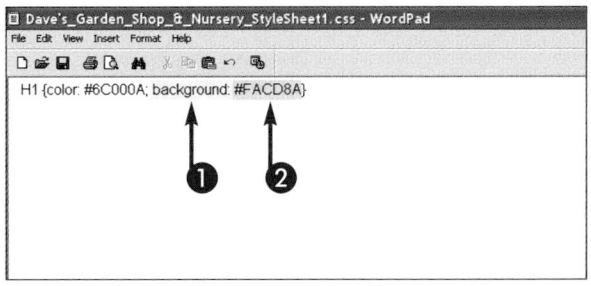

The Web browser uses the assigned background color for the element to which the tag is applied.

● In this example, the <H1> tag has a background color assigned.

Add a Border

You can add a border to a Web page element using the `border` property. A border can help separate the element from other Web page objects. You can specify a thickness value yourself, or you can specify one of three descriptive values: `thin`, `medium`, or `thick`.

You can specify a style for your border, choosing from `solid`, `double`, `groove`, `ridge`, `inset`, `outset`, `dotted`, or `dashed`. You can also assign a color value to a border. See the Appendix for a complete list of hexadecimal values for colors.

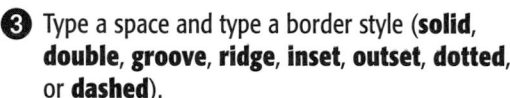

① Click inside the tag declaration and type **border:** and a blank space.

② Type a thickness value in pixels, or specify a thickness (**thin**, **medium**, or **thick**).

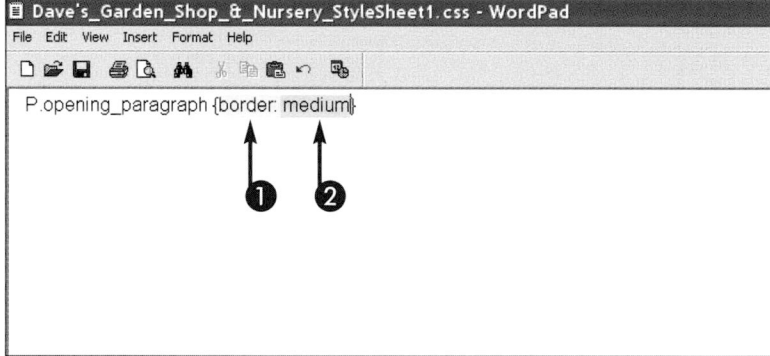

③ Type a space and type a border style (**solid**, **double**, **groove**, **ridge**, **inset**, **outset**, **dotted**, or **dashed**).

Note: If you do not set a border style with the `border` property, the browser will not display a border.

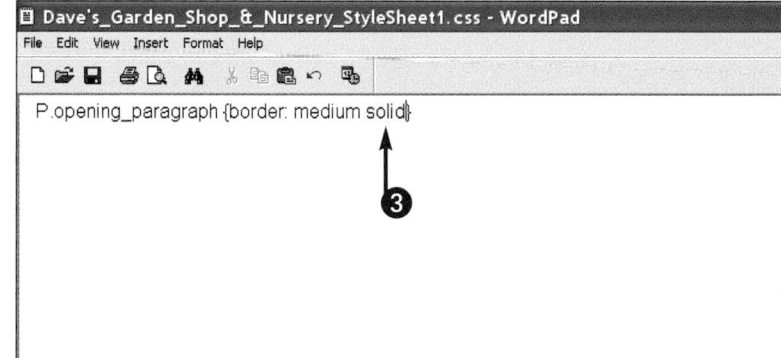

④ To add a color to the border, type a space and the color value.

Note: *To see a full list of color values, see the Appendix at the back of this book.*

● In many instances, you will need to add some padding between the content and the border; you can use the `padding` property to do so.

Note: *See the section "Add Padding" to learn more.*

The Web browser uses the assigned border for the element to which the tag is applied.

● In this example, a border is added to a paragraph class.

Note: *See Chapter 5 to learn more about creating classes in your style sheets.*

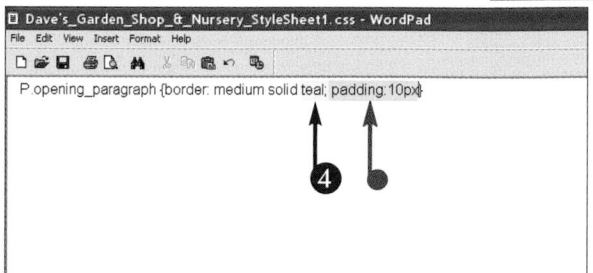

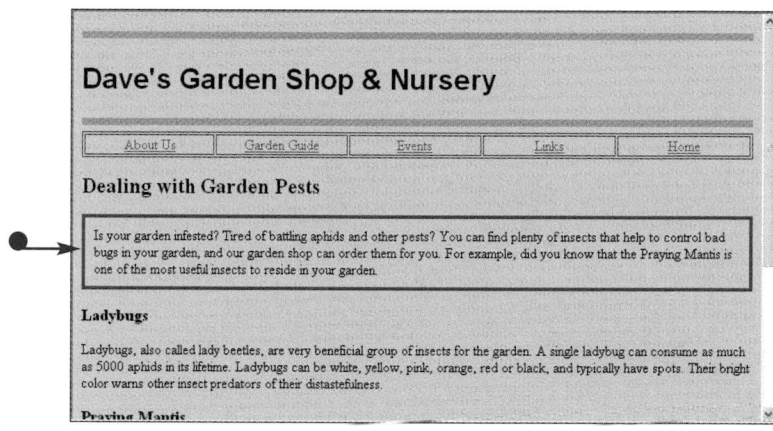

TIPS

Can I add a border to certain sides of an element instead of the entire element?

Yes. You can use the `border-left`, `border-right`, `border-top`, and `border-bottom` properties to designate which sides you want to add a border to. Your code may look like this:

`H3 {border-left: double 5px; border-right: double 5 px}`

In this example, a double border is added to the left and right sides of the heading.

Is there a way to remove all the borders on my page?

Yes. To remove borders, such as those that appear by default around linked images, you can use the border property and set the value to none. Your code looks similar to this:

`IMG {border: none}`

Control Element Position

You can position an element on your Web page absolutely or relatively. Typically, elements are positioned with respect to the surrounding elements, that is the element preceding and following the element in the document.

When you set an *absolute* position, you control the distance from the other elements, but setting an absolute position may cause other elements to shift on the page and overlap. When you set a *relative* position, you can move the element without moving surrounding elements.

Control Element Position

SET AN ABSOLUTE POSITION

① Click inside the tag declaration and type **position: absolute;**.

② Type the direction you want to move (**top**, **bottom**, **right**, or **left**) and a colon (:).

③ Type a space and type the absolute distance, in pixels, you want to move the element away from the surrounding elements.

To move the element in more than one direction, add another direction separated by a semicolon (;).

The Web browser displays the element in the new position.

● In this example, the <IMG> tag is positioned absolutely on the page, causing the <P> and <H3> tags to overlap it.

Note: Learn how to add images in Chapter 7.

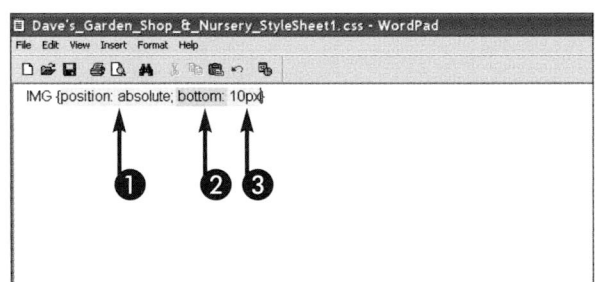

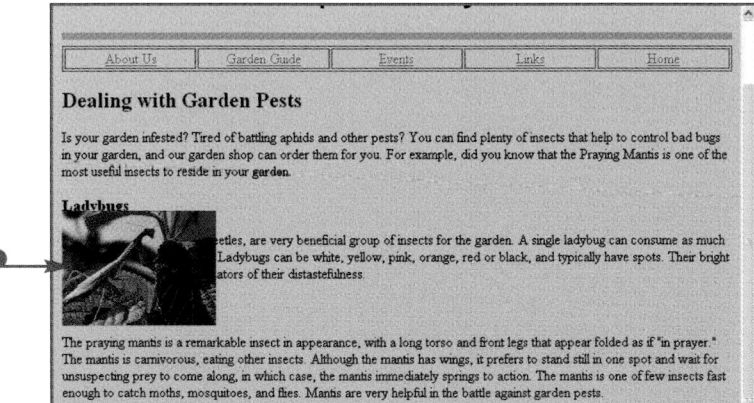

SET A RELATIVE POSITION

1 Click inside the tag declaration and type **position: relative;**.

2 Type the direction you want to offset (**top**, **bottom**, **right**, or **left**) followed by a colon (:).

3 Type a space and type the distance, in pixels, you want to offset the element.

The Web browser displays the element in the new position.

● In this example, the `<IMG>` tag is positioned relatively on the page, and the `<P>` and `<H3>` tags flow with the image.

Note: *Learn how to add images in Chapter 7.*

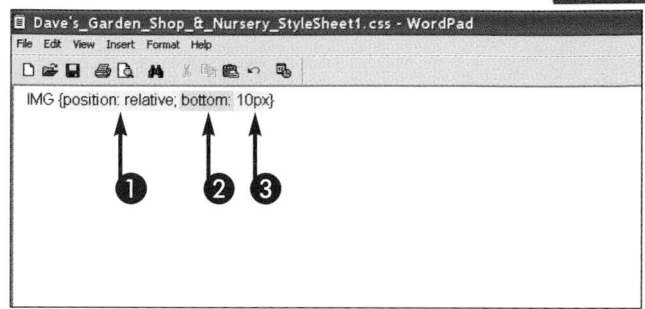

IMG {position: relative; bottom: 10px}

❶ ❷ ❸

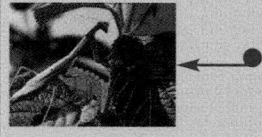

Dealing with Garden Pests

Is your garden infested? Tired of battling aphids and other pests? You can find plenty of insects that help to control bad bugs in your garden, and our garden shop can order them for you. For example, did you know that the Praying Mantis is one of the most useful insects to reside in your garden.

Ladybugs

Ladybugs, also called lady beetles, are very beneficial group of insects for the garden. A single ladybug can consume as much as 5000 aphids in its lifetime. Ladybugs can be white, yellow, pink, orange, red or black, and typically have spots. Their bright color warns other insect predators of their distastefulness.

Praying Mantis

The praying mantis is a remarkable insect in appearance, with a long torso and front legs that appear folded as if "in prayer."

TIPS

Can I make an element stay fixed on the screen while the user scrolls?

Yes. You can keep an element stationary, or fixed. You might use this property to keep a navigation button or list in view at all times whether the user scrolls up or down the page.
To apply the property, your style sheet rule might look similar to this:

```
#navigation
{position: fixed;
left: 10px}
```

Warning: not all browsers support the fixed positioning property. You may prefer to use frames to keep content in view. See Chapter 10.

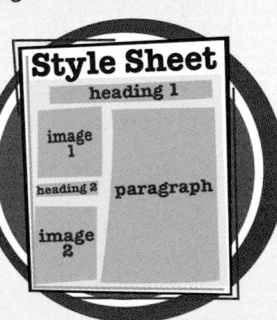

In what ways can a style sheet control the elements on my Web page?

Your Web page elements flow from one to the next based on the order in which they are entered. Much like a page layout program, CSS assigns each element its own space on the page, similar to an invisible box. As such, you can control the content inside the box, the area surrounding the content, the border, and the space around the border. You can position an element by leaving it in the original flow order, removing it from the flow and positioning it exactly (absolute positioning), or moving it in respect to its original position in the flow (relative positioning).

Style Sheet
heading 1
image 1
heading 2 paragraph
image 2

Wrap Text around Elements

You can use the `float` property to control how text wraps around the elements on your Web page. The `left` value controls the left side of an element, and the `right` value controls the right side of an element. To ensure proper text wrapping, the floating element should appear directly before the text you want to wrap.

The `float` property does not work with elements for which you have assigned an absolute or fixed position.

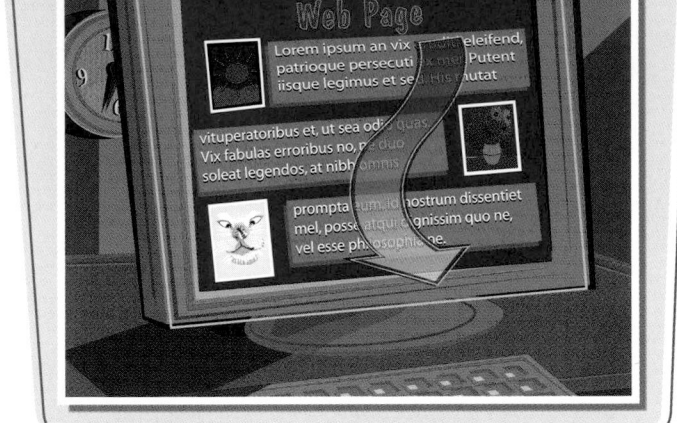

1. Click inside the tag declaration you want to control and type **float:** and a space.

2. Type **left** to set the element to the left side of the text, or type **right** to set the element to the right side of the text.

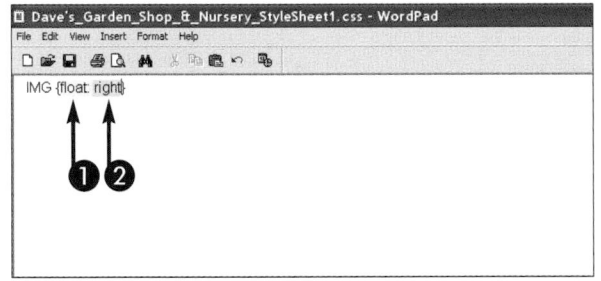

   The Web browser floats the element as directed.

● In this example, the `<IMG>` tag floats to the right of the text tags.

Note: *Learn how to add images in Chapter 7.*

You can control the vertical positioning of elements on your page using the `vertical-align` property. You can choose from six different vertical alignments: `baseline`, `text-top`, `text-bottom`, `middle`, `top`, or `bottom`.

Change Vertical Alignment

① Click inside the tag declaration and type **vertical-align: ?**, replacing *?* with the vertical alignment option you want to assign (**baseline**, **text-top**, **text-bottom**, **middle**, **top**, or **bottom**).

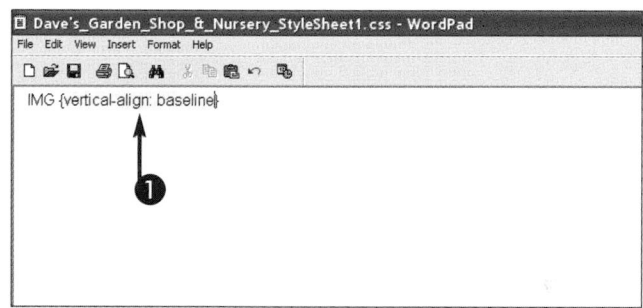

The Web browser displays the element using the assigned vertical alignment.

● In this example, the `<IMG>` tag sits at the baseline of the text.

Note: Learn how to add images in Chapter 7.

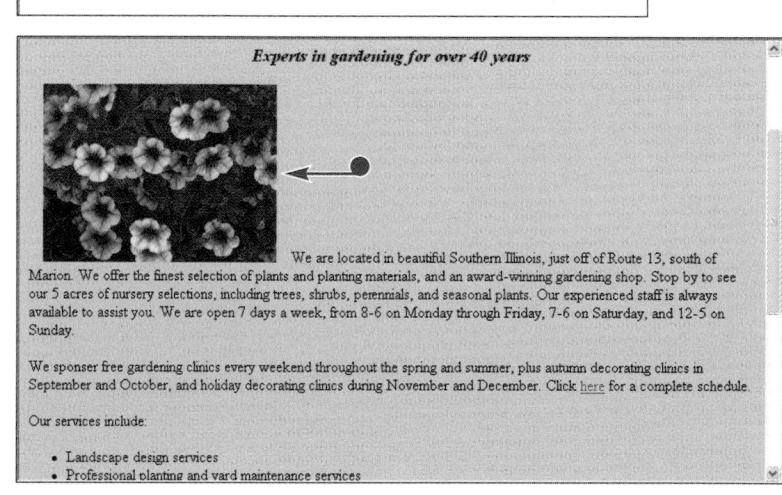

Set Width and Height for an Element

You can use the `width` and `height` properties in your style sheet to set width and height sizes for your Web page elements. For example, if you want all the `<IMG>` tags to share the same dimensions, you can apply the `width` and `height` properties in the style sheet to size all the images. See Chapter 7 to learn more about images.

You can specify width and height values in points (pt), pixels (px), millimeters (mm), centimeters (cm), inches (in), picas (pc), x-height (ex), or em. You can also specify a size based on a percentage.

Set Width and Height for an Element

① Click inside the tag declaration and type **width: ?, height: ?**, replacing *?* with a size for the width and height.

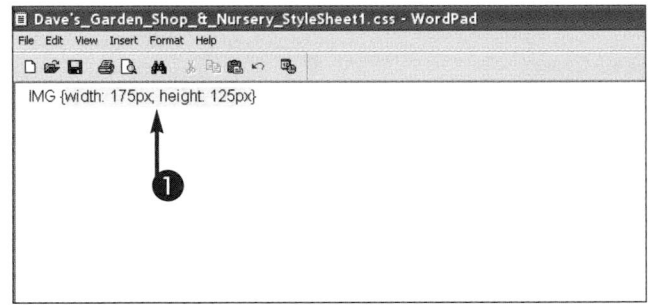

The Web browser displays the element with the designated width and height.

● In this example, all the `<IMG>` tags are resized to the same width and height.

Note: *Learn how to add images in Chapter 7.*

Add a Background Color to an Element

You can use the `background` property to change the color that appears behind an element without changing the entire page's background.

Use caution when assigning a background color to an element, making sure the color does not clash with the element or obscure the legibility.

Add a Background Color to an Element

① Click inside the tag declaration and type **background:** and a space.

② Type a color name or hexadecimal value for the color you want to assign.

If adding more than one property to a tag, remember to separate properties with a semicolon (;).

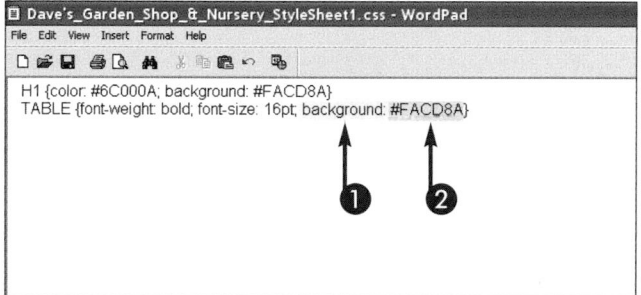

The Web browser uses the assigned background color for the element to which the tag is applied.

In this example, background color is added to the <TABLE> element.

Note: Learn how to add tables in Chapter 9.

Add a Background Image to an Element

You can add a background image to an element using a style sheet rule. To specify a background image, you must know the name and location of the image file. If the image size is small, the browser repeats, or tiles, the image to fill the background area. You can control the repeat using the `repeat` values.

Always be careful when assigning a background image; make sure your text is clearly legible over the top of the background. You may need to change the text color. See the section "Add Color to Text" to learn more.

Add a Background Image to an Element

① Click inside the tag declaration and type **background:** and a space.

If adding more than one property to a tag, remember to separate properties with a semicolon (;).

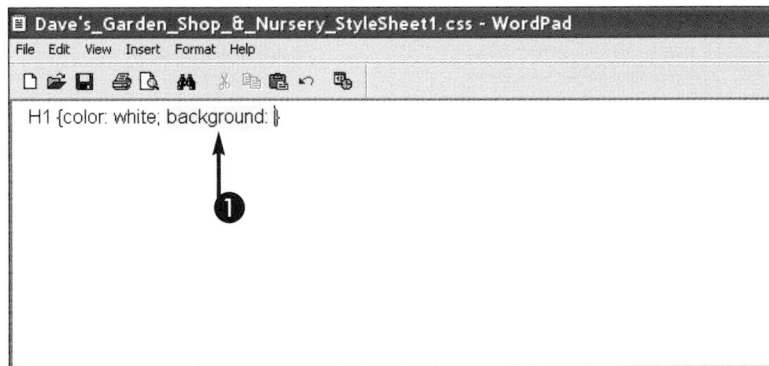

② Type **url("?")** and a space, replacing *?* with the location and name of the image file you want to use as a background.

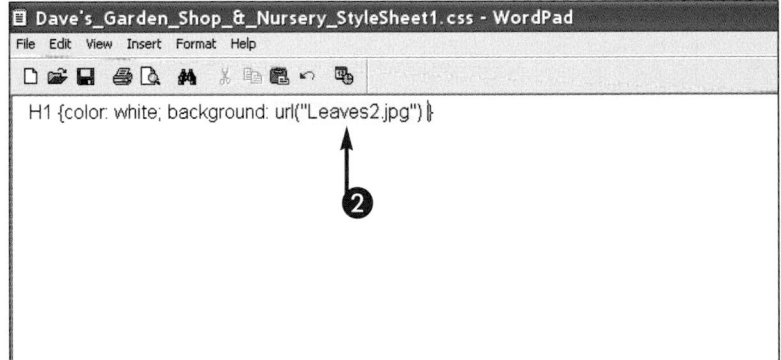

③ Type a repeat option for the image:

repeat repeats the image to fill the background (default).

repeat-x tiles the image horizontally.

repeat-y tiles the image vertically.

no-repeat prevents a background image from repeating.

The Web browser displays the background image as designated in the style rule.

● In this example, a background image is added to the `<H1>` tag.

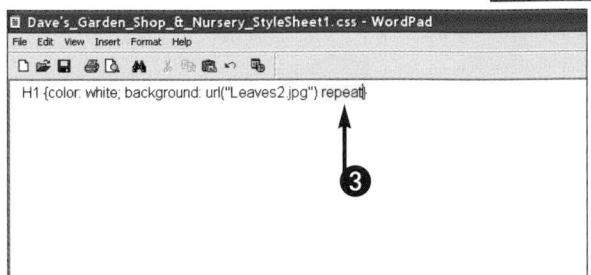

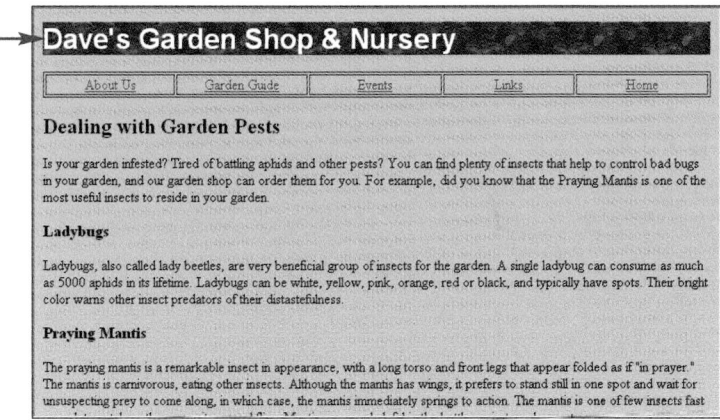

Dave's Garden Shop & Nursery

| About Us | Garden Guide | Events | Links | Home |

Dealing with Garden Pests

Is your garden infested? Tired of battling aphids and other pests? You can find plenty of insects that help to control bad bugs in your garden, and our garden shop can order them for you. For example, did you know that the Praying Mantis is one of the most useful insects to reside in your garden.

Ladybugs

Ladybugs, also called lady beetles, are very beneficial group of insects for the garden. A single ladybug can consume as much as 5000 aphids in its lifetime. Ladybugs can be white, yellow, pink, orange, red or black, and typically have spots. Their bright color warns other insect predators of their distastefulness.

Praying Mantis

The praying mantis is a remarkable insect in appearance, with a long torso and front legs that appear folded as if "in prayer." The mantis is carnivorous, eating other insects. Although the mantis has wings, it prefers to stand still in one spot and wait for unsuspecting prey to come along, in which case, the mantis immediately springs to action. The mantis is one of few insects fast

TIPS

Where can I find good background images to use with my Web pages?

If you do not have images to use as backgrounds, you can try finding free ones on the Web. Many sites offer texture images, such as marble backgrounds, water, and more. For example, BackgroundCity.com (www.backgroundcity.com), Absolute Background Textures Archive (www.grsites.com/textures/), and Free-Backgrounds.com (www.free-backgrounds.com/) are good places to start. Try conducting a Web search on the keywords "free background images."

If the user has images turned off in his or her browser, can the user see the background image for an element?

No. However, you can insert both a background color and a background image. While the image downloads, the browser displays the background color. If the user has images turned off, he or she still sees the background color. Be sure to type the color property before the URL. Your style rule will look similar to this:

```
P {background: yellow url
("images/peaches10.jpg")}
```

Change Link Colors

You can control the appearance of links throughout your Web pages using a style rule. You can change the color of unvisited, visited, and active links. You can also remove the default underlining that normally appears beneath a link.

Change Link Colors

① Type **A:? {}** to identify the link tag, replacing *?* with the type of link you want to change (**link**, **visited**, or **active**).

Note: *To learn more about writing style sheets and rules, see Chapter 5.*

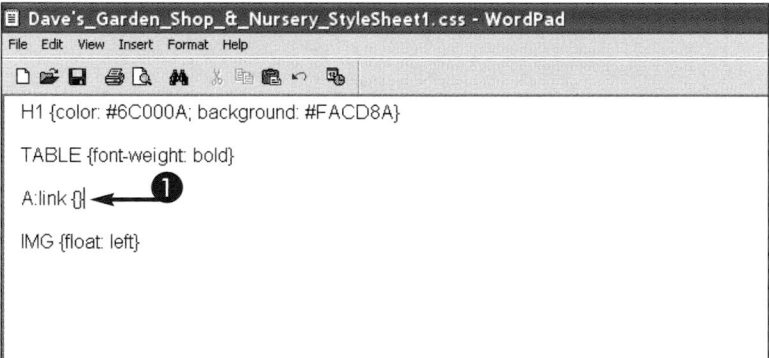

② Click between the {} and type **color:** and a space.

③ Type the color name or value you want to assign.

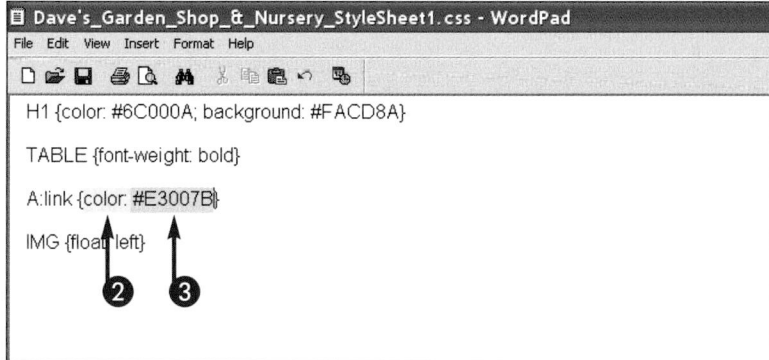

④ Type a semicolon (;) followed by a space.

⑤ Type **text-decoration: none** to remove the link underline.

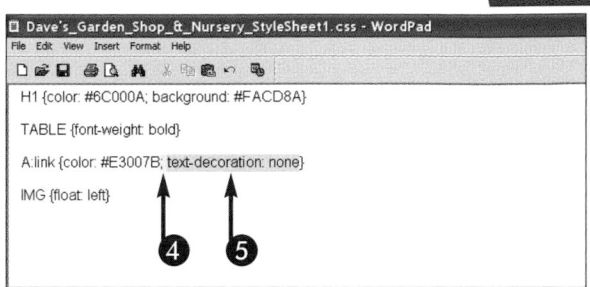

The Web browser displays the link in the color you specified.

● In this example, color is assigned to the links in the navigation bar.

 TIPS

What other style sheet properties can I apply to links?

You can use the background and font-family properties to control the appearance of text and backgrounds of your links. Any time you enter more than one value in a style rule, be sure to insert a semicolon. Here is an example of a style rule with other properties assigned:

```
A:link {background:
yellow; font-family:
"Arial"}
```

Can I change the link color that appears when the user moves the mouse over the link?

Yes. You can use the hover class to control the appearance of a link when the user positions the mouse pointer directly over a link. For example, you may want the link to change fonts or color, alerting users that they are pointing at a link. Here is an example of the hover class in a style rule:

```
A:hover {color: fuchsia}
```

Not all browsers support the hover property. See Chapter 5 to learn more about CSS classes.

Change Bullet or Number Styles

You can use the `list-style` property to change the bullet or number style for your unordered or ordered lists. You can choose from three bullet styles and five number styles.

Bullets come in three flavors: circle (○), disc (●), or square (■). Disc is the default bullet style. Numbers include decimal (1, 2, 3), lower-alpha (a,b,c), upper-alpha (A, B, C), lower-roman (i, ii, iii), or upper-roman (I, II, III). Decimal is the default number style.

CHANGE THE BULLET STYLE

① Click inside the UL tag declaration and type **list-style** followed by a space.

② Type the bullet style you want to apply (**circle**, **disc**, or **square**).

Note: To learn more about creating lists, see Chapter 3.

The Web browser displays the bullet style you specified in the style rule.

● In this example, the bulleted list shows square bullets.

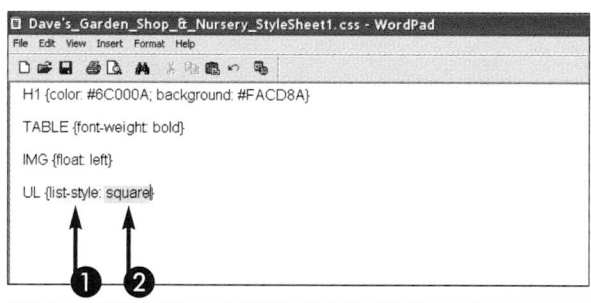

CHANGE THE NUMBER STYLE

① Click inside the OL tag declaration and type **list-style** followed by a space.

② Type the number style you want to apply (**decimal**, **lower-alpha**, **upper-alpha**, **lower-roman**, or **upper-roman**).

Note: *To learn more about creating lists, see Chapter 3.*

The Web browser uses the number style you specified in the style rule.

● In this example, the numbered list shows lower-roman numbers.

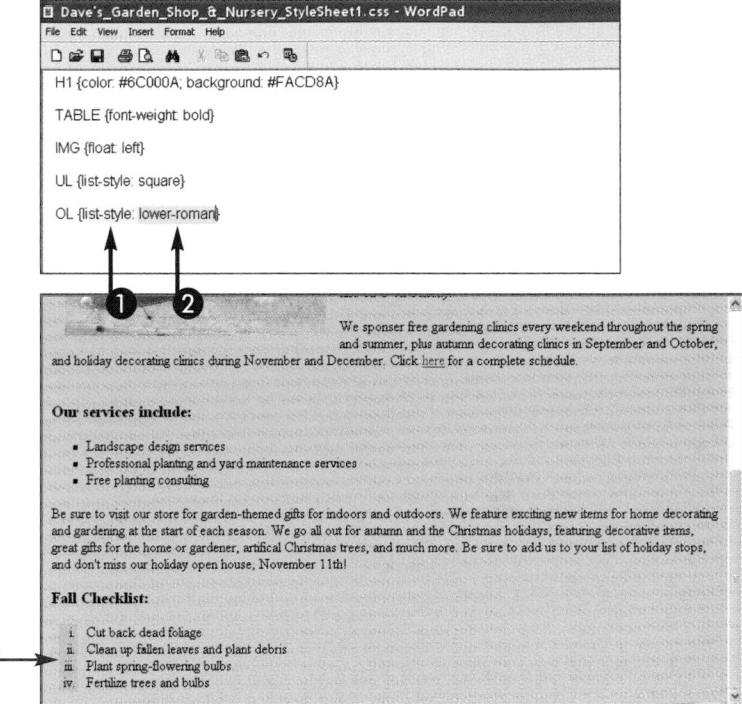

TIPS

Can I use an Image for a bullet?

Yes. To use an image as a bullet, you must include the url value to designate the location and name of the image. Your style rule may look similar to this:

```
UL {list-style: url
("images/flower1.gif")
circle}
```

You can locate numerous bullet images on the Web; many are free for downloading. Visit sites like The Shockzone.com (www.theshockzone .com), Grapholina (www.grapholina.com/Graphics), and CreateAFree Website (www.createafreewebsite.net/ free_bullets.html) to find picture bullets you can use in your bulleted lists.

Can I control the position of bullets or numbers in my lists?

Yes. You can use the inside or outside value to position bullets or numbers in your lists. You can use the inside value to wrap text beneath the bullet or number marker. The outside value indents all the text to line up neatly to the inside of the markers. Here is an example of the inside value applied in a style rule:

```
OL {list-style: decimal;
inside}
```

Adding Images

Are you ready to add images to your Web page? Images include everything from photographs, logos, clip art, and other visual objects you can add to a Web page. This chapter shows you how to add and control images, including photographs, graphic files, and background images.

Understanding Web Page Images 112

Prepare Your Images for the Web 114

Insert an Image 116

Specify an Image Size 118

Add Alternative Text 120

Create an Image Label 121

Add Copyright Text to Images 122

Align an Image Horizontally 123

Align an Image Vertically 124

Center an Image 125

Wrap Text between Images 126

Stop Text Wrap 127

Set an Image Border 128

Add Space around an Image 129

Add a Background Image 130

Create an Image Banner 131

Understanding Web Page Images

You can use images in a variety of ways on your HTML pages. Images include everything from graphics and clip art, to photographs and other visual objects. Images can illustrate text, show a product, or act as navigational tools for a Web site. An important part of using images effectively on your own site is to understand how browsers display the images for others to view.

Image File Formats

Although there are numerous file types used for images, JPEG and GIF are the two most popular types used on the Web. Both formats are cross-platform and offer file compression. PNG is a newer arrival in the image file format world and is gaining popularity among Web developers. However, not all older browsers can support PNG.

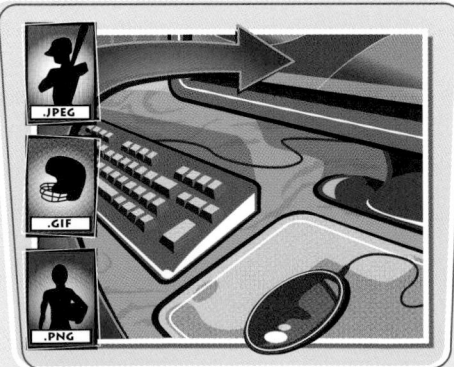

JPEG

JPEG, or JPG, which stands for *Joint Photographic Experts Group*, supports 24-bit color, allowing for millions of colors. The JPEG format is commonly used with complex images, such as photos or graphics that use millions of colors and feature lots of detail. JPEG is not a good choice for simple artwork because it results in a larger overall file size, which in turn, takes longer to display on Web pages.

GIF

GIF, which stands for *Graphics Interchange Format*, supports up to 256 colors. The GIF format is more common with simple images, such as simple graphics utilizing basic shapes and lines, and logos. If your image or graphic contains few colors and not a lot of detail, GIF is a good file format choice.

PNG

The PNG format, which stands for *Portable Network Graphics*, offers rich color support and advanced compression schemes, and is a good choice for any kind of images, from graphics to photographs. PNG supports 24-bit color, like JPEG, but greater file compression. Choose PNG if your intended audience most likely uses a new browser version.

Downloading Considerations

Browsers must first download an image before users can view it on the Web page. Large images can take a long time to display, especially with slower Internet connection speeds. For this reason, you need to consider the overall file size of an image when deciding whether to add it to a Web page. Do not populate your page with many large pictures, or the download time will be excessive.

Optimize Images

Most image-editing programs allow you to make adjustments to the quality or resolution of the image to control file size. For best results, make sure your image file size does not exceed 60K, a good size for Web page images; if you use larger image files, many users will not wait for extended periods of time for the picture to download on-screen. You can also reduce the number of colors in an image to reduce the file size.

Prepare Your Images for the Web

You can use image editing software or a graphics program to edit your images and make them Web-ready. Whether you plan to use photographs or graphics on an HTML page, you can save yourself some time and effort by preparing the images in another program first, and then inserting them onto your pages using HTML coding.

For more on images and the formats they use, see the section "Understanding Web Page Images."

Image Editing Programs

You can find numerous image-editing and graphics-editing programs for editing your image files. Programs, such as Adobe's Photoshop Elements and JACS's Paint Shop Pro, are very affordable, retailing for less than $100, and allow you to reduce the overall file size of an image, as well as save it to a Web-friendly file format.

Reduce the Image Width and Height

Image size is an important consideration for placing an image on a Web page. Images wider than 620 pixels may not be viewable on some computers. You can use an editing program to resize an image. You should also crop out any areas of the image you do not want to appear on the final image. This can help reduce the overall image file size.

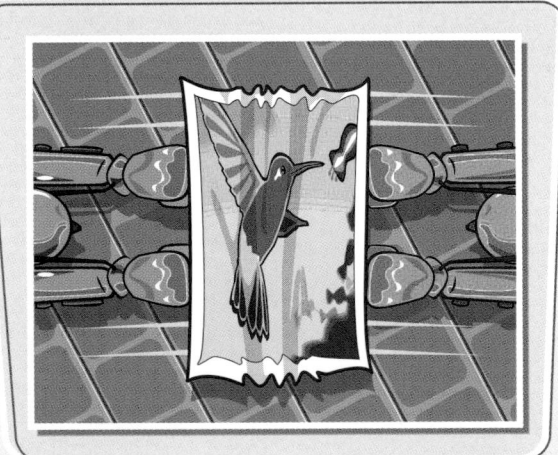

Image Resolution

Although higher resolution images are sharper in detail, you do not need incredibly sharp photos for a Web page. Lowering the resolution setting to less than 72 dpi (dots per inch) can help reduce the overall file size and reduce the amount of time to download the image onto a page.

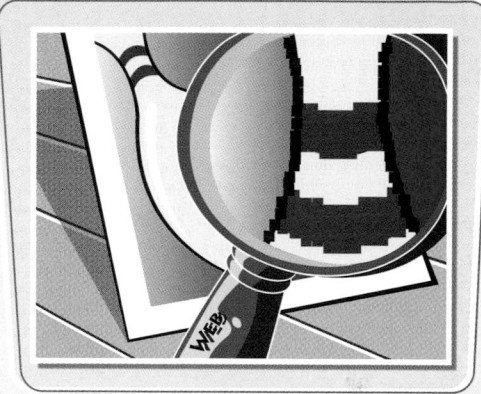

Image Compression

Image editing programs allow you to save your image to a specific file type and set a compression level. File compression allows you to reduce the file by up to 90 percent of the original file size. Many programs allow you to view the image both before and after compression to see a difference in quality levels.

Alternative Text

For some Web users, turning off the image display setting in a browser can help speed up the viewing of Web pages. To anticipate such users viewing your pages, be sure to include alternative text to describe the images you insert. Alternative text appears in place of the image and allows you to keep the page layout intact in spite of the nondisplay of images. Learn how to add alternative text in the section "Add Alternative Text."

Insert an Image

You can add images to your Web page to add interest or illustrate a topic. For example, you can add a photograph or a graphic to your page. In HTML coding, images are inline elements, which means they appear within the body of the page along with text elements.

You can use image files from a digital camera or scanner, or files you create with a graphics program. If you are not the original author of the image, you need permission to use the image before placing it on a Web site. (Using an image without permission violates copyright laws and exposes you to potential prosecution.) You can also find free clip art images on the Web.

Insert an Image

INSERT A PHOTOGRAPH

① Type **<IMG SRC="?">** where you want to insert a photographic image, replacing the *?* with the full path to the file you want to insert.

```
<HTML>
<HEAD>
<TITLE>Dave's Garden Shop & Nursery</TITLE>
<BASE TARGET="_blank">
</HEAD>
<BODY BGCOLOR="#CCFFCC">

<H1 ALIGN="center"><FONT FACE="Arial">Dave's Garden Shop & Nursery</FONT></H1>
<HR>

<IMG SRC="Garden_Supplies.jpg">  ◄——— ①

<P><B><I>Experts in gardening for over 40 years</B></I></P>

<P>We offer the finest selection of plants and planting materials, and an award-winning gardening shop. Stop by to see our 5 acres of nursery selections, including trees, shrubs, perennials, and seasonal plants. Our experienced staff is always available to assist you.</P>

<P>Be sure to visit our store for garden-themed gifts for indoors and out. We feature exciting new items for home decorating and gardening each season.</P>

</BODY>

</HTML>
```

● The Web browser displays the image on the page.

Dave's Garden Shop & Nursery

Experts in gardening for over 40 years

We offer the finest selection of plants and planting materials, and an award-winning gardening shop. Stop by to see our 5 acres of nursery selections, including trees, shrubs, perennials, and seasonal plants. Our experienced staff is always available to assist you.

Be sure to visit our store for garden-themed gifts for indoors and out. We feature exciting new items for home decorating and gardening each season.

INSERT A GRAPHIC FILE

1 Type **\<IMG SRC="*?*">** where you want to insert a graphic, replacing the *?* with the full path to the file you want to insert.

```
<!DOCTYPE HTML PUBLIC "-/W3C/DTD HTML 4.0 Tranistional//EN"
"http://www.w3.org/TR/REC-html40/loose.dtd">

<HTML>
<HEAD>
<TITLE>Kinkoph Designs</TITLE>
<META NAME="author" CONTENT="Greg Kinkoph">
<META NAME="description" CONTENT="Kinkoph Designs">
<META NAME="keywords" CONTENT="woodworking, custom woodworking, custom furniture, furniture
building">
<META NAME="copyright" CONTENT="2004">
</HEAD>
<BODY BGCOLOR="#FFFFCC">

<IMG SRC="Greg_Logo.gif">   ◄——1

<HR>
<P><FONT SIZE="5"><B><I>Custom woodworking and furniture designs to suit your home and office</FONT>
</B></I></P>

<IMG SRC="Sofa_Table.jpg" WIDTH="175" HEIGHT="175" HSPACE="20" ALIGN="center"> <IMG
SRC="Built_ins.jpg" WIDTH="175" HEIGHT="175" HSPACE="20" ALIGN="center"> <IMG
SRC="Corner_Table.jpg" WIDTH="175" HEIGHT="175" HSPACE="20" ALIGN="center">


<P><B>Whether you are looking for a unique furniture piece or a custom copy, we can create a timeless
classic you will treasure<BR>
```

● The Web browser displays the graphic on the page.

Custom woodworking and furniture designs to suit your home and office

TIPS

What file types can I use for Web images?

The most common file type for photographs is JPG, or JPEG files. The most common type for simple graphics is GIF files. PNG is also gaining popularity as a cross-platform file type for image files; however, older browser programs do not support PNG. You can use an image-editing or graphics program to save your images to specific file types. Most programs also offer options for optimizing the file size to create a smaller image file that downloads much faster. Consult your program's documentation to learn more.

When I insert an image, it appears too large on the Web page. How do I reduce its size?

You can use the Height and Width attributes within the \<IMG> tag to set a specific display size for your image. For example, you may want to make your image 160 pixels wide and 210 pixels tall. See the section "Specify an Image Size" to learn more about applying these attributes to an image.

Specify an Image Size

If your image appears too big or too small on a Web page, you can use HTML coding to change the size with image attributes. You can set a size for the width and height of an image. The width and height is measured in pixels, or you can set the size as a percentage value of the overall window size.

Specify an Image Size

① Click inside the `<IMG>` tag and type **WIDTH="?"**, replacing the *?* with the width measurement you want to set.

```
<HTML>
<HEAD>
<TITLE>Dave's Garden Shop & Nursery</TITLE>
<BASE TARGET="_blank">
</HEAD>
<BODY BGCOLOR="#CCFFCC">

<H1 ALIGN="center"><FONT FACE="Arial">Dave's Garden Shop & Nursery</FONT></H1>
<HR>

<IMG SRC="Garden_Supplies.jpg" WIDTH="300">

<P><B><I>Experts in gardening for over 40 years</B></I></P>

<P>We offer the finest selection of plants and planting materials, and an award-winning gardening shop. Stop by to see our 5 acres of nursery selections, including trees, shrubs, perennials, and seasonal plants. Our experienced staff is always available to assist you.</P>

<P>Be sure to visit our store for garden-themed gifts for indoors and out. We feature exciting new items for home decorating and gardening each season.</P>


</BODY>

</HTML>
```

② Type a blank space.

③ Type **HEIGHT="?"**, replacing the *?* with the height measurement you want to set.

```
<HTML>
<HEAD>
<TITLE>Dave's Garden Shop & Nursery</TITLE>
<BASE TARGET="_blank">
</HEAD>
<BODY BGCOLOR="#CCFFCC">

<H1 ALIGN="center"><FONT FACE="Arial">Dave's Garden Shop & Nursery</FONT></H1>
<HR>

<IMG SRC="Garden_Supplies.jpg" WIDTH="300" HEIGHT="200">

<P><B><I>Experts in gardening for over 40 years</B></I></P>

<P>We offer the finest selection of plants and planting materials, and an award-winning gardening shop. Stop by to see our 5 acres of nursery selections, including trees, shrubs, perennials, and seasonal plants. Our experienced staff is always available to assist you.</P>

<P>Be sure to visit our store for garden-themed gifts for indoors and out. We feature exciting new items for home decorating and gardening each season.</P>


</BODY>

</HTML>
```

- You can also set the attribute value as a percentage. This tells the browser to display the image at a percentage of the browser window size.

  When setting a percentage value, be sure to add a percent (%) sign after the value.

```
<HTML>
<HEAD>
<TITLE>Dave's Garden Shop & Nursery</TITLE>
<BASE TARGET="_blank">
</HEAD>
<BODY BGCOLOR="#CCFFCC">

<H1 ALIGN="center"><FONT FACE="Arial">Dave's Garden Shop & Nursery</FONT></H1>
<HR>

<IMG SRC="Garden_Supplies.jpg" WIDTH="50%" HEIGHT="30%">

<P><B><I>Experts in gardening for over 40 years</B></I></P>

<P>We offer the finest selection of plants and planting materials, and an award-winning gardening shop. Stop by
to see our 5 acres of nursery selections, including trees, shrubs, perennials, and seasonal plants. Our experienced
staff is always available to assist you.</P>

<P>Be sure to visit our store for garden-themed gifts for indoors and out. We feature exciting new items for home
decorating and gardening each season.</P>


</BODY>

</HTML>
```

- The Web browser displays the specified image size on the page.

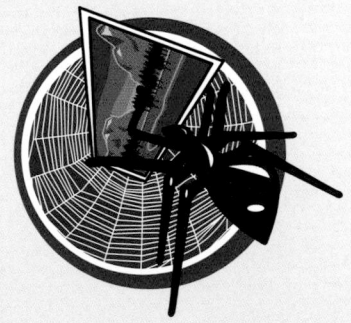

Dave's Garden Shop & Nursery

Experts in gardening for over 40 years

We offer the finest selection of plants and planting materials, and an award-winning gardening shop. Stop by to see our 5 acres of nursery selections, including trees, shrubs, perennials, and seasonal plants. Our experienced staff is always available to assist you.

Be sure to visit our store for garden-themed gifts for indoors and out. We feature exciting new items for home decorating and gardening each season.

TIPS

What size should I set for a Web page image?

The size of the image really depends on how you want to use it on the Web page. The average Web page measures approximately 600 pixels wide. For best results, set the image less than 40–50 percent of the page size, and keep the width and height values proportional. It is easier to scale a large image to a smaller size. If you make a small image too large, it appears grainy.

Is it better to resize an image in an editing program or use HTML coding?

Using an image-editing or graphics program is the best way to resize an image for the Web. These types of programs give you complete control over an image and allow you to set several optimizing options for an image so it is well suited for Web viewing.

Add Alternative Text

For users who do not have images turned on in their browser windows, you can add alternative text that identifies the images on your page. Alternative text, sometimes called placeholder text, helps describe the image and is an important addition to your Web page markup.

Add Alternative Text

1 Click inside the <IMG> image tag and type **ALT="?"**, replacing the *?* with the alternative text describing the image.

● If the user's browser has downloaded images turned off, the Web browser displays the alternative text in lieu of an image.

You can add a label that appears
whenever the user moves the mouse
pointer over the image on the Web
page. You might use labels to detail
information about the image.

**Labels work differently than alternative text.
Alternative text appears on the page itself,
while a label appears in a pop-up box when
the user moves the mouse over the image.**

Create an Image Label

1 Within the `<IMG>` tag, type **TITLE="?"**, replacing
the *?* with the image label you want to use.

```
<HTML>
<HEAD>
<TITLE>Dave's Garden Shop & Nursery</TITLE>
<BASE TARGET="_blank">
</HEAD>
<BODY BGCOLOR="#CCFFCC">

<H1 ALIGN="center"><FONT FACE="Arial">Dave's Garden Shop & Nursery</FONT></H1>
<HR>

<IMG SRC="Garden_Supplies.jpg" WIDTH="300" HEIGHT="200" ALT="Image of Gardening Tool">

<P><B><I>Experts in gardening for over 40 years</B></I></P>

<P>We offer the finest selection of plants and planting materials, and an award-winning gardening shop. Stop
by to see our 5 acres of nursery selections, including trees, shrubs, perennials, and seasonal plants. Our
experienced staff is always available to assist you.</P>

<IMG SRC="Million_Bells2.jpg" TITLE="Million Bells Petunia Variety"> <IMG SRC="Mixed_Plantings2.jpg">
<IMG SRC="Butterfly3.jpg">

<P>Be sure to visit our store for garden-themed gifts for indoors and out. We feature exciting new items for
home decorating and gardening each season.</P>

</BODY>

</HTML>
```

● The label appears when you move the mouse
pointer over the image in the browser window.

Add Copyright Text to Images

You can add copyright text below or next to an image to give yourself credit as the author. If you are using an image from another source, be sure to ask permission first; then use the copyright text to credit the correct author or source of the image.

1 Type **©** to create the copyright symbol.

2 Type a blank space, and then type the copyright text you want to add.

Note: *You can control the font and font size using tags. See Chapter 4 to learn more.*

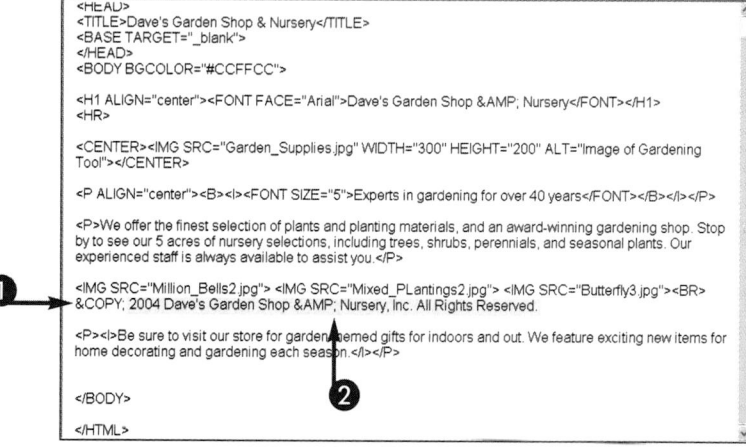

```
<HEAD>
<TITLE>Dave's Garden Shop & Nursery</TITLE>
<BASE TARGET="_blank">
</HEAD>
<BODY BGCOLOR="#CCFFCC">

<H1 ALIGN="center"><FONT FACE="Arial">Dave's Garden Shop &AMP; Nursery</FONT></H1>
<HR>

<CENTER><IMG SRC="Garden_Supplies.jpg" WIDTH="300" HEIGHT="200" ALT="Image of Gardening
Tool"></CENTER>

<P ALIGN="center"><B><I><FONT SIZE="5">Experts in gardening for over 40 years</FONT></B></I></P>

<P>We offer the finest selection of plants and planting materials, and an award-winning gardening shop. Stop
by to see our 5 acres of nursery selections, including trees, shrubs, perennials, and seasonal plants. Our
experienced staff is always available to assist you.</P>

<IMG SRC="Million_Bells2.jpg"> <IMG SRC="Mixed_PLantings2.jpg"> <IMG SRC="Butterfly3.jpg"><BR>
&COPY; 2004 Dave's Garden Shop &AMP; Nursery, Inc. All Rights Reserved.

<P><I>Be sure to visit our store for garden-themed gifts for indoors and out. We feature exciting new items for
home decorating and gardening each season.</I></P>

</BODY>

</HTML>
```

● The copyright text appears in the browser window.

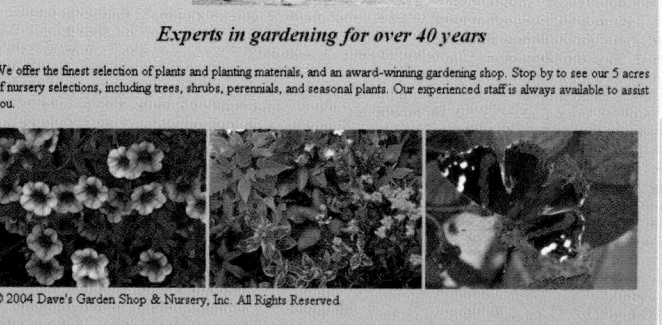

Align an Image Horizontally

You can use the alignment attributes to control the horizontal positioning of an image on a page. The alignment attributes include Left and Right. By default, the image aligns to the left. The alignment attributes also control the way in which text wraps around the image.

You can also align an image vertically on a page. See the section "Align an Image Vertically" to learn more.

Align an Image Horizontally

1 Click inside the `<IMG>` image tag and type **ALIGN="?"**, replacing the *?* with the alignment you want to apply, either **Left** or **Right**.

```
<HTML>
<HEAD>
<TITLE>Dave's Garden Shop & Nursery</TITLE>
<BASE TARGET="_blank">
</HEAD>
<BODY BGCOLOR="#CCFFCC">

<H1 ALIGN="center"><FONT FACE="Arial">Dave's Garden Shop & Nursery</FONT></H1>
<HR>

<P><B><I>Experts in gardening for over 40 years</B></I></P>

<IMG SRC="Garden_Supplies.jpg" WIDTH="300" HEIGHT="200" ALT="Image of Gardening Tool"
ALIGN="Right">



</BODY>

</HTML>
```

The Web browser aligns the image as specified.

● In this example the image is aligned to the right.

Note: For greater control over image alignment, consider placing your images in tables. Learn more about using tables in Chapter 9.

Dave's Garden Shop & Nursery

Experts in gardening for over 40 years

Align an Image Vertically

You can use the alignment attributes to control the vertical positioning of an image on a page. The alignment attributes include Top, Middle, and Bottom. These attributes are especially useful when you want to align the image with corresponding text on a page.

Align an Image Vertically

① Click inside the `<IMG>` image tag and type **ALIGN="?"**, replacing the *?* with the alignment you want to apply, either **Middle**, **Top**, or **Bottom**.

If the image shares the same line as text, you can use the alignment attribute to control the position of the image as it relates to the text.

```
<HTML>
<HEAD>
<TITLE>Dave's Garden Shop & Nursery</TITLE>
<BASE TARGET="_blank">
</HEAD>
<BODY BGCOLOR="#CCFFCC">

<H1 ALIGN="center"><FONT FACE="Arial">Dave's Garden Shop & Nursery</FONT></H1>
<HR>

<IMG SRC="Garden_Supplies.jpg" WIDTH="300" HEIGHT="200" ALT="Image of Gardening Tool"
ALIGN="Middle"><B><I><ALIGN="Center">   Experts in gardening for over 40 years</B></I>




</BODY>

</HTML>
```

The Web browser aligns the image as specified.

● In this example, the image is middle-aligned with existing text.

Note: *For greater control over image alignment, consider placing your images in tables. Learn more about using tables in Chapter 9.*

Center an Image

You can center your image on the page using tags. Centering an image can give it more emphasis and help the image stand out from the text or other page elements.

Center an Image

1 Click in front of the <IMG> tag and type **<CENTER>**.

2 Click at the end of the image tag and type **</CENTER>**.

```
<HTML>
<HEAD>
<TITLE>Dave's Garden Shop & Nursery</TITLE>
<BASE TARGET="_blank">
</HEAD>
<BODY BGCOLOR="#CCFFCC">

<H1 ALIGN="center"><FONT FACE="Arial">Dave's Garden Shop & Nursery</FONT></H1>
<HR>

<CENTER><IMG SRC="Garden_Supplies.jpg" WIDTH="300" HEIGHT="200" ALT="Image of Gardening Tool">
</CENTER>

<CENTER><P><B><I>Experts in gardening for over 40 years</B></I></P></CENTER>

<P>We offer the finest selection of plants and planting materials, and an award-winning gardening shop. Stop by
to see our 5 acres of nursery selections, including trees, shrubs, perennials, and seasonal plants. Our experienced
staff is always available to assist you.</P>

<P>Be sure to visit our store for garden-themed gifts for indoors and outdoors. We feature exciting new items for
home decorating and gardening at the start of each season.</P>

</BODY>

</HTML>
```

● The image appears centered on the Web page.

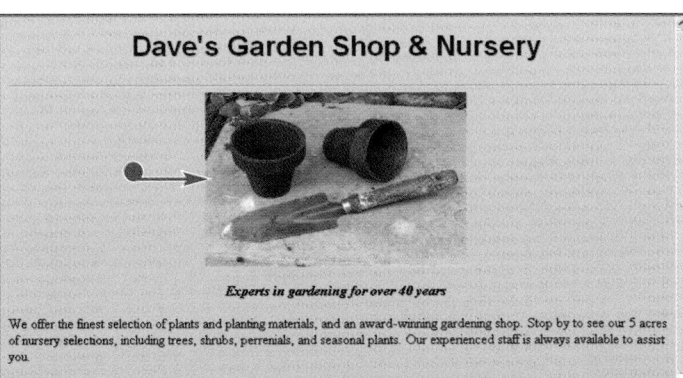

Wrap Text between Images

You can place two images side by side and wrap text between the two. To create this effect, you align one image to the left and the other to the right.

Wrap Text between Images

1 Insert the two images above the text you want to wrap.

2 Click inside the first <IMG> tag and type **ALIGN="Left"**.

3 Click inside the second <IMG> tag and type **ALIGN="Right"**.

```
<TITLE>Dave's Garden Shop & Nursery</TITLE>
<BASE TARGET="_blank">
</HEAD>
<BODY BGCOLOR="#CCFFCC">

<H1 ALIGN="center"><FONT FACE="Arial">Dave's Garden Shop & Nursery</FONT></H1>
<HR>

<CENTER><IMG SRC="Garden_Supply.jpg" WIDTH="300" HEIGHT="200" ALT="Image of Gardening
Tool"></CENTER>

<CENTER><P><B><I>Experts in gardening for over 40 years</B></I></P></CENTER>

<IMG SRC="Million_Bells2.jpg" ALIGN="Left">
<IMG SRC="Butterfly3.jpg" ALIGN="Right">

<P>We offer the finest selection of plants and planting materials, and an award-winning gardening shop. Stop
by to see our 5 acres of nursery selections, including trees, shrubs, perennials, and seasonal plants. Our
experienced staff is always available to assist you.</P>

<P>Be sure to visit our store for garden-themed gifts for indoors and outdoors. We feature exciting new items
for home decorating and gardening at the start of each season.</P>


</BODY>

</HTML>
```

● The text wraps between the two images on the Web page.

Note: See the section "Add Space around an Image" to learn how to add space between an image and surrounding text.

You can stop text wrapping
around your images using the
line break tag along with the
`Clear` attribute.

1 Click where you want to end the text wrap
and type **<BR CLEAR="?">**, replacing the *?*
with the margin you want to clear, either
Left, **Right**, or **All**.

```
<TITLE>Dave's Garden Shop & Nursery</TITLE>
<BASE TARGET="_blank">
</HEAD>
<BODY BGCOLOR="#CCFFCC">

<H1 ALIGN="center"><FONT FACE="Arial">Dave's Garden Shop & Nursery</FONT></H1>
<HR>

<CENTER><IMG SRC="Garden_Supplies.jpg" WIDTH="300" HEIGHT="200" ALT="Image of Gardening
Tool"></CENTER>

<CENTER><P><B><I>Experts in gardening for over 40 years</B></I></P></CENTER>

<IMG SRC="Million_Bells2.jpg" ALIGN="Left">
<IMG SRC="Butterfly3.jpg" ALIGN="Right">

<P>We offer the finest selection of plants and planting materials, and an award-winning gardening shop. Stop
by to see our 5 acres of nursery selections, including trees, shrubs, perennials, and seasonal plants. Our
experienced staff is always available to assist you.</P><BR CLEAR="All">|

<P>Be sure to visit our store for garden-themed gifts for indoors and outdoors. We feature exciting new items
for home decorating and gardening at the start of each season.</P>

</BODY>

</HTML>
```

The text wrapping ends at the selected point
on the page.

● In this example, the next paragraph starts
on a different line than the images.

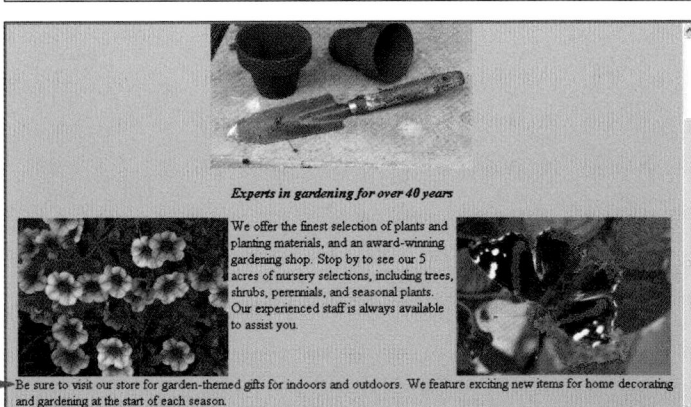

Experts in gardening for over 40 years

We offer the finest selection of plants and
planting materials, and an award-winning
gardening shop. Stop by to see our 5
acres of nursery selections, including trees,
shrubs, perennials, and seasonal plants.
Our experienced staff is always available
to assist you.

Be sure to visit our store for garden-themed gifts for indoors and outdoors. We feature exciting new items for home decorating
and gardening at the start of each season.

Set an Image Border

You can add a border to an image to give it added emphasis or make the image more attractive on the page. You can define the thickness of the border, measured in pixels.

Set an Image Border

① Click inside the `<IMG>` image tag and type **BORDER="?"**, replacing the *?* with thickness value you want to apply.

To remove a border you no longer want, replace the *?* with **0**.

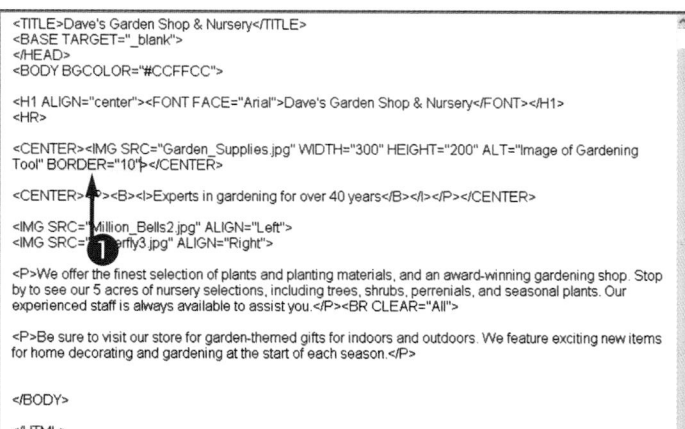

```
<TITLE>Dave's Garden Shop & Nursery</TITLE>
<BASE TARGET="_blank">
</HEAD>
<BODY BGCOLOR="#CCFFCC">

<H1 ALIGN="center"><FONT FACE="Arial">Dave's Garden Shop & Nursery</FONT></H1>
<HR>

<CENTER><IMG SRC="Garden_Supplies.jpg" WIDTH="300" HEIGHT="200" ALT="Image of Gardening
Tool" BORDER="10"></CENTER>

<CENTER><P><B><I>Experts in gardening for over 40 years</B></I></P></CENTER>

<IMG SRC="Million_Bells2.jpg" ALIGN="Left">
<IMG SRC="Butterfly3.jpg" ALIGN="Right">

<P>We offer the finest selection of plants and planting materials, and an award-winning gardening shop. Stop
by to see our 5 acres of nursery selections, including trees, shrubs, perrenials, and seasonal plants. Our
experienced staff is always available to assist you.</P><BR CLEAR="All">

<P>Be sure to visit our store for garden-themed gifts for indoors and outdoors. We feature exciting new items
for home decorating and gardening at the start of each season.</P>

</BODY>

</HTML>
```

● The Web browser displays a border around the image.

Note: *You can also set a color for a border. See Chapter 4 to learn more about color attributes.*

Add Space around an Image

Most Web browsers display only a small amount of space between images and text. You can increase the amount of space, also called padding, to make the page more visually appealing and easier to read. You can use the HSPACE attribute to control horizontal padding to an image, which adds space to the left and right of an image. You can use the VSPACE attribute to add padding above and below an image.

The value used with the horizontal and vertical spacing attributes is measured in pixels. For example, a value of 25 adds 25 pixels.

Add Space around an Image

① Click inside the <IMG> image tag and type **HSPACE="?"** or **VSPACE="?"**, replacing the *?* with the amount of space you want to insert.

You can add one or both attributes to an image.

If adding both attributes, separate them with a space in the HTML coding.

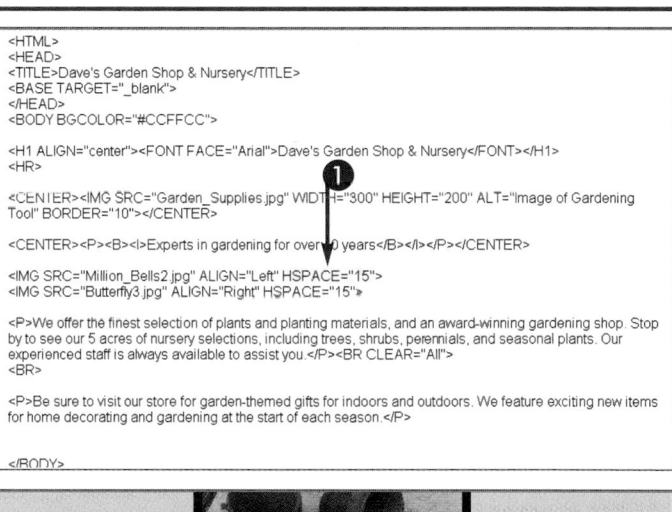

```
<HTML>
<HEAD>
<TITLE>Dave's Garden Shop & Nursery</TITLE>
<BASE TARGET="_blank">
</HEAD>
<BODY BGCOLOR="#CCFFCC">

<H1 ALIGN="center"><FONT FACE="Arial">Dave's Garden Shop & Nursery</FONT></H1>
<HR>

<CENTER><IMG SRC="Garden_Supplies.jpg" WIDTH="300" HEIGHT="200" ALT="Image of Gardening
Tool" BORDER="10"></CENTER>

<CENTER><P><B><I>Experts in gardening for over 40 years</B></I></P></CENTER>

<IMG SRC="Million_Bells2.jpg" ALIGN="Left" HSPACE="15">
<IMG SRC="Butterfly3.jpg" ALIGN="Right" HSPACE="15">

<P>We offer the finest selection of plants and planting materials, and an award-winning gardening shop. Stop
by to see our 5 acres of nursery selections, including trees, shrubs, perennials, and seasonal plants. Our
experienced staff is always available to assist you.</P><BR CLEAR="All">
<BR>

<P>Be sure to visit our store for garden-themed gifts for indoors and outdoors. We feature exciting new items
for home decorating and gardening at the start of each season.</P>

</BODY>
```

● The Web browser displays the specified amount of space around the image.

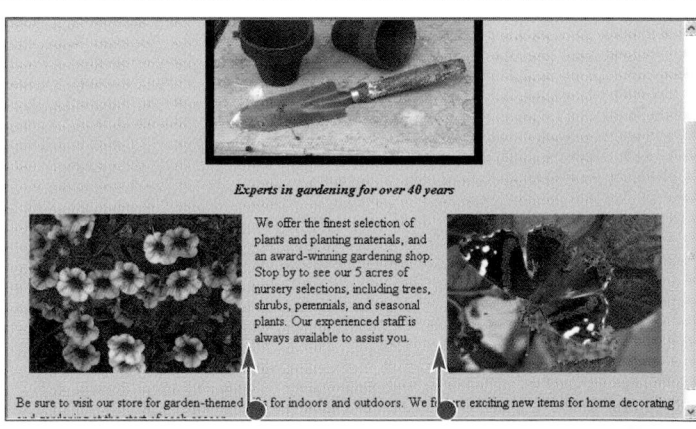

Add a Background Image

You can turn an image into a background for your Web page. Any time you select an image for a background, you must factor in how your text appears against the image. You may need to change the text color to make the text legible.

If you use a large image file, it fills the entire background. If you use a small size image, the browser window tiles the image across the page to fill the background with a repeating pattern.

Add a Background Image

1 Click inside the `<BODY>` tag and type **BACKGROUND="?"**, replacing the *?* with the path to the image file you want to use.

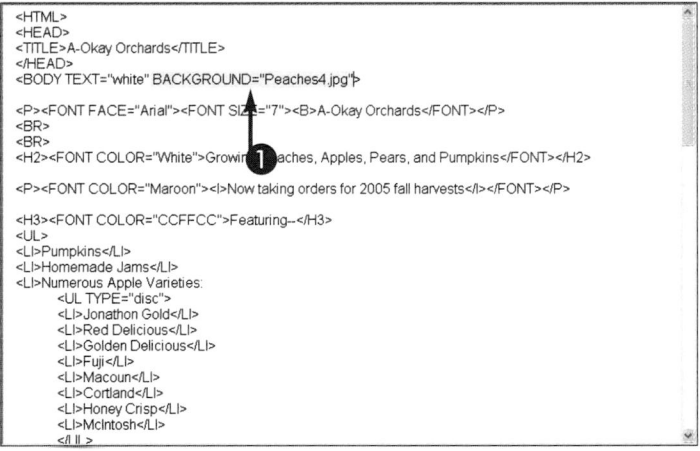

● The Web browser displays the image as the page background.

Note: See Chapter 4 to learn how to change the text color.

Create an Image Banner

You can use banners at the top of your Web pages to advertise a product or service, or to give your Web site a consistent look and feel. You can use a GIF image as a banner.

Full banners are typically 468 pixels wide and 60 pixels tall; however, yours might vary in size to suit your site. You can assign the banner size while creating the banner in a graphics editing program, or you can set an image size using HTML coding. To learn how to set image height and width, see the section "Specify an Image Size" earlier in this chapter.

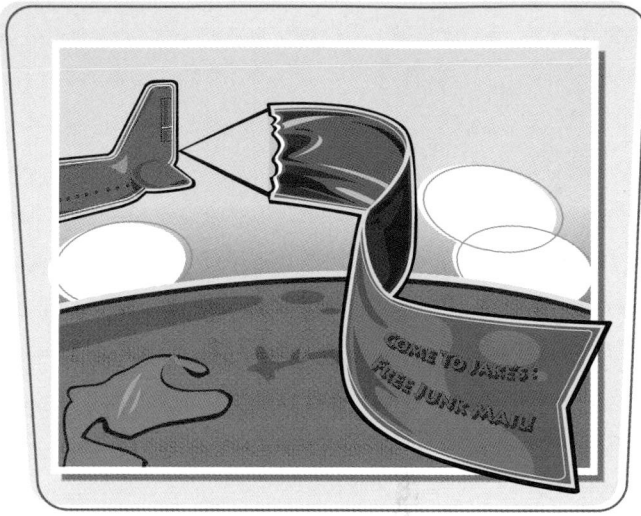

Create an Image Banner

1 At the top of the page, before any body text, type **<IMG SRC="?">**, replacing the *?* with the path and name of the banner file you want to use.

If you have not specified a width, type **WIDTH="?"** within the <IMG> tag, replacing the *?* with a value, such as 450.

Width and height values for an image are measured in pixels.

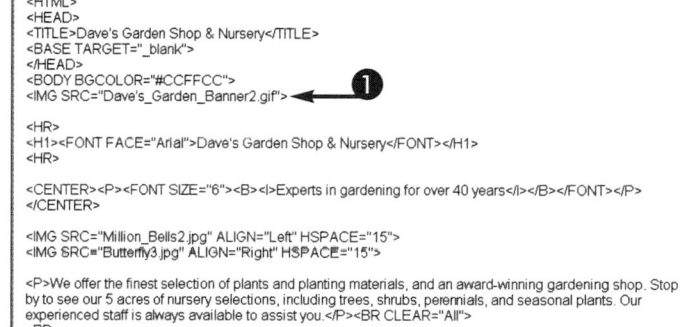

● The Web browser displays the image as a banner at the top of the page.

Note: See Chapter 14 to learn how to create an image map at the top of your Web pages.

CHAPTER 8

Adding Links

Are you ready to start adding links to your Web pages? This chapter shows you how to create all kinds of links in your HTML documents to allow users to jump to other pages or pages within your own site. You also learn how to add e-mail links and control the appearance of links.

Understanding Links..**134**

Understanding URLS...**136**

Insert a Link to Another Page **138**

Insert a Link to a New Window.....................**140**

Insert a Link to an Area on the
    Same Page **142**

Link to Another File Type **144**

Link to an E-mail Address.............................**146**

Change Link Colors...**148**

Hyperlinks, or *links* for short, are the heart and soul of Web pages. Links enable users to navigate from one topic to the next, and from one page to another. The user simply clicks the link and the browser immediately opens the designated page.

Types of Links

Links can be text or images. Most commonly, links appear as underlined text on a page. However, images also make good links. For example, graphical site maps and navigation bars that appear at the top or side of a page make it easy to link to other pages on the same Web site. When a user hovers his or her mouse pointer over a link, the pointer takes the shape of a pointing hand, indicating the presence of an active link.

Link to Other Web Pages

You can use links on your Web page to direct users to other pages on the Internet. For example, you might include a link on your company Web page to a local city directory detailing available activities and hotels in the area. Or you might add a link on a product page to the manufacturer's Web site.

Link to Other Pages on Your Site

If your Web site consists of more than one page, you can include links to other pages on the site. For example, your main page may provide links to pages about your business, products, and ordering information, and a map of your location.

Absolute and Relative Links

You can use two types of links in your HTML documents: absolute and relative. *Absolute links* use a complete URL to point to a specific page on the Web. *Relative links* use a shorthand to reference a page. You generally use relative links to reference documents on the same Web site.

Link to Other Areas on the Same Page

If your Web page is particularly long, you can provide links to different areas on the same page. For example, you might include links to each topic heading or photo on the page. This allows the user to jump right to the information he or she wants to view.

Anchor Element

The HTML element you use to create a link is called an anchor element. Anchor elements are identified by the `<A>` and `</A>` tags. The `HREF` attribute works within the opening anchor tag to define the URL to which you want to link. You can learn more about using URLs in the next section, "Understanding URLs."

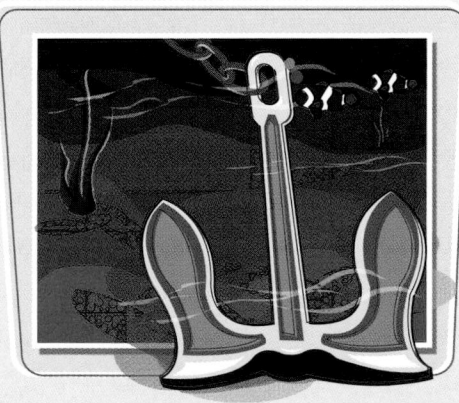

Understanding URLs

Every page on the Web has a unique address, called a URL. Short for *Uniform Resource Locator*, an URL identifies the domain name or host server where the page resides, and the directory path to the file. Absolute URLs link to a complete Web page address, whereas relative URLs link to Web pages relative to the current page in which the link is embedded.

HTTP Prefix

All URLs you type into an HTML document must include the standard HTTP prefix, such as http://www.myweb .com. The HTTP protocol identifies the URL as a Web page. Most browsers insert the prefix for you when you surf the Web, but when you design your own Web pages, you must include the full prefix to make the URL valid. If you are linking to a file transfer site (FTP) or e-mail address, you can use the FTP or MAILTO prefixes.

FTP or MAILTO Prefix

If you are linking to a file transfer site (FTP) or e-mail address, you can use the FTP or MAILTO prefixes instead of the HTTP prefix. For example, you might add a link to your e-mail address so that visitors can e-mail you about the Web site. You can also link to non-HTML resources, such as word processing documents and compressed files.

Host Name

Immediately following the identifying prefix is the name of the host server or domain name. Typically, host names are the name of the server or company storing your Web page files. Hosts can include commercial companies, educational institutions, and government agencies. In the URL http://www.mycompany.com, mycompany.com is the name of the domain.

Directory Path and Filename

If the page is stored in a directory on the server, the address generally includes a directory path to the file. For example, in the URL http://www.mycompany .com/webdocs/home.html, the slashes and directory names help define the path to the document file, home.html. In this example, the file is located within the webdocs directory. Directories act like folders found on your computer's hard disk drive.

Common URL Mistakes

One of the easiest ways to add an error to your Web page is to type the wrong URL for a link. A broken link that leads to an error page is very frustrating for users visiting your Web site. Be very careful to check over your URLs, paying careful attention to typos. You should also pay attention to the filenames and extensions. One misplaced letter in a filename can create a broken link.

Insert a Link to Another Page

You can create a link on your HTML document that, when clicked, takes the visitor to another page on the Web. You can link to a page on your own Web site, or to a page elsewhere on the Web.

In order to create a link, you must first know the URL of the page to which you want to link, such as `http://www.wiley.com`.

Insert a Link to Another Page

INSERT A TEXT LINK

1 Type the text you want to use as a link.

2 Type **<A HREF="?">** in front of the text, replacing *?* with the URL of the page to which you want to link.

3 Type **</A>** at the end of the link text.

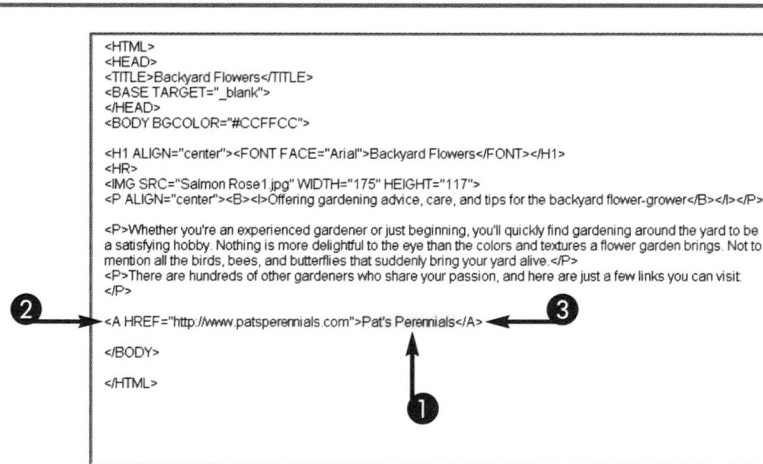

● The Web browser displays the text as an underlined link.

● Anytime the user moves the mouse pointer (⤣) over the link, it takes the shape of a hand pointer (🖑), indicating a link.

● The URL for the link appears on the status bar.

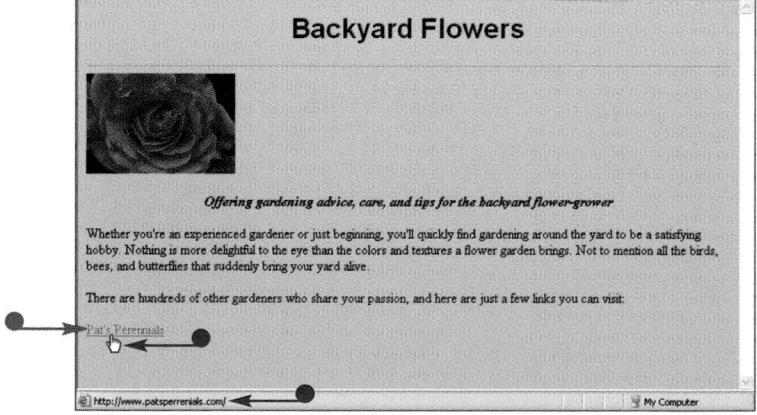

INSERT AN IMAGE LINK

1 Add the image you want to use as a link.

Note: See Chapter 5 to learn how to add images to a page.

2 Type **<A HREF="*?*">** in front of the image coding, replacing *?* with the URL of the page to which you want to link.

3 Type **</A>** at the end of the image coding.

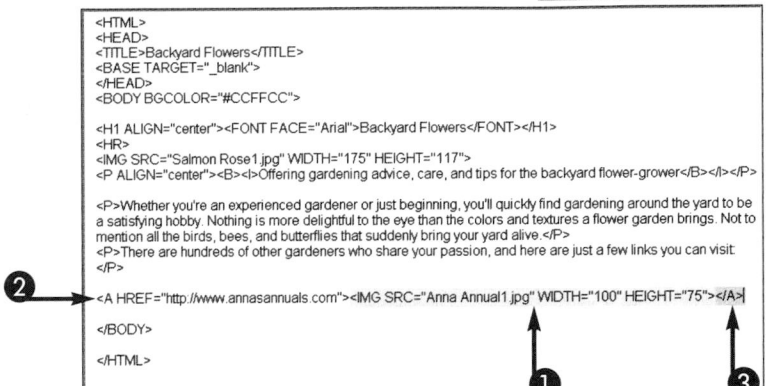

```
<HTML>
<HEAD>
<TITLE>Backyard Flowers</TITLE>
<BASE TARGET="_blank">
</HEAD>
<BODY BGCOLOR="#CCFFCC">

<H1 ALIGN="center"><FONT FACE="Arial">Backyard Flowers</FONT></H1>
<HR>
<IMG SRC="Salmon Rose1.jpg" WIDTH="175" HEIGHT="117">
<P ALIGN="center"><B><I>Offering gardening advice, care, and tips for the backyard flower-grower</B></I></P>

<P>Whether you're an experienced gardener or just beginning, you'll quickly find gardening around the yard to be
a satisfying hobby. Nothing is more delightful to the eye than the colors and textures a flower garden brings. Not to
mention all the birds, bees, and butterflies that suddenly bring your yard alive.</P>
<P>There are hundreds of other gardeners who share your passion, and here are just a few links you can visit:
</P>

<A HREF="http://www.annasannuals.com"><IMG SRC="Anna Annual1.jpg" WIDTH="100" HEIGHT="75"></A>|

</BODY>

</HTML>
```

● The Web browser displays the image as a link.

● Anytime the user moves the mouse pointer (⇖) over the link, it takes the shape of a hand pointer (👆), indicating a link.

● The URL for the link appears on the status bar.

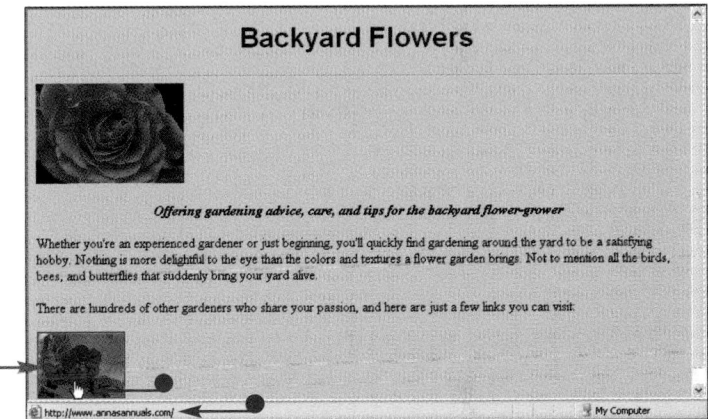

TIPS

How do I link to another page on my Web site?

You can link to another page on your site using a relative URL. Relative URLs allow you to simply list the name of the page file without needing to list the entire directory path, such as <A HREF= "vacationphotos.html">. The page must be stored in the same directory or folder as the current page. If the page is stored in a subfolder, you must identify the name of the subfolder or subdirectory first, such as familyphotos/ vacationphotos.html.

My link image includes a border. How do I remove the border?

When you turn an image into a link, a border automatically surrounds the image. To remove the border, type **BORDER="0"** in the <IMG> tag, such as <A HREF=http:// www.mypage.com> <IMG SRC="vacation1. jpg" BORDER="0"></A>.

Insert a Link to a New Window

You can add instructions to an HTML link that tell the browser to open the link page in a new browser window. You may add this instruction if you want to keep a window to your own site open so the user can easily return to your page.

You use a `target` **attribute within the link anchor element (<A>) to open links in new windows. By assigning the** `target` **the value** `_blank`**, it instructs the browser to keep your page open while opening a new unnamed window for the URL. To make all the links on your page open in new windows, you can use the** `BASE` **element. To learn more about how links and URLs work, see the sections at the beginning of this chapter.**

Insert a Link to a New Window

LINK TO A NEW WINDOW

1 Click within the <A> tag for the link you want to edit and type **TARGET="?"**, replacing *?* with a name for the new window.

To target a new, unnamed window, type "**_blank**".

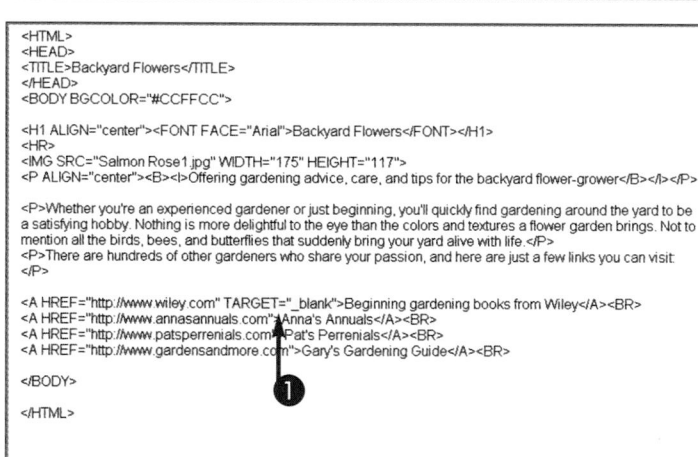

```
<HTML>
<HEAD>
<TITLE>Backyard Flowers</TITLE>
</HEAD>
<BODY BGCOLOR="#CCFFCC">

<H1 ALIGN="center"><FONT FACE="Arial">Backyard Flowers</FONT></H1>
<HR>
<IMG SRC="Salmon Rose1.jpg" WIDTH="175" HEIGHT="117">
<P ALIGN="center"><B><I>Offering gardening advice, care, and tips for the backyard flower-grower</B></I></P>

<P>Whether you're an experienced gardener or just beginning, you'll quickly find gardening around the yard to be
a satisfying hobby. Nothing is more delightful to the eye than the colors and textures a flower garden brings. Not to
mention all the birds, bees, and butterflies that suddenly bring your yard alive with life.</P>
<P>There are hundreds of other gardeners who share your passion, and here are just a few links you can visit:
</P>

<A HREF="http://www.wiley.com" TARGET="_blank">Beginning gardening books from Wiley</A><BR>
<A HREF="http://www.annasannuals.com">Anna's Annuals</A><BR>
<A HREF="http://www.patsperrenials.com">Pat's Perrenials</A><BR>
<A HREF="http://www.gardensandmore.com">Gary's Gardening Guide</A><BR>

</BODY>

</HTML>
```

● When the link is clicked, a new browser window opens.

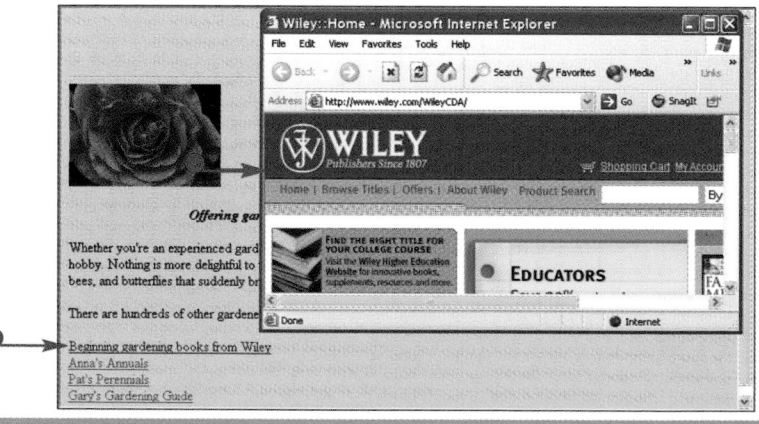

MAKE ALL LINKS OPEN NEW WINDOWS

1 Click within the `<HEAD>` and `</HEAD>` tags and type **`<BASE TARGET="?">`**, replacing *?* with a name for the new window, such as **main**.

To target a new, unnamed window, type **"_blank"**.

```
<HTML>
<HEAD>
<TITLE>Backyard Flowers</TITLE>
<BASE TARGET="_blank">                    1
</HEAD>
<BODY BGCOLOR="#CCFFCC">

<H1 ALIGN="center"><FONT FACE="Arial">Backyard Flowers</FONT></H1>
<HR>
<IMG SRC="Salmon Rose1.jpg" WIDTH="175" HEIGHT="117">
<P ALIGN="center"><B><I>Offering gardening advice, care, and tips for the backyard flower-grower</B></I></P>

<P>Whether you're an experienced gardener or just beginning, you'll quickly find gardening around the yard to be a
satisfying hobby. Nothing is more delightful to the eye than the colors and textures a flower garden brings. Not to
mention all the birds, bees, and butterflies that suddenly bring your yard alive with life.</P>
<P>There are hundreds of other gardeners who share your passion, and here are just a few links you can visit:
</P>

<A HREF="http://www.wiley.com">Beginning gardening books from Wiley</A><BR>
<A HREF="http://www.annasannuals.com">Anna's Annuals</A><BR>
<A HREF="http://www.patsperrenials.com">Pat's Perrenials</A><BR>
<A HREF="http://www.gardensandmore.com">Gary's Gardening Guide</A><BR>

</BODY>

</HTML>
```

● When a user clicks any of the links on the page, a new browser window opens.

Backyard Flowers

Offering gardening advice, care, and tips for the backyard flower-grower

Whether you're an experienced gardener or just beginning, you'll quickly find gardening around the yard to be a satisfying hobby. Nothing is more delightful to the eye than the colors and textures a flower garden brings. Not to mention all the birds, bees, and butterflies that suddenly bring your yard alive.

There are hundreds of other gardeners who share your passion, and here are just a few links you can visit:

Beginning gardening books from Wiley
Anna's Annuals
Pat's Perrenials
Gary's Gardening Guide

TIPS

Do I need to specify a name for the new window?

No. Rather than worry about what to name a new window, it is often easier to leave the window unnamed. Always use the `TARGET="_blank"` attribute if you do not want to create a window name.

Do I need to open new windows for every link?

No. If a new window opens every time a user clicks a link on your page, the user might become very irritated with the number of windows. For ease of use, keep the new windows to a minimum, and only when the links visit a page outside your own Web site.

Insert a Link to an Area on the Same Page

You can add links to your page that, when clicked, take the user to another area on the same page. This is particularly useful for longer documents. For example, you can add links that take the user to different headings throughout your document.

The key to linking on the same page is assigning names to the various areas to which you want to link. You can do this with the NAME **attribute. Keep your naming system simple, using only letters and numbers to name the sections throughout your document.**

Insert a Link to an Area on the Same Page

NAME AN AREA

① Click in front of the section of text to which you want to create a link and type **<A NAME="?">**, replacing the *?* with a unique name for the area.

```
<H4><A NAME="Section3">Section. 3.</H4>
<H4>Clause 1: The Senate of the United States shall be composed of two Senators from each State, chosen
by the Legislature thereof, for six Years; and each Senator shall have one Vote.</H4>
<H4>Clause 2: Immediately after they shall be assembled in Consequence of the first Election, they shall be
divided as equally as may be into three Classes. The Seats of the Senators of the first Class shall be vacated
at the Expiration of the second Year, of the second Class at the Expiration of the fourth Year, and of the third
Class at the Expiration of the sixth Year, so that one third may be chosen every second Year; and if Vacancies
happen by Resignation, or otherwise, during the Recess of the Legislature of any State, the Executive thereof
may make temporary Appointments until the next Meeting of the Legislature, which shall then fill such
Vacancies.</H4>
<H4>Clause 3: No Person shall be a Senator who shall not have attained to the Age of thirty Years, and been
nine Years a Citizen of the United States, and who shall not, when elected, be an Inhabitant of that State for
which he shall be chosen.</H4>
<H4>Clause 4: The Vice President of the United States shall be President of the Senate, but shall have no
Vote, unless they be equally divided.</H4>
<H4>Clause 5: The Senate shall choose their other Officers, and also a President pro tempore, in the Absence
of the Vice President, or when he shall exercise the Office of President of the United States.</H4>
<H4>Clause 4: The Senate shall have the sole Power to try all Impeachments. When sitting for that Purpose,
they shall be on Oath or Affirmation. When the President of the United States is tried, the Chief Justice shall
preside: And no Person shall be convicted without the Concurrence of two thirds of the Members present.</H4>
<H4>Clause 7: Judgment in Cases of Impeachment shall not extend further than to removal from Office, and
disqualification to hold and enjoy any Office of honor, Trust or Profit under the United States: but the Party
convicted shall nevertheless be liable and subject to Indictment, Trial, Judgment and Punishment, according to
Law.</H4>
<H4>Section. 4 </H4>
```

② Type **</A>** at the end of the section.

```
<H4><A NAME="Section3"></A>Section. 3.</H4>
<H4>Clause 1: The Senate of the United States shall be composed of two Senators from each State, chosen
by the Legislature thereof, for six Years; and each Senator shall have one Vote.</H4>
<H4>Clause 2: Immediately after they shall be assembled in Consequence of the first Election, they shall be
divided as equally as may be into three Classes. The Seats of the Senators of the first Class shall be vacated
at the Expiration of the second Year, of the second Class at the Expiration of the fourth Year, and of the third
Class at the Expiration of the sixth Year, so that one third may be chosen every second Year; and if Vacancies
happen by Resignation, or otherwise, during the Recess of the Legislature of any State, the Executive thereof
may make temporary Appointments until the next Meeting of the Legislature, which shall then fill such
Vacancies.</H4>
<H4>Clause 3: No Person shall be a Senator who shall not have attained to the Age of thirty Years, and been
nine Years a Citizen of the United States, and who shall not, when elected, be an Inhabitant of that State for
which he shall be chosen.</H4>
<H4>Clause 4: The Vice President of the United States shall be President of the Senate, but shall have no
Vote, unless they be equally divided.</H4>
<H4>Clause 5: The Senate shall choose their other Officers, and also a President pro tempore, in the Absence
of the Vice President, or when he shall exercise the Office of President of the United States.</H4>
<H4>Clause 4: The Senate shall have the sole Power to try all Impeachments. When sitting for that Purpose,
they shall be on Oath or Affirmation. When the President of the United States is tried, the Chief Justice shall
preside: And no Person shall be convicted without the Concurrence of two thirds of the Members present.</H4>
<H4>Clause 7: Judgment in Cases of Impeachment shall not extend further than to removal from Office, and
disqualification to hold and enjoy any Office of honor, Trust or Profit under the United States: but the Party
convicted shall nevertheless be liable and subject to Indictment, Trial, Judgment and Punishment, according to
Law.</H4>
<H4>Section. 4 </H4>
```

CREATE A LINK TO THE AREA

1 In front of the text or image you want to turn into a link, type **<A HREF="#?">**, replacing *?* with a name of the section to which you want to link.

Note: *Be careful not to leave out the pound sign (#) when linking to other areas of a page.*

2 Type **</A>** after the link text.

Note: *You can also use an image as a link. See the section "Insert a Link to Another Page" to learn more.*

● When a user clicks the link, the browser scrolls to the designated section of the page.

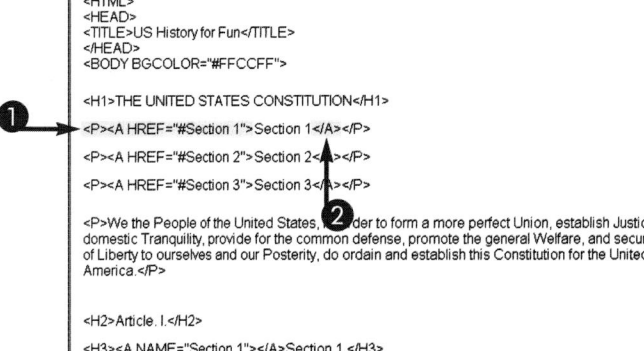

THE UNITED STATES CONSTITUTION

Section 1
Section 2
Section 3

We the People of the United States, in Order to form a more perfect Union, establish Justice, insure domestic Tranquility, provide for the common defense, promote the general Welfare, and secure the Blessings of Liberty to ourselves and our Posterity, do ordain and establish this Constitution for the United States of America.

Article. I.

Section 1.

All legislative Powers herein granted shall be vested in a Congress of the United States, which shall consist of a Senate and House of Representatives.

Section. 2.

Clause 1: The House of Representatives shall be composed of Members chosen every second Year by the People

TIPS

Can I place a link at the bottom of my page that returns the user to the top of the page?

Yes. It is always a good idea to add links to the bottom of a long document page to help the user navigate to the top again. To create such a link, first name the top section of the page following the steps shown in this section. Then include link text that describes the link, such as Return to Top or Back to Top, and add a link that takes the user to the named section at the top of the document.

How do I link to a specific location on another page on my Web site?

You can use the same technique shown in this section to link to another page on your site. Make sure you name the spot on the other page using the **<A NAME=" ? ">** tag and attribute.

Link to Another File Type

You can add links to non-HTML resources, such as Word document files, spreadsheet files, image files, compressed files, and more. The key to linking to non-HTML pages is to include the file in the same location as your Web pages. For example, if you store your Web pages on your Internet service provider's server, be sure to store a copy of the file on the server as well.

When a user clicks a link to a non-HTML file, the browser first attempts to display the page, and then it attempts to open the file on the user's computer. The user may then be prompted to save or open the file.

Link to Another File Type

1 Type the text you want to use as a link.

It is always good form to include a description with the link that clearly identifies what sort of file the link opens.

2 Type **<A HREF="?">**, replacing *?* with the full path and name of the file.

```
<HTML>
<HEAD>
<TITLE>Backyard Flowers</TITLE>
<BASE TARGET="_blank">
</HEAD>
<BODY BGCOLOR="#CCFFCC" LINK="#FF00FF" ALINK="008000" VLINK="#000080">

<H1 ALIGN="center"><FONT FACE="Arial">Backyard Flowers</FONT></H1>
<HR>
<IMG SRC="Salmon Rose1.jpg" WIDTH="175" HEIGHT="117">
<P ALIGN="center"><B><I>Offering gardening advice, care, and tips for the backyard flower-grower</B></I></P>

<P>Whether you're an experienced gardener or just beginning, you'll quickly find gardening around the yard to be a satisfying hobby. Nothing is more delightful to the eye than the colors and textures a flower garden brings. Not to mention all the birds, bees, and butterflies that bring your yard to life.</P>

<P>Here are some recent JPEG pictures from my own backyard you can download:</P>

<A HREF="Flower_Pictures.zip">Download Now<BR>
<BR>You will need to unzip the files to view them.


</BODY>

</HTML>
```

3 Type **</A>** at the end of the link text.

```
<HTML>
<HEAD>
<TITLE>Backyard Flowers</TITLE>
<BASE TARGET="_blank">
</HEAD>
<BODY BGCOLOR="#CCFFCC" LINK="#FF00FF" ALINK="008000" VLINK="#000080">

<H1 ALIGN="center"><FONT FACE="Arial">Backyard Flowers</FONT></H1>
<HR>
<IMG SRC="Salmon Rose1.jpg" WIDTH="175" HEIGHT="117">
<P ALIGN="center"><B><I>Offering gardening advice, care, and tips for the backyard flower-grower</B></I></P>

<P>Whether you're an experienced gardener or just beginning, you'll quickly find gardening around the yard to be a satisfying hobby. Nothing is more delightful to the eye than the colors and textures a flower garden brings. Not to mention all the birds, bees, and butterflies that bring your yard to life.</P>

<P>Here are some recent JPEG pictures from my own backyard you can download:</P>

<A HREF="Flower_Pictures.zip">Download Now</A><BR>
<BR>You will need to unzip the files to view them.


</BODY>

</HTML>
```

● The link appears on the Web page.

When the link is clicked, the browser may display the file in the browser window.

Note: *See the section "Insert a Link to a New Window" to open the file in a new window.*

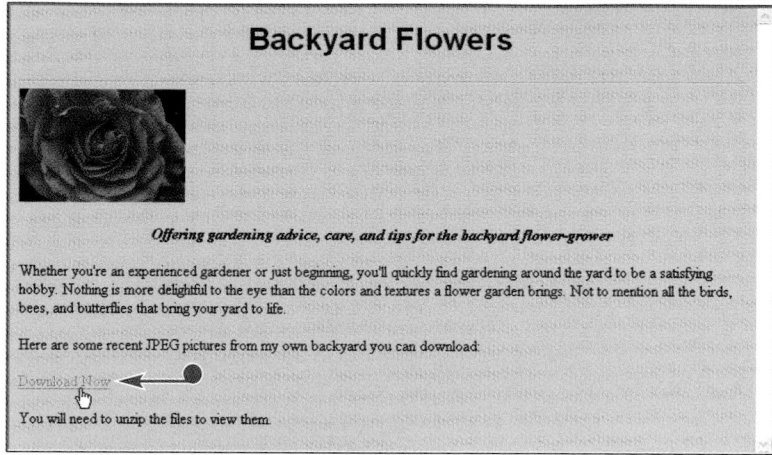

Depending on the file type, the File Download dialog box may appear, allowing the user to download the file to a designated folder on his or her computer.

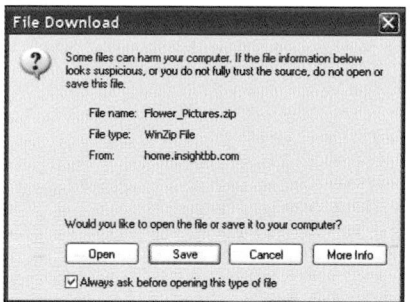

TIPS

Can I include a link to a downloadable file, such as a program file?

Yes, you can include a link to a downloadable file on your Web page. For example, if your company distributes a software product online, you can create a link that helps users start the downloading process.

What happens if the user cannot download the file?

If the user encounters problems with the download, his or her browser or computer displays an error message. To help with possible problems that might occur, be sure to include information about the file format and size on the Web page; also include any useful tools to help the user work with the file. You might also consider adding a link to a help page or other documentation to help troubleshoot file downloading problems.

Link to an E-mail Address

You can add a link to your Web page that allows users to send you an e-mail message. Adding e-mail links is a good way to solicit feedback from your Web site visitors, as well as enable them to ask questions about you or your site.

Link to an E-mail Address

1 Type the text you want to use as an e-mail link.

It is a good idea to mention the name or title of the person to whom you want the e-mails to go, or clearly indicate the link is an e-mail link.

2 In front of the link text, type **<A HREF="mailto:?">**, replacing *?* with the e-mail address you want to use.

3 Type **</A>** at the end of the link text.

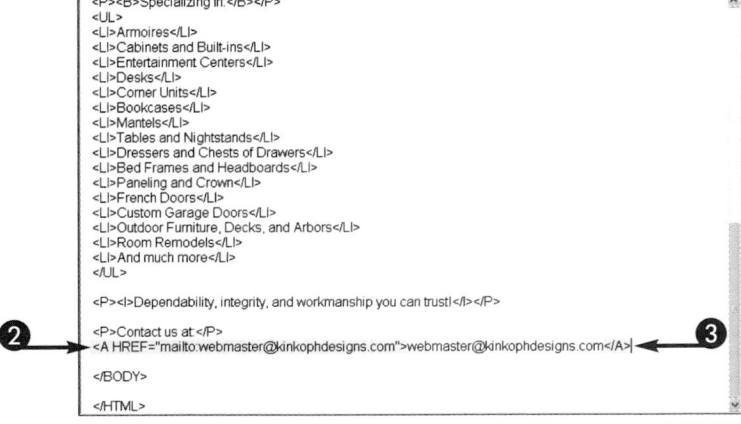

● The link appears in the Web browser.

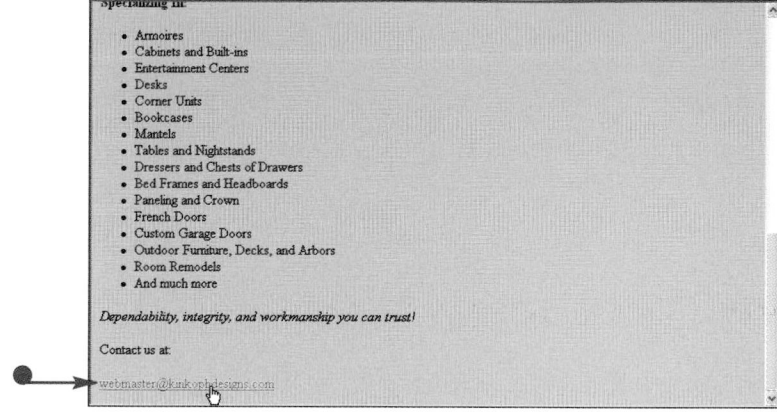

● When the link is clicked, the user's e-mail editor opens with the To address filled in with the address you specified.

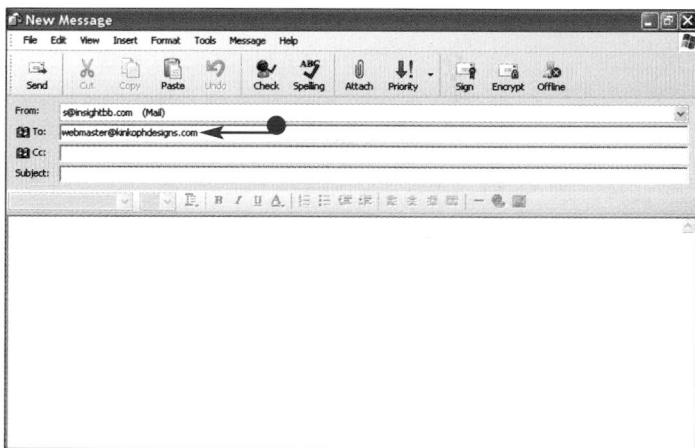

TIPS

Can I preset a subject for an e-mail message?

Yes. You can use the `?subject` attribute within the link tag to include a subject line with the e-mail message. When the user clicks the link to open his or her e-mail client, the subject area is already filled in. You might use this technique to help recognize e-mail generated from your Web site. For example:

```
<A HREF="MAILTO:jdoe@myemail.com
?subject=comments">Web Site Comments</>
```

Is it safe to use my e-mail address in a link?

You should always use caution when thinking about placing a personal e-mail address online. E-mail addresses are notorious magnets for spamming. For this reason, you may want to create a special e-mail account just for your Web-generated e-mail messages. See your service provider for more information.

Change Link Colors

You can control the color of links on a page. When a user clicks a link, the link changes color. This helps users to keep track of which links they have already selected.

You can assign link colors in the <BODY> tag. Use the LINK attribute to assign a color to all the links on the page that the user has not clicked. Use the ALINK attribute, which stands for *active link,* to change the color of active links, which appear when the user is in the process of selecting the link. Use the VLINK attribute, which stands for *visited link,* to change the color of links users have previously selected.

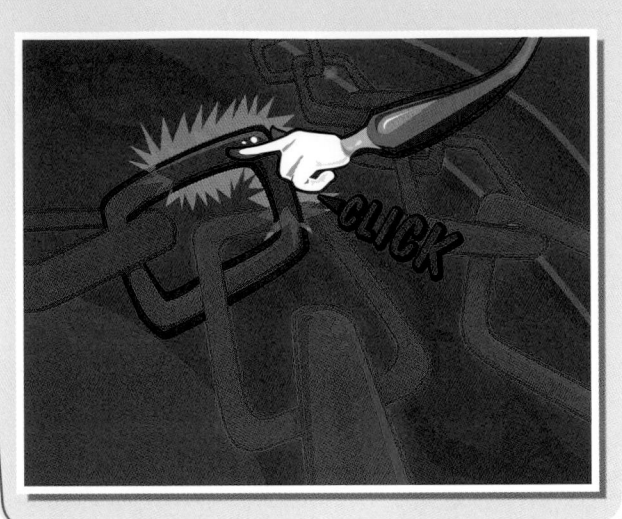

Change Link Colors

1 Click within the <BODY> tags and type **LINK="?"**, replacing *?* with the color value you want to apply to the unselected links on your page.

2 Type an empty space.

```
<HTML>
<HEAD>
<TITLE>Backyard Flowers</TITLE>
<BASE TARGET="_blank">
</HEAD>
<BODY BGCOLOR="#CCFFCC" LINK="#FF00FF">

<H1 ALIGN="center"><FONT FACE="Arial">Backyard Flowers</FONT></H1>
<HR>
<IMG SRC="Salmon_Rose1.jpg" WIDTH="175" HEIGHT="117">
<P ALIGN="center"><B><I>Offering gardening advice, care, and tips for the backyard flower-grower</B></I></P>

<P>Whether you're an experienced gardener or just beginning, you'll quickly find gardening around the yard to be a satisfying hobby. Nothing is more delightful to the eye than the colors and textures a flower garden brings. Not to mention all the birds, bees, and butterflies that bring your yard to life.</P>

<P>Here are some recent JPEG pictures from my own backyard you can download:</P>

<A HREF="Flower_Pictures.zip">Download Now</A><BR>
<BR>You will need to unzip the files to view them.


</BODY>

</HTML>
```

3 Type **ALINK="?"**, replacing *?* with the color value you want to apply to active links on your page.

4 Type an empty space.

```
<HTML>
<HEAD>
<TITLE>Backyard Flowers</TITLE>
<BASE TARGET="_blank">
</HEAD>
<BODY BGCOLOR="#CCFFCC" LINK="#FF00FF" ALINK="#008000">

<H1 ALIGN="center"><FONT FACE="Arial">Backyard Flowers</FONT></H1>
<HR>
<IMG SRC="Salmon_Rose1.jpg" WIDTH="175" HEIGHT="117">
<P ALIGN="center"><B><I>Offering gardening advice, care, and tips for the backyard flower-grower</B></I></P>

<P>Whether you're an experienced gardener or just beginning, you'll quickly find gardening around the yard to be a satisfying hobby. Nothing is more delightful to the eye than the colors and textures a flower garden brings. Not to mention all the birds, bees, and butterflies that bring your yard to life.</P>

<P>Here are some recent JPEG pictures from my own backyard you can download:</P>

<A HREF="Flower_Pictures.zip">Download Now</A><BR>
<BR>You will need to unzip the files to view them.


</BODY>

</HTML>
```

5 Type **VLINK="?"**, replacing *?* with the color value you want to apply to the previously selected links on your page.

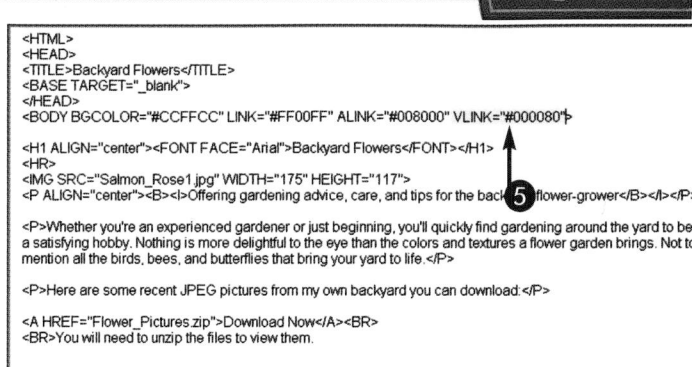

```
<HTML>
<HEAD>
<TITLE>Backyard Flowers</TITLE>
<BASE TARGET="_blank">
</HEAD>
<BODY BGCOLOR="#CCFFCC" LINK="#FF00FF" ALINK="#008000" VLINK="#000080">

<H1 ALIGN="center"><FONT FACE="Arial">Backyard Flowers</FONT></H1>
<HR>
<IMG SRC="Salmon_Rose1.jpg" WIDTH="175" HEIGHT="117">
<P ALIGN="center"><B><I>Offering gardening advice, care, and tips for the backyard flower-grower</B></I></P>

<P>Whether you're an experienced gardener or just beginning, you'll quickly find gardening around the yard to be
a satisfying hobby. Nothing is more delightful to the eye than the colors and textures a flower garden brings. Not to
mention all the birds, bees, and butterflies that bring your yard to life.</P>

<P>Here are some recent JPEG pictures from my own backyard you can download:</P>

<A HREF="Flower_Pictures.zip">Download Now</A><BR>
<BR>You will need to unzip the files to view them.

</BODY>

</HTML>
```

● The browser displays the new color choices for links.

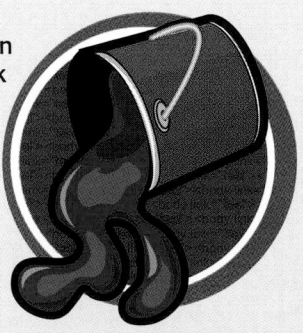

 TIPS

Can I type in color names rather than hexadecimal values?

Yes. You can use any of the 16 Web-safe colors by name rather than by hexadecimal value to change link colors. For example, you can type:

```
<BODY LINK="teal" VLINK=
"gray" ALINK="red">
```

and achieve the same effect as typing:

```
<BODY LINK="#008080"
VLINK="#808080"
ALINK="#FF0000">
```

How do I remove underlines from my text links?

The only way to remove the default underlining browsers display for links is to use cascading style sheets, or CSS. CSS gives you greater formatting controls for your Web page text. To learn more about CSS, see Chapter 12.

CHAPTER

9

Working with Tables

Are you looking for a method to organize data on a page? Need a way to control your page layout? Tables can help. This chapter shows you how to use tables as receptacles for different types of data.

Understanding Table Structure......................152

Add a Table 154

Assign a Table Border................................156

Adjust Cell Padding and Spacing..................158

Adjust Cell Width and Height.......................160

Add Column Labels......................................162

Create Newspaper-Style Columns................163

Add a Table Header 164

Add a Table Caption 165

Control Which Borders to Display................166

Adjust the Table Size 168

Change Cell Alignment................................170

Span Cells across Columns and Rows 172

Create Column and Row Groups 174

Add Background Color to Cells 178

Add a Background Color to a Table 179

Insert an Image in a Cell 180

Insert a Table Background Image 181

Change Table Alignment 182

Control Text Wrapping in Cells....................184

Nest a Table within a Table 185

Understanding Table Structure

Tables offer a unique way to hold data in a tabular format. With the advent of Web pages, developers quickly took advantage of table structures to help with complicated page layouts. Although CSS now allows users to create layouts without tables, HTML tables are still a popular way to organize and present Web page data and images.

Table Structure

Every table is built on a basic structure of a square containing four borders. Within the table, intersecting columns and rows create *cells* to hold data. Each cell is also surrounded by four borders. You can resize various borders in a table to increase the size of cells. Borders may or may not be visible in the table structure as it appears on the Web page.

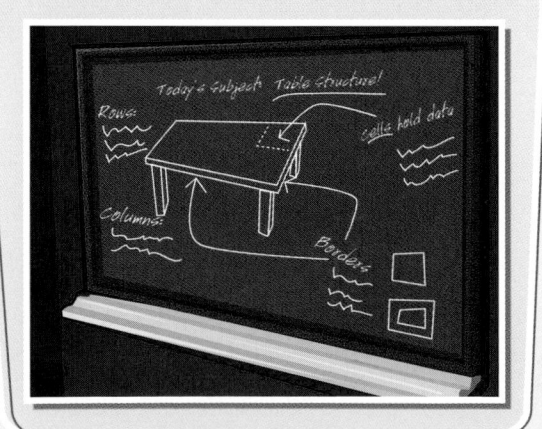

Cell Spanning

Cells can span two or more columns or rows to form bigger containers for data. For example, a table may include a cell at the top that spans multiple columns across the table, or a cell that spans downward across several rows. When you span cells in a table, you add or delete interior cell walls to create a larger cell.

Traditional Tables

You can use traditional tables on a Web page to present data in a tabular format. For example, you might insert a table to hold a list of products and prices, or to display a roster of classes. One way to create a traditional table is to define a set width and depth for the table. When you define an exact size for a table, a user cannot resize the table; the table appears just as it was created.

Table Elements

The building blocks of HTML tables are the <TABLE>, <TR>, and <TD> codes. The <TABLE> element defines the table component. The <TR> tag defines a table row. The <TD> tag defines the table data, or cell content. In addition to these codes, you can assign table headers, captions, and column groups. You can also create tables within tables, called *nested tables*.

Presentation Tables

You can use a presentation-style table to showcase your data more dynamically. Instead of defining an exact size, you can specify a table size using percentages. Whenever the user resizes his or her browser window, the table resizes as well. This allows for a more "liquid" layout. This type of table is good for page layouts as well as regular data tables.

Preparing for a Table

Before you start the task of creating any kind of table, whether it is strictly for data or to control the page layout, stop and sketch out what you want the table to look like and what type of data you want each cell to hold. A little planning beforehand can help you build your table faster and more accurately using the HTML coding.

You can insert a table onto your page to organize data or control the entire page layout. Tables offer a manageable structure for creating a layout for your page. You can assign different page elements to different cells to control the positioning of elements on the page. Cells can hold text data, images, and other Web page elements.

Add a Table

① Type **<TABLE>** where you want to insert a table.

② Type **<TR>** to start the first row in the table.

To make the tag easier to distinguish between rows, type each row tag on a new line.

③ Type **<TD>** for the first cell you want to create.

④ Type the cell data.

Note: *If you want your first row to include column labels, you can use the* <TH> *tag instead of* <TD>. *See the section "Add Column Labels" to learn more.*

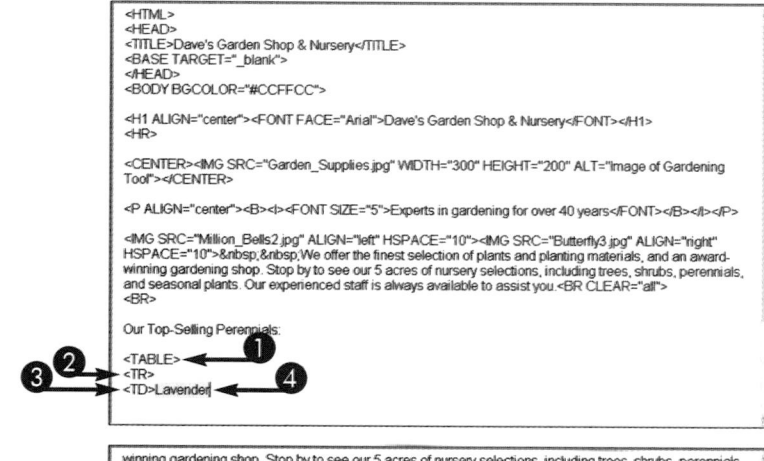

⑤ Type **</TD>** to complete the cell.

⑥ Repeat steps **3** to **5** to add additional cells.

To make it easier to distinguish between cells, you can place each cell on a new line in your HTML document.

⑦ Type **</TR>** at the end of the first row.

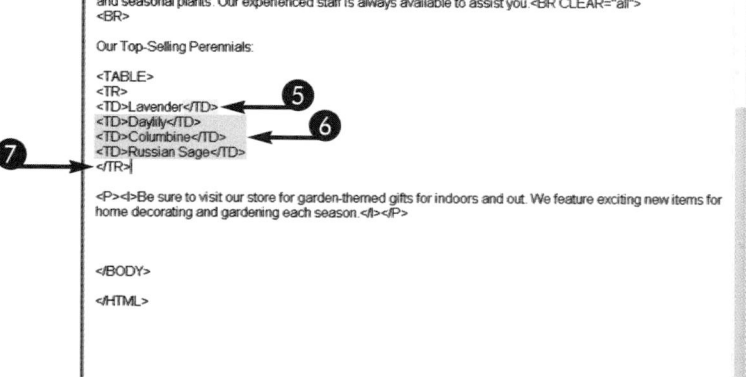

8 Continue adding rows and cell data as needed.

9 Type **</TABLE>** at the end of the table data.

Note: The </TABLE> tag is not an optional tag. Netscape Navigator does not display a table without the tag.

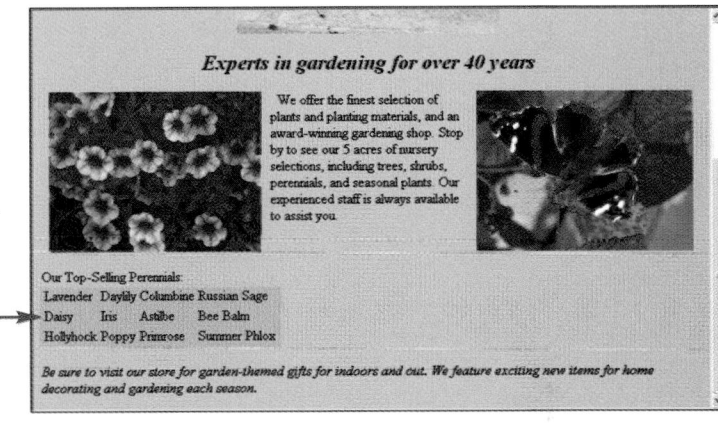

The Web browser displays the data in a tabular format.

● In this example, the table cells need some padding and spacing or borders displayed.

Note: See the sections "Assign a Table Border" and "Adjust Cell Padding and Spacing" to learn more.

TIPS

How do I set an exact size for a table?

If you want your table to appear in a set width, you can measure how wide the table should be on the page and then divide the value by how wide you want each column. For best results, do not set your table width any wider than 600 pixels to ensure the table is viewable at lower screen resolutions. See the section "Adjust the Table Size" to learn how to write HTML coding for an exact width using pixels or percentages.

What is the best procedure for building a table?

Before you type up your table coding, it is helpful to draw it out on paper first to organize the cell contents, designate column headers and rows, and determine a general layout and size of a table. When you are ready to enter the table coding, start with a skeleton of the page, typing just the tags to define the table structure, including the number of rows and columns. You can check the structure in a Web browser to see how it looks, and then return to your editor and start filling in the actual cell data.

Assign a Table Border

You can use table borders to make your cells easier to distinguish and give the table more structure on a page. A table border is simply a line that appears around a table as well as around each cell within the table. By default, a table does not have an actual border unless you specify one. You can use the BORDER attribute to turn table borders on or off.

When you set a border thickness, it applies only to the outer edge of the table, not to the cells within the table. Border thickness is measured in pixels. Borders appear gray unless you specify a color. See the section "Adjust Cell Padding and Spacing" to learn how to control interior borders.

Assign a Table Border

1 In the `<TABLE>` tag, type **BORDER="?"**, replacing the *?* with the value for the border thickness you want to set.

Note: *See the section "Add a Table" to learn how to create a basic table.*

```
Our Top-Selling Perennials:

<TABLE BORDER="5">
<TR>
<TD>Lavender</TD>
<TD>Daylily</TD>
<TD>Columbine</TD>
<TD>Russian Sage</TD>
</TR>
<TR>
<TD>Daisy</TD>
<TD>Iris</TD>
<TD>Astilbe</TD>
<TD>Bee Balm</TD>
</TR>
<TR>
<TD>Hollyhock</TD>
<TD>Poppy</TD>
<TD>Primrose</TD>
<TD>Summer Phlox</TD>
</TR>
</TABLE>

<P><I>Be sure to visit our store for garden-themed gifts for indoors and out. We feature exciting new items for
home decorating and gardening each season.</I></P>
```

● To set a border color, type **BORDERCOLOR="?"** in the `<TABLE>` tag, replacing the *?* with the color value you want to apply.

```
Our Top-Selling Perennials:

<TABLE BORDER="5" BORDERCOLOR="teal">
<TR>
<TD>Lavender</TD>
<TD>Daylily</TD>
<TD>Columbine</TD>
<TD>Russian Sage</TD>
</TR>
<TR>
<TD>Daisy</TD>
<TD>Iris</TD>
<TD>Astilbe</TD>
<TD>Bee Balm</TD>
</TR>
<TR>
<TD>Hollyhock</TD>
<TD>Poppy</TD>
<TD>Primrose</TD>
<TD>Summer Phlox</TD>
</TR>
</TABLE>

<P><I>Be sure to visit our store for garden-themed gifts for indoors and out. We feature exciting new items for
home decorating and gardening each season.</I></P>
```

● In this example, the browser displays a table with a default gray border.

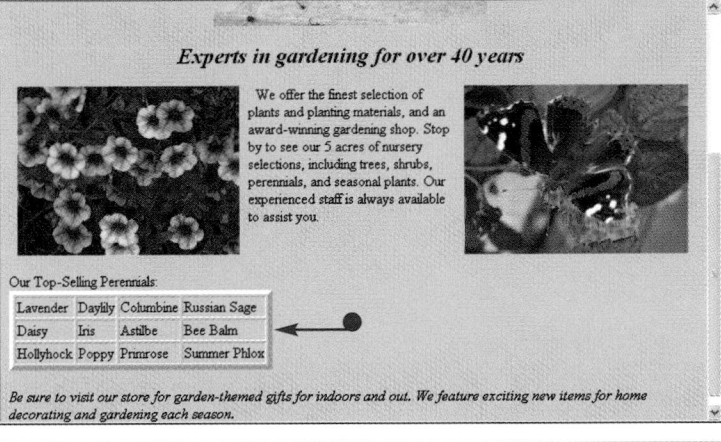

● In this example, the browser displays the same table with a color border.

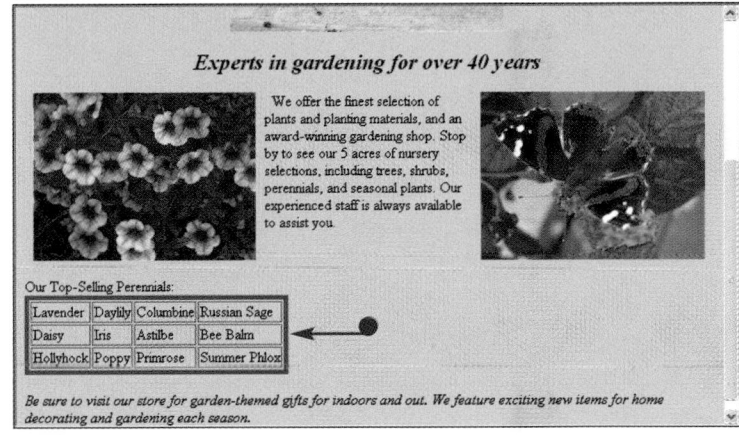

Can I specify a border with a style sheet?

Yes. In your style sheet, type **TABLE** or **TD**, or the selector that denotes the portion of the table to which you want to apply a border. Then type **{BORDER:VALUE}**, with BORDER defining the border property and VALUE defining the border type. See Chapters 5 and 6 to learn more about applying style sheets to your Web pages.

Do I need to add borders if I am using a table as a layout for my Web page?

No. It is not a good idea to invoke the BORDER attribute for table layouts. With a layout, you want the table structure to define different sections of the page. If you assign a border, it adds a border to every section, which can distract from your page content.

Adjust Cell Padding and Spacing

You can use padding to add space between the border and the contents of a cell. You can use spacing to increase the border size or width between cells. Padding and spacing size is measured in pixels.

SET CELL PADDING

1 In the `<TABLE>` tag, type **CELLPADDING="?"**, replacing the *?* with the pixel value you want to assign.

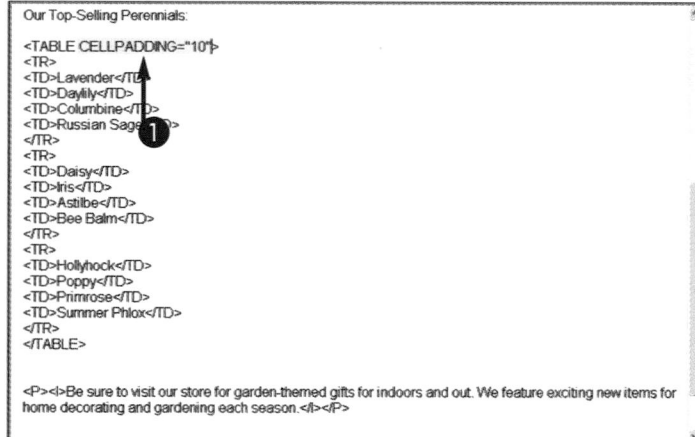

● The Web browser displays the designated amount of space between the contents and the cell borders.

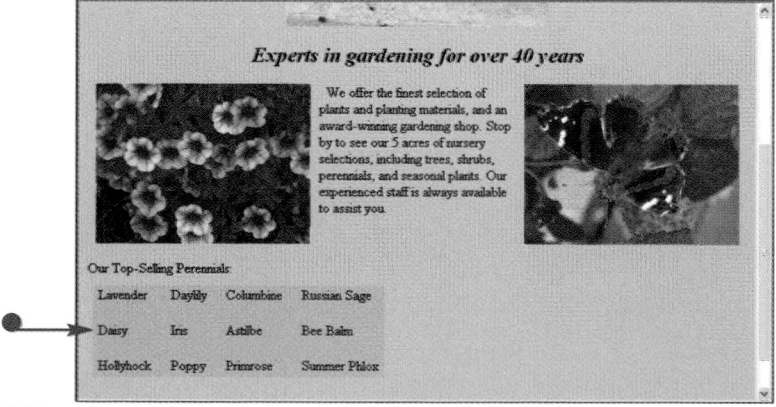

SET CELL SPACING

1 In the `<TABLE>` tag, type **CELLSPACING="?"**, replace the *?* with the pixel value you want to assign.

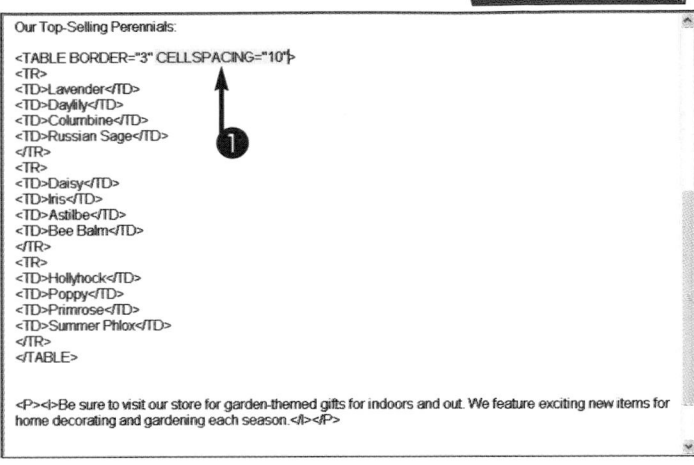

● The Web browser displays the designated amount of space for the cell borders.

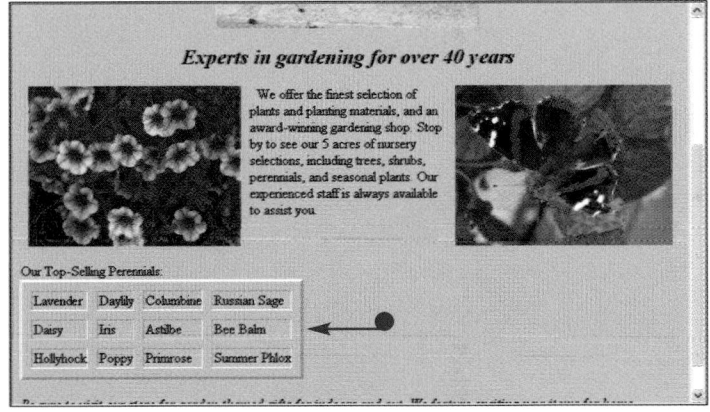

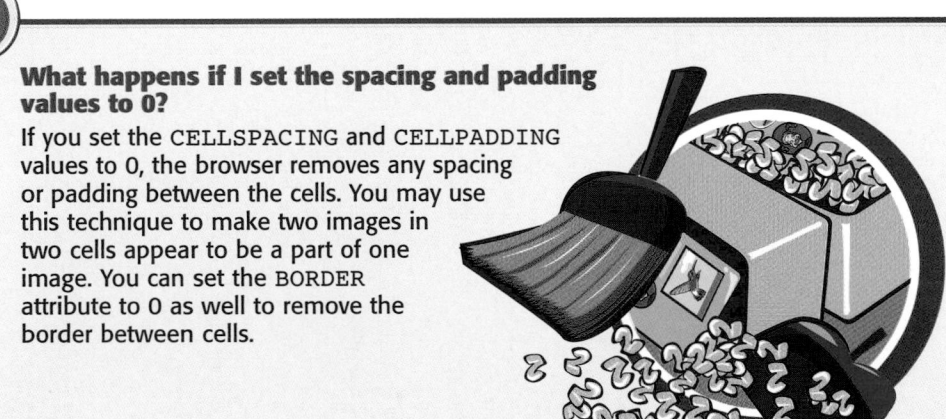

TIP

What happens if I set the spacing and padding values to 0?

If you set the CELLSPACING and CELLPADDING values to 0, the browser removes any spacing or padding between the cells. You may use this technique to make two images in two cells appear to be a part of one image. You can set the BORDER attribute to 0 as well to remove the border between cells.

Adjust Cell Width and Height

You can control the width of a cell using the WIDTH attribute and the height of a cell using the HEIGHT attribute. Typically, the content of the cell determines the cell's width. For example, if the cell contains a long line of text, the cell appears wide enough in the browser window to hold all the text in the cell.

For greater control, you can specify a width based on a percentage of the browser window, or you can set an exact number of pixels. You can also control the depth of a cell using the HEIGHT attribute.

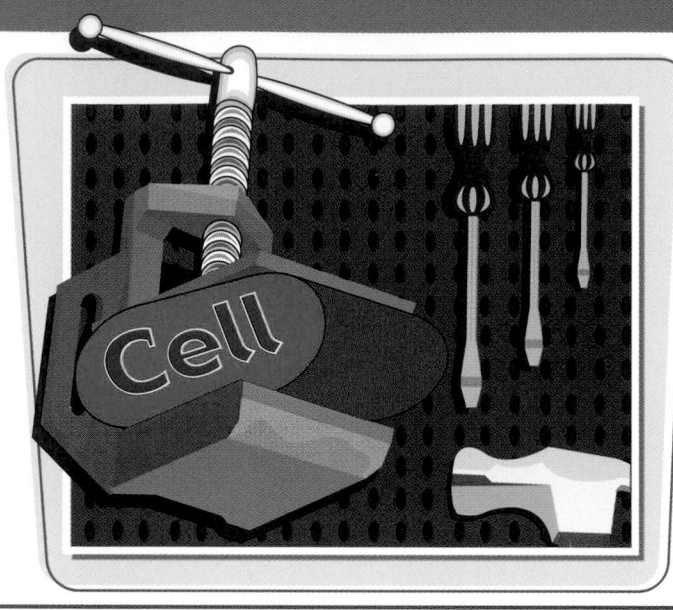

Adjust Cell Width and Height

SET CELL WIDTH

1 In the `<TD>` tag, type **WIDTH="?"**, replacing the *?* with the value or percentage you want to set for the cell.

To set the same cell width for the entire table, type the WIDTH attribute within the `<TABLE>` tag.

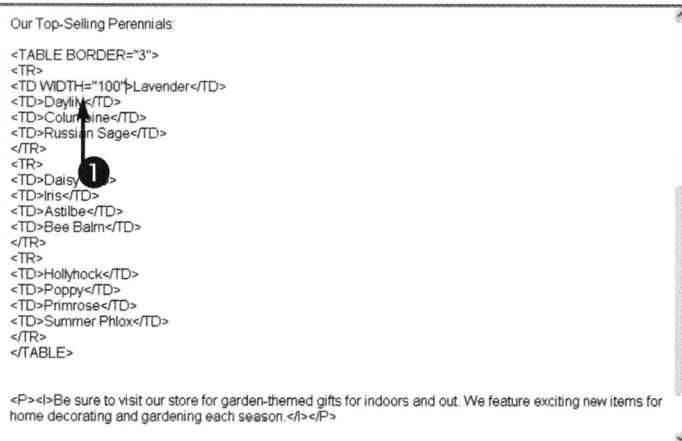

```
Our Top-Selling Perennials:

<TABLE BORDER="3">
<TR>
<TD WIDTH="100">Lavender</TD>
<TD>Daylily</TD>
<TD>Columbine</TD>
<TD>Russian Sage</TD>
</TR>
<TR>
<TD>Daisy</TD>
<TD>Iris</TD>
<TD>Astilbe</TD>
<TD>Bee Balm</TD>
</TR>
<TR>
<TD>Hollyhock</TD>
<TD>Poppy</TD>
<TD>Primrose</TD>
<TD>Summer Phlox</TD>
</TR>
</TABLE>

<P><I>Be sure to visit our store for garden-themed gifts for indoors and out. We feature exciting new items for home decorating and gardening each season.</I></P>
```

● The Web browser displays a set width for the cell, as well as all the other cells in the same column.

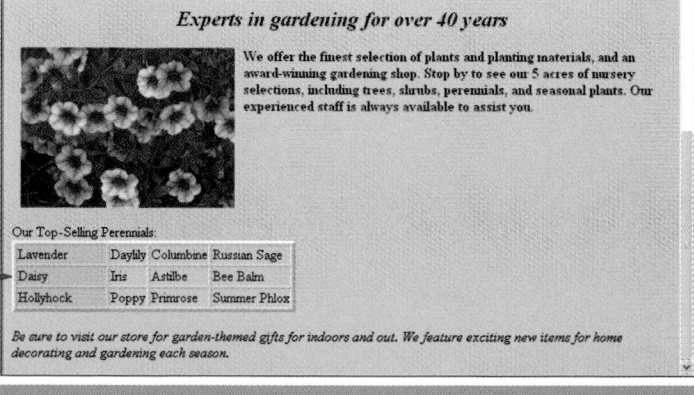

Experts in gardening for over 40 years

We offer the finest selection of plants and planting materials, and an award-winning gardening shop. Stop by to see our 5 acres of nursery selections, including trees, shrubs, perennials, and seasonal plants. Our experienced staff is always available to assist you.

Our Top-Selling Perennials:

Lavender	Daylily	Columbine	Russian Sage
Daisy	Iris	Astilbe	Bee Balm
Hollyhock	Poppy	Primrose	Summer Phlox

Be sure to visit our store for garden-themed gifts for indoors and out. We feature exciting new items for home decorating and gardening each season.

SET CELL HEIGHT

1 In the `<TD>` tag, type **HEIGHT="?"**, replacing the *?* with the pixel value or percentage you want to set for the cell.

To set the height for the entire table, type the HEIGHT attribute within the `<TABLE>` tag.

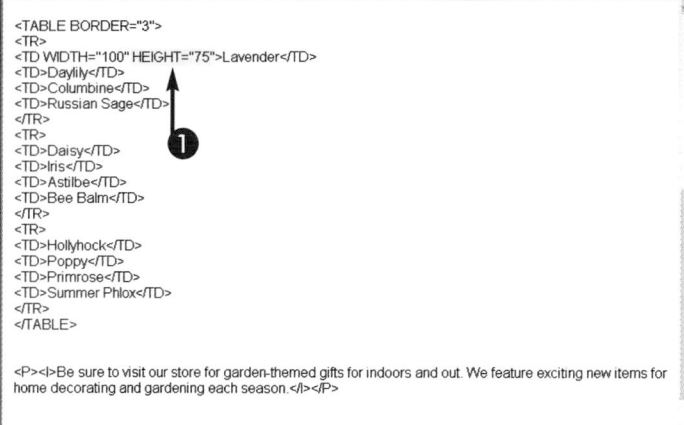

```
<TABLE BORDER="3">
<TR>
<TD WIDTH="100" HEIGHT="75">Lavender</TD>
<TD>Daylily</TD>
<TD>Columbine</TD>
<TD>Russian Sage</TD>
</TR>
<TR>
<TD>Daisy</TD>
<TD>Iris</TD>
<TD>Astilbe</TD>
<TD>Bee Balm</TD>
</TR>
<TR>
<TD>Hollyhock</TD>
<TD>Poppy</TD>
<TD>Primrose</TD>
<TD>Summer Phlox</TD>
</TR>
</TABLE>

<P><I>Be sure to visit our store for garden-themed gifts for indoors and out. We feature exciting new items for home decorating and gardening each season.</I></P>
```

● The Web browser displays a set height for the cell, as well as all the other cells in the same row.

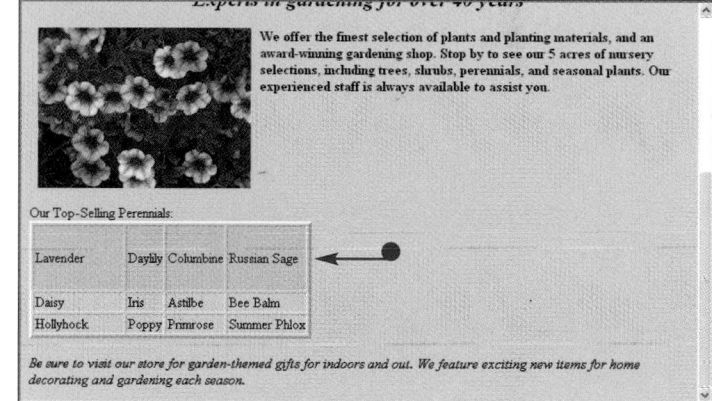

TIPS

Which is more important, setting cell height or setting cell width?

Setting the cell width is more important than setting the cell height. The content of your cells typically define the height of the cell. You may never need to assign a cell height. Technically, the HEIGHT attribute is not normally associated with the `<TABLE>` tags. Some browsers do not support the attribute in tables, and as such, unpredictable results may occur when displaying the table in the browser window.

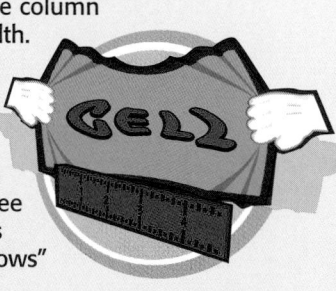

Can I set the width for a single cell and not affect the other cells?

When you change the width of a cell, all the cells in the same column adjust to the same width. If you want one cell to span across one or more columns, you can use another set of codes to control the individual cell width. See the section "Span Cells across Columns and Rows" to learn more.

Add Column Labels

If you are building a table to populate with data, you can add labels, also called *headers*, to the top of each column to identify column contents. Any time you want to make your cell text bold and centered, you can use the <TH> tag. For example, if your table lists products and prices, column headers might include labels such as Product Number, Product Name, and Price. Column headers appear in bold type and are centered within each cell.

You can also give your table a title using the same <TH> tag. See the section "Add a Table Header" to learn more.

Add Column Labels

① After the <TR> tag for the row you want to use as column labels, type **<TH>**.

Note: *See the section "Add a Table" to learn how to create a basic table.*

② Type the first column label text.

③ Type **</TH>** at the end of the label.

④ Repeat steps **1** to **3** to add as many column labels as you need, ending the row with the **</TR>** tag.

● The Web browser displays the labels as column headers in the table.

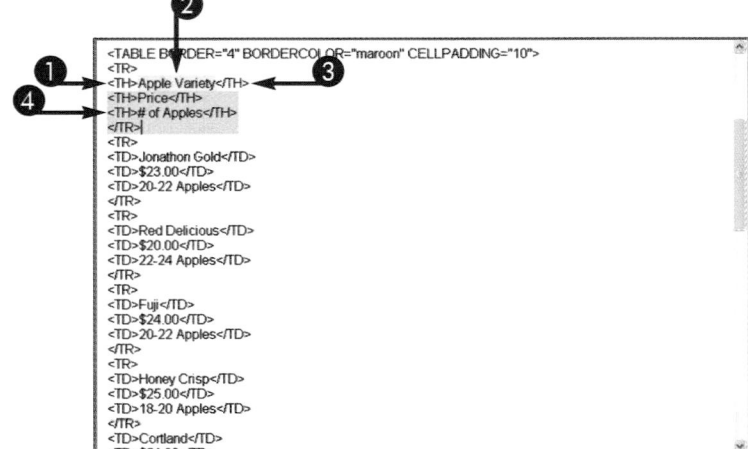

Create Newspaper-Style Columns

You can use the table format to present columns of text on your Web page, much like a newspaper. For example, you may want to present your text in a two-column or three-column format. Paragraphs of text are contained within each column.

You can use the vertical alignment attribute to make each column align at the top of the table.

Create Newspaper-Style Columns

1 Within the `<TR>` and `</TR>` tags, type **<TD VALIGN="top">** to start the first column of text.

Note: See the section "Add a Table" to learn how to create a basic table.

2 Type your column text.

3 Type **</TD>** at the end of the text.

4 Repeat steps **2** and **3** to add more columns and text.

```
<HR NOSHADE SIZE="8">
<BR CLEAR="all">

<TABLE CELLPADDING="10">
<TR>
<TD VALIGN="top">Whether you are looking for a unique furniture piece or a custom copy, we can create a
timeless classic you will treasure for years to come. Offering old-world craftsmanship at a quality price, we build
a wide variety of beautiful furniture pieces, cabinetry, and built-ins to fit any home or office design and style.
</TD>
<TD VALIGN="top">At Kinkoph Designs, you'll experience dependability, integrity, and workmanship you can
trust. We do not send out a piece until it has met our rigid quality control checks. We also offer a lifetime
guarantee--unlike other furniture companies, we guarantee our pieces for the duration of your lifetime.
</TD>
<TD VALIGN="top">We offer a variety of building options suited to your pricing needs. We're happy to match
stains and paint from other pieces in your room, plus we offer a vast palette of our own custom shades. We also
sell unfinished furniture to allow our customers to paint or stain to fit their own decorating schemes.
</TD>
</TR>
</TABLE>

</BODY>

</HTML>
```

The Web browser displays the text as columns on the page.

Kinkoph Designs

Custom woodworking and furniture designs to suit your home and office.

Whether you are looking for a unique furniture piece or a custom copy, we can create a timeless classic you will treasure for years to come. Offering old-world craftsmanship at a quality price, we build a wide variety of beautiful furniture pieces, cabinetry, and built-ins to fit any home or office design and style.

At Kinkoph Designs, you'll experience dependability, integrity, and workmanship you can trust. We do not send out a piece until it has met our rigid quality control checks. We also offer a lifetime guarantee--unlike other furniture companies, we guarantee our pieces for the duration of your lifetime.

We offer a variety of building options suited to your pricing needs. We're happy to match stains and paint from other pieces in your room, plus we offer a vast palette of our own custom shades. We also sell unfinished furniture to allow our customers to paint or stain to fit their own decorating schemes.

You can add a table header to the top of the table to give your table a title row. Text you type as a table header appears bold and centered. Table headers can help identify the content or purpose of a data table.

You can learn how to add captions, which sit outside the table borders, in the next section.

Add a Table Header

1 Type **<TH>** at the top of the table.

Note: See the section "Add a Table" to learn how to create a basic table.

2 Type the table header text.

3 Type **</TH>** at the end of the header text.

```
<TABLE BORDER="4" BORDERCOLOR=" aroon" CELLPADDING="10">
<TH>Fall Apple Pricing</TH>|
<TR>
<TH>Apple Variety</TH>
<TH>Price</TH>
<TH># of Apples</TH>
</TR>
<TR>
<TD>Jonathon Gold</TD>
<TD>$23.00</TD>
<TD>20-22 Apples</TD>
</TR>
<TR>
<TD>Red Delicious</TD>
<TD>$20.00</TD>
<TD>22-24 Apples</TD>
</TR>
<TR>
<TD>Fuji</TD>
<TD>$24.00</TD>
<TD>20-22 Apples</TD>
</TR>
<TR>
<TD>Honey Crisp</TD>
<TD>$25.00</TD>
<TD>18-20 Apples</TD>
</TR>
```

● The Web browser displays the text as a table header.

Growing Peaches, Apples, Pears, and Pumpkins

Now taking orders for 2005 fall harvests

Fall Apple Pricing		
Apple Variety	**Price**	**# of Apples**
Jonathon Gold	$23.00	20-22 Apples
Red Delicious	$20.00	22-24 Apples
Fuji	$24.00	20-22 Apples
Honey Crisp	$25.00	18-20 Apples
Cortland	$21.00	20-22 Apples

How to Order:

1. Specify an apple variety, pear variety, or pumpkin type and size

Add a Table Caption

You can add a caption to your table to help users identify the information contained within the table. Table captions can appear at the top or bottom of the table. By default, captions appear above the table unless you specify another alignment attribute. Captions always appear as a separate line of text from the table.

You can add formatting to your caption text using the HTML formatting tags. See Chapter 4 to learn more.

Matt Zigaitis in victory lane after 3rd consecutive HTML 500 win

Add a Table Caption

① Add a new line directly below the `<TABLE>` tag.

Note: See the section "Add a Table" to learn how to create a basic table.

② Type **`<CAPTION>`**.

To place the caption below the table, type **ALIGN="bottom"** within the `<CAPTION>` tag.

③ Type the caption text.

④ Type **`</CAPTION>`** at the end of the caption text.

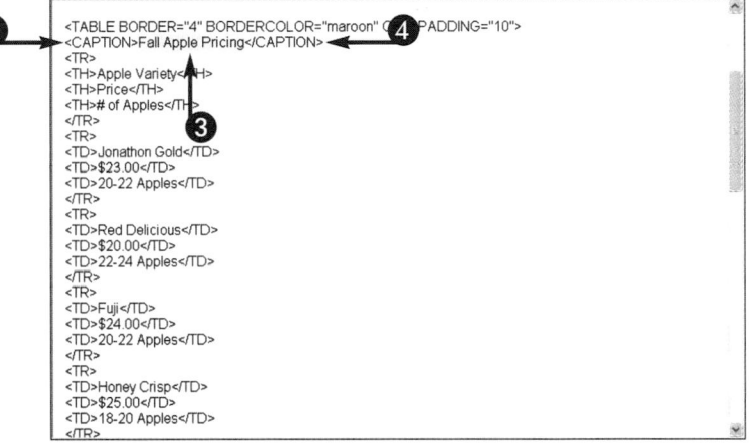

● The Web browser displays the caption above or below the table.

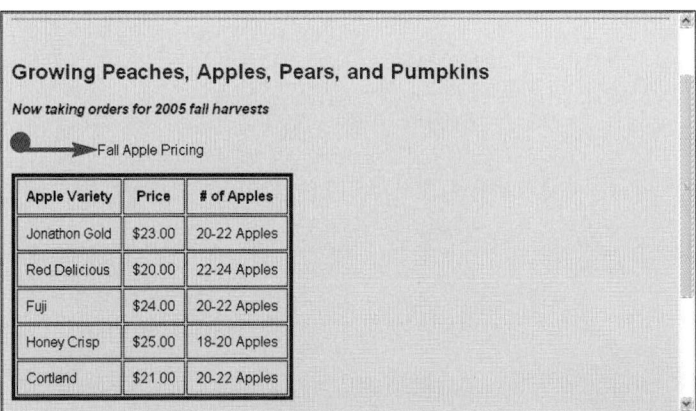

Growing Peaches, Apples, Pears, and Pumpkins

Now taking orders for 2005 fall harvests

Fall Apple Pricing

Apple Variety	Price	# of Apples
Jonathon Gold	$23.00	20-22 Apples
Red Delicious	$20.00	22-24 Apples
Fuji	$24.00	20-22 Apples
Honey Crisp	$25.00	18-20 Apples
Cortland	$21.00	20-22 Apples

Control Which Borders to Display

Ordinarily, when you assign a border to a table, it surrounds the outside of the table as well as separates each cell. You can control which internal and external borders appear in your table using the FRAME attribute. For example, you can turn off the top and bottom borders of a cell or display the entire right side of the table without a border. By controlling which borders appear, you can create a custom table.

This section includes a list of all external and internal border values for your quick reference.

Control Which Borders to Display

CONTROL EXTERNAL BORDERS

1 In the BORDER attribute for the table, type **FRAME="?"**, replacing the *?* with the value for the border display you want to set (**void**, **above**, **below**, **rhs**, **lhs**, **hsides**, **vsides**, or **border**).

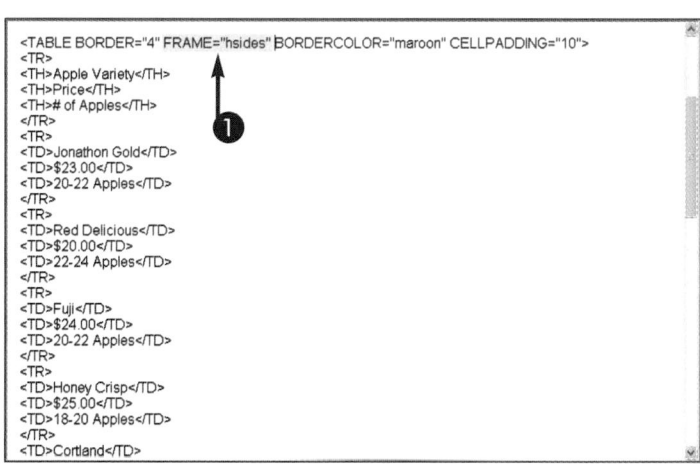

```
<TABLE BORDER="4" FRAME="hsides" BORDERCOLOR="maroon" CELLPADDING="10">
<TR>
<TH>Apple Variety</TH>
<TH>Price</TH>
<TH># of Apples</TH>
</TR>
<TR>
<TD>Jonathon Gold</TD>
<TD>$23.00</TD>
<TD>20-22 Apples</TD>
</TR>
<TR>
<TD>Red Delicious</TD>
<TD>$20.00</TD>
<TD>22-24 Apples</TD>
</TR>
<TR>
<TD>Fuji</TD>
<TD>$24.00</TD>
<TD>20-22 Apples</TD>
</TR>
<TR>
<TD>Honey Crisp</TD>
<TD>$25.00</TD>
<TD>18-20 Apples</TD>
</TR>
<TD>Cortland</TD>
```

The Web browser displays the table with the external borders you specified.

● In this example, the sides of the table are hidden.

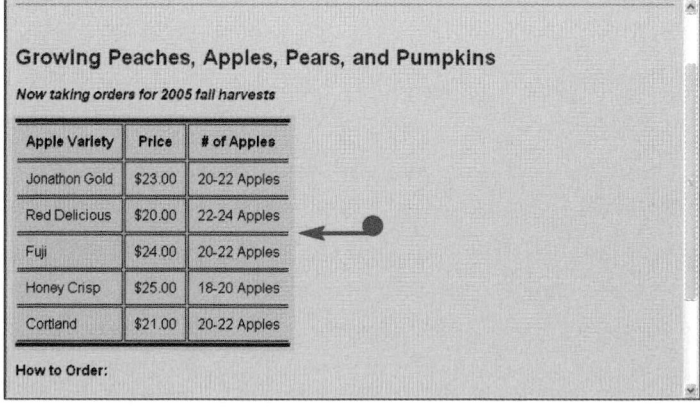

Growing Peaches, Apples, Pears, and Pumpkins

Now taking orders for 2005 fall harvests

Apple Variety	Price	# of Apples
Jonathon Gold	$23.00	20-22 Apples
Red Delicious	$20.00	22-24 Apples
Fuji	$24.00	20-22 Apples
Honey Crisp	$25.00	18-20 Apples
Cortland	$21.00	20-22 Apples

How to Order:

CONTROL INTERNAL BORDERS

1 In the BORDER attribute for the table, type **RULES="?"**, replacing the *?* with the value for the border display you want to set (**none**, **cols**, **rows**, **groups**, or **all**).

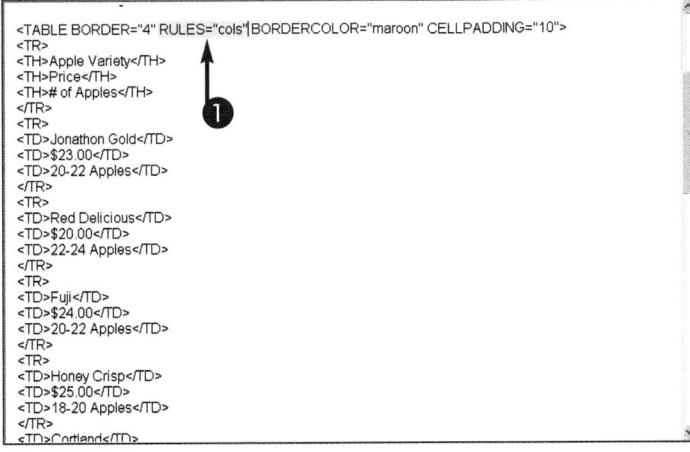

The Web browser displays the table with the internal borders you specified.

● In this example, the inside row borders are hidden.

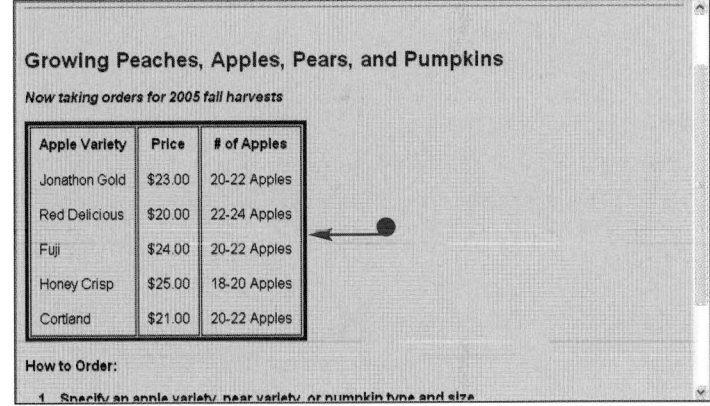

TIPS

What values do I use to define external or internal borders?

External Borders	
Value	**Display**
VOID	No external borders
ABOVE	A border above the table
BELOW	A border below the table
RHS	A border on the right side of the table
LHS	A border on the left side of the table
HSIDES	Borders on the top and bottom of the table
VSIDES	Borders on the left and right sides of the table
BORDER	Borders on every side of the table (default)

Internal Borders	
Value	**Display**
NONE	No internal borders
COLS	Borders between columns
ROWS	Borders between rows
GROUPS	Borders between column and row groups
ALL	Borders throughout the table cells (default)

You can control the exact size of a table using the WIDTH and HEIGHT attributes in the <TABLE> tag. You can specify a table size in pixels or set the size as a percentage of the browser window.

When setting a size in pixels, set the value to 600 pixels or less to ensure the table fits on the screen. If you prefer a more flexible table, set the size in percentages. This allows the table to be resized along with any resizing of the browser window.

Adjust the Table Size

SET A TABLE SIZE IN PIXELS

1 In the <TABLE> tag, type **WIDTH="?"**, replacing the *?* with the pixel value you want to assign.

2 Type a space.

3 Type **HEIGHT="?"**, replacing the *?* with the pixel value you want to assign.

Note: *The HEIGHT attribute is not as well supported as the WIDTH attribute and may not display properly on all browsers.*

```
<TABLE BORDER="4" BORDERCOLOR="maroon" WIDTH="600" HEIGHT="400" CELLPADDING="10">
<TR>
<TH>Apple Variety</TH>
<TH>Price</TH>
<TH># of Apples</TH>
</TR>
<TR>
<TD>Jonathon Gold</TD>
<TD>$23.00</TD>
<TD>20-22 Apples</TD>
</TR>
<TR>
<TD>Red Delicious</TD>
<TD>$20.00</TD>
<TD>22-24 Apples</TD>
</TR>
<TR>
<TD>Fuji</TD>
<TD>$24.00</TD>
<TD>20-22 Apples</TD>
</TR>
<TR>
<TD>Honey Crisp</TD>
<TD>$25.00</TD>
<TD>18-20 Apples</TD>
</TR>
<TD>Cortland</TD>
<TD>$21.00</TD>
```

①②③

● The Web browser displays the table in the specified size.

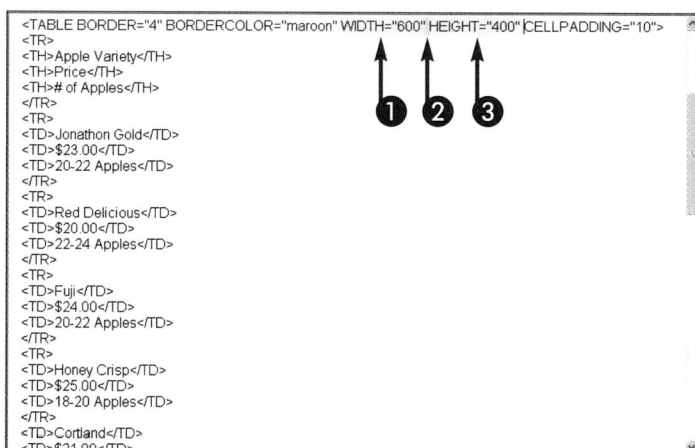

Now taking orders for 2005 fall harvests

Apple Variety	Price	# of Apples
Jonathon Gold	$23.00	20-22 Apples
Red Delicious	$20.00	22-24 Apples
Fuji	$24.00	20-22 Apples
Honey Crisp	$25.00	18-20 Apples
Cortland	$21.00	20-22 Apples

SET A TABLE SIZE AS A PERCENTAGE

1 In the `<TABLE>` tag, type **WIDTH="?"**, replacing the *?* with the percentage value you want to assign.

Optionally, you can add a height setting if your table needs one by typing **HEIGHT="?"** in the `<TABLE>` tag to set a table height.

Note: *The* HEIGHT *attribute is not as well supported as the* WIDTH *attribute and may not display properly on all browsers.*

```
<TABLE BORDER="4" BORDERCOLOR="maroon" WIDTH="100%" CELLPADDING="10">
<TR>
<TH>Apple Variety</TH>
<TH>Price</TH>
<TH># of Apples</TH>
</TR>
<TR>
<TD>Jonathon Gold</TD>
<TD>$23.00</TD>
<TD>20-22 Apples</TD>
</TR>
<TR>
<TD>Red Delicious</TD>
<TD>$20.00</TD>
<TD>22-24 Apples</TD>
</TR>
<TR>
<TD>Fuji</TD>
<TD>$24.00</TD>
<TD>20-22 Apples</TD>
</TR>
<TR>
<TD>Honey Crisp</TD>
<TD>$25.00</TD>
<TD>18-20 Apples</TD>
</TR>
<TD>Cortland</TD>
<TD>$21.00</TD>
```

● The Web browser displays the table in the specified size.

Now taking orders for 2005 fall harvests

Apple Variety	Price	# of Apples
Jonathon Gold	$23.00	20-22 Apples
Red Delicious	$20.00	22-24 Apples
Fuji	$24.00	20-22 Apples
Honey Crisp	$25.00	18-20 Apples
Cortland	$21.00	20-22 Apples

How to Order:

1. Specify an apple variety, pear variety, or pumpkin type and size.
2. Fill out your shipping information.
3. Select a payment method.
4. Submit your order.
5. Receive a confirmation e-mail

TIPS

Is it possible to set a table too small for its contents?

No. If you do accidentally set a size too small for the contents, the browser ignores the measurements and tries to make the table fit as best it can. On the other hand, if you set a table too wide, users are forced to scroll to see parts of the table. For best results, do not make a table wider than 600 pixels.

What size does a browser set my table to if I do not specify an exact width?

If you do not set a width, the browser automatically determines the width by looking at the cell contents. It expands the table to fit the longest contents or the edge of the browser window, whichever is reached first. Cell text is stretched out until the first line break or end of the paragraph, which can make the table appear off balance. To exert control over the table size, you can set a width and add paragraph or line breaks to control the appearance of text within the cells.

You can control the alignment of data within your table cells using the ALIGN and VALIGN attributes. The ALIGN attribute controls horizontal alignment: left, center, and right. By default, all table data you enter into cells is left-aligned. The VALIGN attribute controls vertical alignment: top, middle, and bottom. By default, the table data is vertically aligned to appear in the middle of each cell.

You can add alignment attributes to a single cell, a row, or all the data in the table. To learn how to position a table on the page, see the section "Change Table Alignment."

Change Cell Alignment

SET HORIZONTAL ALIGNMENT

① Click inside the cell, row, or table tag you want to align.

Note: You can also align column or row groups. See the section "Create Column and Row Groups" to learn more.

② Type **ALIGN="?"**, replacing the ? with the horizontal alignment attribute: **left**, **center**, or **right**.

```
<TABLE BORDER="4" BORDERCOLOR="maroon" WIDTH="100%" CELLPADDING="10">
<TR>
<TH>Apple Variety</TH>
<TH>Price</TH>
<TH># of Apples</TH>
</TR>
<TR>
<TD>Jonathon Gold</TD>
<TD ALIGN="center">$23.00</TD>
<TD>20-22 Apples</TD>
</TR>
<TR>
<TD>Red Delicious</TD>
<TD>$20.00</TD>
<TD>22-24 Apples</TD>
</TR>
<TR>
<TD>Fuji</TD>
<TD>$24.00</TD>
<TD>20-22 Apples</TD>
</TR>
<TR>
<TD>Honey Crisp</TD>
<TD>$25.00</TD>
<TD>18-20 Apples</TD>
</TR>
<TD>Cortland</TD>
```

The Web browser displays the alignment in the table.

● In this example, the contents of a single cell are centered.

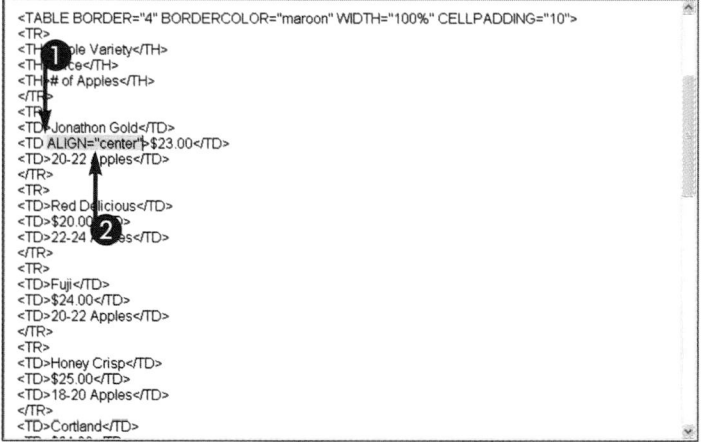

Growing Peaches, Apples, Pears, and Pumpkins

Now taking orders for 2005 fall harvests

Apple Variety	Price	# of Apples
Jonathon Gold	$23.00	20-22 Apples
Red Delicious	$20.00	22-24 Apples
Fuji	$24.00	20-22 Apples
Honey Crisp	$25.00	18-20 Apples
Cortland	$21.00	20-22 Apples

How to Order:

SET VERTICAL ALIGNMENT

1 Click inside the cell, row, or table tag you want to align.

Note: You can also align column or row groups. See the section "Create Column and Row Groups" to learn more.

2 Type **VALIGN="?"**, replacing the *?* with the horizontal alignment attribute: **top**, **middle**, or **bottom**.

```
<TABLE BORDER="4" BORDERCOLOR="maroon" WIDTH="600" HEIGHT="400" CELLPADDING="10">
<TR>
<TH>Apple Variety</TH>
<TH VALIGN="top">Price</TH>
<TH># of Apples</TH>
</TR>
<TR>
<TD>Jonathon Gold</TD>
<TD>$23.00</TD>
<TD>20-22 Apples</TD>
</TR>
<TR>
<TD>Red Delicious</TD>
<TD>$20.00</TD>
<TD>22-24 Apples</TD>
</TR>
<TR>
<TD>Fuji</TD>
<TD>$24.00</TD>
<TD>20-22 Apples</TD>
</TR>
<TR>
<TD>Honey Crisp</TD>
<TD>$25.00</TD>
<TD>18-20 Apples</TD>
</TR>
<TD>Cortland</TD>
```

The Web browser displays the alignment in the table.

● In this example, a single column heading is top-aligned.

Now taking orders for 2005 fall harvests

Apple Variety	Price	# of Apples
Jonathon Gold	$23.00	20-22 Apples
Red Delicious	$20.00	22-24 Apples
Fuji	$24.00	20-22 Apples
Honey Crisp	$25.00	18-20 Apples
Cortland	$21.00	20-22 Apples

TIPS

Can I override an alignment for a column or row group with a different alignment?

Yes. You can set the alignment for a column or row and then override the alignment for an individual cell within the group. Simply add the alignment attribute to the cell. See the section "Create Column and Row Groups" to learn more.

How do I justify data in a table cell?

Justification sets both a left and right alignment and stretches the text to spread out between the two cell borders. Although there is an HTML attribute for justification, JUSTIFY, Web browsers do not currently support the setting.

Span Cells across Columns and Rows

You can create a larger cell in your table by spanning the cell across two or more columns or rows. Spanning cells, also called merging cells, allows you to create unique cell structures within your table. For example, you might include a large cell across the top of a table to hold a heading or an image.

Span Cells across Columns and Rows

SPAN CELLS ACROSS COLUMNS

1 Click inside the cell tag you want to span.

2 Type **COLSPAN="?"**, replacing the *?* with the number of columns you want to span across.

```
<TABLE BORDER="4" BORDERCOLOR="maroon" WIDTH="600" CELLPADDING="10">
<TR>
<TH COLSPAN="3">Fall Apple Pricing</TH>
</TR>
<TR>
<TH>Apple Variety</TH>
<TH>Price</TH>
<TH># of Apples</TH>
</TR>
<TR>
<TD>Jonathon Gold</TD>
<TD>$23.00</TD>
<TD>20-22 Apples</TD>
</TR>
<TR>
<TD>Red Delicious</TD>
<TD>$20.00</TD>
<TD>22-24 Apples</TD>
</TR>
<TR>
<TD>Fuji</TD>
<TD>$24.00</TD>
<TD>20-22 Apples</TD>
</TR>
<TR>
<TD>Honey Crisp</TD>
<TD>$25.00</TD>
```

The Web browser displays the cell across the designated number of columns.

● In this example, a heading column spans across the top of the table.

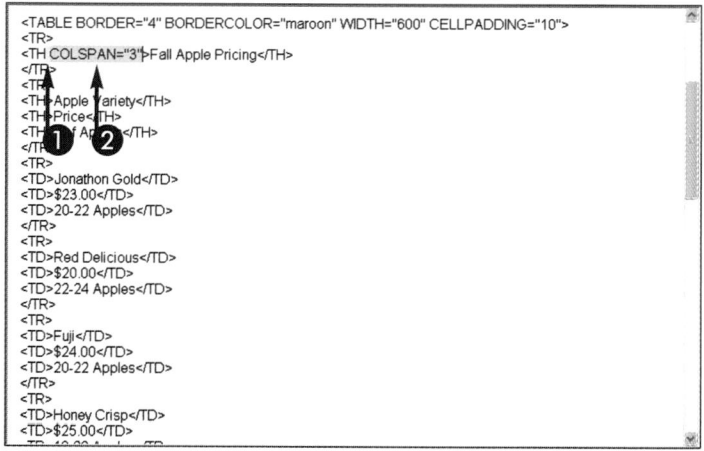

SPAN CELLS ACROSS ROWS

1 Click inside the cell tag you want to span.

2 Type **ROWSPAN="?"**, replacing the *?* with the number of rows you want to span across.

```
<TABLE BORDER="4" BORDERCOLOR="maroon" WIDTH="600" CELLPADDING="10">
<TR>
<TH COLSPAN="4">Fall Apple Pricing</TH>
</TR>
<TR>
<TH ROWSPAN="6">Available Crop</TH>
<TH>Apple Variety</TH>
<TH>Price</TH>
<TH># of Apples</TH>
</TR>
<TR>
<TD>Jonathon Gold</TD>
<TD>$23.00</TD>
<TD>20-22 Apples</TD>
</TR>
<TR>
<TD>Red Delicious</TD>
<TD>$20.00</TD>
<TD>22-24 Apples</TD>
</TR>
<TR>
<TD>Fuji</TD>
<TD>$24.00</TD>
<TD>20-22 Apples</TD>
</TR>
<TR>
<TD>Honey Crisp</TD>
<TD>$25.00</TD>
```

The Web browser displays the cell across the designated number of rows.

● In this example, a heading spans six rows down the side of the table.

Now taking orders for 2005 fall harvests

Fall Apple Pricing			
Available Crop	**Apple Variety**	**Price**	**# of Apples**
	Jonathon Gold	$23.00	20-22 Apples
	Red Delicious	$20.00	22-24 Apples
	Fuji	$24.00	20-22 Apples
	Honey Crisp	$25.00	18-20 Apples
	Cortland	$21.00	20-22 Apples

How to Order:

1. Specify an apple variety, pear variety, or pumpkin type and size.
2. Fill out your shipping information.
3. Select a payment method.

TIP

Can I span a cell across columns and rows at the same time?

Yes. If you add the COLSPAN and ROWSPAN attributes to the same row or header, you can make a cell span across and down in the table. Just remember to remove cells in the columns and rows into which you want to span the current cell.

Create Column and Row Groups

You can divide your table into column or row groups to more easily format groups of cells. For example, if your table lists products, you might group product numbers and descriptions and format them in a particular font and size. Rather than having to apply individual formatting to each cell, column and row groups allow you to format select cells in one fell swoop.

Columns can use structural groups, which divide a table into sections you design, or nonstructural groups. Structural groups use the <COLGROUP> tag, while nonstructural groups use the <COL> tag.

Create Column and Row Groups

CREATE A STRUCTURAL COLUMN GROUP

1 Add a line where you want to insert a new column group and type **<COLGROUP SPAN="?">**, replacing the *?* with the number of columns you want to include in the group.

● You can type any formatting attributes you want to assign the group within the <COLGROUP> tag.

2 Type **</COLGROUP>** to end the group.

3 Repeat steps **1** and **2** for each column group you want to create.

Any formatting you assign to the group is applied to every cell in the group.

● In this example, one group has a gray background color, while the other has a white background color.

Note: *See the section "Add Background Color to Cells" to learn more about adding color to tables.*

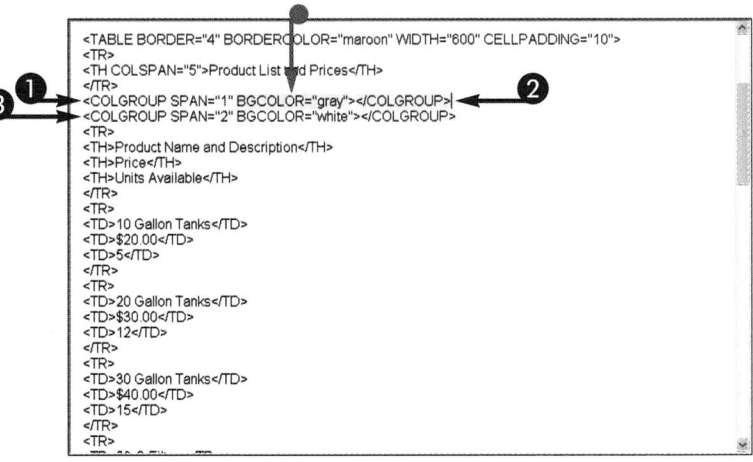

```
<TABLE BORDER="4" BORDERCOLOR="maroon" WIDTH="600" CELLPADDING="10">
<TR>
<TH COLSPAN="5">Product List and Prices</TH>
</TR>
<COLGROUP SPAN="1" BGCOLOR="gray"></COLGROUP>
<COLGROUP SPAN="2" BGCOLOR="white"></COLGROUP>
<TR>
<TH>Product Name and Description</TH>
<TH>Price</TH>
<TH>Units Available</TH>
</TR>
<TR>
<TD>10 Gallon Tanks</TD>
<TD>$20.00</TD>
<TD>5</TD>
</TR>
<TR>
<TD>20 Gallon Tanks</TD>
<TD>$30.00</TD>
<TD>12</TD>
</TR>
<TR>
<TD>30 Gallon Tanks</TD>
<TD>$40.00</TD>
<TD>15</TD>
</TR>
<TR>
```

supplies

Product List and Prices		
Product Name and Description	**Price**	**Units Available**
10 Gallon Tanks	$20.00	5
20 Gallon Tanks	$30.00	12
30 Gallon Tanks	$40.00	15
20-G Filters	$15.00	20
Goldfish 1"	$.10	52
Goldfish 3"	$.25	78
Goldfish 5"	$.50	30

CREATE A NONSTRUCTURAL COLUMN GROUP

① Add a line where you want to insert a new column group and type **<COL SPAN="?">**, replacing the *?* with the number of columns you want to include in the group.

● You can type any formatting attributes you want to assign the group within the <COL> tag.

You do not need a closing tag for nonstructural groups.

② Repeat step **1** for each column group you want to create in the table.

Any formatting you assign to the group is applied to every cell in the group.

● In this example, one group has a silver background color, while the other has a white background color.

Note: *See the section "Add Background Color to Cells" to learn more about adding color to tables.*

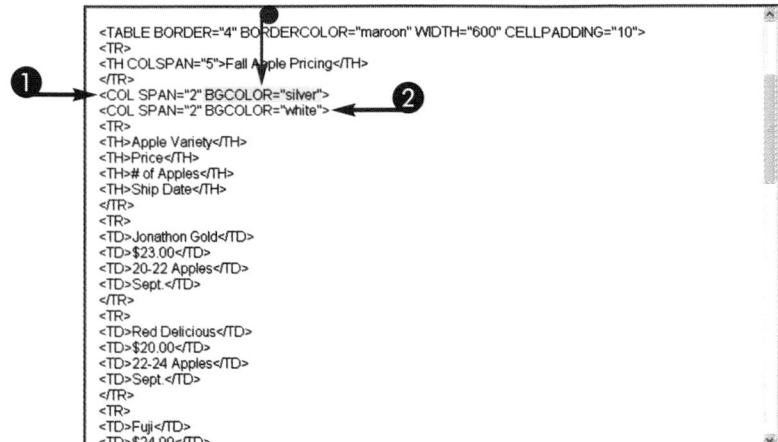

```
<TABLE BORDER="4" BORDERCOLOR="maroon" WIDTH="600" CELLPADDING="10">
<TR>
<TH COLSPAN="5">Fall Apple Pricing</TH>
</TR>
<COL SPAN="2" BGCOLOR="silver">
<COL SPAN="2" BGCOLOR="white">
<TR>
<TH>Apple Variety</TH>
<TH>Price</TH>
<TH># of Apples</TH>
<TH>Ship Date</TH>
</TR>
<TR>
<TD>Jonathon Gold</TD>
<TD>$23.00</TD>
<TD>20-22 Apples</TD>
<TD>Sept.</TD>
</TR>
<TR>
<TD>Red Delicious</TD>
<TD>$20.00</TD>
<TD>22-24 Apples</TD>
<TD>Sept.</TD>
</TR>
<TR>
<TD>Fuji</TD>
<TD>$24.00</TD>
```

Growing Peaches, Apples, Pears, and Pumpkins

Now taking orders for 2005 fall harvests

Fall Apple Pricing			
Apple Variety	**Price**	**# of Apples**	**Ship Date**
Jonathon Gold	$23.00	20-22 Apples	Sept.
Red Delicious	$20.00	22-24 Apples	Sept.
Fuji	$24.00	20-22 Apples	Oct.
Honey Crisp	$25.00	18-20 Apples	Sept.
Cortland	$21.00	20-22 Apples	Aug./Sept.

How to Order:

TIPS

After I assign a column or row group, how do I align every cell in the group?

You can add the ALIGN attribute to the <THEAD>, <TFOOT>, or <TBODY> tags to assign alignment to the entire group. For example, if you type **<TBODY ALIGN= "right">** all the cell content in the group aligns to the right of the cells.

If my column group includes a column header and I assign an alignment to the group, does the header alignment change, too?

No. Header cells are not affected by alignment you assign to the column group. Browsers read the <TH> tag and automatically set center alignment and bold text. You can, however, align the cell separately using the alignment attributes. See the section "Change Cell Alignment" to learn how to add alignment coding to a table cell.

continued

You can use row groups to divide a table into horizontal sections. You can create row groups using the <THEAD> and <TBODY> tags. The <THEAD> tag creates a header for the row group. You use the <TBODY> tag to define the actual row groups. If the row group requires a footer, you can add one with the <TFOOT> tag.

Create Column and Row Groups *(continued)*

CREATE A ROW GROUP

1 Before the header row you want to include in a row group, type **<THEAD>**.

You can add any formatting you want to apply to the group within the <THEAD> tag.

Note: See the section "Add Background Color to Cells" to learn more about adding color to tables.

2 Type **</THEAD>** after the last row you want to include in a group.

3 Type **<TBODY>** above each row you want to include in the group.

● You can type any formatting attributes you want to assign the group within the <TBODY> tag.

4 Type **</TBODY>** after the last row to include in the group.

To create multiple row groups, repeat steps **3** and **4** for the other rows you want to group together in the table.

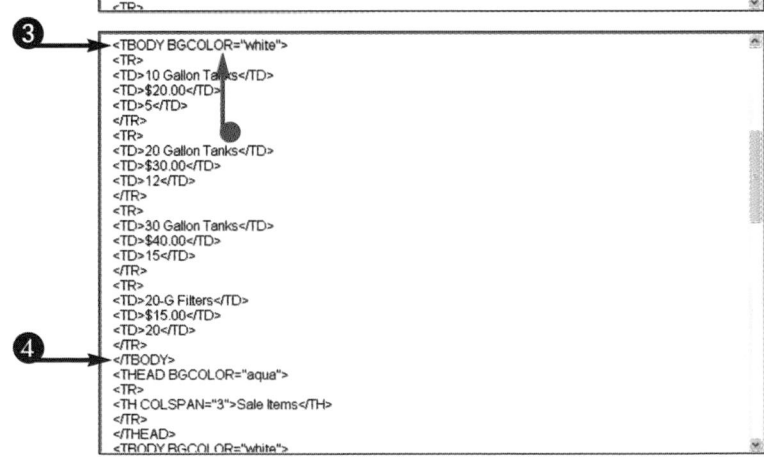

● Optionally, to include a footer below the row group, type **<TFOOT>** and **</TFOOT>** before and after the row you want to use as the footer.

```
<TR>
<TH COLSPAN="3">Sale Items</TH>
</TR>
</THEAD>
<TBODY BGCOLOR="white">
<TR>
<TD>Goldfish 1"</TD>
<TD>$.10</TD>
<TD>52</TD>
</TR>
<TR>
<TD>Goldfish 3"</TD>
<TD>$.25</TD>
<TD>78</TD>
</TR>
<TR>
<TD>Goldfish 5"</TD>
<TD>$.50</TD>
<TD>30</TD>
</TR>
</TBODY>
<TFOOT BGCOLOR="gray">
<TR>
<TH COLSPAN="3">All Prices Subject to Change</TH>
</TR>
</TFOOT>
</TABLE>
```

The Web browser displays the row groups in the table.

In this example, row groups are assigned different background colors to help distinguish each group.

Product List and Prices		
Product Name and Description	Price	Units Available
10 Gallon Tanks	$20.00	5
20 Gallon Tanks	$30.00	12
30 Gallon Tanks	$40.00	15
Sale Items		
Goldfish 1"	$.10	52
Goldfish 3"	$.25	78
Goldfish 5"	$.50	30
All Prices Subject to Change		

TIPS

Can my table include both structural and nonstructural column and row groups?

Yes. For example, your table might include a group of rows in the middle of the table set aside for certain data, while the remaining cells remain nonstructured.

How do I add lines between my groups?

You can specify exactly which cell and table borders appear in your table using the FRAME attribute. For example, you might set a thick, color border at the top and bottom of a row group to make the group stand out from the rest of the table. See the section "Control Which Borders to Display" earlier in this chapter to learn more.

Add Background Color to Cells

You can add color to individual cells in your table or to select rows and columns. You can use background color to draw attention to the cell contents.

When applying a background color, be careful not to choose a color that makes the table data difficult to read. See Chapter 4 to learn more about setting color values in HTML.

Add Background Color to Cells

① Click in the cell or row tag to which you want to add a background color.

② Type **BGCOLOR="?"**, replacing the *?* with the color value you want to assign.

Note: See Chapter 4 to learn more about assigning color values.

To add color to a particular column, you can add the color attribute to each cell in the column or insert the attribute in a column group tag.

Note: See the section "Create Column and Row Groups" to learn more.

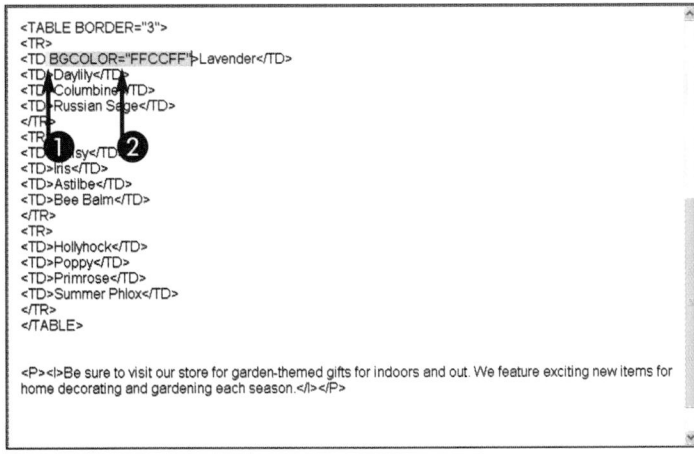

The Web browser displays the background color in the cell, row, or column.

● In this example, a color is added to a single cell.

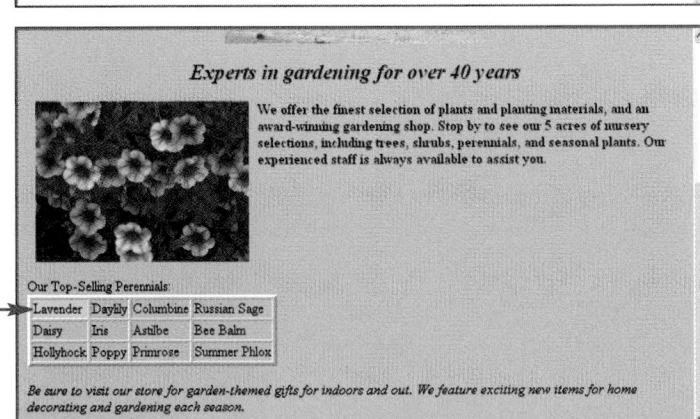

Add a Background Color to a Table

You can add a background color to appear behind the entire table of data. You can use a background color to make the table stand out from the rest of the Web page.

When applying a background color, be careful not to choose a color that makes the table data difficult to read. See Chapter 4 to learn more about setting color values in HTML.

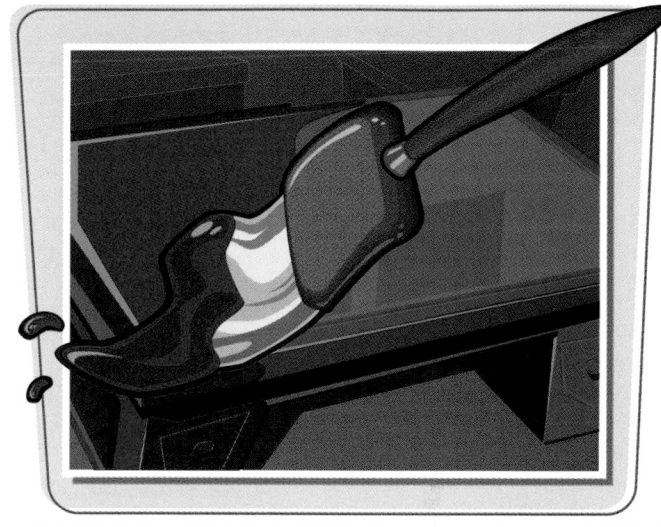

Add a Background Color to a Table

① Within the `<TABLE>` tag, type **BGCOLOR="?"**, replacing the *?* with the color value you want to assign.

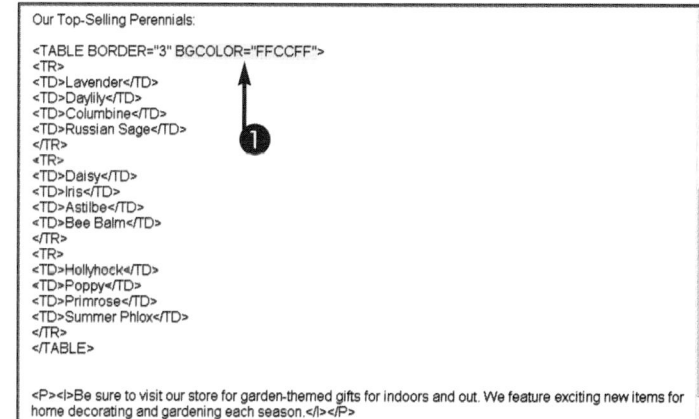

Our Top-Selling Perennials:

```
<TABLE BORDER="3" BGCOLOR="FFCCFF">
<TR>
<TD>Lavender</TD>
<TD>Daylily</TD>
<TD>Columbine</TD>
<TD>Russian Sage</TD>
</TR>
<TR>
<TD>Daisy</TD>
<TD>Iris</TD>
<TD>Astilbe</TD>
<TD>Bee Balm</TD>
</TR>
<TR>
<TD>Hollyhock</TD>
<TD>Poppy</TD>
<TD>Primrose</TD>
<TD>Summer Phlox</TD>
</TR>
</TABLE>

<P><I>Be sure to visit our store for garden-themed gifts for indoors and out. We feature exciting new items for home decorating and gardening each season.</I></P>
```

● The Web browser displays the table with the specified background color.

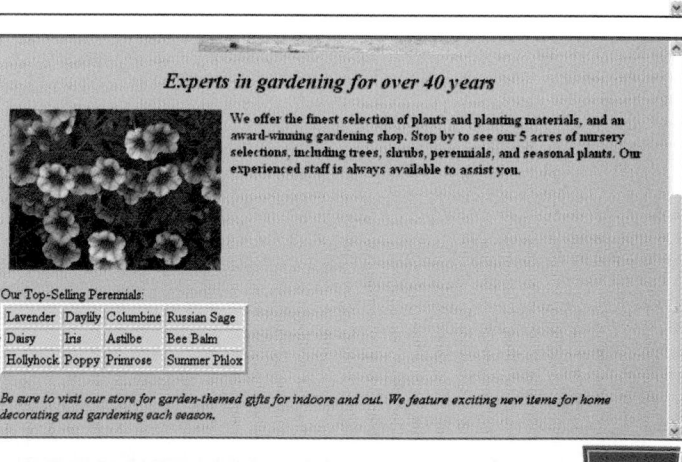

Insert an Image in a Cell

You can add an image to any cell in your table. If you are using a table as a page layout structure, for example, you might place images in different cells to illustrate your page. If you are using a table strictly to hold data, you might insert an image of your content, such as a product picture.

You can also use the BACKGROUND **attribute to add an image to a single cell or the entire table. See the section "Insert a Table Background Image" to learn more.**

Insert an Image in a Cell

① Click within the cell in which you want to add an image, right after the opening `<TD>` tag, and type **<IMG SRC="?">**, replacing the *?* with the name and path to the image file you want to use.

Note: See Chapter 7 to learn how to add and work with images.

```
<B>We offer the finest selection of plants and planting materials, and an award-winning gardening shop. Stop
by to see our 5 acres of nursery selections, including trees, shrubs, perennials, and seasonal plants. Our
experienced staff is always available to assist you.</B>
<BR>

<H3>Our Top-Selling Annuals:</H3>
<BR>

<TABLE BORDER="3" WIDTH="450" CELLPADDING="5">
<TR>
<TD><IMG SRC="Million_Bells2.jpg"></TD>
<TD>Million Bells Petunia</TD>
</TR>
<TR>
<TD><IMG SRC="Blue_Salvia2.jpg"></TD>
<TD>Blue Salvia</TD>
</TR>
</TABLE>

<P><I>Be sure to visit our store for garden-themed gifts for indoors and out. We feature exciting new items for
home decorating and gardening each season.</I></P>

</BODY>
```

The Web browser displays the cell with the specified image.

Insert a Table Background Image

You can add a background image to appear behind your entire table. Background images can give your table an interesting design.

When using an image as a background, be careful the design and colors do not conflict with the table data. You may need to change the text color to make it stand out from the underlying background image. See Chapter 4 to learn how to assign color to text.

Insert a Table Background Image

1 Click in the `<TABLE>` tag and type **BACKGROUND="?"**, replacing the *?* with the name and path to the image file you want to use.

Note: See Chapter 7 to learn how to add and work with images.

```
<TABLE BORDER="3" WIDTH="600" HEIGHT="450" CELLPADDING="5"
BACKGROUND="Salmon_Rose5.jpg">
<TR>
<TD><B>Lavender</B></TD>
<TD><B>Hollyhock</B></TD>
<TD><B>Daisy</B></TD>
<TD><B>Columbine</B></TD>
</TR>
<TR>
<TD><B>Daylily</B></TD>
<TD><B>Primrose</B></TD>
<TD><B>Poppy</B></TD>
<TD><B>Bee Balm</B></TD>
</TR>
<TR>
<TD><B>Peony</B></TD>
<TD><B>Astilbe</B></TD>
<TD><B>Iris</B></TD>
<TD><B>Coneflower</B></TD>
</TR>
</TABLE>

<P><I>Be sure to visit our store for garden-themed gifts for indoors and out. We feature exciting new items for home decorating and gardening each season.</I></P>
```

The Web browser displays the table with the specified background image.

Change Table Alignment

You can control the positioning of a table on your Web page using the ALIGN attribute. You can use the ALIGN attribute to center a table or align it to the right or left sides of the page. The ALIGN attribute also determines the way in which text wraps around your table element. For example, if you align the table to the right, text wraps around the left side of the table.

① Click in the `<TABLE>` tag and type **ALIGN="?"**, replacing the *?* with the alignment you want to apply: **left**, **right**, or **center**.

Note: *Text does not wrap around a centered table, but it will wrap around those that are left- or right-aligned.*

To stop text from wrapping, type **<BR CLEAR="?"** before the text, replacing *?* with the alignment value you want to clear.

```
<TABLE BORDER="4" BORDERCOLOR="maroon" WIDTH="575" CELLPADDING="10" ALIGN="right">
<TR>
<TH COLSPAN="5">Fall Apple Pricing</TH>
</TR>
<COL SPAN="2" BGCOLOR="silver">
<COL SPAN="2" BGCOLOR="white">
<TR>
<TH>Apple Variety</TH>
<TH>Price</TH>
<TH># of Apples</TH>
<TH>Ship Date</TH>
</TR>
<TR>
<TD>Jonathon Gold</TD>
<TD>$23.00</TD>
<TD>20-22 Apples</TD>
<TD>Sept.</TD>
</TR>
<TR>
<TD>Red Delicious</TD>
<TD>$20.00</TD>
<TD>22-24 Apples</TD>
<TD>Sept.</TD>
</TR>
<TR>
<TD>Fuji</TD>
<TD>$24.00</TD>
<TD>20-22 Apples</TD>
```

The Web browser displays the table with wrapping text.

● In this example, the table is right-aligned, with text wrapping around the left side.

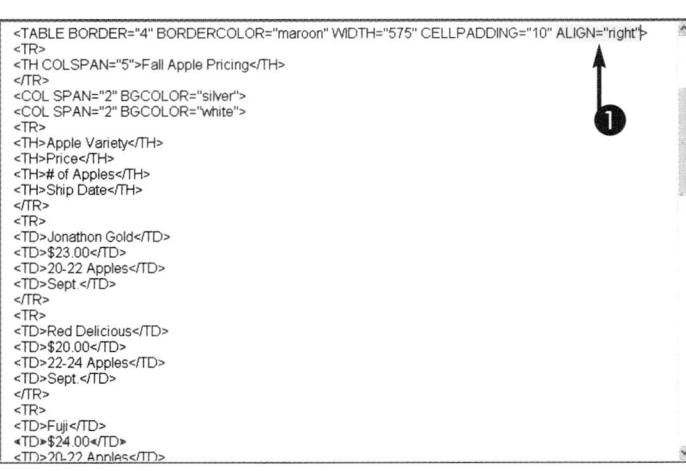

Growing Peaches, Apples, Pears, and Pumpkins

Now taking orders for 2005 fall harvests

Fall Apple Pricing			
Apple Variety	Price	# of Apples	Ship Date
Jonathon Gold	$23.00	20-22 Apples	Sept.
Red Delicious	$20.00	22-24 Apples	Sept.
Fuji	$24.00	20-22 Apples	Oct.
Honey Crisp	$25.00	18-20 Apples	Sept.
Cortland	$21.00	20-22 Apples	Aug./Sept.

● In this example, the table is left-aligned, with text wrapping around the right side.

Note: *Left alignment is the default alignment unless you specify an alignment value.*

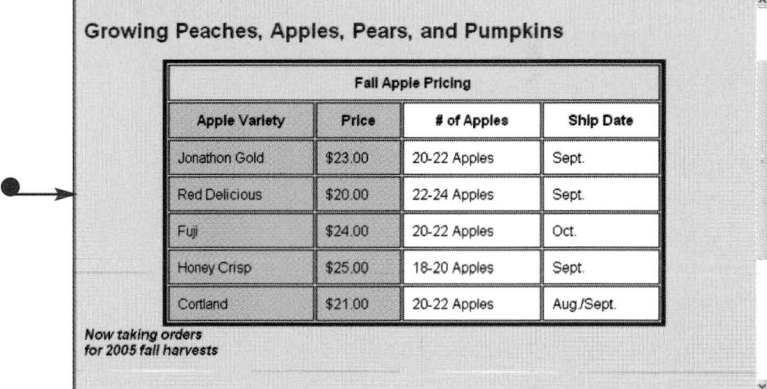

● In this example, the table is center-aligned, and no text wrapping occurs.

TIPS

How do I control line breaks in a cell?

You can use the `<BR>` tag to create a new line break in a cell. You can also use the `<P>` tag to create a line break. You can use the same text formatting tags and attributes used for regular page text to control the text within table cells. See Chapters 3 and 4 to learn more about line breaks and other text formatting. See the next section "Control Text Wrapping in Cells" to learn how to control the way in which text wraps within a table cell.

Can I center a table using a style sheet?

Yes. You can type `MARGIN-RIGHT: AUTO` or `MARGIN-LEFT: AUTO` in the table's style rule to center a table. However, you need to specify the table width first. See Chapters 5 and 6 to learn more about CSS. See the section "Adjust the Table Size" to learn how to set a table width.

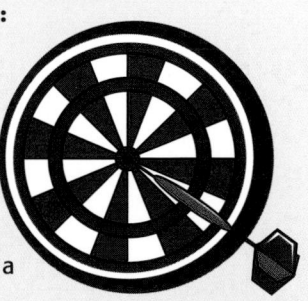

Control Text Wrapping in Cells

Depending on the size of the table, Web browsers automatically wrap text in cells when needed. You can control the wrapping by using line breaks within the cell, or you can turn off text wrapping completely.

Control Text Wrapping in Cells

1 Click inside the cell tag for the text you want to control and type **NOWRAP**.

To specify where a line breaks, type **
**.

You can also use the <P> tag to control line breaks in a cell.

```
<TABLE BORDER="4" BORDERCOLOR="maroon" WIDTH="575" CELLPADDING="10">
<TR>
<TH COLSPAN="5">Class Schedule</TH>
</TR>
<TR>
<TH NOWRAP>Class Description</TH>
<TH>Teacher</TH>
<TH>Days</TH>
<TH>Time</TH>
<TH>Location</TH>
</TR>
<TR>
<TD NOWRAP>Beginning Digital Photography 101</TD>
<TD>Ansel Edwards</TD>
<TD>Tuesdays and Thursdays</TD>
<TD>7:00 p.m.</TD>
<TD>Room B, Tech Building, Broward St.</TD>
</TR>
<TR>
<TD>Beginning Digital Photography 101</TD>
<TD>Susan Harding</TD>
<TD>Mondays and Wednesdays</TD>
<TD>7:00 p.m.</TD>
<TD>Room C, Tech Building, Broward St.</TD>
</TR>
<TR>
<TD>Beginning Digital Photography 102</TD>
<TD>David Willard</TD>
```

● The Web browser displays the text without breaking the line automatically.

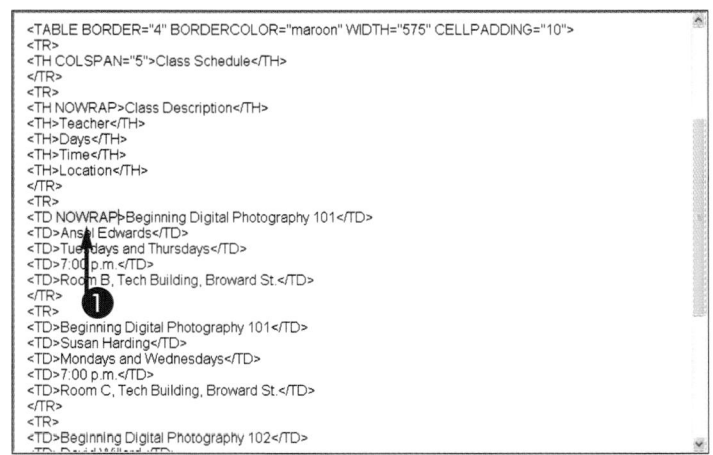

Class Schedule				
Class Description	**Teacher**	**Days**	**Time**	**Location**
Beginning Digital Photography 101	Ansel Edwards	Tuesdays and Thursdays	7:00 p.m.	Room B, Tech Building, Broward St.
Beginning Digital Photography 101	Susan Harding	Mondays and Wednesdays	7:00 p.m.	Room C, Tech Building, Broward St.
Beginning Digital Photography 102	David Willard	Mondays and Wednesdays	10:00 a.m.	Room E, Tech Building, Broward St.

You can create a table within a table, called *nested tables*. Nested tables allow you to create a more complex table layout.

Nest a Table within a Table

1 Within the main table, add a line in the cell in which you want to add another table.

2 Create the nested table just like a regular table.

Note: *See the section "Add a Table" to learn how to create a basic HTML table.*

To help distinguish the nested table from the main table, consider using indents or new lines to enter the nested table data.

● The Web browser displays the table within the main table.

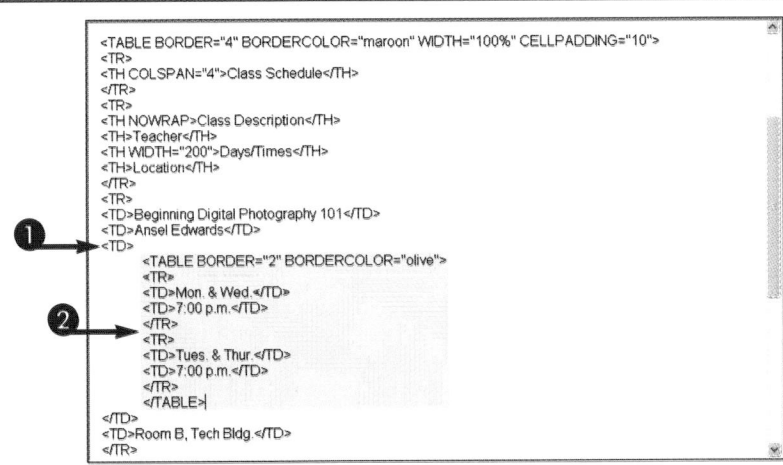

```
<TABLE BORDER="4" BORDERCOLOR="maroon" WIDTH="100%" CELLPADDING="10">
<TR>
<TH COLSPAN="4">Class Schedule</TH>
</TR>
<TR>
<TH NOWRAP>Class Description</TH>
<TH>Teacher</TH>
<TH WIDTH="200">Days/Times</TH>
<TH>Location</TH>
</TR>
<TR>
<TD>Beginning Digital Photography 101</TD>
<TD>Ansel Edwards</TD>
<TD>
    <TABLE BORDER="2" BORDERCOLOR="olive">
    <TR>
    <TD>Mon. & Wed.</TD>
    <TD>7:00 p.m.</TD>
    </TR>
    <TR>
    <TD>Tues. & Thur.</TD>
    <TD>7:00 p.m.</TD>
    </TR>
    </TABLE>
</TD>
<TD>Room B, Tech Bldg.</TD>
</TR>
```

Photography for Fun

Offering classes for the beginner photographer

Class Schedule			
Class Description	**Teacher**	**Days/Times**	**Location**
Beginning Digital Photography 101	Ansel Edwards	Mon. & Wed. 7:00 p.m. / Tues. & Thur. 7:00 p.m.	Room B, Tech Bldg.
Beginning Digital Photography 102	David Willard	Mon. & Wed. 10:00 a.m. / Tues. & Thur. 10:00 a.m.	Room , Tech Bldg.

Working with Frames

Looking for a way to enhance your Web site layout? Frames can help you present multiple pages to your Web site visitors all on one screen. This chapter shows you how to create framesets and add frames to your Web site.

Understanding Frames **188**

Create Frames **190**

Customize Frame Borders **192**

Control Frame Margins **194**

Add Alternative Text **195**

Prevent Frame Resizing **196**

Hide or Display Frame Scroll Bars **197**

Target a Link **198**

Create a Nesting Frameset **200**

Create an Inline Frame **201**

Understanding Frames

You can use frames to divide your Web page into sections and allow users to access different pages in your Web site from one screen. Although frames are not as widely used as they once were, they can still serve as a valuable tool to help you create a dynamic structure for your Web site.

Frame Basics

Browser windows typically hold a single frame to display an HTML document. If a page's content exceeds the size of the frame, scroll bars appear allowing the user to view different parts of the page. With multiple frames, the browser window displays several HTML documents at one time, each frame acting as a separate screen. Each frame can display its own scroll bars to allow users to view different portions of the Web page appearing within the frame.

Ways to Use Frames

You can find numerous uses for frames with a multipage Web site. You can use frames to display a fixed page at the top of the screen and a scrollable page in the remainder of the screen. For example, you might use a navigation page at the top with links to pages on your site. When a user clicks a link in the top frame, the frame below displays the content. Or you might use side-by-side frames to display a picture in one frame and text in another.

Frame Advantages

When deciding whether to use frames in your Web site, take time to examine the pros and cons of frames. On the pro side, frames are really helpful with larger Web sites, especially when you want to keep certain information in view at all times. Frames offer a great way to display a navigation bar in one location without needing to include navigational links on every Web page in your site. Frames can make it easier for users to navigate a large Web site.

Frame Disadvantages

On the con side, users might not see your frame content as you envision; monitor resolution settings vary and what you think is the perfect size for a frame may not be so on another user's screen. Depending on the Web page, not all page content looks good in smaller frames. Although newer browsers support the use of frames, some older versions do not. You may need to design a nonframes version of your site to accommodate users without frame support. Frames can also complicate your HTML page coding, and when frames are not working properly, can cause user frustration. For example, you must test that the content of all frames in a three-frame set up work properly; improper loading may result in a user's not being able to view the navigation tools in one frame resulting in a less than satisfactory visiting experience.

Framesets and Frames

You use several documents to create frames for your Web site. The frameset document, which is a part of HTML, defines the number and size of your frames. Within each frame you must target content, so you need separate HTML documents to appear within the frames. You can save the frameset document as a separate file and link other pages from your site to the frame structure. See the section "Create Frames" to learn how to make a frameset document.

Nesting and Inline Frames

If your Web site requires a more complex frame structure, you can nest a frameset within the original frameset. This gives you the flexibility of dividing a frame into more frames. Learn how to create nesting framesets in the section "Create a Nesting Frameset." You can also insert a single frame within any Web page on your site without needing to define a frameset document. See the section "Create an Inline Frame" to learn more.

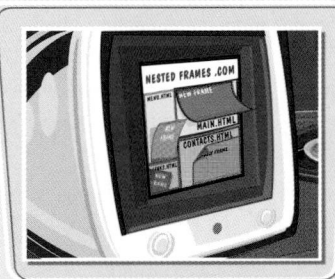

Create Frames

You can use frames to divide the Web browser window into sections. This allows you to display different pages in your site on the screen at the same time. For example, you might use one frame to display a navigational page that helps viewers access other parts of your site, and then show the content of a page in another frame.

You can use the `<FRAMESET>` **and** `<FRAME>` **tags to define the frame structure. The** `<FRAMESET>` **tag creates a frameset, dividing the window into sections, while the** `<FRAME>` **tag specifies which page goes into which frame. You can define the size of each frame using an absolute value, measured in pixels, or a relative value, measured as a percentage.**

Create Frames

① Create and save a new HTML document, including only the basic `<HTML>`, `<HEAD>`, and `<TITLE>` tags.

Note: See Chapter 2 to learn how to create HTML documents.

② Below the `</HEAD>` tag, type **<FRAMESET** and a blank space.

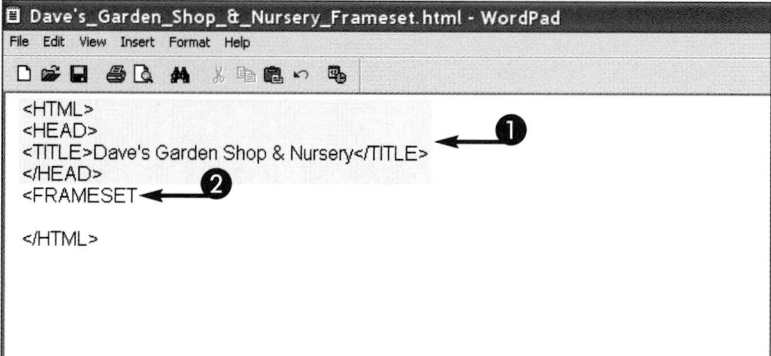

③ Define the frameset to include two or more rows or columns and specify a size for the rows or columns.

To create frames in rows, type **ROWS="?,?">**, replacing *?* with the height of each row in your frameset.

To create frames in columns, type **COLS="?,?">**, replacing *?* with the width of each column in your frameset.

You can also set a row or column size as a percentage by simply typing the value followed by a percentage sign, such as **30%**.

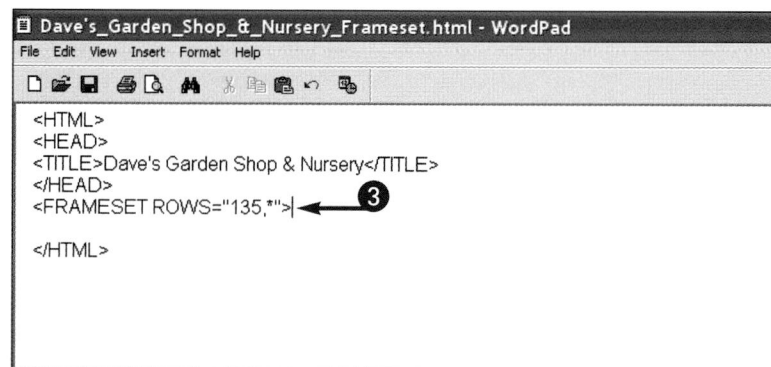

④ Type **<FRAME NAME="?"**, replacing *?* with a name for the frame.

⑤ Type a space and **SRC="?">**, replacing *?* with the name and location of the Web page you want to appear in the frame.

⑥ Repeat steps **4** and **5** for each frame you specified in step **3**.

⑦ Type **</FRAMESET>**.

The Web browser displays the frames.

In this example, two frames appear in the browser window.

You can use a nested frameset to combine both rows and columns in a frameset.

Note: *See the section "Create a Nesting Frameset" for more on nested framesets.*

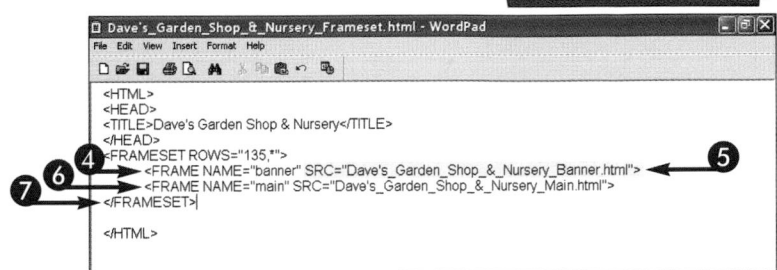

TIPS

Do I need to declare my frameset document somewhere on the Web page?

It is good practice to include a DOCTYPE declaration on your page. Frameset is a type of HTML document, and adding a statement specifying what version of HTML you are using can help identify the document type to others. Your DOCTYPE declaration might look like this:

```
<!DOCTYPE HTML PUBLIC "-
//W3C/DTD HTML 4.0
Frameset//EN"
```

```
http://www.w3.org/TR/
REC-html40/frameset.dtd>
```

See Chapter 2 to learn more about document declarations.

Do I have to specify a row height or column width for each frame?

After you define the first frame size, you can use an asterisk (*) to assign the remaining window space to other frames. The asterisk specifies the size as a variable. For example:

```
<FRAMESET
ROWS="65,*,60">
```

In this frameset, the middle frame is sized to fit the remaining space left after the other two absolute frames.

Customize Frame Borders

You can change the thickness of your frame borders using the BORDER attribute. By default, Web browsers display the borders around your frames at a thickness of 6 pixels. You can set your frame borders to another size as well as control the color of the borders.

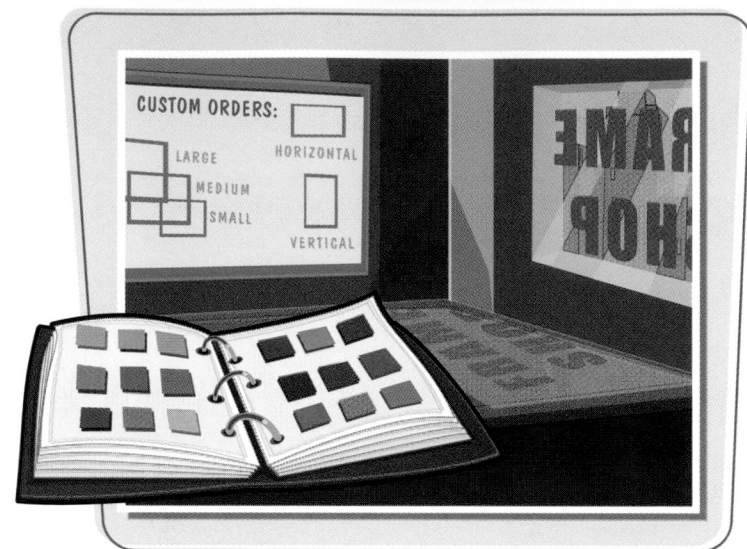

Customize Frame Borders

CHANGE THE FRAME BORDERS

1 Within the `<FRAMESET>` tag, type **BORDER="?"**, replacing *?* with a thickness value, measured in pixels.

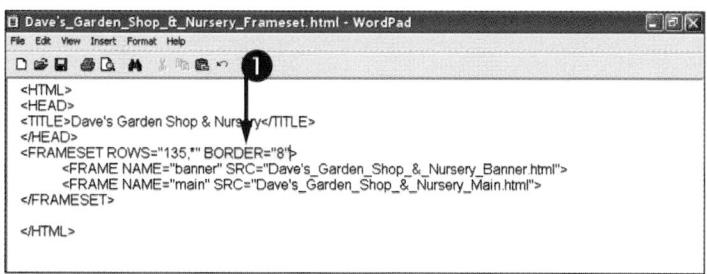

● The Web browser displays the frames with the designated border thickness.

192

CHANGE THE BORDER COLOR

1 Within the <FRAMESET> tag, type **BORDERCOLOR="?"**, replacing *?* with a color value.

Note: See Appendix A for a full chart of color codes.

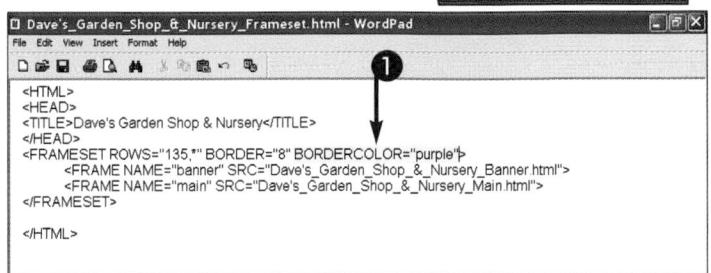

- The Web browser displays the frames with the designated color.

TIPS

Is there a way to hide my frame borders completely?

Yes. To hide all the frame borders, type **FRAMEBORDER="0"** in the <FRAMESET> tag. This coding makes the content of each separate frame blend together to seemingly make one large Web page. You may experience a small space between the pages. To rid the frame of this space, simply type **BORDER="0"** in the <FRAMESET> tag.

Is there another way I can control frame border thickness?

Yes. You can also use the FRAMESPACING attribute to control the thickness of frame borders. However, only Internet Explorer supports the FRAMESPACING attribute; the attribute is not part of the formal HTML standard. To set a border thickness, type **FRAMESPACING="?"** in the <FRAMESET> tag, replacing *?* with the thickness value you want to set. Border thickness is measured in pixels.

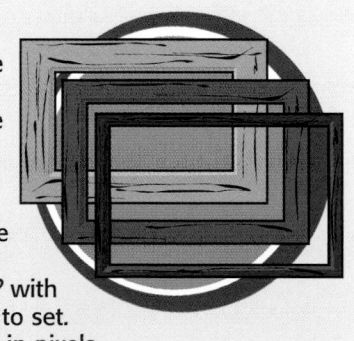

Control Frame Margins

You can control the amount of space that appears between a frame border and the contents of the frame. Using the MARGINWIDTH and MARGINHEIGHT attributes, you can set margins for the top, bottom, left, and right side of your frames. Margin space is measured in pixels.

① Within the `<FRAME>` tag, type **MARGINWIDTH="?"**, replacing *?* with the amount of space you want to set for the left and right margins.

② Type a space and **MARGINHEIGHT="?"**, replacing *?* with the amount of space you want to set for the top and bottom margins.

The Web browser displays the frames with the designated margins.

● In this example, the second frame now has increased margins all around the inside of the frame.

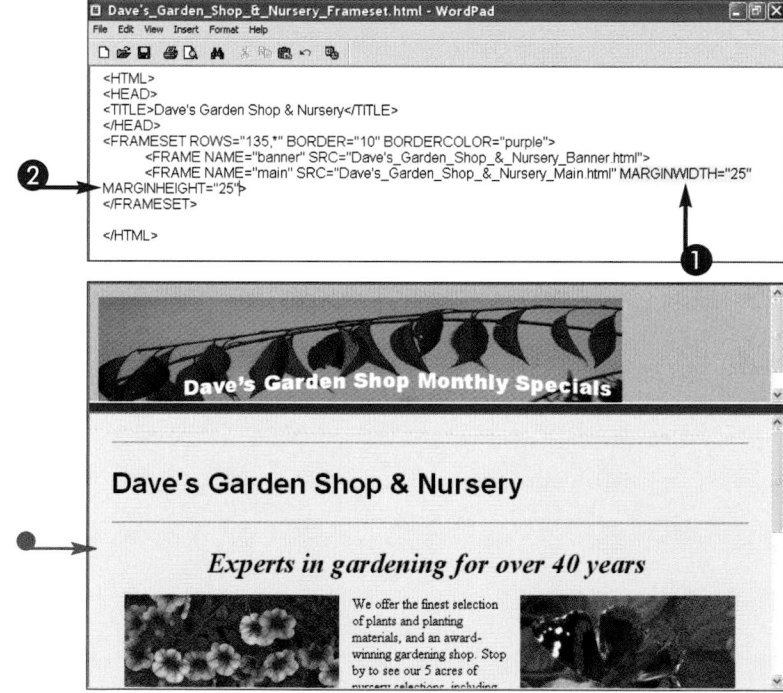

You can use the <NOFRAMES> tag to insert alternative text for users whose browsers do not support frames. In some cases, the user may turn off frame display on purpose. Alternative text can alert them to the missing pages.

Add Alternative Text

① Directly above the </FRAMESET> tag, add a line and type **<NOFRAMES>**.

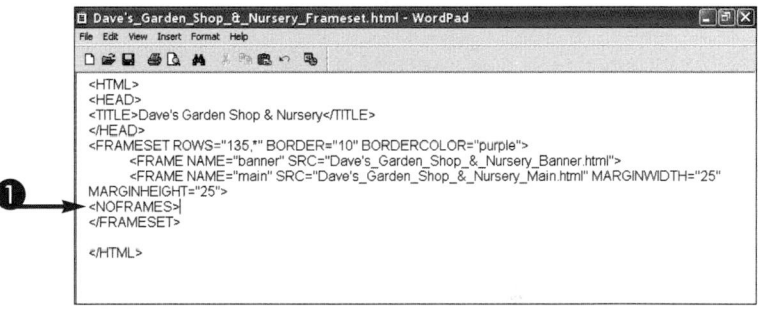

② Type in any alternative text you want to appear.

③ Type **</NOFRAMES>**.

If the user's browser does not support frames, or the frame display is turned off, a page appears with the alternative text.

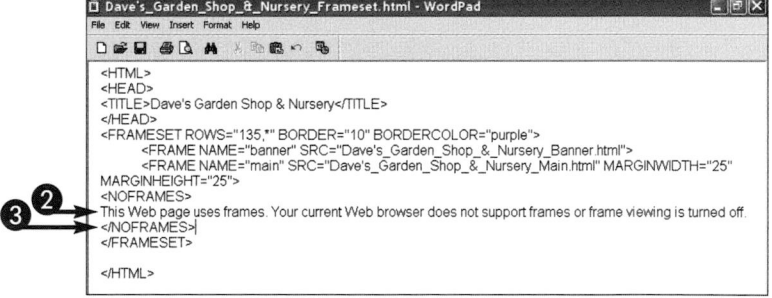

Prevent Frame Resizing

By default, users can resize the frames in your Web page, allowing them to view more information in a frame. You can control your page layout by restricting frame resizing.

Prevent Frame Resizing

1. Type **NORESIZE** inside the `<FRAME>` tag of the frame you want to control.

2. Repeat step **1** for any other frames for which you want to prevent resizing.

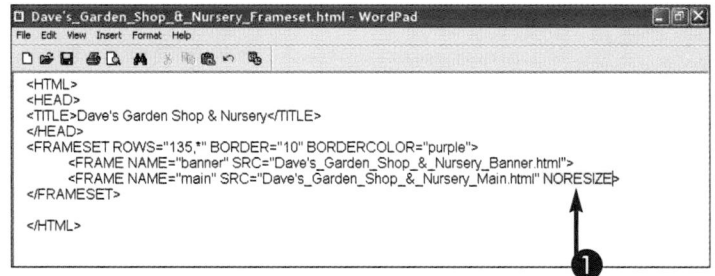

The user is not able to resize the frame in the browser window.

● In this example, resizing is turned off in the second frame.

Web browsers automatically display scroll bars if a frame's content exceeds the size of the frame. You can use the SCROLLING attribute to control when scroll bars appear. A Yes value displays scroll bars, while a No value hides the scroll bars.

Hide or Display Frame Scroll Bars

① Click inside the <FRAME> tag of the frame you want to control.

② Type **SCROLLING="?"**, replacing *?* with **Yes** to display scroll bars, or **No** to hide scroll bars.

You can repeat steps **1** and **2** to control the scroll bars in other frames.

The browser displays or hides scroll bars as instructed.

● In this example, the scroll bars are hidden for the top frame.

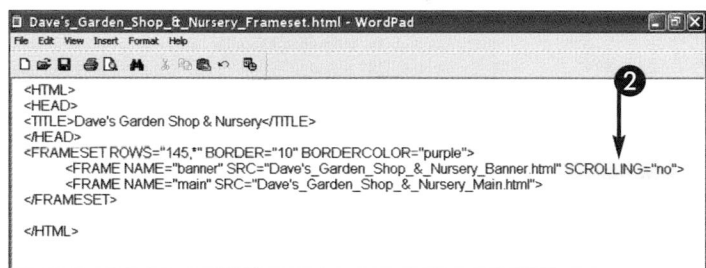

You can make other pages from your Web site appear in a frame in addition to the initial frameset content. To target links to particular frames, you must identify each frame with a unique name.

To learn how to assign names to frames, see the section "Create Frames."

Target a Link

1 Open the Web page where the link should appear.

2 Click where you want to insert the link and type **<A HREF="?"**, replacing *?* with the target page.

Note: Be sure to name the frame before targeting a link. See the section "Create Frames" to learn how to name frames in the frameset document.

```
<HTML>
<HEAD>
<TITLE>Dave's Garden Shop & Nursery</TITLE>
</HEAD>
<BODY BGCOLOR="#A4D4B0">

<H3>Our Top-Selling Perennials:</H3>
<BR>

<TABLE BORDER="2" CELLPADDING="5" CELLSPACING="5">
<TR>
<TD><A HREF="daylily.html"</TD>
</TR>
<TR>
<TD>Poppy</TD>
</TR>
<TR>
<TD>Monkshood</TD>
</TR>
<TR>
<TD>Coreopsis</TD>
</TR>
<TR>
<TD>Bee Balm</TD>
</TR>
</TABLE>
```

3 Type a space and **TARGET="?">**, replacing *?* with the frame name you assigned in step **1**.

```
<HTML>
<HEAD>
<TITLE>Dave's Garden Shop & Nursery</TITLE>
</HEAD>
<BODY BGCOLOR="#A4D4B0">

<H3>Our Top-Selling Perennials:</H3>
<BR>

<TABLE BORDER="2" CELLPADDING="5" CELLSPACING="5">
<TR>
<TD><A HREF="daylily.html" TARGET="main"></TD>
</TR>
<TR>
<TD>Poppy</TD>
</TR>
<TR>
<TD>Monkshood</TD>
</TR>
<TR>
<TD>Coreopsis</TD>
</TR>
<TR>
<TD>Bee Balm</TD>
</TR>
</TABLE>
```

④ Type the link text.

⑤ Type **</A>**.

You can repeat steps **1** to **6** to target more links.

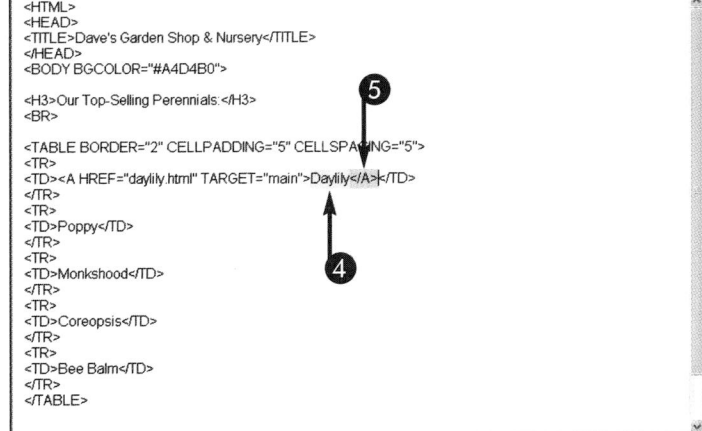

```
<HTML>
<HEAD>
<TITLE>Dave's Garden Shop & Nursery</TITLE>
</HEAD>
<BODY BGCOLOR="#A4D4B0">

<H3>Our Top-Selling Perennials:</H3>
<BR>

<TABLE BORDER="2" CELLPADDING="5" CELLSPACING="5">
<TR>
<TD><A HREF="daylily.html" TARGET="main">Daylily</A></TD>
</TR>
<TR>
<TD>Poppy</TD>
</TR>
<TR>
<TD>Monkshood</TD>
</TR>
<TR>
<TD>Coreopsis</TD>
</TR>
<TR>
<TD>Bee Balm</TD>
</TR>
</TABLE>
```

● The browser displays the link.

● When the user clicks the link, the page opens in the frame you specified.

TIPS

Can I make all the links open in the same frame?

Yes. To make all the Web page links open in the same frame, you can add the target frame to the <HEAD> and </HEAD> tags. Simply click within the <HEAD> tags and type **<BASE TARGET="?">**, replacing *?* with the name of the target frame. You must name the target frame in the frameset document in order to reference the name in the <BASE TARGET> tag.

Can I make the target link open a new window?

Yes. You can use the TARGET attribute to instruct the browser to open the target link in a new window. To open the linked page in a new unnamed window, use the _blank value. To open the linked page in the current window, use the _top value. For example:

```
<A HREF="mypage.html"
TARGET="_blank">Click
here to view the page</A>
```

In this code, when the user clicks the link, the document mypage.html opens in a new browser window.

Create a Nesting Frameset

You can nest a frameset within another frameset, creating a combined frameset. For example, you might place a two-frame frameset within the largest frame of your main frameset.

You use the same procedure for creating an initial frameset to create an additional, nested frameset. See the section "Create Frames" to learn more about creating a frameset document and defining frames.

Create a Nesting Frameset

① In the frameset document, add a line where you want to insert a nested frameset.

② Type **<FRAMESET ROWS="?,?">** to insert rows or **<FRAMESET COLS="?,?">** to insert columns, replacing *?* with the row or column values for your frames.

③ Add the frame tags for the frame name and target page.

④ Type **</FRAMESET>** to complete the nested frameset.

The Web browser displays the frameset within the original frameset.

● In this example, the nested frameset is two columns that appear below a row frame.

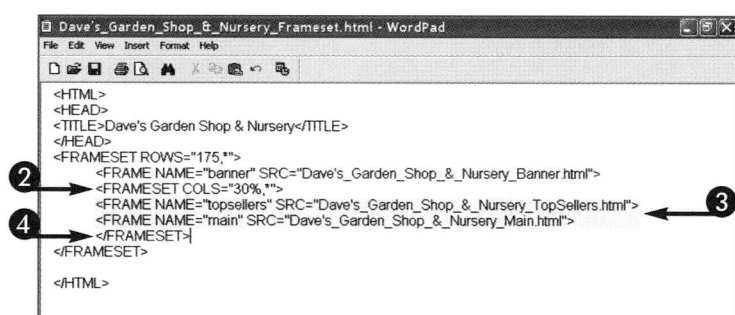

Create an Inline Frame

You can create a floating frame, also called an inline frame, that appears within the content of a Web page. Inline frames do not require a frameset.

Create an Inline Frame

① Type **<IFRAME SRC="?"** where you want to insert an inline frame, replacing ? with the name and location of the page you want to appear within the inline frame.

② Type a space and **NAME="?"**, replacing ? with the name for the inline frame.

③ Type a space and **WIDTH="?" HEIGHT="?">**, replacing ? with width and height values.

④ Type **</IFRAME>**.

```
<HTML>
<HEAD>
<TITLE>Dave's Garden Shop & Nursery</TITLE>
<BASE TARGET="_blank">
</HEAD>
<BODY BGCOLOR="#EBF4EA">
<HR>
<H1><FONT FACE="Arial">Dave's Garden Shop & Nursery</FONT></H1>
<HR>

<CENTER><P><FONT SIZE="6"><B><I>Experts in gardening for over 40 years</I></B></FONT></P>
</CENTER>

<IMG SRC="Million_Bells2.jpg" ALIGN="Left" HSPACE="15">

<P>We offer the finest selection of plants and planting materials, and an award-winning gardening shop. Stop
by to see our 5 acres of nursery selections, including trees, shrubs, perennials, and seasonal plants. Our
experienced staff is always available to assist you.</P><BR CLEAR="All">
<BR>

<IFRAME SRC="Daylily.html" NAME="daylily" WIDTH="50%" HEIGHT="25%">
</IFRAME>

<P>Be sure to visit our store for garden-themed gifts for indoors and outdoors. We feature exciting new items
for home decorating and gardening at the start of each season.</P>

<IMG SRC="Garden_Supplies.jpg" WIDTH="300" HEIGHT="200" ALT="Image of Gardening Tool">
```

● The Web browser displays the inline frame.

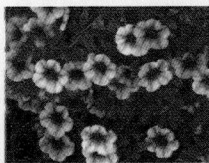

Experts in gardening for over 40 years

We offer the finest selection of plants and planting materials, and an award-winning gardening shop. Stop by to see our 5 acres of nursery selections, including trees, shrubs, perennials, and seasonal plants. Our experienced staff is always available to assist you.

The Daylily is one of our top-selling perennials. It comes in a variety of colors and blooms during the summer. Some varieties bloom throughout the summer

Be sure to visit our store for garden-themed gifts for indoors and outdoors. We feature exciting new items for home decorating and gardening at the start of each season.

Creating Forms

Looking for a way to allow your Web site visitors to communicate with you? This chapter shows you how to build forms to gather information from users and teaches you about the various ways to process the information.

Understanding Forms **204**

Types of Form Elements **206**

Gather Form Data **208**

Create a Form **210**

Send Form Data to an E-mail Address **211**

Add a Text Box **212**

Add a Large Text Area **214**

Add Check Boxes **216**

Add Radio Buttons **218**

Add a Menu List **220**

Add a Submit Button **222**

Add a Reset Button **223**

Add Active Labels **224**

Change the Tab Order **225**

Add a File Upload Element **226**

Group Form Elements **228**

Understanding Forms

You can use forms to collect information from the people who visit your Web site. For example, you might gather answers or feedback from your Web visitors, or enable them to purchase goods or services from your Web site. Before you jump into building your own forms, take a moment to study how forms work and the various ways you can use them on your own Web site.

How Forms Work

Forms use input elements to collect data from a user, such as text fields and check boxes. Once the user fills in the data, he or she can submit the form. As the Web developer, it is up to you to decide how to handle the data. You can write a script to manage form data, receive the data via e-mail, or send the data to a database. Most form data is processed by CGI scripts on the Web server. You can learn more about various ways to process your data in the section "Gather Form Data" later in this chapter.

HTML for Forms

Forms are comprised of three important parts: the <FORM> tag, the form elements, and the submit button. When designing and building a form, you can write HTML to define the form structure and appearance as well as define the different input objects you want to include on the form, such as text fields or radio buttons. All forms should include a Submit button to send the data for processing. You can place your forms directly on a Web page or save them as a separate HTML document and link to the form.

Form Design

Before typing up a form, spend time thinking about how you want the user to interact with the form, what sort of data you want to collect, and how you want the form to appear. Be sure to add label text to your form elements that explains what type of information you want from the user, and give users enough space to enter their input.

Types of Forms

There are several different types of forms you can create. For example, you can add a search form to allow your users to search through your Web site for key information. You can add data collection forms to gather information from users, such as name and e-mail addresses. Your form may be as simple as a guest book or as complex as a detailed survey. You can use forms to customize a user's content, such as displaying the user's name when he or she logs onto your site. You can also use forms to help customers make a purchase on your site.

Controlling Data Entry

You can control how a user enters data into your form input elements. For example, you can guide the user from one input field to the next by controlling the tab order. See the section "Change the Tab Order" to learn more. You can also control the types of data entered into a field. For example, if your form collects phone numbers, you can limit the phone number text element to just inputting numbers instead of characters. You can use JavaScripts to help alert users to invalid form data. See Chapter 13 to learn more about JavaScripts.

Confirmation

After the form data is processed, the script usually displays a message in the browser window noting whether the form data was sent successfully or not. You might also write your own script to send a confirmation message by e-mail. It is always good practice when collecting form data to provide visitors with a confirmation or assurance that some sort of action will be taken based on their contribution.

Forms are comprised of a variety of elements. As you think about how users enter data into a form, you can ascertain the types of elements you might need to include on your own forms.

Text Boxes

Text boxes are input fields designed specifically for users to type data into, such as typing a name or comment. Text boxes can be small to collect limited characters, such as phone numbers, or very large to collect paragraphs of input from the user. You might use text boxes to gather information such as names, addresses, e-mail addresses, feedback comments, and more.

Check Boxes

Check boxes enable a user to make a choice out of a group of choices by activating a value. For example, if you want to collect information on whether the Web site visitor is male or female, you can add two check box options to your form. The users click a box to indicate their answer. You can allow users to select just one box or multiple check boxes. For example, you might offer users check box options regarding their musical preferences, allowing them to select several different styles.

Radio Buttons

Radio buttons are the tiny circle buttons found on forms, named for their resemblance to the buttons found on automobile radios in decades past. You use radio buttons in a group of options. Unlike check boxes, however, users are allowed to choose only one button to make their choice. For example, if you include a feedback form on your page that rates your Web site, you might present radio buttons for the values Excellent, Good, Average, and Poor. The user can choose only one of the four options.

Menus

Menus are a great way to present a list of choices to a Web page visitor. You can present menus as drop-down lists to free up space on your form. Like radio buttons, users can choose only one item from the menu list. A drop-down list of states, for example, is a common menu found on collection forms. The user scrolls through the list and selects his or her state from the menu.

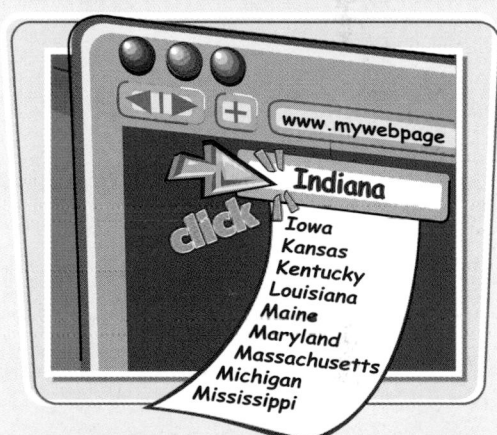

Submit and Reset Buttons

Every form needs a button users can press to submit their data. Known as the Submit button, this button sends the data to the Web server for processing. Until the user clicks this button, the data is not collected. You might also consider adding a Reset button to your page that allows the user to clear all the input fields and start over.

Gather Form Data

After the user enters data into the form, you must determine how to handle the information. Before you begin creating your form, you need to know how the collected data will be processed. Take time to examine your options and set up any necessary procedures with your Web host or on your server.

CGI Scripts

CGI scripts process most data that you collect with forms. CGI, short for Common Gateway Interface, is a script written in a language such as Perl or Java, that runs on a Web server. CGI scripts take form data submitted by the user and make it useful, such as putting it into a database, writing it to a file, creating customized HTML, or sending the information to an e-mail address.

Finding CGI Scripts

You can write your own CGI scripts if you know an appropriate programming language, such as Perl or AppleScript, or you can adapt one of the hundreds of free CGI scripts available on the Web. Sites like The CGI Resource Index (http://cgi.resourceindex.com/), Matt's Script Archive (www.scriptarchive.com/), and ScriptSearch (www.scriptsearch.com) are good places to start. You should also check with your Web host to see what they provide.

CGI and Web Servers

Many Web servers offer CGI scripts for processing form data, but you need to check with your Web host to find out if they feature such processing. If they do, you need to find out the location of the server's CGI-bin. A CGI-bin is a type of directory found on Web servers and may be called something else on different servers. Not all Web hosts allow CGI scripts. If yours does not, you might consider using a form hosting service instead, to process your form results. You can search the Web for form hosting services. Sites such as Creative Digital Resources (www.creative-dr.com) and Response-O-Matic (www.response-o-matic.com) offer free form processing.

Preparing a Script

To make a CGI script ready for your own form, you need to make adjustments to the script variables and path names to suit your Web server. You must also transfer the CGI script to your server, using FPT (File Transfer Protocol). Be sure to check with the Web host regarding where to store the CGI file. Some prefer to store scripts in a central CGI-bin directory, while others let you store scripts in your own folders as long as they utilize a particular file extension.

Sending Data to Databases

Another use for CGI scripts is to send form data to a database. Database programs are designed to store and manage large amounts of data. Client-server databases run 24/7 to process requests from Web users. CGI scripts translate requests from the Web server to a format read by a database, whether the database is located on the same server or in another location. If you plan to use your form data in conjunction with a database, you need to learn more about how databases work with the Web. There are quite a few good books on the subject, including *Web Database Publishing For Dummies* or *Intranet and Web Databases For Dummies*, both from Wiley Publishing, Inc.

Sending Data to an E-mail Address

If you do not want to use a CGI script, you can use an action method to send form data to an e-mail address. This action returns a list of field names and the values entered in each. This option is useful only if the form is simple in nature. More complex forms require scripts or databases to process and make sense of the information. To learn more about sending form data via e-mail, see the section "Send Form Data to an E-mail Address."

Create a Form

You can use a form to gather information from the people who visit your Web site. To create a form, you use the <FORM> tags to define the CGI scripts that will process the form, define the form elements, and define a Submit button to send the data to the CGI script.

Most forms use a CGI script to instruct the Web server to process the collected information. Consult your Web host to find out the location of a CGI script or CGI-bin on the server. You can also forego a CGI script and send the form data to an e-mail address. See the section "Send Form Data to an E-mail Address" to learn more.

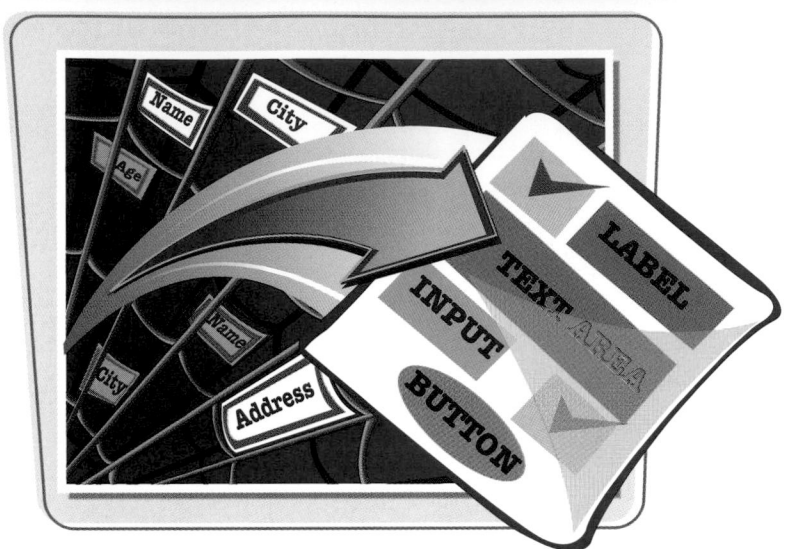

Create a Form

① Click where you want to insert a form and type **<FORM METHOD="post"**.

② Type a space and **ACTION="?">**, replacing *?* with the name and location of the CGI script you want to use to process the form data.

Note: You may need to contact your Web host to determine the name and path of the CGI script.

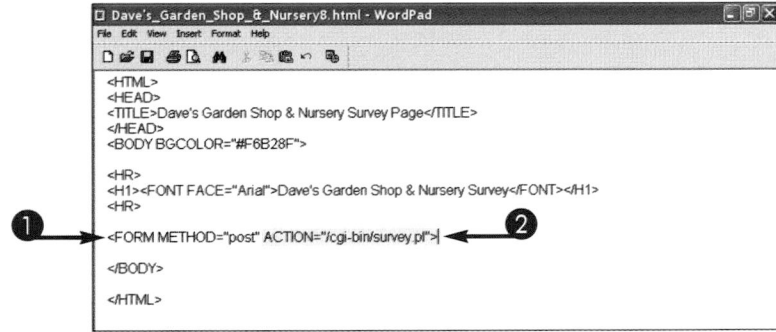

③ Type **</FORM>**.

You can now add input elements to your form.

Note: See the remaining sections in this chapter to learn more about building your form.

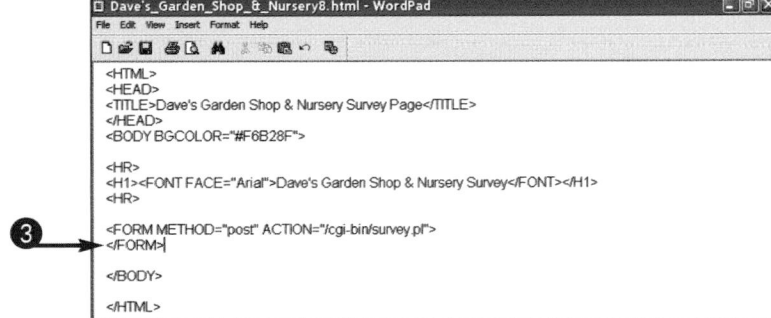

You can instruct the browser to send form data to an e-mail address. You might pursue this route if you are creating a simple form or if your Web server does not support CGI scripts.

Send Form Data to an E-Mail Address

① Click where you want to insert a form and type **<FORM METHOD="post"**.

② Type a space and **ENCTYPE="text/plain"**.

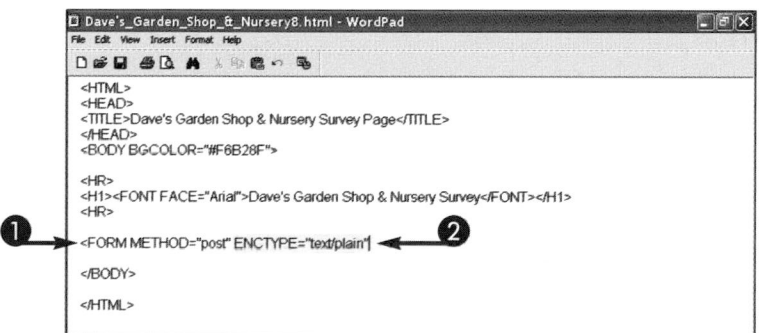

③ Type a space and **ACTION="mailto:?">**, replacing *?* with the e-mail address to which you want to send the form data.

④ Type **</FORM>**.

You can now add input elements to your form.

Note: See the remaining sections in this chapter to learn more about building your form.

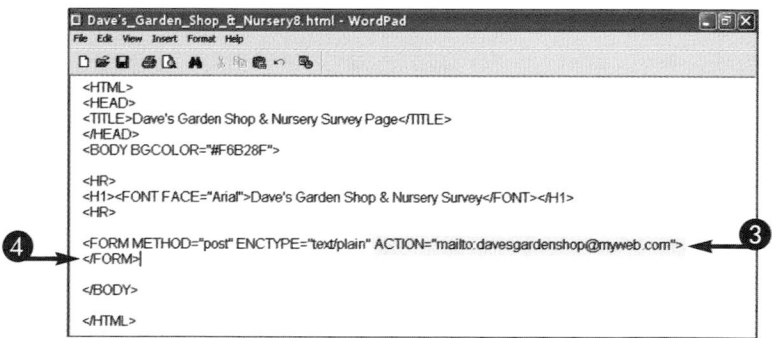

Add a Text Box

You can add a text box to your form to allow users to type in a single line reply or response. When creating a text box, you must identify the input field with a unique name. You can also control the size and number of characters a user enters into the field.

By default, browsers display the text box field at a width of 20 characters. You can set a wider text box using the SIZE **attribute. You can control the number of characters allowed in a text box by specifying a value with the** MAXLENGTH **attribute.**

Add a Text Box

① Between the `<FORM>` and `</FORM>` tags add a new line for the text box.

② Type **<INPUT TYPE="text"**.

③ Type a space and **NAME="?"**, replacing *?* with a unique identifier for the text box.

```
<HTML>
<HEAD>
<TITLE>Dave's Garden Shop & Nursery Survey Page</TITLE>
</HEAD>
<BODY BGCOLOR="#F6B28F">

<HR>
<H1><FONT FACE="Arial"><FONT COLOR="004E4A">Dave's Garden Shop & Nursery Survey</FONT></H1>
<HR>

<FORM METHOD="post" ACTION="cgi-bin/survey.pl">
<H3>Thanks for visiting our site. Please take a moment and fill out our survey. Your input will help us to create a better Web site.</H3>

<BR>Where do you purchase most of your gardening materials and supplies?
<INPUT TYPE="text" NAME="purchase"|

</FORM>

</BODY>

</HTML>
```

④ Type a space and **SIZE="?"**, replacing *?* with the width in characters you want to assign to the text box.

```
<HTML>
<HEAD>
<TITLE>Dave's Garden Shop & Nursery Survey Page</TITLE>
</HEAD>
<BODY BGCOLOR="#F6B28F">

<HR>
<H1><FONT FACE="Arial"><FONT COLOR="004E4A">Dave's Garden Shop & Nursery Survey</FONT></H1>
<HR>

<FORM METHOD="post" ACTION="cgi-bin/survey.pl">
<H3>Thanks for visiting our site. Please take a moment and fill out our survey. Your input will help us to create a better Web site.</H3>

<BR>Where do you purchase most of your gardening materials and supplies?
<INPUT TYPE="text" NAME="purchase" SIZE="45"

</FORM>

</BODY>

</HTML>
```

⑤ To define a maximum number of characters for the field, type **MAXLENGTH="?">**, replacing *?* with the maximum number of characters allowed.

Note: Do not forget to type a closing bracket (>) at the end of your input element tag.

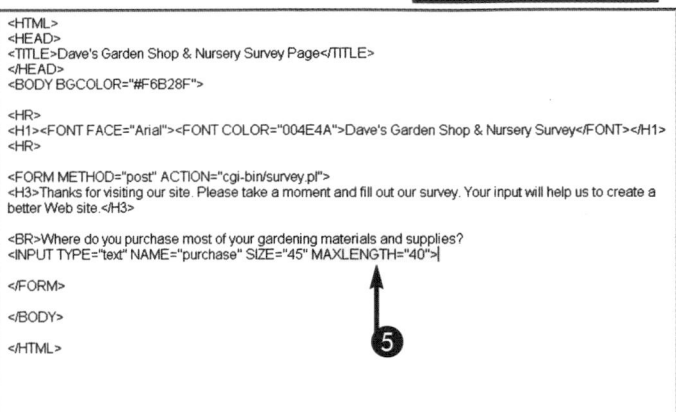

```
<HTML>
<HEAD>
<TITLE>Dave's Garden Shop & Nursery Survey Page</TITLE>
</HEAD>
<BODY BGCOLOR="#F6B28F">

<HR>
<H1><FONT FACE="Arial"><FONT COLOR="004E4A">Dave's Garden Shop & Nursery Survey</FONT></H1>
<HR>

<FORM METHOD="post" ACTION="cgi-bin/survey.pl">
<H3>Thanks for visiting our site. Please take a moment and fill out our survey. Your input will help us to create a
better Web site.</H3>

<BR>Where do you purchase most of your gardening materials and supplies?
<INPUT TYPE="text" NAME="purchase" SIZE="45" MAXLENGTH="40">|

</FORM>

</BODY>

</HTML>
```

● The Web browser displays the text box in the form.

● The user can click inside the text box and type the required information.

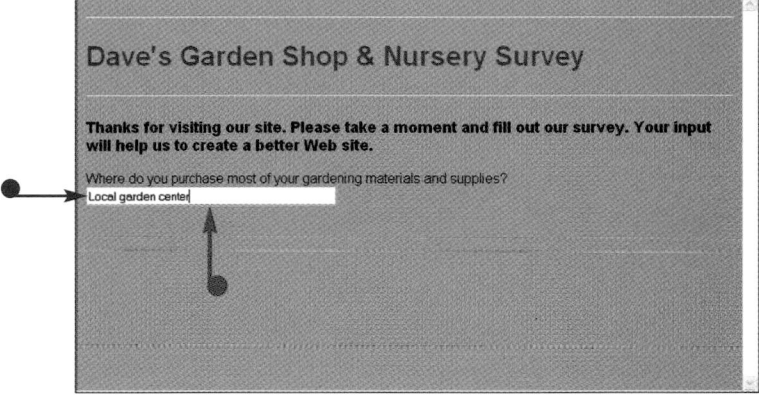

Dave's Garden Shop & Nursery Survey

Thanks for visiting our site. Please take a moment and fill out our survey. Your input will help us to create a better Web site.

Where do you purchase most of your gardening materials and supplies?
Local garden center|

TIPS

Can I add a default value to a text box?

Yes. A default value is text that already appears in the text box when the user views the form. You can use default values to display instructions about the type of data required, give users an example of what data you are looking for, or specify a popular choice or response. To specify a default, you can add the VALUE attribute to the <INPUT> tag. For example:

```
<FORM METHOD="post"
ACTION="/cgi-bin/feedback.pl">

<INPUT TYPE="text" NAME="email"
VALUE="Enter your e-mail address">

</FORM>
```

How do I create a password text box?

Browsers handle password text boxes a bit differently than regular text boxes. Instead of seeing what is typed in the input field, the data appears as asterisks (*) instead of characters. This prevents others from seeing the password text. To create a text box for password entry, you specify the password type in the <INPUT> tag. Your code might look like this:

```
<FORM METHOD="post" ACTION="/
cgi-bin/feedback.pl">

<INPUT TYPE="password"
NAME="password" SIZE="45">

</FORM>
```

Add a Large Text Area

If your form requires a larger text entry box, you can create a large text area for multiple lines of text. For example, if you create a feedback form, you can use a large text area to allow users to type paragraphs of text.

When defining a text area, you can control the size of the text box and how text wraps within the field. Text area size is measured in rows and columns, based on character height.

Add a Large Text Area

① Between the `<FORM>` and `</FORM>` tags, add a new line for the large text box.

② Type **<TEXTAREA**.

③ Type a space and **NAME="?"**, replacing *?* with a unique name for the text area.

Note: You can use the `<BR>` or `<P>` tags to separate input elements onto new lines in your form.

```
<HTML>
<HEAD>
<TITLE>Dave's Garden Shop & Nursery Survey Page</TITLE>
</HEAD>
<BODY BGCOLOR="#F6B28F">

<HR>
<H1><FONT FACE="Arial"><FONT COLOR="004E4A">Dave's Garden Shop & Nursery Survey</FONT></H1>
<HR>

<FORM METHOD="post" ACTION="cgi-bin/survey.pl">
<H3>Thanks for visiting our site. Please take a moment and fill out our survey. Your input will help us to create a
better Web site.</H3>

<BR>What gardening information would you like to see on our site?
<TEXTAREA NAME="gardeninfo">

<BR>Where do you purchase most of your gardening materials and supplies?
<INPUT TYPE="text" NAME="purchase" SIZE="45" MAXLENGTH="40">

</FORM>

</BODY>

</HTML>
```

④ Type a space and **ROWS="?"**, replacing *?* with the number of rows you want to specify to determine the height of the text area.

⑤ Type a space and type **COLS="?"**, replacing *?* with the number of character columns you want to specify to determine the width of the text area.

```
<HTML>
<HEAD>
<TITLE>Dave's Garden Shop & Nursery Survey Page</TITLE>
</HEAD>
<BODY BGCOLOR="#F6B28F">

<HR>
<H1><FONT FACE="Arial"><FONT COLOR="004E4A">Dave's Garden Shop & Nursery Survey</FONT></H1>
<HR>

<FORM METHOD="post" ACTION="cgi-bin/survey.pl">
<H3>Thanks for visiting our site. Please take a moment and fill out our survey. Your input will help us to create a
better Web site.</H3>

<BR>What gardening information would you like to see on our site?
<TEXTAREA NAME="gardeninfo" ROWS="10" COLS="70">

<BR>Where do you purchase most of your gardening materials and supplies?
<INPUT TYPE="text" NAME="purchase" SIZE="45" MAXLENGTH="40">

</FORM>

</BODY>

</HTML>
```

6 Type a space and **WRAP="*?*">**, replacing *?* with a text wrap control:

soft wraps text within the text area but will not wrap text in the form results.

hard wraps text both within the text area and the form results.

off turns off text wrapping, forcing users to create new lines of text as they type.

7 Type **</TEXTAREA>**.

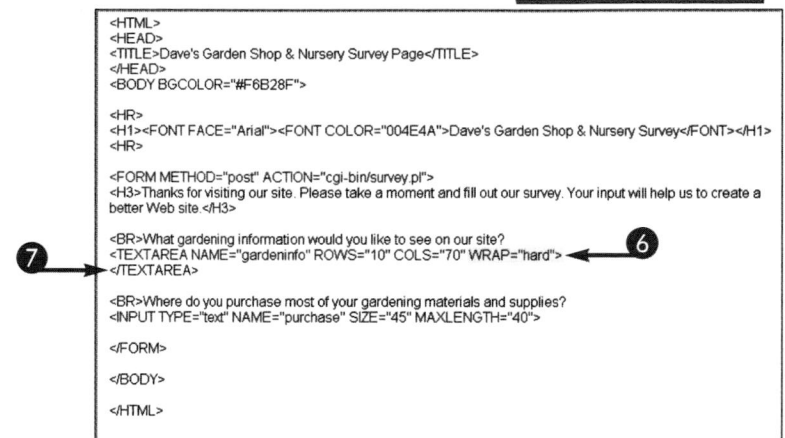

```
<HTML>
<HEAD>
<TITLE>Dave's Garden Shop & Nursery Survey Page</TITLE>
</HEAD>
<BODY BGCOLOR="#F6B28F">

<HR>
<H1><FONT FACE="Arial"><FONT COLOR="004E4A">Dave's Garden Shop & Nursery Survey</FONT></H1>
<HR>

<FORM METHOD="post" ACTION="cgi-bin/survey.pl">
<H3>Thanks for visiting our site. Please take a moment and fill out our survey. Your input will help us to create a
better Web site.</H3>

<BR>What gardening information would you like to see on our site?
<TEXTAREA NAME="gardeninfo" ROWS="10" COLS="70" WRAP="hard">
</TEXTAREA>

<BR>Where do you purchase most of your gardening materials and supplies?
<INPUT TYPE="text" NAME="purchase" SIZE="45" MAXLENGTH="40">

</FORM>

</BODY>

</HTML>
```

● The Web browser displays the text box in the form.

● The user can click inside the text box and type information.

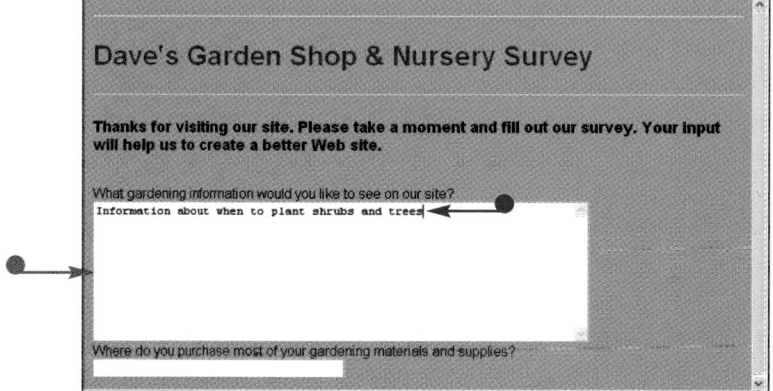

Dave's Garden Shop & Nursery Survey

Thanks for visiting our site. Please take a moment and fill out our survey. Your input will help us to create a better Web site.

What gardening information would you like to see on our site?

Information about when to plant shrubs and trees

Where do you purchase most of your gardening materials and supplies?

TIPS

What happens if the user types more than can be viewed in the text area?

If the user types more text than what is visible in the text area, scroll bars appear active at the side of the text box. Scroll bars allow the user to scroll and view the text. The text area automatically holds as much text as the user needs to type, up to 32,700 characters.

Is there a way to keep users from entering text into a large text area?

Yes. You can use the READONLY attribute if you want to type default text into a text area and do not want users to move or edit the text. For example, you might use a large text area to explain something about your form or offer detailed instructions. You can place the READONLY attribute within the <TEXTAREA> and </TEXTAREA> tags.

You can add check boxes to your
form to allow users to select
from one or more options. You
can group the check boxes under
a single NAME attribute.

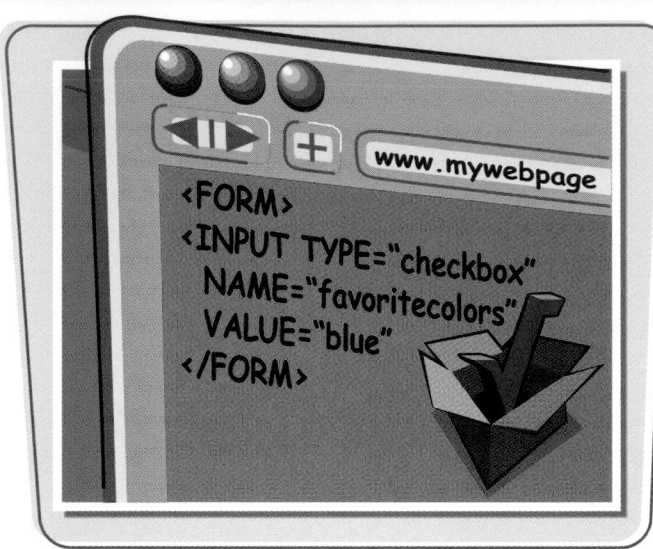

Add Check Boxes

1 Between the <FORM> and </FORM> tags, type
<INPUT TYPE="checkbox".

2 Type a space and **NAME="?"**, replacing *?* with a
unique name for the check box or check box group.

```
<HTML>
<HEAD>
<TITLE>Dave's Garden Shop & Nursery Survey Page</TITLE>
</HEAD>
<BODY BGCOLOR="#F6B28F">

<HR>
<H1><FONT FACE="Arial"><FONT COLOR="004E4A">Dave's Garden Shop & Nursery Survey</FONT>
</H1>
<HR>

<FORM METHOD="post" ACTION="cgi-bin/survey.pl">
<H3>Thanks for visiting our site. Please take a moment and fill out our survey. Your input will help us to create a
better Web site.</H3>

<BR>How did you learn about our site?

<BR>Did you find the information you were looking for?
<BR><INPUT TYPE="checkbox" NAME="find"

<BR>What gardening information would you like to see on our site?
<TEXTAREA NAME="gardeninfo" ROWS="10" COLS="70" WRAP="hard">
</TEXTAREA>

<BR>Where do you purchase most of your gardening materials and supplies?
<INPUT TYPE="text" NAME="purchase" SIZE="45" MAXLENGTH="40">

</FORM>
```

3 Type a space and **VALUE="?">**, replacing *?* with a
value describing the check box.

Note: The check box value does not appear on the form.

```
<HTML>
<HEAD>
<TITLE>Dave's Garden Shop & Nursery Survey Page</TITLE>
</HEAD>
<BODY BGCOLOR="#F6B28F">

<HR>
<H1><FONT FACE="Arial"><FONT COLOR="004E4A">Dave's Garden Shop & Nursery Survey</FONT>
</H1>
<HR>

<FORM METHOD="post" ACTION="cgi-bin/survey.pl">
<H3>Thanks for visiting our site. Please take a moment and fill out our survey. Your input will help us to create a
better Web site.</H3>

<BR>How did you learn about our site?

<BR>Did you find the information you were looking for?
<BR><INPUT TYPE="checkbox" NAME="find" VALUE="yesanswer">

<BR>What gardening information would you like to see on our site?
<TEXTAREA NAME="gardeninfo" ROWS="10" COLS="70" WRAP="hard">
</TEXTAREA>

<BR>Where do you purchase most of your gardening materials and supplies?
<INPUT TYPE="text" NAME="purchase" SIZE="45" MAXLENGTH="40">

</FORM>
```

④ Type the text you want to appear beside the check box.

⑤ Repeat steps **1** to **4** to create more check boxes for a group of check box options.

Note: *You can use the*
 or <P> *tags to separate input elements onto new lines in your form.*

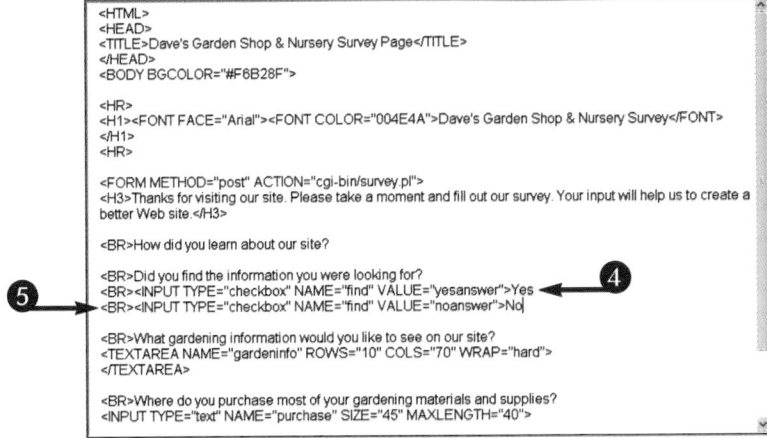

```
<HTML>
<HEAD>
<TITLE>Dave's Garden Shop & Nursery Survey Page</TITLE>
</HEAD>
<BODY BGCOLOR="#F6B28F">

<HR>
<H1><FONT FACE="Arial"><FONT COLOR="004E4A">Dave's Garden Shop & Nursery Survey</FONT>
</H1>
<HR>

<FORM METHOD="post" ACTION="cgi-bin/survey.pl">
<H3>Thanks for visiting our site. Please take a moment and fill out our survey. Your input will help us to create a
better Web site.</H3>

<BR>How did you learn about our site?

<BR>Did you find the information you were looking for?
<BR><INPUT TYPE="checkbox" NAME="find" VALUE="yesanswer">Yes          ④
<BR><INPUT TYPE="checkbox" NAME="find" VALUE="noanswer">No

<BR>What gardening information would you like to see on our site?
<TEXTAREA NAME="gardeninfo" ROWS="10" COLS="70" WRAP="hard">
</TEXTAREA>

<BR>Where do you purchase most of your gardening materials and supplies?
<INPUT TYPE="text" NAME="purchase" SIZE="45" MAXLENGTH="40">
```

● The Web browser displays the check box in the form.

● The user can click the box to insert a check mark.

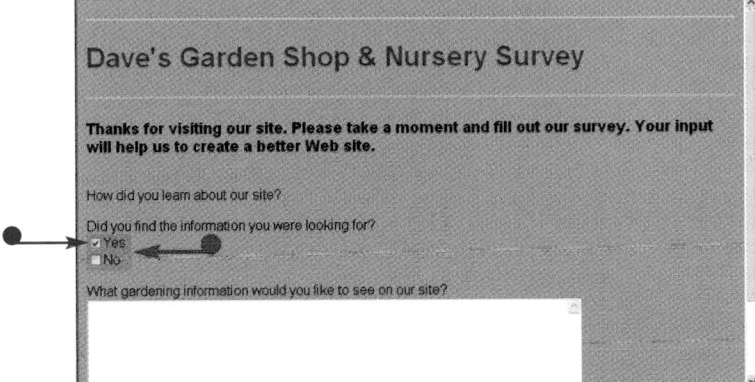

Dave's Garden Shop & Nursery Survey

Thanks for visiting our site. Please take a moment and fill out our survey. Your input will help us to create a better Web site.

How did you learn about our site?

Did you find the information you were looking for?
☑ Yes
☐ No

What gardening information would you like to see on our site?

TIPS

How do I automatically show the check box selected?

You can use the CHECKED attribute. For example, to show the check box selected if the option is popular, add the CHECKED attribute to the <INPUT> tag:

```
<FORM METHOD="post"
ACTION="/cgi-bin/questionnaire.pl">

<INPUT TYPE="checkbox" NAME=
"favoritecolors" VALUE="Blue"
CHECKED>

</FORM>
```

How do I separate my check boxes onto separate lines?
You can use the <P> or <BR> tags. Your code might look like this:

```
<FORM METHOD="post" ACTION="/cgi-bin/
questionnaire.pl">

<P>What type of movie do you like the best?</P>

<INPUT TYPE="checkbox"
NAME="genre" VALUE="Drama">

<BR><INPUT TYPE="checkbox"
NAME="genre" VALUE="Comedy">

<BR><INPUT TYPE="checkbox"
NAME="genre" VALUE="Action">

<BR><INPUT TYPE="checkbox"
NAME="genre" VALUE="Horror">

</FORM>
```

Add Radio Buttons

You can use radio buttons if you want to present a choice of items on a form yet allow the user to choose only one item from the group. The user clicks a button to activate the selection.

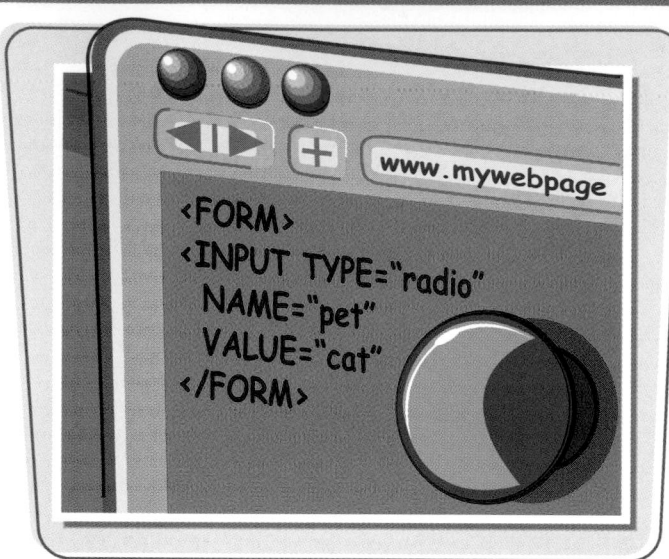

Add Radio Buttons

① Between the <FORM> and </FORM> tags, type **<INPUT TYPE="radio"**.

② Type a space and **NAME="?"**, replacing *?* with a unique name for the radio button group.

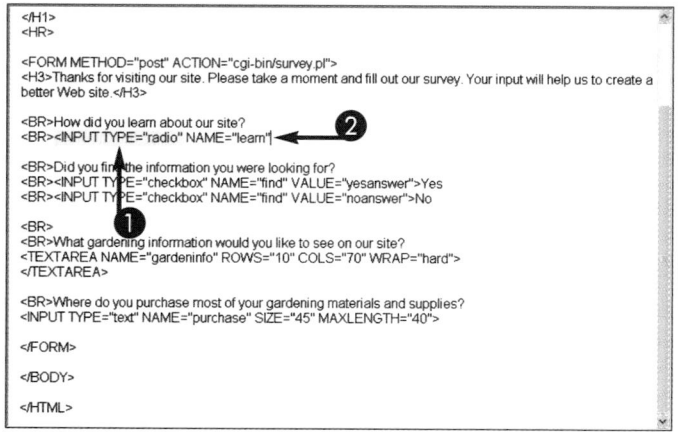

```
</H1>
<HR>

<FORM METHOD="post" ACTION="cgi-bin/survey.pl">
<H3>Thanks for visiting our site. Please take a moment and fill out our survey. Your input will help us to create a
better Web site.</H3>

<BR>How did you learn about our site?
<BR><INPUT TYPE="radio" NAME="learn"|          ② 

<BR>Did you find the information you were looking for?
<BR><INPUT TYPE="checkbox" NAME="find" VALUE="yesanswer">Yes
<BR><INPUT TYPE="checkbox" NAME="find" VALUE="noanswer">No

<BR>
<BR>What gardening information would you like to see on our site?
<TEXTAREA NAME="gardeninfo" ROWS="10" COLS="70" WRAP="hard">
</TEXTAREA>

<BR>Where do you purchase most of your gardening materials and supplies?
<INPUT TYPE="text" NAME="purchase" SIZE="45" MAXLENGTH="40">

</FORM>

</BODY>

</HTML>
```

①

③ Type a space and **VALUE="?">**, replacing *?* with a value describing the radio button.

Note: *The radio button value does not appear on the form.*

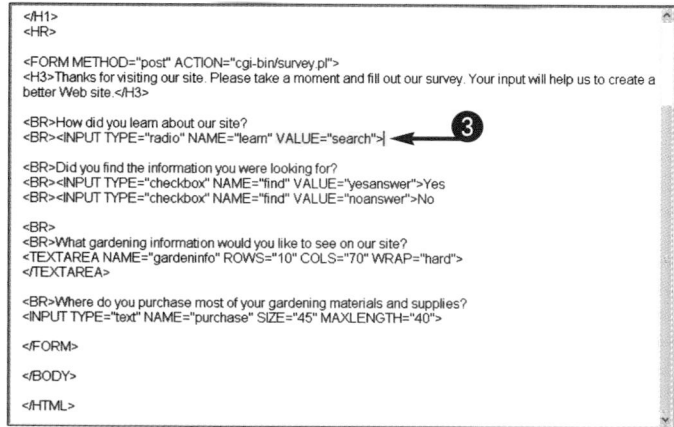

```
</H1>
<HR>

<FORM METHOD="post" ACTION="cgi-bin/survey.pl">
<H3>Thanks for visiting our site. Please take a moment and fill out our survey. Your input will help us to create a
better Web site.</H3>

<BR>How did you learn about our site?
<BR><INPUT TYPE="radio" NAME="learn" VALUE="search">|          ③

<BR>Did you find the information you were looking for?
<BR><INPUT TYPE="checkbox" NAME="find" VALUE="yesanswer">Yes
<BR><INPUT TYPE="checkbox" NAME="find" VALUE="noanswer">No

<BR>
<BR>What gardening information would you like to see on our site?
<TEXTAREA NAME="gardeninfo" ROWS="10" COLS="70" WRAP="hard">
</TEXTAREA>

<BR>Where do you purchase most of your gardening materials and supplies?
<INPUT TYPE="text" NAME="purchase" SIZE="45" MAXLENGTH="40">

</FORM>

</BODY>

</HTML>
```

④ Type the text you want to appear beside the radio button.

⑤ Repeat steps **1** to **4** to add more radio buttons to the group.

Note: *You can use the*
 or <P> *tags to separate input elements onto new lines in your form.*

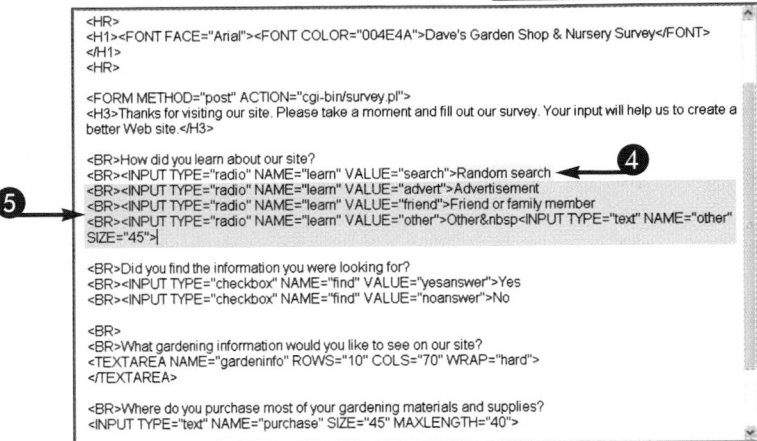

```
<HR>
<H1><FONT FACE="Arial"><FONT COLOR="004E4A">Dave's Garden Shop & Nursery Survey</FONT>
</H1>
<HR>

<FORM METHOD="post" ACTION="cgi-bin/survey.pl">
<H3>Thanks for visiting our site. Please take a moment and fill out our survey. Your input will help us to create a better Web site.</H3>

<BR>How did you learn about our site?
<BR><INPUT TYPE="radio" NAME="learn" VALUE="search">Random search
<BR><INPUT TYPE="radio" NAME="learn" VALUE="advert">Advertisement
<BR><INPUT TYPE="radio" NAME="learn" VALUE="friend">Friend or family member
<BR><INPUT TYPE="radio" NAME="learn" VALUE="other">Other <INPUT TYPE="text" NAME="other"
SIZE="45">

<BR>Did you find the information you were looking for?
<BR><INPUT TYPE="checkbox" NAME="find" VALUE="yesanswer">Yes
<BR><INPUT TYPE="checkbox" NAME="find" VALUE="noanswer">No

<BR>
<BR>What gardening information would you like to see on our site?
<TEXTAREA NAME="gardeninfo" ROWS="10" COLS="70" WRAP="hard">
</TEXTAREA>

<BR>Where do you purchase most of your gardening materials and supplies?
<INPUT TYPE="text" NAME="purchase" SIZE="45" MAXLENGTH="40">
```

● The Web browser displays the radio buttons in the form.

● The user can click the box to insert a check mark.

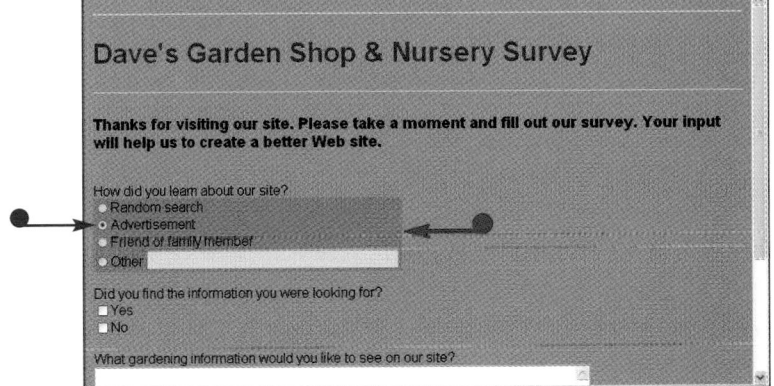

Dave's Garden Shop & Nursery Survey

Thanks for visiting our site. Please take a moment and fill out our survey. Your input will help us to create a better Web site.

How did you learn about our site?
○ Random search
○ Advertisement
○ Friend or family member
○ Other
Did you find the information you were looking for?
□ Yes
□ No

What gardening information would you like to see on our site?

TIPS

Should the radio button value be the same text as the NAME attribute?

Not necessarily. You use the NAME attribute to group related items and identify the radio button in the processing script. The VALUE attribute is the text sent to the server if a user selects the button. If you do not set the VALUE attribute, the word "on" is sent to the script, which does not tell you which button the user selected. For simplicity's sake, Web developers usually assign the same name to both the NAME attribute and the VALUE attribute.

Can I show a particular radio button selected by default?

Yes. You can use the CHECKED attribute to show one radio button in the group selected by default. You can add the CHECKED attribute after the VALUE attribute in your HTML code. Your code might look like this:

```
<FORM METHOD="post"
ACTION="/cgi-bin/questionnaire.pl">

<INPUT TYPE="radio" NAME="agerange"
VALUE="40-50" CHECKED>

</FORM>
```

You can add a menu to a form to give users a list of choices. Menu lists allow you to display choices as a drop-down list that displays only when the user selects the list. By storing choices in a drop-down list, you can free up space for other input items on the form.

Add a Menu List

1. Between the `<FORM>` and `</FORM>` tags, type **`<SELECT NAME="?"`**, replacing *?* with a unique name for the menu.

2. Type a space and **`SIZE="?">`**, replacing *?* with the height, measured in character lines, for the menu input.

   If you want to display a drop-down menu, set the height to 1.

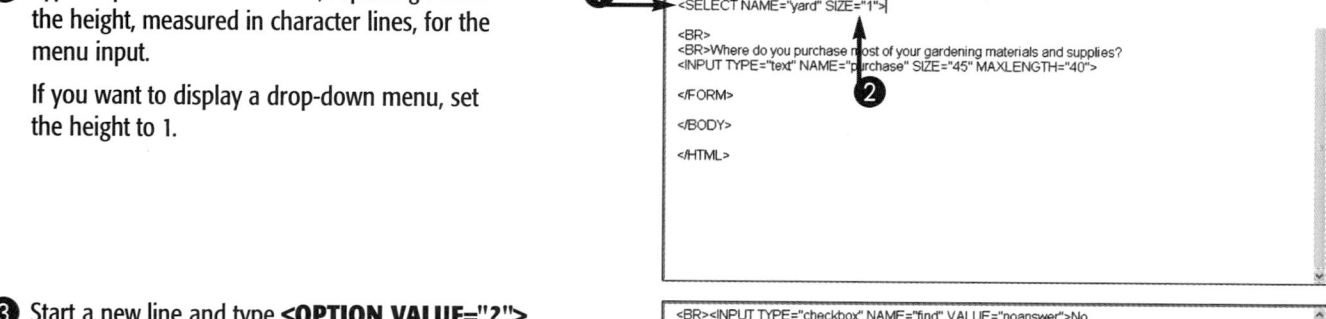

3. Start a new line and type **`<OPTION VALUE="?">`**, replacing *?* with a descriptive word for the menu item.

4. Type the text you want to appear in the menu list.

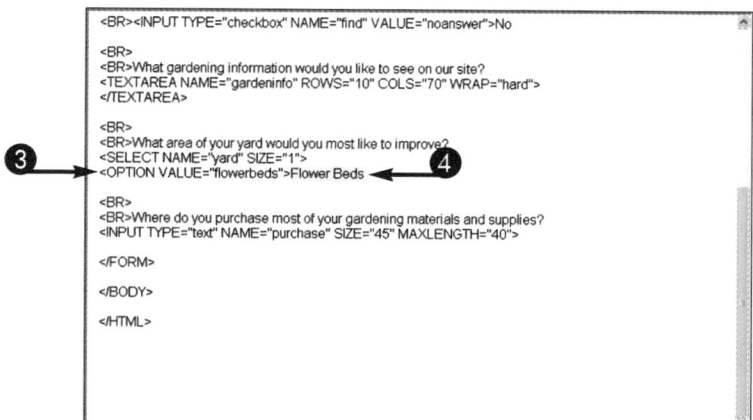

⑤ Repeat steps **3** and **4** to add more menu items to the list.

⑥ To make one menu item appear selected in the list, type **SELECTED** after the VALUE attribute.

⑦ Type **</SELECT>**.

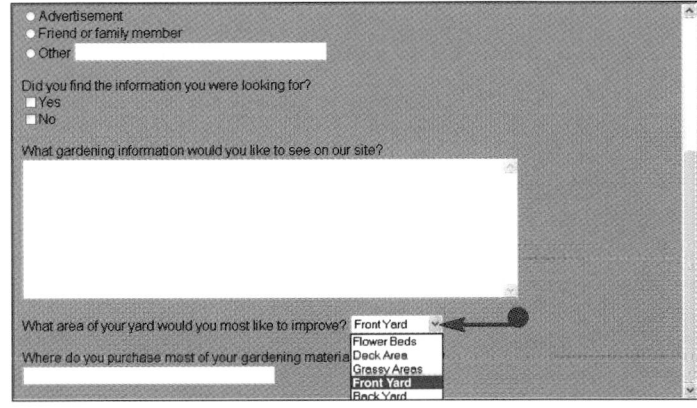

```
<BR><INPUT TYPE="checkbox" NAME="find" VALUE="noanswer">No

<BR>
<BR>What gardening information would you like to see on our site?
<TEXTAREA NAME="gardeninfo" ROWS="10" COLS="70" WRAP="hard">
</TEXTAREA>

<BR>
<BR>What area of your yard would you most like to improve?
<SELECT NAME="yard" SIZE="1">
<OPTION VALUE="flowerbeds">Flower Beds
<OPTION VALUE="deck">Deck Area
<OPTION VALUE="grass">Grassy Areas
<OPTION VALUE="frontyard" SELECTED>Front Yard
<OPTION VALUE="backyard">Back Yard
<OPTION VALUE="sideyard">Side Yard
</SELECT>

<BR>
<BR>Where do you purchase most of your gardening materials and supplies?
<INPUT TYPE="text" NAME="purchase" SIZE="45" MAXLENGTH="40">

</FORM>

</BODY>

</HTML>
```

The Web browser displays the menu on the form.

● The user can click to display the drop-down list and click to make a selection.

How do I display the entire menu in my form?

Simply enter the number of menu entries as the SIZE attribute value. This makes the menu appear at a height that shows all the items in the list. If the menu list is long, you may end up taking up more room than you like on the form, making users scroll to view the selections. If you prefer to save room on your form, keep the menu size at 1. This creates a drop-down menu list.

How can I create a submenu?

Use the <OPTGROUP> tag and the LABEL attribute:

```
<P>What is favorite flower?</P>
<SELECT NAME="favoriteflower">
<OPTGROUP LABEL="Perennial">
<OPTION VALUE="Daisy">Daisy
<OPTION VALUE="Lily">Lily
<OPTION VALUE="Rose">Rose
</OPTGROUP>
<OPGROUP LABEL="Annual">
<OPTION VALUE="Petunia">Petunia
<OPTION VALUE="Impatiens">Impatiens
<OPTION VALUE="Pansy">Pansy
</OPTGROUP>
</SELECT>
```

Not all browsers support the <OPTGROUP> tag.

Add a Submit Button

Add a submit button to your form so users can send you the data they enter. Most Web page developers add the submit button to the bottom of the form. You can choose any label you like for the button, as long as it is easy for users to understand that they need to click it to submit their data.

Add a Submit Button

① Between the `<FORM>` and `</FORM>` tags, type **<INPUT TYPE="submit"**.

② Type a space and type **VALUE="?">**, replacing *?* with the text you want to appear on the button.

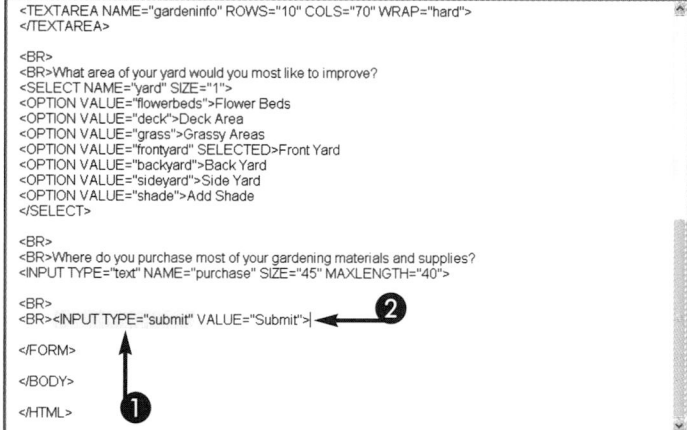

● The browser displays the button on the form.

When the user clicks the button, the form data is processed as specified in the `<FORM>` tag.

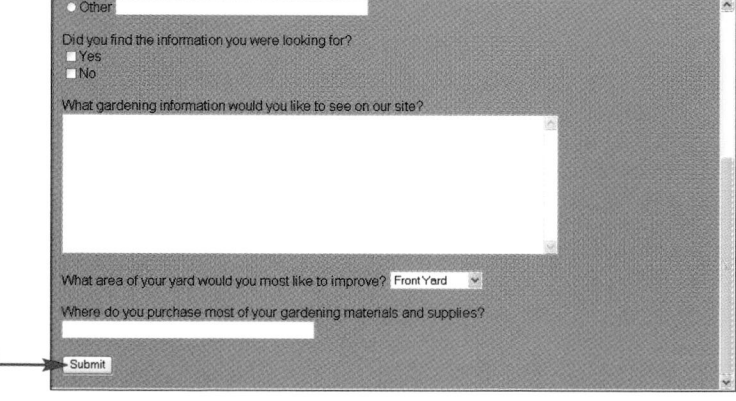

Add a Reset Button

You can add a reset button to your form to allow users to clear the data. For example, the user may want to enter a different set of information, or change his or her mind about submitting the information. A reset button lets users erase all the information they entered into the various input fields.

Add a Reset Button

① Between the `<FORM>` and `</FORM>` tags type **<INPUT TYPE="reset"**.

② Type a space and type **VALUE="?">**, replacing *?* with the text you want to appear on the button.

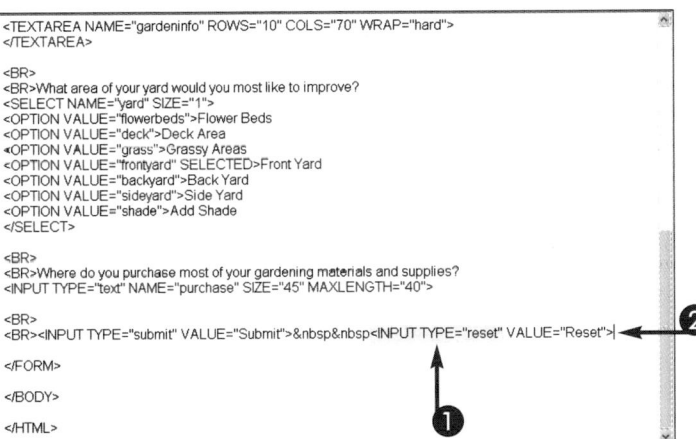

```
<TEXTAREA NAME="gardeninfo" ROWS="10" COLS="70" WRAP="hard">
</TEXTAREA>

<BR>
<BR>What area of your yard would you most like to improve?
<SELECT NAME="yard" SIZE="1">
<OPTION VALUE="flowerbeds">Flower Beds
<OPTION VALUE="deck">Deck Area
<OPTION VALUE="grass">Grassy Areas
<OPTION VALUE="frontyard" SELECTED>Front Yard
<OPTION VALUE="backyard">Back Yard
<OPTION VALUE="sideyard">Side Yard
<OPTION VALUE="shade">Add Shade
</SELECT>

<BR>
<BR>Where do you purchase most of your gardening materials and supplies?
<INPUT TYPE="text" NAME="purchase" SIZE="45" MAXLENGTH="40">

<BR>
<BR><INPUT TYPE="submit" VALUE="Submit">  <INPUT TYPE="reset" VALUE="Reset">

</FORM>

</BODY>

</HTML>
```

● The browser displays the button on the form.

When the user clicks the button, the form is reset to its original settings.

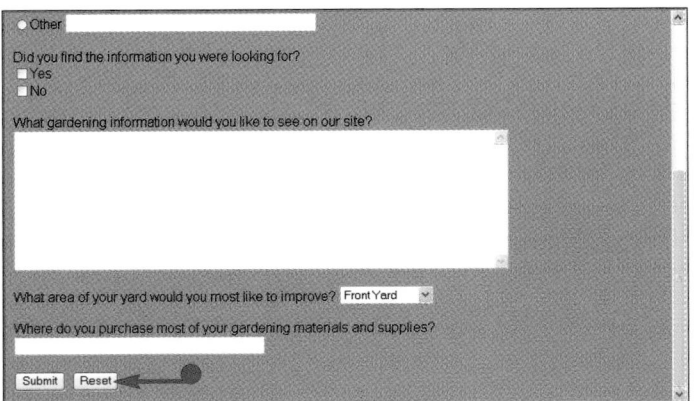

Add Active Labels

To make your form easier to use, you can identify the text beside an input element as a label. The browser treats the text as an active form element, which means if the user clicks it, the input element changes to reflect the selection. For example, if you make the text next to a check box a label, the user can click the text as well as the check box to select the option.

Add Active Labels

① Click inside the tag for the form element you want to label and type **ID="?"**, replacing ? with a descriptive word for the element.

② Before the text, type **<LABEL FOR="?">**, replacing ? with the word you assigned in step **1**.

③ Type **</LABEL>** following the text.

You can repeat steps **1** and **2** to add more labels.

```
<BR>How did you learn about our site?
<BR><INPUT TYPE="radio" NAME="learn" VALUE="search" ID="search"><LABEL FOR="search">Random
search</LABEL>
<BR><INPUT TYPE="radio" NAME="learn" VALUE="advert">Advertisement
<BR><INPUT TYPE="radio" NAME="learn" VALUE="friend">Friend or family member
<BR><INPUT TYPE="radio" NAME="learn" VALUE="other">Other <INPUT TYPE="text" NAME="other"
SIZE="45">

<BR>
<BR>Did you find the information you were looking for?
<BR><INPUT TYPE="checkbox" NAME="find" VALUE="yesanswer">Yes
<BR><INPUT TYPE="checkbox" NAME="find" VALUE="noanswer">No

<BR>
<BR>What gardening information would you like to see on our site?
<TEXTAREA NAME="gardeninfo" ROWS="10" COLS="70" WRAP="hard">
</TEXTAREA>

<BR>
<BR>What area of your yard would you most like to improve?
<SELECT NAME="yard" SIZE="1">
<OPTION VALUE="flowerbeds">Flower Beds
<OPTION VALUE="deck">Deck Area
<OPTION VALUE="grass">Grassy Areas
<OPTION VALUE="frontyard" SELECTED>Front Yard
<OPTION VALUE="backyard">Back Yard
<OPTION VALUE="sideyard">Side Yard
```

● The user can move the mouse pointer over the label to make the input element active as well as click to activate the input element.

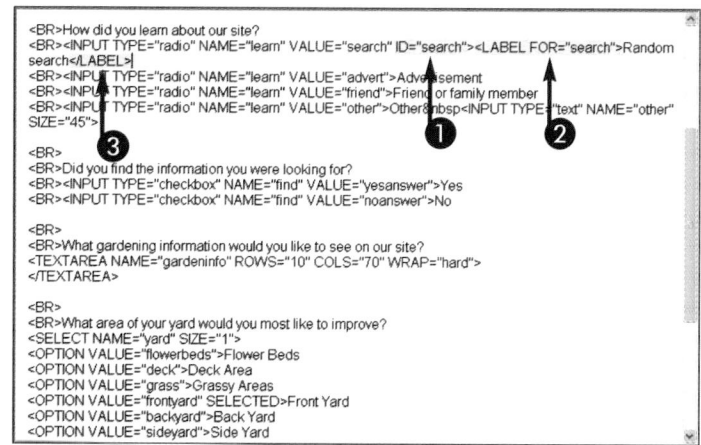

Web site visitors filling out your form can navigate from one input element to the next by clicking on the element or pressing the Tab key. By default the Tab key follows the order in which you entered the input elements in your HTML document. You can change the tab order to move the user around the form in a different order.

Change the Tab Order

① Click inside the first form element tag and type **TABINDEX="?"**, replacing *?* with a number representing the element's position in the tab order.

```
<FORM METHOD="post" ACTION="cgi-bin/survey.pl">
<H3>Thanks for visiting our site. Please take a moment and fill out our survey. Your input will help us to create a
better Web site.</H3>

<BR>How did you learn about our site?
<BR><INPUT TYPE="radio" NAME="learn" VALUE="search" ID="search" TABINDEX="1"><LABEL
FOR="search">Random search</LABEL>
<BR><INPUT TYPE="radio" NAME="learn" VALUE="advert" ID="advert"><LABEL FOR="advert">
Advertisement</LABEL>
<BR><INPUT TYPE="radio" NAME="learn" VALUE="friend" ID="friend"><LABEL FOR="friend">Friend or
family member</LABEL>
<BR><INPUT TYPE="radio" NAME="learn" VALUE="other" ID="other"><LABEL FOR="other">Other 
</LABEL><INPUT TYPE="text" NAME="other" SIZE="45">

<BR>
<BR>Did you find the information you were looking for?
<BR><INPUT TYPE="checkbox" NAME="find" VALUE="yesanswer">Yes
<BR><INPUT TYPE="checkbox" NAME="find" VALUE="noanswer">No

<BR>
<BR>What gardening information would you like to see on our site?
<TEXTAREA NAME="gardeninfo" ROWS="10" COLS="70" WRAP="hard">
</TEXTAREA>

<BR>
<BR>What area of your yard would you most like to improve?
<SELECT NAME="yard" SIZE="1">
```

② Repeat step **1** for the remaining elements.

Note: *You can enter a negative number to exclude an input element from the tab order.*

Users can move through your form using the tab order you specified.

```
<FORM METHOD="post" ACTION="cgi-bin/survey.pl">
<H3>Thanks for visiting our site. Please take a moment and fill out our survey. Your input will help us to create a
better Web site.</H3>

<BR>How did you learn about our site?
<BR><INPUT TYPE="radio" NAME="learn" VALUE="search" ID="search" TABINDEX="1"><LABEL
FOR="search">Random search</LABEL>
<BR><INPUT TYPE="radio" NAME="learn" VALUE="advert" ID="advert" TABINDEX="2"><LABEL
FOR="advert">Advertisement</LABEL>
<BR><INPUT TYPE="radio" NAME="learn" VALUE="friend" ID="friend" TABINDEX="3"><LABEL
FOR="friend">Friend or family member</LABEL>
<BR><INPUT TYPE="radio" NAME="learn" VALUE="other" ID="other" TABINDEX="4"><LABEL
FOR="other">Other </LABEL><INPUT TYPE="text" NAME="other" SIZE="45">

<BR>
<BR>Did you find the information you were looking for?
<BR><INPUT TYPE="checkbox" NAME="find" VALUE="yesanswer" TABINDEX="5">Yes
<BR><INPUT TYPE="checkbox" NAME="find" VALUE="noanswer" TABINDEX="6">No

<BR>
<BR>What gardening information would you like to see on our site?
<TEXTAREA NAME="gardeninfo" ROWS="10" COLS="70" WRAP="hard">
</TEXTAREA>

<BR>
<BR>What area of your yard would you most like to improve?
<SELECT NAME="yard" SIZE="1">
```

Add a File Upload Element

If you want users to send you files, such as resumes or photos, you can add a file upload element to your form. When you add the upload element, a Browse button appears with the field, allowing users to quickly locate the file they want to send.

The upload element works only if your `<FORM>` tag's METHOD attribute is set to post. See the section "Create a Form" to learn more about specifying a method.

Add a File Upload Element

1 Make sure the `<FORM>` tag method is set to post.

2 Within the `<FORM>` tag, type **ENCTYPE="multipart/form-data"**.

```
<FORM METHOD="post" ACTION="cgi-bin/survey.pl" ENCTYPE="multipart/form-data">
<H3>Thanks for visiting our site. Please take a moment and fill out our survey. Your input will help us to create a
better Web site.</H3>

<BR>How did you learn about our site?
<BR><INPUT TYPE="radio" NAME="learn" VALUE="search" ID="search"><LABEL FOR="search">Random
search</LABEL>
<BR><INPUT TYPE="radio" NAME="learn" VALUE="advert" ID="advert"><LABEL FOR="advert">
Advertisement</LABEL>
<BR><INPUT TYPE="radio" NAME="learn" VALUE="friend" ID="friend"><LABEL FOR="friend">Friend or
family member</LABEL>
<BR><INPUT TYPE="radio" NAME="learn" VALUE="other" ID="other"><LABEL FOR="other">Other 
</LABEL><INPUT TYPE="text" NAME="other" SIZE="45">

<BR>
<BR>Did you find the information you were looking for?
<BR><INPUT TYPE="checkbox" NAME="find" VALUE="yesanswer">Yes
<BR><INPUT TYPE="checkbox" NAME="find" VALUE="noanswer">No

<BR>
<BR>What gardening information would you like to see on our site?
<TEXTAREA NAME="gardeninfo" ROWS="10" COLS="70" WRAP="hard">
</TEXTAREA>

<BR>
<BR>What area of your yard would you most like to improve?
<SELECT NAME="yard" SIZE="1">
```

3 Type the text you want to appear next to the upload element.

4 Type **`<INPUT TYPE="file"`**.

```
<BR>
<BR>What area of your yard would you most like to improve?
<SELECT NAME="yard" SIZE="1">
<OPTION VALUE="flowerbeds">Flower Beds
<OPTION VALUE="deck">Deck Area
<OPTION VALUE="grass">Grassy Areas
<OPTION VALUE="frontyard" SELECTED>Front Yard
<OPTION VALUE="backyard">Back Yard
<OPTION VALUE="sideyard">Side Yard
<OPTION VALUE="shade">Add Shade
</SELECT>

<BR>
<BR>Where do you purchase most of your gardening materials and supplies?
<INPUT TYPE="text" NAME="purchase" SIZE="45" MAXLENGTH="40">

<BR>
<BR>Send us your favorite flower photos:  <INPUT TYPE="file"

<BR>
<BR><INPUT TYPE="submit" VALUE="Submit">  <INPUT TYPE="reset" VALUE="Reset">

</FORM>

</BODY>

</HTML>
```

⑤ Type a space and then **NAME="?"**, replacing ? with a name for the input field.

⑥ Type a space and **SIZE="?"**, replacing ? with the character length for the size of the input field.

```
<BR>
<BR>What area of your yard would you most like to improve?
<SELECT NAME="yard" SIZE="1">
<OPTION VALUE="flowerbeds">Flower Beds
<OPTION VALUE="deck">Deck Area
<OPTION VALUE="grass">Grassy Areas
<OPTION VALUE="frontyard" SELECTED>Front Yard
<OPTION VALUE="backyard">Back Yard
<OPTION VALUE="sideyard">Side Yard
<OPTION VALUE="shade">Add Shade
</SELECT>

<BR>
<BR>Where do you purchase most of your gardening materials and supplies?
<INPUT TYPE="text" NAME="purchase" SIZE="45" MAXLENGTH="40">

<BR>
<BR>Send us your favorite flower photos:  <INPUT TYPE="file" NAME="photos" SIZE="50">|

<BR>
<BR><INPUT TYPE="submit" VALUE="Submit">  <INPUT TYPE="reset" VALUE="Reset">

</FORM>

</BODY>

</HTML>
```

● The Web browser displays the upload element on the form.

Users can type the path to the file they want to upload, or click **Browse** to locate the file.

 TIPS

Where does the uploaded file go?

You need a CGI script to process the uploaded file on your server. Unless your Web host offers an uploading script, you may need to adapt a script from the Internet. You can find numerous free CGI scripts on the Internet. Visit www.cgi-resources.com or www.hotscripts.com to search for an upload script.

What if my Web server is limited to certain file types for uploads?

You can use the ACCEPT attribute to list what files the server can process. Your HTML code may look like this:

```
<FORM METHOD="post"
ACTION="/cgi-bin/
feedback.pl" ENCTYPE=
"multipart/form-data">

<INPUT TYPE="file" NAME=
"userfiles" ACCEPT="image/
gif, image/jpeg, image/png">

</FORM>
```

Be sure to separate each MIME (Multi-purpose Internet Mail Extensions) type with a comma. Note that not all browsers support the ACCEPT attribute.

Group Form Elements

If your form is particularly long, you can organize the different parts into groups. For example, you might group personal information separately from questionnaire data. Groups appear roped together with a border. You can assign a title to the group to distinguish the form elements from other input fields on the form.

Not all browsers support the <FIELDSET> **and** <LEGEND> **tags.**

Group Form Elements

① Type **<FIELDSET>** above the first input element you want to place in a group.

② Type **</FIELDSET>** after the last input element you want to place in the group.

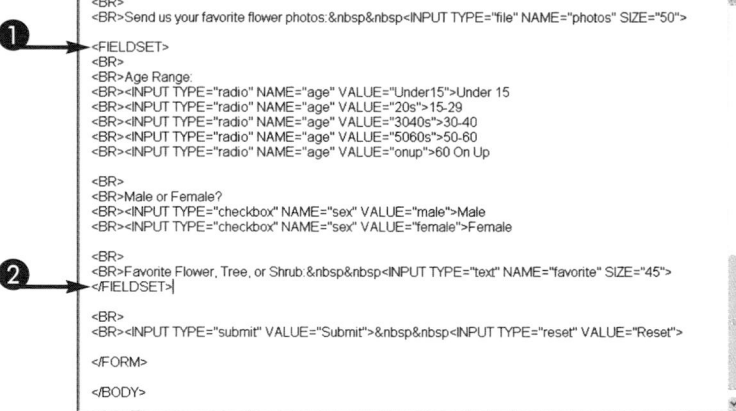

③ Below the <FIELDSET> tag, type **<LEGEND**.

④ Type a space and **ALIGN="?">**, replacing *?* with an alignment for the group title (**left**, **right**, **top**, or **bottom**).

5 Type a title for the group.

6 Type **</LEGEND>**.

You can repeat steps **1** to **6** to define other groups of input elements on your form.

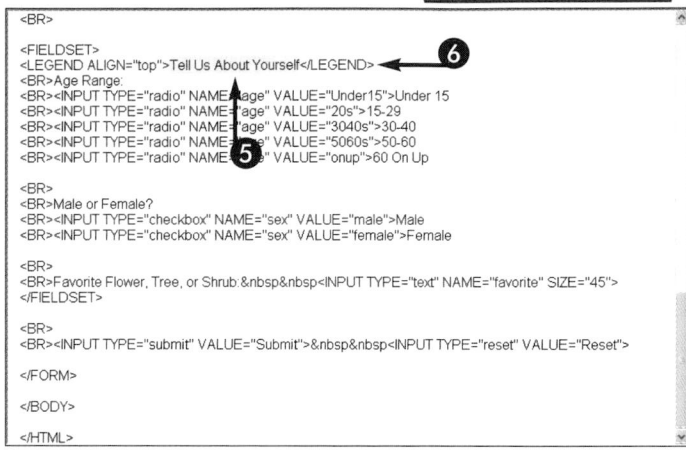

• The Web browser displays the grouped elements together.

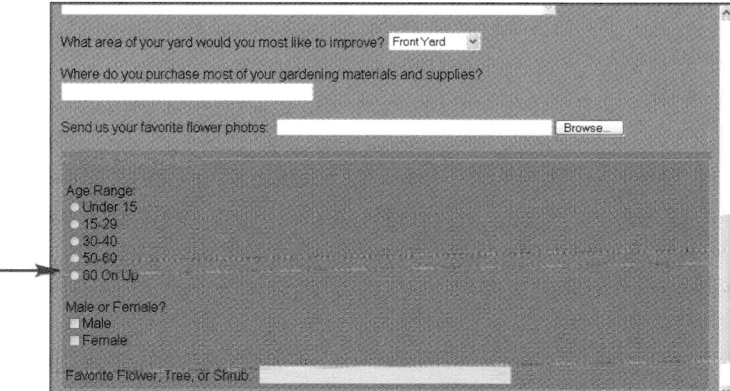

 TIPS

Is there another way to organize my form elements besides the `<FIELDSET>` tag?

You can also arrange your form elements into tables on your Web page. For example, a table row makes a nice receptacle for a related group of input fields. You can size a table cell to fit as many form fields as you require. To learn more about creating HTML tables, see Chapter 9.

Can I disable a form element?

Yes. You can add the DISABLED attribute to an input element's tag to display the field. For example:

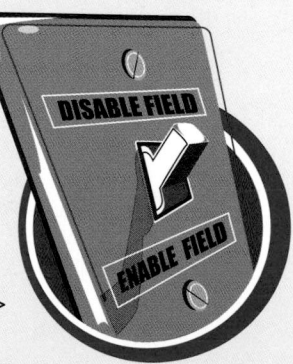

```
<FORM METHOD="post"
ACTION="/cgi-bin/feedback.pl"
ENCTYPE="multipart/form-data">

<INPUT TYPE="file"
NAME="userfiles"
ACCEPT="image/gif, image/jpeg,
image/png" DISABLED="disabled">

</FORM>
```

For example, you may want to disable a field until a later time, or disable it until the user fills out all the other required data. You can then add a JavaScript to enable it again. See Chapter 13 to learn more about JavaScripts.

Adding Sounds and Videos

You can make your Web pages more exciting by adding multimedia elements. This chapter shows you how to add sound and video files to your HTML pages.

Understanding Multimedia Elements..........**232**

Understanding Plug-ins and Players **234**

Link to Audio or Video Files..........................**236**

Embed an Audio File **238**

Embed a Video File..**240**

Embed a Flash Movie......................................**242**

Set Up Background Audio...............................**243**

Understanding Multimedia Elements

The term *multimedia* encompasses all kinds of dynamic visual and audio data on the Internet and computers in general. Graphics, sound, animation, and movies are all examples of multimedia elements. You can incorporate your own multimedia elements onto your HTML pages. Before attempting to add your own multimedia elements, first make sure you understand how such elements work among Web pages, as well as how such elements will affect the person viewing the page.

Ways to Use Multimedia

You can use media files in a variety of ways on your Web page. Media can create an ambiance for the site, enhance your site's message, illustrate a product or service, or simply entertain. When choosing a media file and format to add to your page, always consider the main target audience for your pages. Be sure to include information about the multimedia elements on your page in case the user wants to turn them off or is unable to view or play them.

Delivering Media Files

You can deliver multimedia files to the users viewing your pages in several ways. You can link to an external media file, embed the file into your page, or stream the file. The method you choose depends on the way in which you want the user to interact with the file. Regardless of the method, you must specify the location of the file and include the file on the server in which you publish your Web page.

External Media Files

One way to incorporate a multimedia element into your page is to supply a link to an external media file. For example, you might allow a visitor to click a link and download a slide show of your vacation pictures, or download a music file of your latest song. If the user decides to access the file, the browser helps him or her determine how to conduct the download and where to store the file. Once the file is downloaded, the user can play the file in a separate window using the appropriate media player or program.

Embedded Files

You can integrate a multimedia file directly onto your page by embedding the file. When the user activates the file, it plays as part of the Web page. For example, you might embed a video file to play in an area on the Web page. Depending on the file type and setup, the file may play immediately when the user displays the page, or when the user activates a button or other feature on the page.

Streaming Media

With streaming media, the user can immediately start viewing or hearing the file as the rest of it continues to download. The data starts downloading into a buffer and then the media player begins playing the file. Adding streaming media to your page is similar to linking or embedding a file, yet instead of referencing the actual file, you define a meta file that contains information about the target file's location.

Understanding Plug-ins and Players

A wide variety of media formats exist on the Internet, but in order to actually play these formats, the end user needs a plug-in or media player. When determining what type of media file you want to include with your page, think about how your target audience will interact with the file. Do they need a special plug-in or player program to play the file? If so, you need to add information on your page about the requirements along with access to the actual media file.

Plug-ins

Plug-ins are specialized applications that work along with the browser to play a media file, typically focusing on a particular file format. If users do not have a particular plug-in for the type of file you offer, they can easily download it, install it, and use it as part of their Web browser. First introduced by Netscape, plug-ins are now popular among all the browsers.

Media Players

Media players are separate programs designed to handle numerous types of media files. Often called *all-in-one players*, media players can work both separately and alongside browsers to play multimedia files encountered on and off the Web. Popular media players include Microsoft's Windows Media Player, RealNetworks RealOne Player, and Apple's QuickTime player. Users can download copies of these popular media players from the Internet, or you can provide links to the sites.

Dueling HTML Elements

Establishing standards for Web page development is an ongoing task for the World Wide Web Consortium (W3C). Currently, two popular elements exist for showing multimedia files on Web pages, the EMBED and OBJECT elements. Netscape created the nonstandard EMBED element, while the W3C introduced the standard OBJECT element. Microsoft added ActiveX controls to the OBJECT element. Today's browser versions support different degrees of these elements. For the widest support, many developers combine the OBJECT element with the nonstandard EMBED element.

Embed with ActiveX Controls

Another way you can embed video clips into your pages is using ActiveX controls along with the <OBJECT> element. ActiveX uses a CLASSID attribute control number to define which data type the browser loads for playback. The CLASSID attribute for QuickTime, for example, is a different number than that for Windows Media Player. Once you define the proper player, you can set the parameters for the clip's playback.

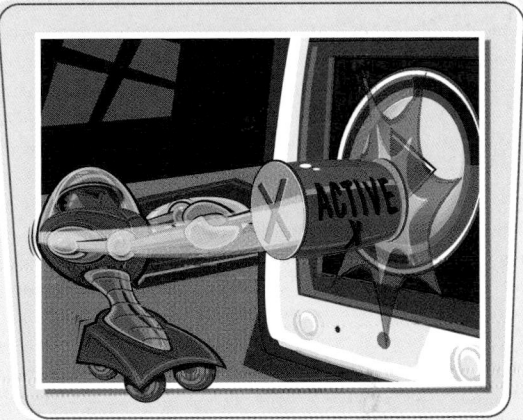

Finding Media Players and Plug-ins

Player	Web Site
Windows Media Player	www.microsoft.com/downloads
QuickTime	www.apple.com/quicktime
RealOne Player	www.real.com
Macromedia Flash Player	www.macromedia.com
Macromedia Shockwave Player	www.macromedia.com
Adobe Acrobat Reader	www.adobe.com/products/acrobat/main.html
Netscape Plug-ins	http://channels.netscape.com/ns/browsers/plugins.jsp

Link to Audio or Video Files

You can insert links on your Web page that, when clicked, download and play an audio or video file. When you link to a file, the file opens to play in a separate window. Linking is the easiest way to deliver multimedia files to your Web page visitor.

When publishing your HTML page to a Web server, make sure you upload the audio or video file along with the document.

Link to Audio or Video Files

① Type the text you want to use as a link.

② Type **<A HREF="?">** in front of the link text, replacing the *?* with the location and name of the audio or video file to which you want to link.

Note: See Chapter 8 to learn more about creating HTML links.

```
<HR SIZE="3" NOSHADE>
<H1><FONT FACE="Arial">Dave's Garden Shop & Nursery</FONT></H1>
<HR SIZE="3" NOSHADE>

<CENTER><P><FONT SIZE="4"><B><I>Experts in gardening for over 40 years</I></B></FONT></P>
</CENTER>

<IMG SRC="Million_Bells2.jpg" ALIGN="Left" HSPACE="15">
<IMG SRC="Butterfly3.jpg" ALIGN="Right" HSPACE="15">

<P>We offer the finest selection of plants and planting materials, and an award-winning gardening shop. Stop
by to see our 5 acres of nursery selections, including trees, shrubs, annuals, perennials, and seasonal plants.
Our experienced staff is always available to assist you.</P><BR CLEAR="All">
<BR>

<P>Be sure to visit our store for garden-themed gifts for indoors and outdoors. We feature exciting new items
for home decorating and gardening at the start of each season.</P>

<IMG SRC="Garden_Supplies.jpg" WIDTH="300" HEIGHT="200" ALT="Image of Gardening Tool"
ALIGN="middle">   
Click <A HREF="classical1.mp3">here to listen to a selection from our gardening music collection.

</BODY>

</HTML>
```

② ①

③ Type **</A>** at the end of the link text.

```
<HR SIZE="3" NOSHADE>
<H1><FONT FACE="Arial">Dave's Garden Shop & Nursery</FONT></H1>
<HR SIZE="3" NOSHADE>

<CENTER><P><FONT SIZE="4"><B><I>Experts in gardening for over 40 years</I></B></FONT></P>
</CENTER>

<IMG SRC="Million_Bells2.jpg" ALIGN="Left" HSPACE="15">
<IMG SRC="Butterfly3.jpg" ALIGN="Right" HSPACE="15">

<P>We offer the finest selection of plants and planting materials, and an award-winning gardening shop. Stop
by to see our 5 acres of nursery selections, including trees, shrubs, annuals, perennials, and seasonal plants.
Our experienced staff is always available to assist you.</P><BR CLEAR="All">
<BR>

<P>Be sure to visit our store for garden-themed gifts for indoors and outdoors. We feature exciting new items
for home decorating and gardening at the start of each season.</P>

<IMG SRC="Garden_Supplies.jpg" WIDTH="300" HEIGHT="200" ALT="Image of Gardening Tool"
ALIGN="middle">   
Click <A HREF="classical1.mp3">here</A>to listen to a selection from our gardening music collection.

</BODY>

</HTML>
```

③

The Web browser displays the link on the page.

● When the user activates the link, the Web browser attempts to play the audio or video file.

Note: See Chapter 2 to learn more about viewing your HTML document as an offline Web page.

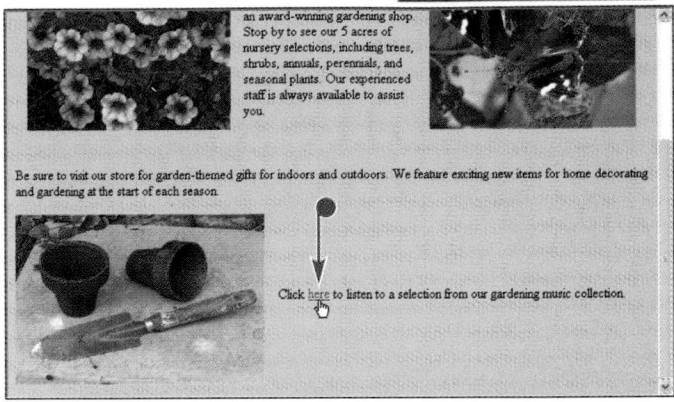

In this example, Windows Media Player opens and plays the audio file.

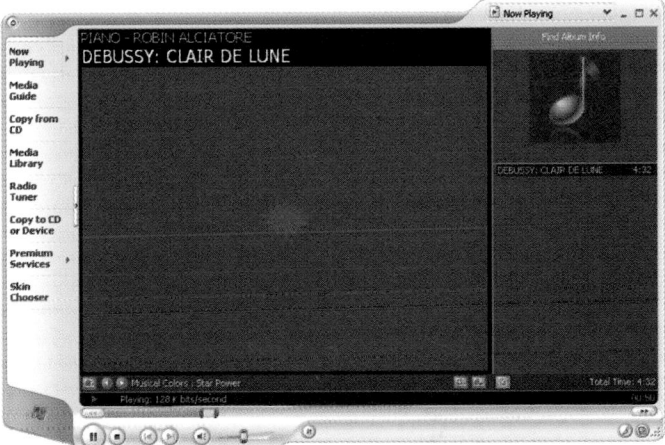

TIPS

Does my page need to include information about the file available for downloading?

It is always good practice to give your Web page visitors all the information they need to know in order to download and view any type of multimedia file. For example, include a brief description of the file, list the file type and size, and provide a link to any plug-ins or media players the user might need in order to play the file.

What happens if the link is broken?

If users attempt to activate a link to an inactive URL, their Web browser displays an error message. Always check your links as part of your Web page maintenance after the page is published. Be careful not to move any referenced files or you will need to rewrite the link to the correct file.

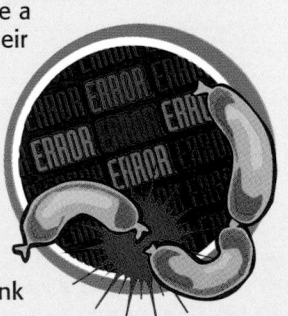

Embed an Audio File

You can add an embedded sound to your HTML page using the <EMBED> tag. Embedded sounds play directly from your page. Playback controls appear on the page allowing the user to start and stop the sound.

You can control the size of the sound controls that appear with an embedded sound file. For example, you can set the width at 170 pixels and the height at 25 pixels to create easy-to-read playback controls.

Embed an Audio File

① Type **<EMBED SRC="?">** where you want to insert sound controls on the page, replacing the *?* with the location and name of the audio file.

```
<HR SIZE="3" NOSHADE>

<CENTER><P><FONT SIZE="4"><B><I>Experts in gardening for over 40 years</I></B></FONT></P>
</CENTER>

<IMG SRC="Million_Bells2.jpg" ALIGN="Left" HSPACE="15">
<IMG SRC="Butterfly3.jpg" ALIGN="Right" HSPACE="15">

<P>We offer the finest selection of plants and planting materials, and an award-winning gardening shop. Stop
by to see our 5 acres of nursery selections, including trees, shrubs, annuals, perennials, and seasonal plants.
Our experienced staff is always available to assist you.</P><BR CLEAR="All">
<BR>

<P>Be sure to visit our store for garden-themed gifts for indoors and outdoors. We feature exciting new items
for home decorating and gardening at the start of each season.</P>

<IMG SRC="Garden_Supplies.jpg" WIDTH="300" HEIGHT="200" ALT="Image of Gardening Tool"
ALIGN="left">   
Music for the Garden<BR>
<EMBED SRC="classical1.mp3">|          ①

</BODY>

</HTML>
```

② Within the <EMBED> tag, type **WIDTH="?" HEIGHT="?"** replacing *?* in both attributes with the width and height values you want to use for the size of the controls.

You can experiment with the values to set just the right size for your page.

```
<HR SIZE="3" NOSHADE>

<CENTER><P><FONT SIZE="4"><B><I>Experts in gardening for over 40 years</I></B></FONT></P>
</CENTER>

<IMG SRC="Million_Bells2.jpg" ALIGN="Left" HSPACE="15">
<IMG SRC="Butterfly3.jpg" ALIGN="Right" HSPACE="15">

<P>We offer the finest selection of plants and planting materials, and an award-winning gardening shop. Stop
by to see our 5 acres of nursery selections, including trees, shrubs, annuals, perennials, and seasonal plants.
Our experienced staff is always available to assist you.</P><BR CLEAR="All">
<BR>

<P>Be sure to visit our store for garden-themed gifts for indoors and outdoors. We feature exciting new items
for home decorating and gardening at the start of each season.</P>

<IMG SRC="Garden_Supplies.jpg" WIDTH="300" HEIGHT="200" ALT="Image of Gardening Tool"
ALIGN="left">   
Music for the Garden<BR>
<EMBED SRC="classical1.mp3" WIDTH="170" HEIGHT="25">          ②

</BODY>

</HTML>
```

- To keep the sound from playing immediately when the page loads, type **AUTOSTART="false"** in the `EMBED` tag.

- To make the sound play continuously, type **LOOP="true"** in the `EMBED` tag.

The Web browser displays the sound controls on the page.

- The user can click the **Play** button (⊡) to start the sound.

The embedded sound controls act like regular controls for playing, pausing, and stopping the sound.

Note: See Chapter 2 to learn more about viewing your HTML document as an offline Web page.

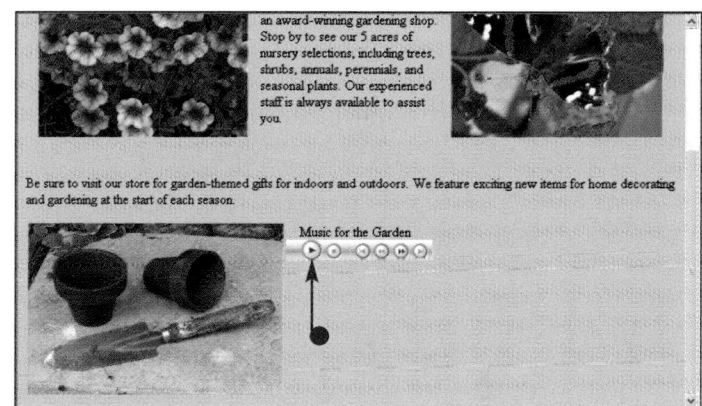

What audio file formats are common on the Web?

Audio file formats come in several flavors, and some formats are more popular on the Web than others. Here is a list of common audio formats supported by most browsers, plug-ins, and media players:

Audio Formats	
Format	**File Extension**
MP3 (MPEG-1, Layer III)	.mp3
MIDI (Musical Instrument Digital Interface)	.mid
AIFF (Audio Interchange File Format)	.aif
WAV (RIEFF WAVE)	.wav
WMA (Windows Media Audio)	.wma
RA (RealAudio)	.ra

Embed a Video File

You can use the `<EMBED>` tag to add an embedded video clip to your HTML page. Embedded videos play directly on your page. Playback controls also appear on the page, allowing the user to start and stop the video.

You can control the size of the video window that appears with an embedded video file. For example, you can set the width at 320 pixels and the height at 240 pixels.

1 Type **`<EMBED SRC="?">`** where you want to insert the video window on the page, replacing the *?* with the location and name of the video file.

by to see our 5 acres of nursery selections, including trees, shrubs, annuals, perennials, and seasonal plants. Our experienced staff is always available to assist you.</P><BR CLEAR="All">

<P>Be sure to visit our store for garden-themed gifts for indoors and outdoors. We feature exciting new items for home decorating and gardening at the start of each season.</P>

<IMG SRC="Garden_Supplies.jpg" WIDTH="300" HEIGHT="200" ALT="Image of Gardening Tool" ALIGN="left">
Music for the Garden
<EMBED SRC="classical1.mp3" WIDTH="170" HEIGHT="25" AUTOSTART="false" LOOP="true">
<BR CLEAR="all">

<HR SIZE="3" NOSHADE>

<H2>Dealing with Garden Pests</H2>

<P>Is your garden infested? Tired of battling aphids and other pests? You can find plenty of insects that help to control bad bugs in your garden, and our garden shop can order them for you. For example, did you know that the Praying Mantis is one of the most useful insects to reside in your garden. Here's an AVI movie clip to show you more:</P>
<EMBED SRC="Green_Mantis.avi">

</BODY>

</HTML>

2 Within the `<EMBED>` tag, type **`WIDTH="?"` `HEIGHT="?"`**, replacing *?* in both attributes with the width and height values you want to use for the size of the window.

by to see our 5 acres of nursery selections, including trees, shrubs, annuals, perennials, and seasonal plants. Our experienced staff is always available to assist you.</P><BR CLEAR="All">

<P>Be sure to visit our store for garden-themed gifts for indoors and outdoors. We feature exciting new items for home decorating and gardening at the start of each season.</P>

<IMG SRC="Garden_Supplies.jpg" WIDTH="300" HEIGHT="200" ALT="Image of Gardening Tool" ALIGN="left">
Music for the Garden
<EMBED SRC="classical1.mp3" WIDTH="170" HEIGHT="25" AUTOSTART="false" LOOP="true">
<BR CLEAR="all">

<HR SIZE="3" NOSHADE>

<H2>Dealing with Garden Pests</H2>

<P>Is your garden infested? Tired of battling aphids and other pests? You can find plenty of insects that help to control bad bugs in your garden, and our garden shop can order them for you. For example, did you know that the Praying Mantis is one of the most useful insects to reside in your garden. Here's an AVI movie clip to show you more:</P>
<EMBED SRC="Green_Mantis.avi" WIDTH="320" HEIGHT="240">

</BODY>

</HTML>

- To make the video play immediately when the page loads, type **AUTOSTART="true"** in the EMBED tag.

  To keep the video from playing immediately when the page loads, type **AUTOSTART="false"** in the EMBED tag.

- To make the video play continuously, type **LOOP="true"** in the EMBED tag.

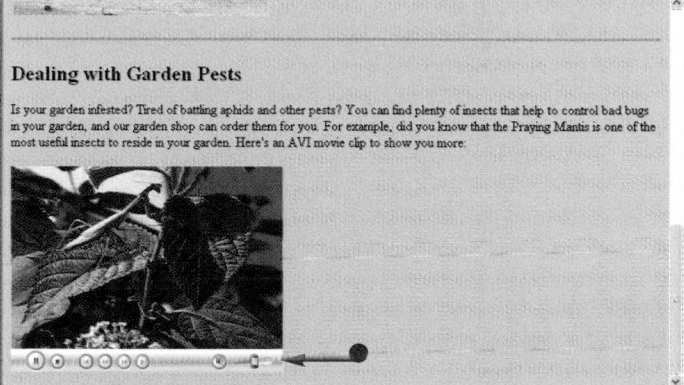

- The Web browser displays the embedded video window and playback controls on the page.

- The embedded controls act like regular controls for playing, pausing, and stopping the video.

Note: See Chapter 2 to learn more about viewing your HTML document as an offline Web page.

What video file formats are commonly found on the Web?
Here is a list of common video formats supported by many browsers, plug-ins, and media players:

Video Formats	
Format	**File Extension**
AVI (Audio/Video Interleaved)	.avi
QT (Apple QuickTime)	.qt
MOV (QuickTime)	.mov
MPG (Motion Picture Experts Group)	.mpg
RV (Real Video)	.rv
DCR (Macromedia Director)	.dcr

Embed a Flash Movie

You can add a Flash animation to your Web page. Using an ActiveX control number along with the OBJECT element, you can instruct the browser with the necessary information to load and play the Flash file.

Embed a Flash Movie

① Type **<OBJECT CLASSID="clsid: D27CDB6E-AE6D-11cf-96B8-4445535 40000"**.

② Type **CODEBASE="http://download. macromedia.com/pub/shockwave/cabs/ flash/swflash.cab#version=6,0,29,0"**.

③ Type **WIDTH="160" HEIGHT="120">**.

④ Type **<PARAM NAME="movie" VALUE="?"/>**, substituting the Flash filename for *?*.

⑤ Type a closing **</OBJECT>**.

● When the user displays your page, the embedded Flash movie plays.

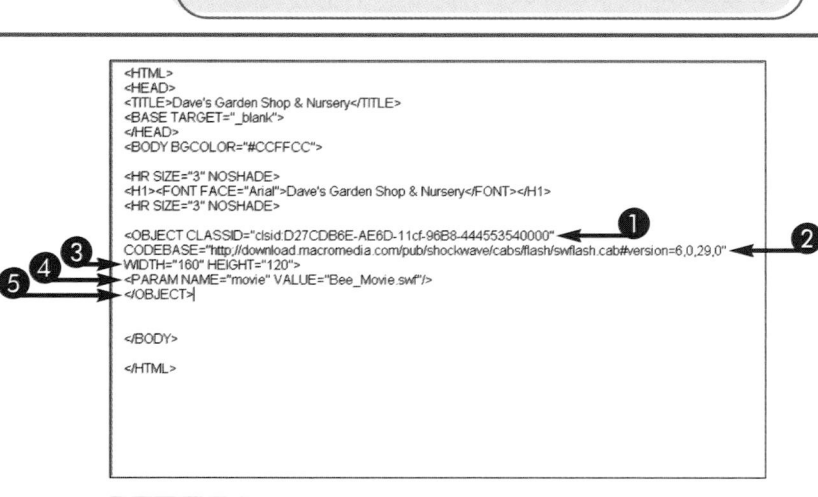

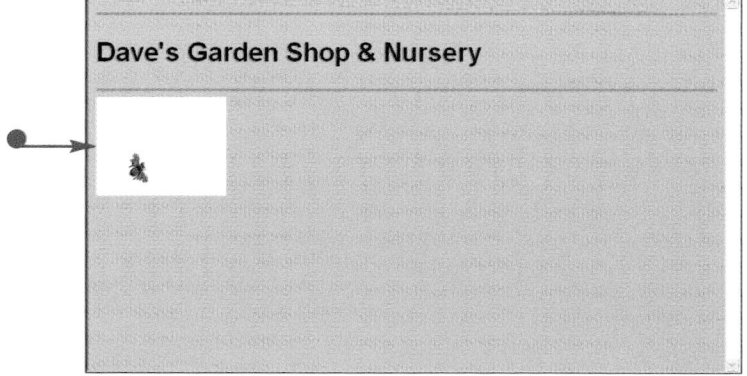

Dave's Garden Shop & Nursery

Set Up Background Audio

You can assign an audio clip to play in the background while users visit your page. Internet Explorer, both Windows and Mac versions, supports a nonstandard tag for playing a sound file automatically when a user displays your page.

Because the <BGSOUND> **element is not part of the HTML standard, you may not want to assign this coding unless you know the majority of your Web page audience uses Internet Explorer as its browser of choice.**

Set Up Background Audio

① Type **<BGSOUND SRC="?">** on your page, replacing the *?* with the location and name of the audio file.

```
<HTML>
<HEAD>
<TITLE>Dave's Garden Shop & Nursery</TITLE>
<BASE TARGET="_blank">
</HEAD>
<BODY BGCOLOR="#CCFFCC">
<BGSOUND SRC="classical1.mp3">      ①

<HR SIZE="3" NOSHADE>
<H1><FONT FACE="Arial">Dave's Garden Shop & Nursery</FONT></H1>
<HR SIZE="3" NOSHADE>

<CENTER><P><FONT SIZE="4"><B><I>Experts in gardening for over 40 years</I></B></FONT></P>
</CENTER>

<IMG SRC="Million_Bells2.jpg" ALIGN="Left" HSPACE="15">
<IMG SRC="Butterfly3.jpg" ALIGN="Right" HSPACE="15">

<P>We offer the finest selection of plants and planting materials, and an award-winning gardening shop. Stop
by to see our 5 acres of nursery selections, including trees, shrubs, annuals, perennials, and seasonal plants.
Our experienced staff is always available to assist you.</P><BR CLEAR="All">
<BR>

<P>Be sure to visit our store for garden-themed gifts for indoors and outdoors. We feature exciting new items
for home decorating and gardening at the start of each season.</P>

<IMG SRC="Garden_Supplies.jpg" WIDTH="300" HEIGHT="200" ALT="Image of Gardening Tool"
ALIGN="left">   
```

● To loop the sound to play continuously, type **LOOP="?"** within the <BGSOUND> tag, replacing *?* with the number of times you want the sound to loop.

You can also set the LOOP value to true to make the sound play continuously, **LOOP="true"**.

When the user displays your page in Internet Explorer, the background audio plays.

```
<HTML>
<HEAD>
<TITLE>Dave's Garden Shop & Nursery</TITLE>
<BASE TARGET="_blank">
</HEAD>
<BODY BGCOLOR="#CCFFCC">
<BGSOUND SRC="classical1.mp3" LOOP="3">

<HR SIZE="3" NOSHADE>
<H1><FONT FACE="Arial">Dave's Garden Shop & Nursery</FONT></H1>
<HR SIZE="3" NOSHADE>

<CENTER><P><FONT SIZE="4"><B><I>Experts in gardening for over 40 years</I></B></FONT></P>
</CENTER>

<IMG SRC="Million_Bells2.jpg" ALIGN="Left" HSPACE="15">
<IMG SRC="Butterfly3.jpg" ALIGN="Right" HSPACE="15">

<P>We offer the finest selection of plants and planting materials, and an award-winning gardening shop. Stop
by to see our 5 acres of nursery selections, including trees, shrubs, annuals, perennials, and seasonal plants.
Our experienced staff is always available to assist you.</P><BR CLEAR="All">
<BR>

<P>Be sure to visit our store for garden-themed gifts for indoors and outdoors. We feature exciting new items
for home decorating and gardening at the start of each season.</P>

<IMG SRC="Garden_Supplies.jpg" WIDTH="300" HEIGHT="200" ALT="Image of Gardening Tool"
ALIGN="left">   
```

Working with JavaScript

Looking for ways to add action and interest to your Web site? JavaScript can help you add interactivity to your HTML documents. This chapter shows you how to use JavaScripts, through a few examples, to make your pages more interesting to Web site visitors.

Understanding JavaScript **246**

**Understanding Script Events
and Handlers** **248**

Add JavaScript to a Web Page **250**

Create a JavaScript File **251**

Hide JavaScript **252**

Add Alternative Text **253**

Insert the Current Date and Time **254**

Display an Alert Message Box **255**

Display a Pop-Up Window **256**

**Customize the Status Bar Message
for a Link** **257**

Create an Image Rollover Effect **258**

Validate Form Data **260**

You can use scripts, such as those written in JavaScript, to add dynamic effects to your Web pages. Scripts can turn a static HTML page into an exciting, interactive page that is sure to attract Web visitors. You can use JavaScripts to display message boxes, change images when a user rolls a mouse over an area of the page, validate form information, and much more.

How Scripts Work

Scripts are little programs you can write to add interactivity to Web pages. Scripting instructions can activate when an event occurs, such as when a user clicks something on the page or moves the mouse pointer over an area of the page. Scripts can also activate automatically when the user downloads your page. Because scripts are written in programming languages, you need to know a little bit about programming if you want to write your own scripts. If you want to learn more about writing scripts, visit www.htmlgoodies.com/primers/jsp.

JavaScript

Most Web page scripts are written in the JavaScript language. JavaScript is supported by a vast majority of newer browsers. Originally developed by Netscape, JavaScript is widely used by Web developers to add action and interactivity to Web pages. If you do decide to add scripting to your pages, JavaScript is the best choice. JavaScript is case-sensitive and requires careful placement of quotes, single quotes, double quotes, and other punctuation, so use care when typing your scripts.

Client-Side and Server-Side Scripts

Because scripts require a program to read them, you have two options for reading Web page scripts: Web browser or Web server. Scripts read by the Web browser are called *client-side scripts*. Most scripts you use to add action to your Web page are client-side scripts. Scripts read by a Web server are called *server-side scripts*. If your Web site uses forms to collect information from visitors, you commonly use server-side scripts. Server-side scripts work with the server to help databases and other applications collect information from Web pages.

Scripting Tips

Many users turn off the JavaScript function in their browsers for security reasons. You can use the <NOSCRIPT> and </NOSCRIPT> tags to include alternative text about the script. For example, you might include a simple message like "Your browser does not support this script." It is also good policy to note your scripting language on your HTML document. You can use the <META> tag to identify the type of scripting language you use. The remaining sections of this chapter show you a few JavaScripts you can try out on your own pages.

Scripting Tools

You can create your own scripts using an HTML editor. Many editors, such as Macromedia Dreamweaver and Adobe GoLive offer built-in toolsets to help you create your own scripts without needing to know a lot about programming. You can also easily incorporate scripts that other users have written and add them to your own HTML documents.

Finding Prewritten Scripts

You can find numerous sites on the Internet that offer JavaScripts you can use on your own Web pages. Be sure to ask permission, if needed. For example, sites such as Java-Scripts.net (www.java-scripts.net), JavaScript City (www.javascriptcity.com), and The JavaScript Source (javascript.internet.com), offer free JavaScripts for Web pages.

Understanding Script Events and Handlers

When using JavaScript to add interactivity to your pages, it helps to understand when and why a script executes. Some scripts run as soon as the page downloads, while others require an action on the part of the Web page visitor. As the Web site developer, you decide when and how a script executes. You can use events and event handlers to control your scripts.

Events

Script *events* are any actions taken by a Web page visitor, such as clicking on an area of the page. The browser can also cause an event, such as loading a page, to occur. For example, mouse events include actions a user performs with a mouse, such as clicking, moving the mouse pointer over an object, or releasing the mouse button after clicking it. Keyboard events include key presses on a keyboard.

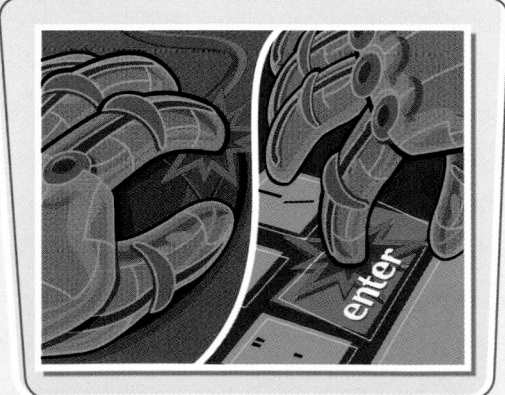

Event Handlers

You can determine what happens after an action by specifying an *event handler*. Event handlers associate an object or Web page element with an event. For example, you can use the onClick event handler to associate a Web page button with a mouse click. Event handlers are not added using the <SCRIPT> tags but, rather, appear within HTML element tags.

Scriptable Events

Event	Trigger
LOAD	Triggers when the page is loaded
UNLOAD	Triggers when the page is unloaded
MOUSEOVER	Triggers when the mouse moves over an object or area on the page
MOUSEOUT	Triggers when the mouse is no longer over an object or area on the page
MOUSEDOWN	Triggers when the mouse is clicked on an object
MOUSEUP	Triggers when the mouse button is released after being clicked
CLICK	Triggers when the user clicks and releases
KEYPRESS	Triggers when a keyboard key is pressed and released
KEYDOWN	Triggers when a keyboard keypress is pressed
KEYUP	Triggers when a keyboard keypress is released
SUBMIT	Triggers when a form button is clicked
RESET	Triggers when a reset form button is clicked

Event Handlers

Event Handler	Action
ONLOAD	A browser loads a page
ONUNLOAD	A browser unloads a page
ONMOUSEOVER	User positions the mouse over an element
ONMOUSEDOWN	User presses the mouse button
ONMOUSEUP	User releases the mouse button
ONMOUSEMOVE	User moves the mouse
ONMOUSEOUT	User moves the mouse away from an element
ONCLICK	User clicks an element
ONDBLCLICK	User double-clicks an element
ONKEYPRESS	User presses and releases a keyboard key
ONKEYDOWN	User presses a key
ONKEYUP	User releases a key
ONSUBMIT	User clicks a Submit button

Add JavaScript to a Web Page

JavaScripts are a great way to add interactivity to your Web pages. You can use the <SCRIPT> and </SCRIPT> tags to add JavaScript to your HTML document. The browser reads anything between the two tags as a script.

To learn more about writing your own JavaScripts, try one of these books: *JavaScript For Dummies, Beginning JavaScript,* or *JavaScript Visual Blueprint,* all from Wiley Publishing, Inc.

Add JavaScript to a Web Page

① Type **<SCRIPT LANGUAGE="javascript">** where you want to insert the script on the page.

② Type the code for the script you want to add.

In this example, the script tells the user the size of their monitor screen.

③ Type **</SCRIPT>** at the end of the script.

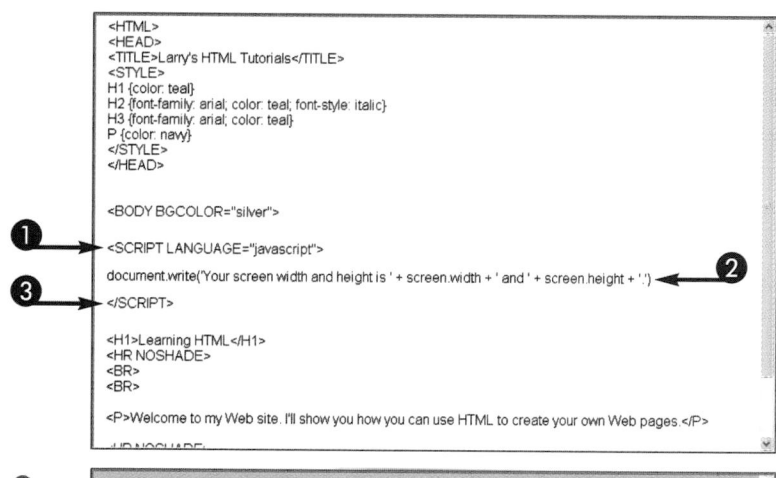

```
<HTML>
<HEAD>
<TITLE>Larry's HTML Tutorials</TITLE>
<STYLE>
H1 {color: teal}
H2 {font-family: arial; color: teal; font-style: italic}
H3 {font-family: arial; color: teal}
P {color: navy}
</STYLE>
</HEAD>

<BODY BGCOLOR="silver">

<SCRIPT LANGUAGE="javascript">

document.write('Your screen width and height is ' + screen.width + ' and ' + screen.height + '.')

</SCRIPT>

<H1>Learning HTML</H1>
<HR NOSHADE>
<BR>
<BR>

<P>Welcome to my Web site. I'll show you how you can use HTML to create your own Web pages.</P>
```

● The Web browser runs the script when the user views your page.

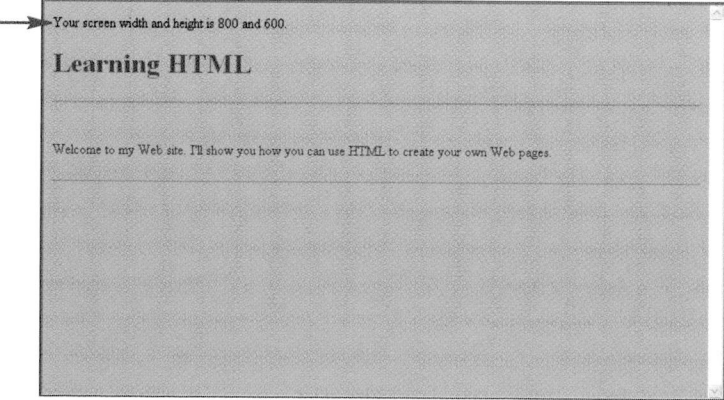

```
Your screen width and height is 800 and 600.

Learning HTML


Welcome to my Web site. I'll show you how you can use HTML to create your own Web pages.
```

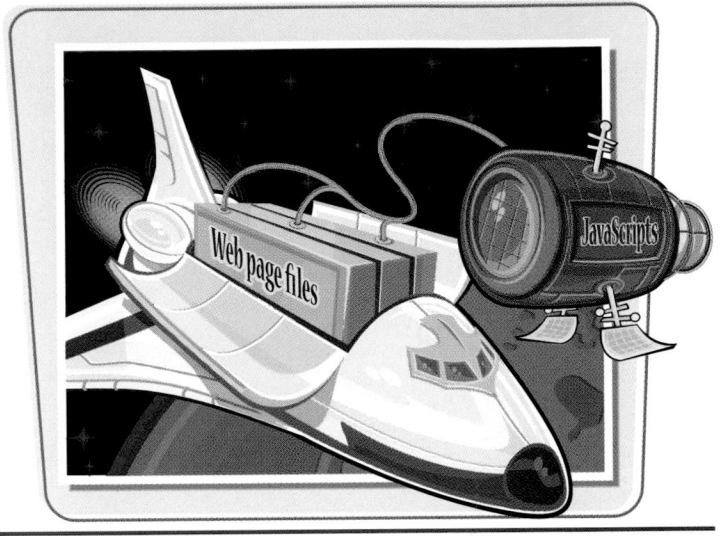

Many developers prefer to save their scripts in a separate text file and link the file to the Web page. Storing your scripts in a separate file can free up your HTML document to focus just on Web page content. When saving a JavaScript file, use the .js file extension.

When you publish your Web pages to a server, be sure to include the linked JavaScript file as part of your file upload. See Chapter 15 to learn more about publishing Web pages.

Create a JavaScript File

1 Create a new document in your text editor.

2 Type your JavaScript code.

Note: *You can find numerous free JavaScripts on the Internet. See the section "Understanding JavaScript" to learn more.*

3 Save the file using the .js file extension.

Note: *See Chapter 2 to learn how to create and save HTML documents.*

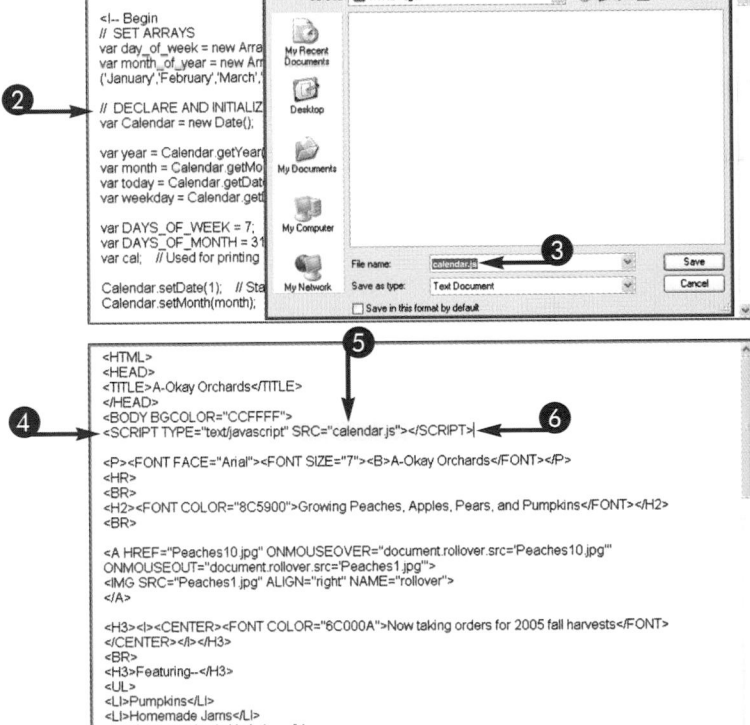

4 In your Web page document, click where you want to insert the script and type **<SCRIPT TYPE="text/javascript"**.

5 Type a blank space and type **SRC="?">**, replacing *?* with the location and name of the JavaScript file.

6 Type **</SCRIPT>**.

The JavaScript file is now linked to the Web page.

Hide JavaScript

You can hide your JavaScript coding from older Web browsers. Ordinarily, if a browser does not support JavaScript, it displays your script coding on the Web page instead of activating the script. To prevent this from happening, you can hide the script using the comment tags.

Hide JavaScript

1 Type **<!--** directly after the opening **<SCRIPT>** tag.

```
<HTML>
<HEAD>
<TITLE>A-Okay Orchards</TITLE>
</HEAD>
<BODY BGCOLOR="CCFFFF" ONLOAD="javascript:window.open('sale.html','Sale',HEIGHT=350,WIDTH=
350')">

<P><FONT FACE="Arial"><FONT SIZE="7"><B>A-Okay Orchards</FONT></P>
<HR>
<BR>
<H2><FONT COLOR="8C5900">Growing Peaches, Apples, Pears, and Pumpkins</FONT></H2>
<BR>

<SCRIPT TYPE="text/javascript">
<!--
document.write(Date())
</SCRIPT>

<IMG SRC="Peaches1.jpg" ALIGN="right">
<H3><I><CENTER><FONT COLOR="6C000A">Now taking orders for 2005 fall harvests</FONT>
</CENTER></I></H3>
<BR>
<H3>Featuring--</H3>
<UL>
<LI>Pumpkins</LI>
<LI>Homemade Jams</LI>
<LI>Numerous Apple Varieties:</LI>
  <LI >
```

2 Type **//-->** directly before the closing **</SCRIPT>** tag.

If an older browser that does not read scripts encounters your page, it does not display the script coding on the page.

You can use these tags to add any type of comments to your JavaScript.

```
<HTML>
<HEAD>
<TITLE>A-Okay Orchards</TITLE>
</HEAD>
<BODY BGCOLOR="CCFFFF" ONLOAD="javascript:window.open('sale.html','Sale',HEIGHT=350,WIDTH=
350')">

<P><FONT FACE="Arial"><FONT SIZE="7"><B>A-Okay Orchards</FONT></P>
<HR>
<BR>
<H2><FONT COLOR="8C5900">Growing Peaches, Apples, Pears, and Pumpkins</FONT></H2>
<BR>

<SCRIPT TYPE="text/javascript">
<!--
document.write(Date())
//-->
</SCRIPT>

<IMG SRC="Peaches1.jpg" ALIGN="right">
<H3><I><CENTER><FONT COLOR="6C000A">Now taking orders for 2005 fall harvests</FONT>
</CENTER></I></H3>
<BR>
<H3>Featuring--</H3>
<UL>
<LI>Pumpkins</LI>
<LI>Homemade Jams</LI>
<LI>Numerous Apple Varieties:</LI>
```

252

Add Alternative Text

Some users turn off JavaScript in their Web browsers for security reasons. You can provide alternative text to describe what the user is missing or to remind users that their scripting feature is turned off.

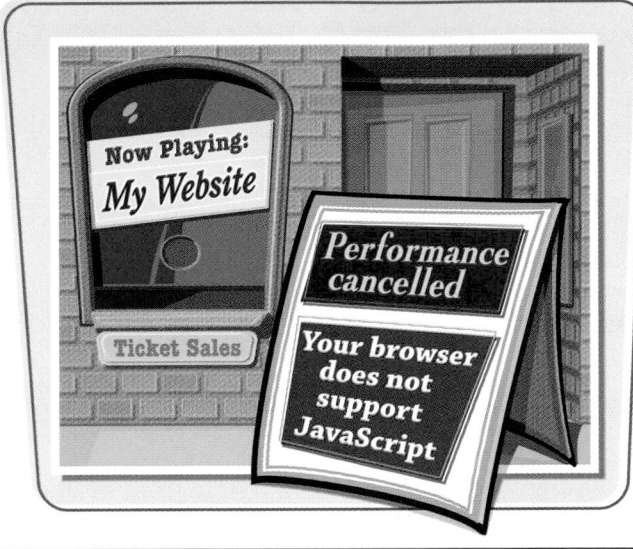

Add Alternative Text

1 Type **<NOSCRIPT>** below the </SCRIPT> tag.

2 Type your alternative text message.

3 Type **</NOSCRIPT>**.

Note: *You can format the alternative text. See Chapter 3 to learn how to add formatting attributes to HTML text.*

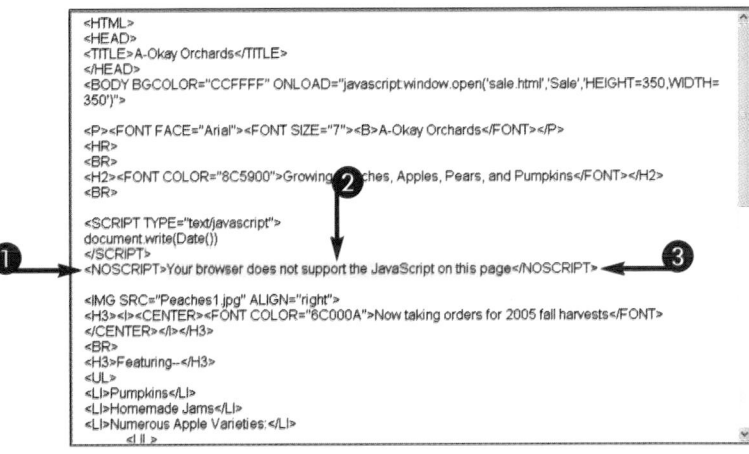

● If the browser's script feature is turned off, the browser displays your alternative text.

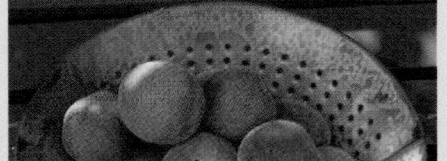

Insert the Current Date and Time

You can use JavaScript to insert the current date and time on your Web page. This can help your page seem current and up-to-date.

Insert the Current Date and Time

① Click where you want to insert the date and time on the page and add a new line.

② Type **\<SCRIPT TYPE="text/javascript"\>**.

③ Type **document.write(Date())**.

④ Type **\</SCRIPT\>**.

You may prefer to keep your script on one line or break it onto multiple lines to make it easier to read.

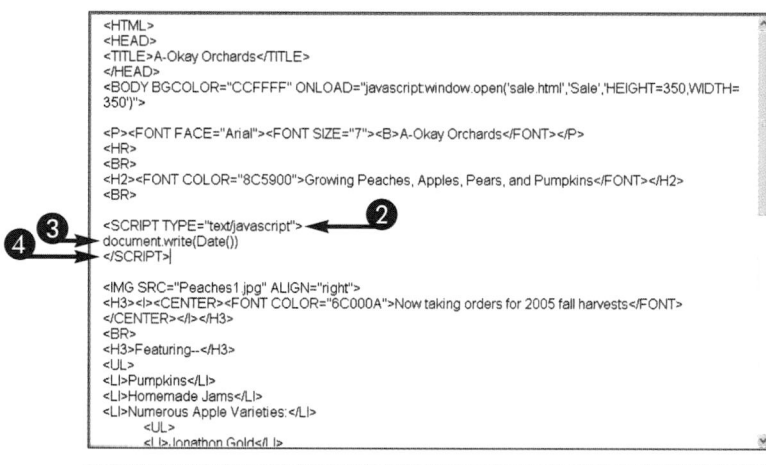

```
<HTML>
<HEAD>
<TITLE>A-Okay Orchards</TITLE>
</HEAD>
<BODY BGCOLOR="CCFFFF" ONLOAD="javascript:window.open('sale.html','Sale',HEIGHT=350,WIDTH=350)">

<P><FONT FACE="Arial"><FONT SIZE="7"><B>A-Okay Orchards</FONT></P>
<HR>
<BR>
<H2><FONT COLOR="8C5900">Growing Peaches, Apples, Pears, and Pumpkins</FONT></H2>
<BR>

<SCRIPT TYPE="text/javascript">
document.write(Date())
</SCRIPT>

<IMG SRC="Peaches1.jpg" ALIGN="right">
<H3><I><CENTER><FONT COLOR="6C000A">Now taking orders for 2005 fall harvests</FONT>
</CENTER></I></H3>
<BR>
<H3>Featuring--</H3>
<UL>
<LI>Pumpkins</LI>
<LI>Homemade Jams</LI>
<LI>Numerous Apple Varieties:</LI>
    <UL>
    <LI>Jonathon Gold</LI>
```

● The Web browser displays the current date and time.

A-Okay Orchards

Growing Peaches, Apples, Pears, and Pumpkins

Mon Nov 08 12:23:30 2004

Now taking orders for 2005 fall harvests

Featuring--
- Pumpkins
- Homemade Jams
- Numerous Apple Varieties:
    - Jonathon Gold
    - Red Delicious
    - Golden Delicious

You can use JavaScript to display an alert message box on your Web page. For example, you might use alert messages to provide special instructions about your site or to alert the user to any important information. After the user reads the message, he or she can close the box.

Display an Alert Message Box

① Type **<SCRIPT TYPE="text/javascript">**.

② Type **alert('?')**, replacing the *?* with the message text you want to appear in the box.

③ Type **</SCRIPT>** to end the JavaScript code.

The placement of your script on the page determines its order of appearance during the page download.

Place it at the top to load first, or at the bottom to load last.

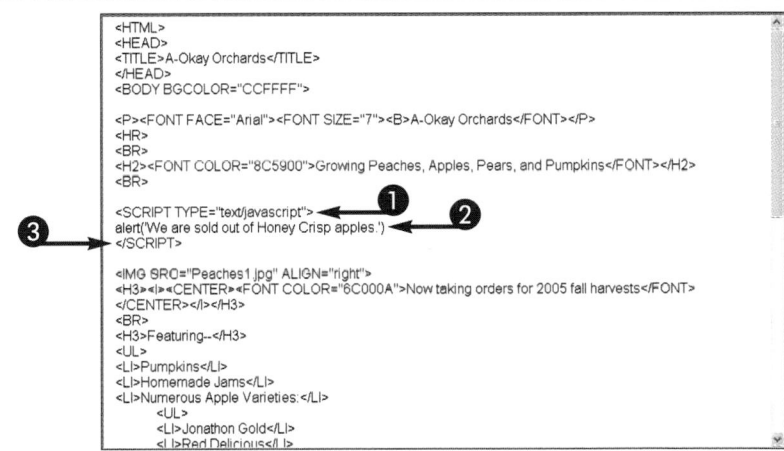

When the user displays your page in a browser, the alert message box appears.

● The user can click here to close the box.

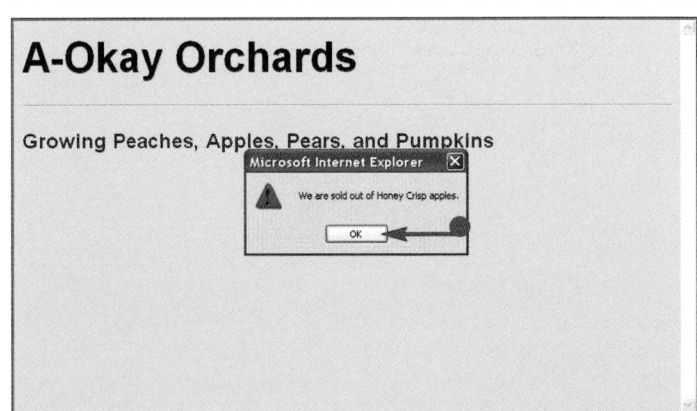

Display a Pop-Up Window

You can use JavaScript to display a pop-up window on your Web page. Pop-up windows are a great way of alerting your Web site visitors to important news about your site, announcing a sale, or describing an upcoming event. The message that appears in the window is actually another Web page created just for the pop-up window.

The pop-up window references a separate HTML file. You will need to create the file before writing the JavaScript. See Chapter 2 to learn more about building HTML documents.

Display a Pop-Up Window

① Within the `<BODY>` tag, type **ONLOAD="javascript:window.open('?',**.

Replace *?* with the location and name of the Web page you want to appear in the pop-up box.

② Type **'?',** replacing *?* with a name for the window.

③ Type **'HEIGHT=?, WIDTH=?')"**, replacing the *?* with a height and width size, measured in pixels, for the pop-up window.

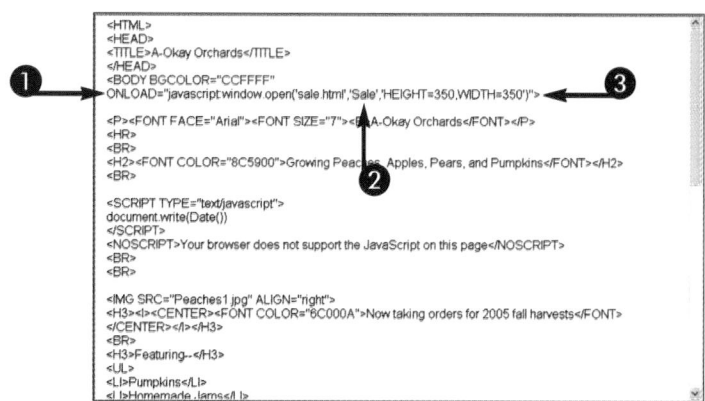

When the user displays your page in a browser, the pop-up window appears.

● The user can click here to close the window.

Note: *Be very careful about the punctuation you type in a JavaScript. A missed comma or quote can cause an error in your script.*

Ordinarily, when the user moves his or her mouse pointer over a link on your page, the browser's status bar displays the address of the link. You can customize the text that appears in the status bar for a link. For example, you might shorten a complex address to something simpler or create your own text message to appear instead.

Always be careful about typing single quotes and double quotes in JavaScript code. Do not inadvertently leave any spaces unless the code requires it. A mistype can cause problems with your script.

Customize the Status Bar Message for a Link

① Within the `<A>` tag for the link you want to change, type **ONMOUSEOVER="window.status=**.

② Type **'** followed by the status bar message text, ending with **'**.

Anything you type between the single quotes appears in the status bar.

③ Type **;return true"**.

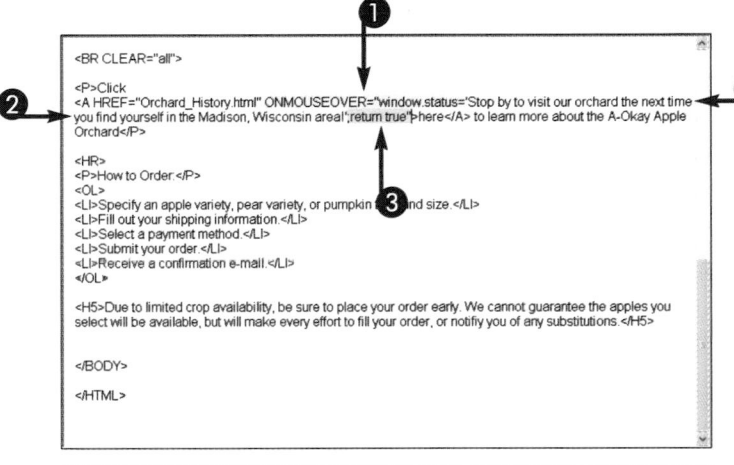

```
<BR CLEAR="all">

<P>Click
<A HREF="Orchard_History.html" ONMOUSEOVER="window.status='Stop by to visit our orchard the next time
you find yourself in the Madison, Wisconsin area!';return true">here</A> to learn more about the A-Okay Apple
Orchard</P>

<HR>
<P>How to Order:</P>
<OL>
<LI>Specify an apple variety, pear variety, or pumpkin type and size.</LI>
<LI>Fill out your shipping information.</LI>
<LI>Select a payment method.</LI>
<LI>Submit your order.</LI>
<LI>Receive a confirmation e-mail.</LI>
</OL>

<H5>Due to limited crop availability, be sure to place your order early. We cannot guarantee the apples you
select will be available, but will make every effort to fill your order, or notify you of any substitutions.</H5>


</BODY>

</HTML>
```

● When the user moves the mouse pointer (👆) over the link, the status bar displays your custom text.

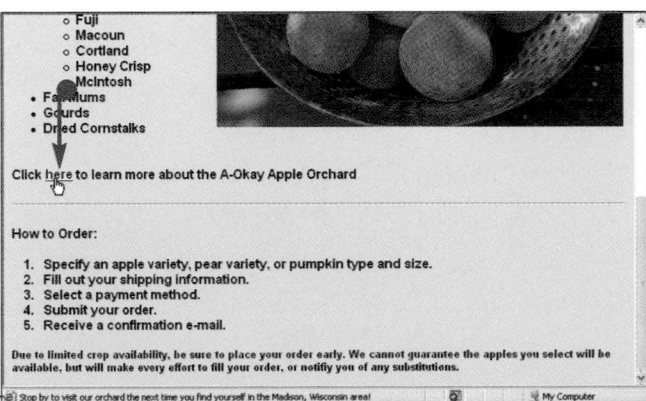

Create an Image Rollover Effect

You can use JavaScript to create an image rollover effect. When the user moves the mouse over the image on the Web page, it is suddenly replaced with a different image. When the user moves the mouse pointer off the image, the image returns to the original image. The image rollover is actually a link to another image file.

To create an image rollover, you must add a link to a second image and type two mouse event handlers on your HTML document. The effect works best if both images share the same dimensions. To learn more about setting image size, see Chapter 7.

Create an Image Rollover Effect

① To add an image to your page, type **<IMG SRC="?"**, replacing the *?* with the name and location of the image you want to appear on the page.

If the image already appears on the page, you can skip to step **2** to add the NAME attribute.

② Type a blank space and then **NAME="rollover">**.

```
<HTML>
<HEAD>
<TITLE>A-Okay Orchards</TITLE>
</HEAD>
<BODY BGCOLOR="CCFFFF"
ONLOAD="javascript:window.open('sale.html','Sale','HEIGHT=350,WIDTH=350')">

<P><FONT FACE="Arial"><FONT SIZE="7"><B>A-Okay Orchards</FONT></P>
<HR>
<BR>
<H2><FONT COLOR="8C5900">Growing Peaches, Apples, Pears, and Pumpkins</FONT></H2>
<BR>

<IMG SRC="Peaches1.jpg" ALIGN="right" NAME="rollover">

<H3><I><CENTER><FONT COLOR="6C000A">Now taking orders for 2005 fall harvests</FONT>
</CENTER></I></H3>
<BR>
<H3>Featuring--</H3>
<UL>
<LI>Pumpkins</LI>
<LI>Homemade Jams</LI>
<LI>Numerous Apple Varieties:</LI>
    <UL>
    <LI>Jonathon Gold</LI>
    <LI>Red Delicious</LI>
    <LI>Golden Delicious</LI>
    <LI>Fuji</LI>
```

③ Before the <IMG> tag, type **<A HREF="?">**, replacing the *?* with the name and location of the image you want to replace the existing image when the user rolls over the picture.

④ After the <IMG> tag, type **</A>**.

```
<HTML>
<HEAD>
<TITLE>A-Okay Orchards</TITLE>
</HEAD>
<BODY BGCOLOR="CCFFFF"
ONLOAD="javascript:window.open('sale.html','Sale','HEIGHT=350,WIDTH=350')">

<P><FONT FACE="Arial"><FONT SIZE="7"><B>A-Okay Orchards</FONT></P>
<HR>
<BR>
<H2><FONT COLOR="8C5900">Growing Peaches, Apples, Pears, and Pumpkins</FONT></H2>
<BR>

<A HREF="Peaches10.jpg">
<IMG SRC="Peaches1.jpg" ALIGN="right" NAME="rollover">
</A>

<H3><I><CENTER><FONT COLOR="6C000A">Now taking orders for 2005 fall harvests</FONT>
</CENTER></I></H3>
<BR>
<H3>Featuring--</H3>
<UL>
<LI>Pumpkins</LI>
<LI>Homemade Jams</LI>
<LI>Numerous Apple Varieties:</LI>
    <UL>
    <LI>Jonathon Gold</LI>
    <LI>Red Delicious</LI>
```

⑤ Within the <A> tag, type
ONMOUSEOVER="document.rollover.src='?'",
replacing the *?* with the name and location of the
image you want to replace the existing image when
the user rolls over the picture.

⑥ Type a space, and then
ONMOUSEOUT="document.rollover.src='?'",
replacing the *?* with the name of the original image.

Note: Be very careful not to leave out any single quotes in the script.

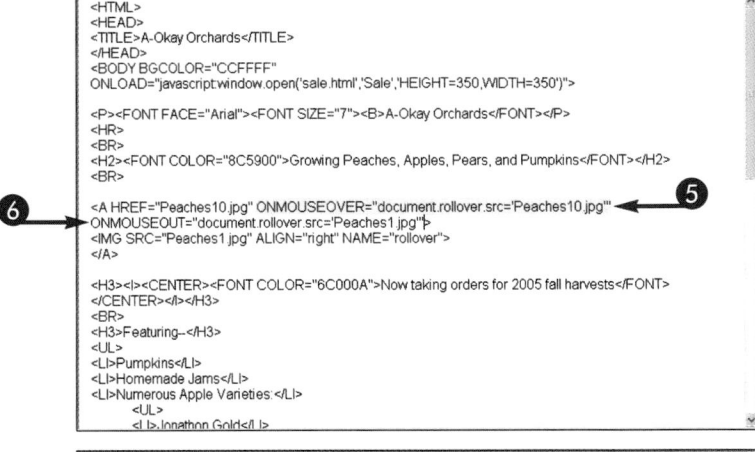

```
<HTML>
<HEAD>
<TITLE>A-Okay Orchards</TITLE>
</HEAD>
<BODY BGCOLOR="CCFFFF"
ONLOAD="javascript:window.open('sale.html','Sale',HEIGHT=350,WIDTH=350')">

<P><FONT FACE="Arial"><FONT SIZE="7"><B>A-Okay Orchards</FONT></P>
<HR>
<BR>
<H2><FONT COLOR="8C5900">Growing Peaches, Apples, Pears, and Pumpkins</FONT></H2>
<BR>

<A HREF="Peaches10.jpg" ONMOUSEOVER="document.rollover.src='Peaches10.jpg'"
ONMOUSEOUT="document.rollover.src='Peaches1.jpg'">
<IMG SRC="Peaches1.jpg" ALIGN="right" NAME="rollover">
</A>

<H3><I><CENTER><FONT COLOR="6C000A">Now taking orders for 2005 fall harvests</FONT>
</CENTER></I></H3>
<BR>
<H3>Featuring--</H3>
<UL>
<LI>Pumpkins</LI>
<LI>Homemade Jams</LI>
<LI>Numerous Apple Varieties:</LI>
    <UL>
    <LI>Jonathon Gold</LI>
```

● When the user moves 👆 over the image, the Web
browser displays the second image you specified.

TIP

How can I instruct the browser to speed up image viewing in my rollover effect?
You can instruct your browser to load both rollover images in the cache to speed things up.
The *cache* is a storage area on your hard drive that contains data and programs for your
computer to easily access. You can write another JavaScript to instruct the browser to load
both images into the browser cache, making the rollover effect seem instantaneous. Write
the following script in a separate text file:

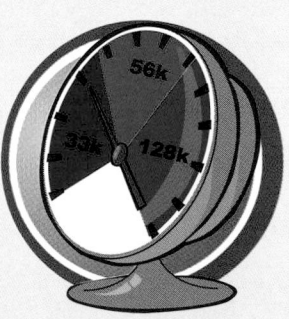

```
LABEL=new Image(h,w)
LABEL.SRC="image.url"
```

Replace *LABEL* with an actual label name for the image, and replace the *h,w* with the
height and width values for the image. Save the file and return to the HTML document.

In the HTML document, add the following script to the <HEAD> tags:

```
<SCRIPT TYPE="text/javascript" language="javascript"
src="filename.js">
</SCRIPT>
```

Replace *filename* with the script file you created.

Validate Form Data

You can use JavaScript to help prompt users on how to enter data into a Web page form. Called form validation, the scripts display prompt boxes instructing the user of any errors. For example, if the user types the wrong data type into a form field, you can display a prompt box alerting the user to the problem.

To learn more about creating Web page forms, see Chapter 11.

Please type numbers, not letters.

Enter your Zip Code:
24368

Validate Form Data

VALIDATE INPUT CHARACTERS

1 In the `<INPUT>` or `<TEXTAREA>` tag you want to validate, type **ONCHANGE="var pattern=/[?]/;**, replacing the *?* with the characters the user is not allowed to enter into the form.

2 Type a space and **if (pattern.test(this.value)) alert('?')"**, replacing the *?* with the error message text you want to display.

In this example, the value prevents users from entering numbers into the form field.

● If the user enters the wrong data type, the validation prompt box appears.

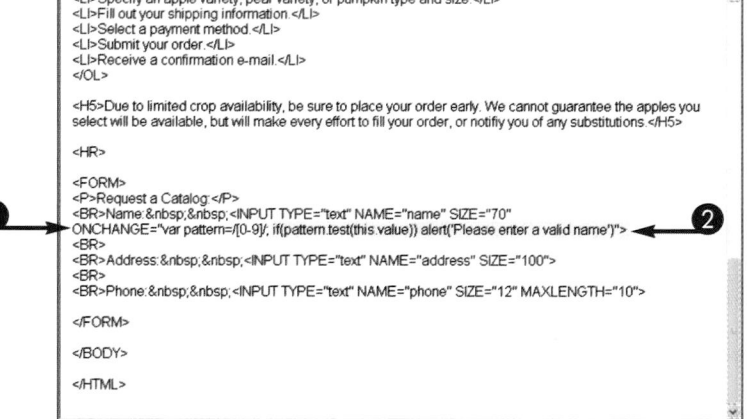

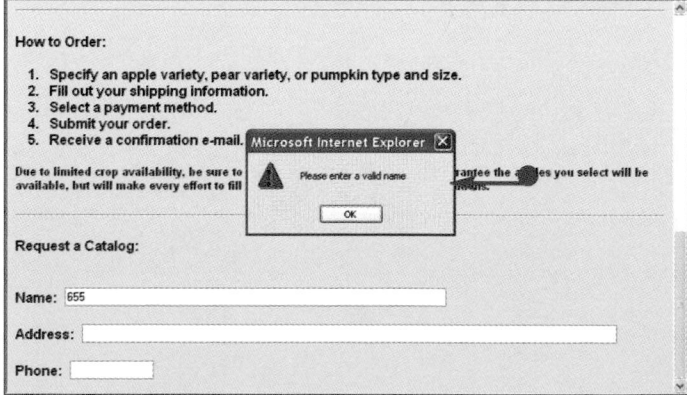

VALIDATE MINIMUM LENGTH

1 In the `<INPUT>` or `<TEXTAREA>` tag you want to validate, type **ONCHANGE="if (this.value.length<?)**, replacing the *?* with the minimum number of characters allowed for the form field.

To set a maximum number, type **>?**, replacing the *?* with the maximum number of characters allowed.

2 Type a space and **alert('?')"**, replacing the *?* with the error message text you want to display.

● If the user exceeds the maximum or has fewer than the minimum number of characters allowed, the validation prompt box appears.

```
<LI>Specify an apple variety, pear variety, or pumpkin type and size.</LI>
<LI>Fill out your shipping information.</LI>
<LI>Select a payment method.</LI>
<LI>Submit your order.</LI>
<LI>Receive a confirmation e-mail.</LI>
</OL>

<H5>Due to limited crop availability, be sure to place your order early. We cannot guarantee the apples you
select will be available, but will make every effort to fill your order, or notify you of any substitutions.</H5>

<HR>

<FORM>
<P>Request a Catalog:</P>
<BR>Name:  <INPUT TYPE="text" NAME="name" SIZE="70" ONCHANGE="var pattern=/[0-9]/; if
(pattern.test(this.value)) alert('Please enter a valid name')">
<BR>
<BR>Address:  <INPUT TYPE="text" NAME="address" SIZE="100">
<BR>
<BR>Phone:  <INPUT TYPE="text" NAME="phone" SIZE="12" MAXLENGTH="10"
ONCHANGE="if (this.value.length<10) alert('Please include your area code')">

</FORM>

</BODY>

</HTML>
```

How to Order:

1. Specify an apple variety, pear variety, or pumpkin type and size.
2. Fill out your shipping information.
3. Select a payment method.
4. Submit your order.
5. Receive a confirmation e-mail.

Due to limited crop availability, be sure to   guarantee the apples you select will be
available, but will make every effort to fill

Microsoft Internet Explorer

⚠ Please include your area code

OK

Request a Catalog:

Name:

Address:

Phone: 555-1230

TIPS

What characters can I control in my form validations?

You can control whether a user is allowed to type upper- or lowercase letters, numbers, and spacing. For example, if you want the user to type only numbers into a field, you can specify characters in the pattern value in step **1**. If you want to limit both upper- and lowercase letters, you must enter both values separately. Use this table to help you enter the correct characters for your form fields:

Value	Users Cannot Enter
A-Z	Uppercase letters
a-z	Lowercase letters
0-9	Any number
\d	Any number
\s	Any spacing
\w	Any letters, numbers, or the underscore character

Where can I find more data validation scripts?

You can find more JavaScripts for validating form data at the following Web sites: javascript.internet.com, www.javascripts.com, www.houseofscripts.com, and www .free-javascripts.com.

14

Adding Extra Touches

Are you ready to add a few extra touches to your Web pages? This chapter shows you how to apply a few complicated features to your HTML documents.

Insert Text over an Image 264

Add ToolTips to Web Page Elements 266

Add a Java Applet 267

Add a Scrolling Marquee 268

Create an Image Map 270

Create Thumbnail Images 274

Automatically Load Another Web Page 276

Insert Text over an Image

You can make text appear on top of an image on your Web page. For example, you may want to superimpose a caption over a photo. You can create this technique using a simple table.

Insert Text over an Image

① Create a table by typing **<TABLE BORDER="0" CELLPADDING="0" CELLSPACING="0">**.

② Start a new line and type **<TR>**.

③ On a new line, type **<TD WIDTH="?" HEIGHT="?"** to create a cell the same size as the image you want to use, replacing *?* with the width and height of the image.

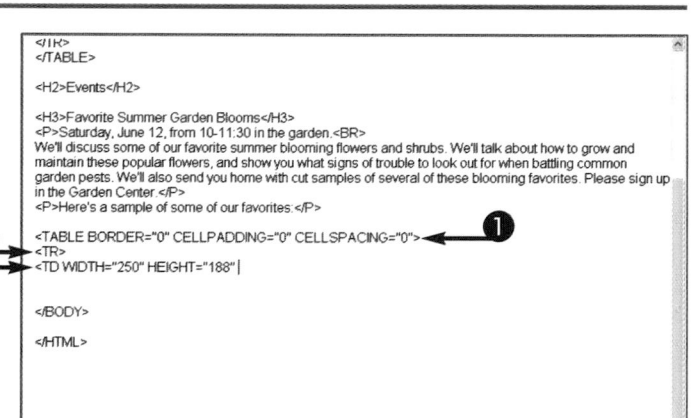

④ Type a space and type **BACKGROUND="?"**, replacing *?* with the name and location of the image.

⑤ Type a space and **VALIGN="?">**, replacing *?* with a vertical alignment for the image (**top**, **middle**, or **bottom**).

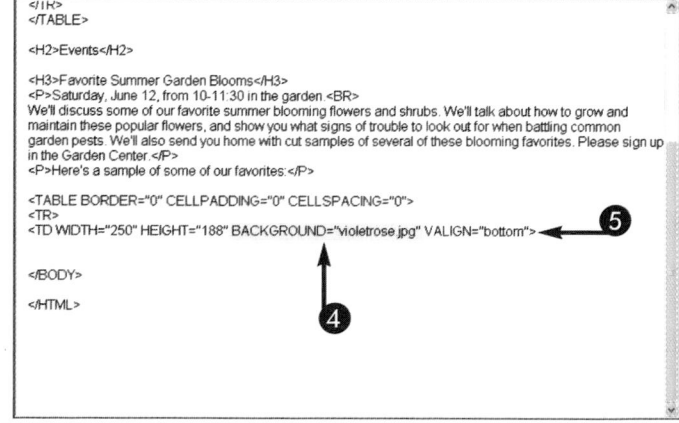

6 Type the text you want to superimpose over the image.

● You can add any formatting tags to the text as needed. For example, you may need to change the text color so it is visible against the image.

7 Type **</TD>** to close the cell.

You can add more cells to the table, as needed.

8 Type **</TR>** to complete the row.

9 Type **</TABLE>**.

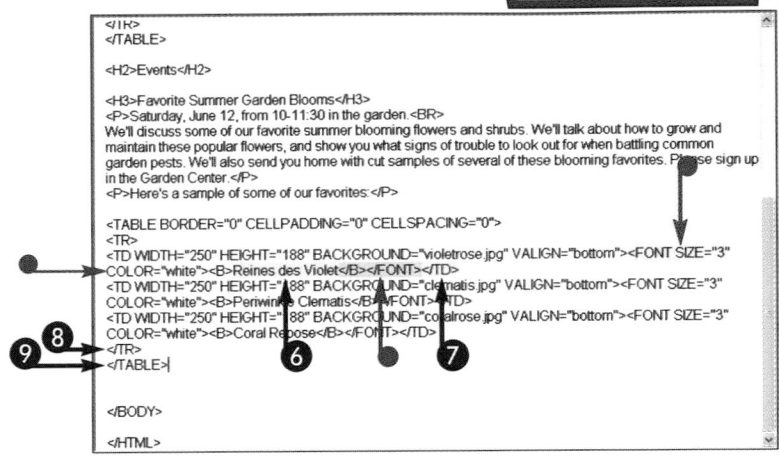

The Web browser displays the text over the image.

In this example, the table format displays three images with superimposed text.

Note: *You may need to change your text color to make it legible over the image. See Chapter 4 to learn more.*

Note: *See Chapter 9 to learn more about creating tables.*

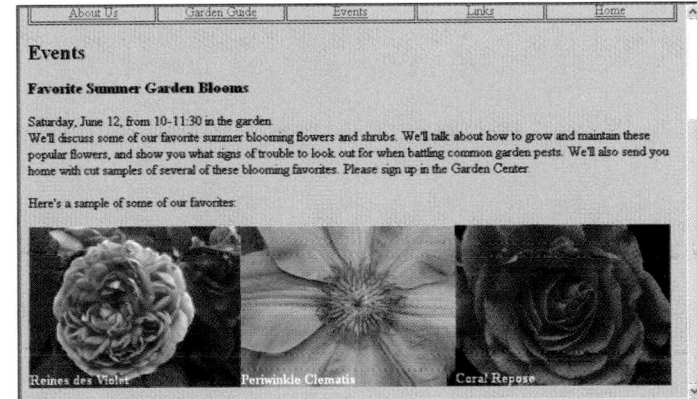

TIPS

Can I use this technique to create a navigation bar?

Yes. Inserting text over an image using a table framework is a good way to build your own navigation bar. Simply add links to the text you add in step **6**. Be very careful your link text is legible against the image background. You can change the text color and size, as needed. See Chapter 4 to learn more.

How do I turn an image into a watermark on my Web page?

You can add an image to the BACKGROUND property and set it as fixed. This keeps the image in place while the remaining Web page elements are scrollable. Use this code to create a watermark:

```
<BODY
BACKGROUND="imagefile.jpg"
BGPROPERTIES="fixed">
```

As with any image that underlies text, you may need to change the text color to make sure it is legible against the background image.

Add ToolTips to Web Page Elements

You can add ToolTips to your Web page elements to provide information about the element. ToolTips are small boxes that contain text. When the user moves the mouse pointer over the element, the ToolTip box appears.

The `TITLE` attribute does not work with the `<BASE>`, `<BASEFONT>`, `<HEAD>`, `<HTML>`, `<META>`, `<PARAM>`, `<SCRIPT>`, **or** `<TITLE>` **tags.**

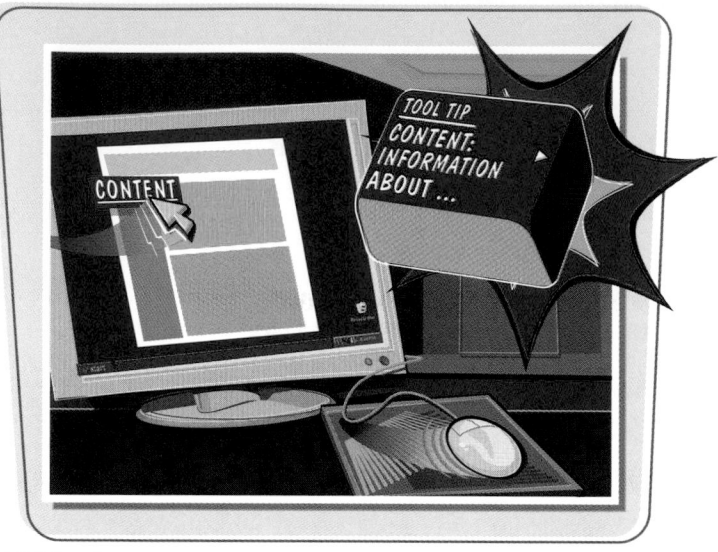

Add ToolTips to Web Page Elements

1 Click inside the element tag to which you want to add a ToolTip.

2 Type **TITLE="?"**, replacing *?* with the text you want to appear in the ToolTip box.

```
<LI>Professional planting and yard maintenance services</LI>
<LI>Free planting consulting</LI>
</UL>

<P>Be sure to visit our store for garden-themed gifts for indoors and outdoors. We feature exciting new items
for home decorating and gardening at the start of each season. We go all out for autumn and the Christmas
holidays, featuring decorative items, great gifts for the home or gardener, artifical Christmas trees, and much
more. Be sure to add us to your list of holiday stops, and don't miss our holiday open house, November 11th!
</P>

<IMG SRC="Garden_Supplies.jpg" WIDTH="300" HEIGHT="200" ALT="Image of Gardening Tool">
<BR CLEAR="all">
<BR>

<P>Click <A HREF="classical1.mp3" TITLE="Debussy: Claire de Lune">here</A> to listen to a selection from
our gardening music collection. Our gardening shop has a wide variety of gift selections, including beautiful
music CDs, and nature DVDs.</P>

</BODY>

</HTML>
```

When the user moves the mouse pointer over the element, the ToolTip box appears.

● In this example, the ToolTip appears with a link.

You can add Java applets to your Web pages to add animation and interactivity. Java applets are programs written in the Java programming language.

You can find numerous Java applets on the Web that you can download for free. The Java Boutique (www.javaboutique.internet.com), and the JavaShareware.com site (www .javashareware.com) are good places to start. You can also conduct a Web search to find more free Java applets.

Add a Java Applet

① Click where you want to insert the applet and type **<APPLET CODE="?">**, replacing *?* with the location and name of the applet.

● Optionally, to control the size of the applet window, type **WIDTH="?" HEIGHT="?"** within the <APPLET> tag, replacing *?* with width and height values.

● You can also add alternative text for browsers that do not run Java applets.

② Type **</APPLET>**.

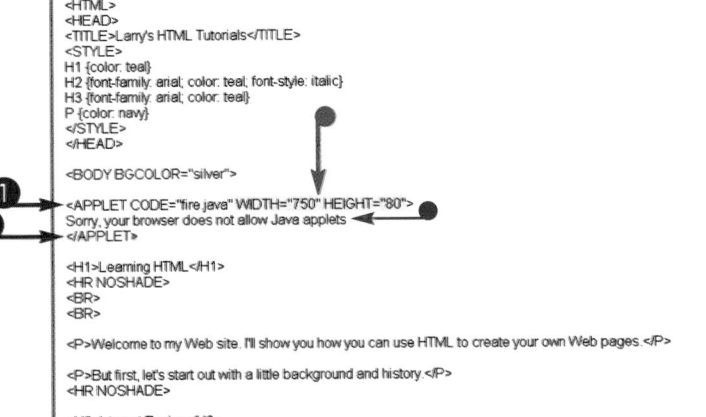

● The Web browser runs the Java applet when the user views your page.

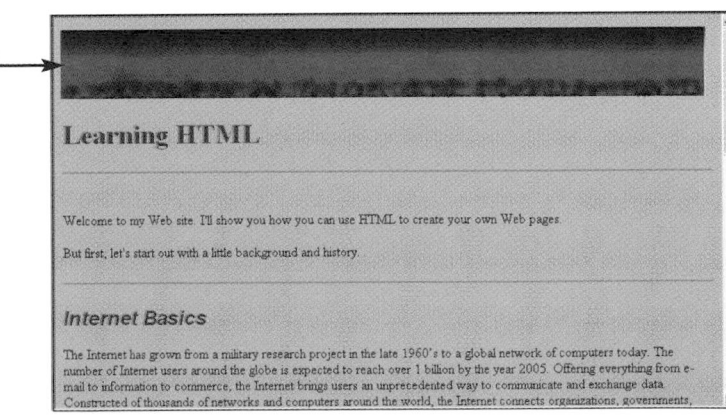

Add a Scrolling Marquee

You can use the `<MARQUEE>` tag to create a marquee that scrolls or slides across the page, much like a stock ticker. This technique is a great way to advertise a product or draw attention to special information.

The `<MARQUEE>` can scroll, slide, or alternate between the two behaviors. You can also control the direction of the scrolling effect and set the effect to occur a specified number of times, or to loop indefinitely. You can even control the number of milliseconds between the repeating message.

Add a Scrolling Marquee

① Add a new line where you want the marquee to appear and type **<MARQUEE** followed by a space.

② Type **BEHAVIOR="?"**, replacing *?* with the scrolling behavior you want to assign (**scroll**, **slide**, or **alternate**).

Note: The behavior you choose dictates which attributes you need to include.

③ Type a space, and then **DIRECTION="left"** or **DIRECTION="right"**.

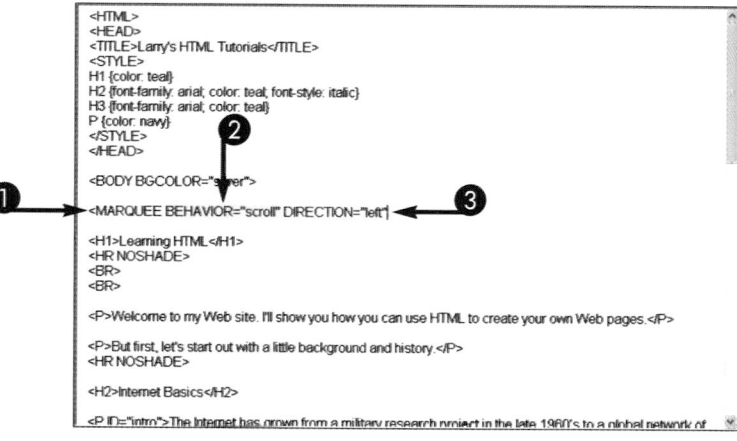

④ Type a space and type **LOOP="?"**, replacing *?* with the number of times you want the message to loop, or type **infinite** to loop indefinitely.

⑤ Type a space, and then **SCROLLAMOUNT="?"**, replacing *?* with the number of pixels you want to move at a time.

This attribute controls the speed of the message.

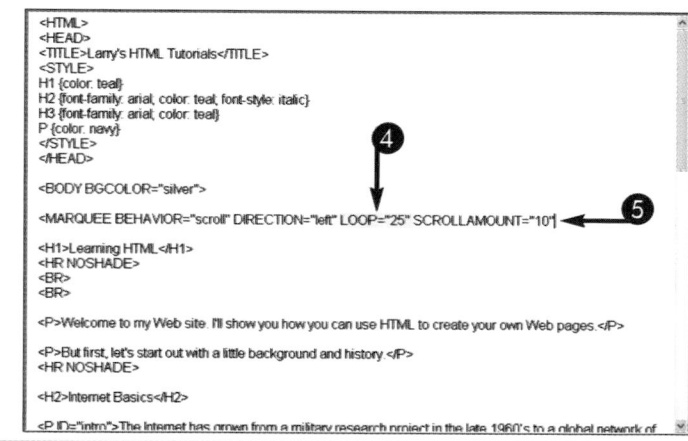

6 Type a space, and then **SCROLLDELAY="?">**, replacing *?* with the number of milliseconds you want to elapse before the message repeats the scrolling effect.

7 Type the marquee text.

You can add formatting tags to the text, as needed.

8 Type **</MARQUEE>**.

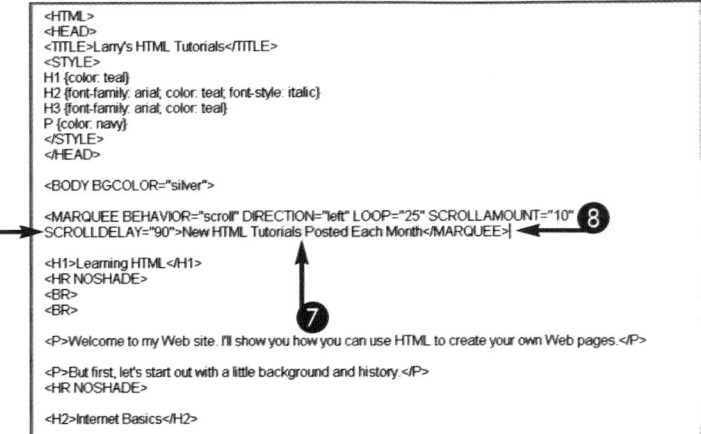

```
<HTML>
<HEAD>
<TITLE>Larry's HTML Tutorials</TITLE>
<STYLE>
H1 {color: teal}
H2 {font-family: arial; color: teal; font-style: italic}
H3 {font-family: arial; color: teal}
P {color: navy}
</STYLE>
</HEAD>

<BODY BGCOLOR="silver">

<MARQUEE BEHAVIOR="scroll" DIRECTION="left" LOOP="25" SCROLLAMOUNT="10"
SCROLLDELAY="90">New HTML Tutorials Posted Each Month</MARQUEE>

<H1>Learning HTML</H1>
<HR NOSHADE>
<BR>
<BR>

<P>Welcome to my Web site. I'll show you how you can use HTML to create your own Web pages.</P>

<P>But first, let's start out with a little background and history.</P>
<HR NOSHADE>

<H2>Internet Basics</H2>
```

The Web browser displays a scrolling marquee.

● In this example, the marquee text is formatted and includes a color background.

Larry's HTML TUTORIALS

New HTML Tutorials Posted Each Month

Learning HTML

Welcome to my Web site. I'll show you how you can use HTML to create your own Web pages.

But first, let's start out with a little background and history.

Internet Basics

The Internet has grown from a military research project in the late 1960's to a global network of computers today. The number of Internet users around the globe is expected to reach over 1 billion by the year 2005. Offering everything from e-mail to information to commerce, the Internet brings users an unprecedented way to communicate and exchange data. Constructed of thousands of networks and computers around the world, the Internet connects organizations, governments,

TIPS

How do I change the size of my marquee?

You can use the WIDTH and HEIGHT attributes to adjust the size of the marquee. You can set the width and height using pixels as your measurement, or you can set the size based on a percentage of the browser window. Simply add the WIDTH and HEIGHT attributes to the <MARQUEE> tag. Changing the marquee size does not change the size of the scrolling text message. You must use text formatting tags and attributes to control the appearance of the text. See Chapter 4 to learn more.

Can I change the background color of a marquee?

Yes. You can add the BGCOLOR attribute to the <MARQUEE> tag to change the background color of a scrolling marquee. Be sure to choose a color that does not conflict with the legibility of the scrolling message text. For a complete palette of HTML color values, see the Appendix. To learn more about assigning background colors, see Chapter 4.

Create an Image Map

You can create an image map that links users to different pages based on where they click on the image. For example, you might use an image map as a navigational tool for your Web site. The key to creating a good image map is finding an image with distinct areas to click.

You can define each clickable area on the map using three shape values: `rect` **(for rectangle),** `circle` **(for circle), or** `poly` **(for polygon, or an irregular shape).**

Create an Image Map

1 Click where you want to insert an image map.

2 Type **<IMG SRC="?"**, replacing *?* with the location and name of the image file.

```
<HTML>
<HEAD>
<TITLE>Dave's Garden Shop & Nursery</TITLE>
<LINK REL="stylesheet" TYPE="text/css" HREF="Dave's_Garden_Shop_&_Nursery_StyleSheet1.css">
</HEAD>
<BODY BGCOLOR="#CCFFCC">

<HR SIZE="2" NOSHADE COLOR=#FACD8A>
<H1><FONT FACE="Arial" COLOR="#6C000A" SIZE="7"><CENTER>Dave's Garden Shop & Nursery
</CENTER></FONT></H1>
<HR SIZE="2" NOSHADE COLOR=#FACD8A>

<BR>

<CENTER><IMG SRC="imagemap2.jpg"<CENTER>

<H3><FONT FACE="Arial">Click a link above to visit a particular page on our site</FONT></H3>

</BODY>

</HTML>
```
2

3 Type a space, and then **USEMAP="#?">**, replacing *?* with a name for the image map.

```
<HTML>
<HEAD>
<TITLE>Dave's Garden Shop & Nursery</TITLE>
<LINK REL="stylesheet" TYPE="text/css" HREF="Dave's_Garden_Shop_&_Nursery_StyleSheet1.css">
</HEAD>
<BODY BGCOLOR="#CCFFCC">

<HR SIZE="2" NOSHADE COLOR=#FACD8A>
<H1><FONT FACE="Arial" COLOR="#6C000A" SIZE="7"><CENTER>Dave's Garden Shop & Nursery
</CENTER></FONT></H1>
<HR SIZE="2" NOSHADE COLOR=#FACD8A>

<BR>

<CENTER><IMG SRC="imagemap2.jpg" USEMAP="#imagemap"><CENTER>

<H3><FONT FACE="Arial">Click a link above to visit a particular page on our site</FONT></H3>

</BODY>

</HTML>
```
3

④ Click where you want to insert the map information and type **<MAP NAME="?"**, replacing *?* with the map name you assigned in step **3**.

```
<HTML>
<HEAD>
<TITLE>Dave's Garden Shop & Nursery</TITLE>
<LINK REL="stylesheet" TYPE="text/css" HREF="Dave's_Garden_Shop_&_Nursery_StyleSheet1.css">
</HEAD>
<BODY BGCOLOR="#CCFFCC">

<HR SIZE="2" NOSHADE COLOR=#FACD8A>
<H1><FONT FACE="Arial" COLOR="#6C000A" SIZE="7"><CENTER>Dave's Garden Shop & Nursery
</CENTER></FONT></H1>
<HR SIZE="2" NOSHADE COLOR=#FACD8A>

<BR>

<CENTER><IMG SRC="imagemap2.jpg" USEMAP="#imagemap"><CENTER>
<MAP NAME="imagemap">

<H3><FONT FACE="Arial">Click a link above to visit a particular page on our site</FONT></H3>

</BODY>

</HTML>
```

④

⑤ Type **<AREA** and a blank space.

⑥ Type **SHAPE="?"** followed by a blank space, replacing *?* with the shape of the area (**rect**, **circle**, or **poly**).

Choose a shape that best fits the clickable area you want to create.

```
<HTML>
<HEAD>
<TITLE>Dave's Garden Shop & Nursery</TITLE>
<LINK REL="stylesheet" TYPE="text/css" HREF="Dave's_Garden_Shop_&_Nursery_StyleSheet1.css">
</HEAD>
<BODY BGCOLOR="#CCFFCC">

<HR SIZE="2" NOSHADE COLOR=#FACD8A>
<H1><FONT FACE="Arial" COLOR="#6C000A" SIZE="7"><CENTER>Dave's Garden Shop & Nursery
</CENTER></FONT></H1>
<HR SIZE="2" NOSHADE COLOR=#FACD8A>

<BR>

<CENTER><IMG SRC="imagemap2.jpg" USEMAP="#imagemap"><CENTER>
<MAP NAME="imagemap">
<AREA SHAPE="rect"

<H3><FONT FACE="Arial">Click a link above to visit a particular page on our site</FONT></H3>

</BODY>

</HTML>
```

⑤ ⑥

TIPS

What is the difference between client-side image maps and server-side image maps?

There are two kinds of image maps, *client-side* and *server-side*. Client-side maps are interpreted by the browser, so the response time is much faster. The user clicks a map area, and the page is loaded. With server-side maps, each mouse click must be sent to the server using a CGI script before the linked page appears. Most Web developers create client-side image maps for use with less-complex Web sites.

How do I prepare an image to be an image map?

You can use a photograph as an image map, or better yet, design your own graphic image map. You can use a drawing program to create a simple image map of several shapes and labels over the shapes. For example, you can take a large shape and divide it into smaller shapes, assigning each a different color and label corresponding to a Web page or content on your site. Regardless of how you create an image map, the map should show logical areas to click.

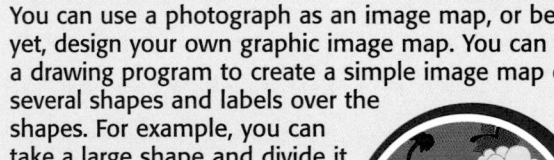

You use the `<AREA>` tag to define the information about each clickable part of your image map. This information includes the shape of the clickable area and the corresponding coordinates on the image. You must also specify which Web page you want to open when each area is clicked on the map.

Create an Image Map *(continued)*

⑦ Type the coordinates for the clickable shape:

For a rectangle, type **COORDS="x1,y1,x2,y2"**, replacing *x1,y1* with the coordinates for the top-left corner and *x2,y2* with the coordinates for the bottom-right corner.

For a circle, type **COORDS="x,y,r"**, replacing *x,y* with the coordinates for the center of the circle and *r* with the radius.

For a polygon, type **COORDS="x1,y1,x2,y2,x3 . . . "**, replacing each with the coordinates for every point on the polygon.

⑧ Type a blank space and **HREF="?">**, replacing *?* with the name and location of the Web page you want to appear when the area is clicked.

```
<HTML>
<HEAD>
<TITLE>Dave's Garden Shop & Nursery</TITLE>
<LINK REL="stylesheet" TYPE="text/css" HREF="Dave's_Garden_Shop_&_Nursery_StyleSheet1.css">
</HEAD>
<BODY BGCOLOR="#CCFFCC">

<HR SIZE="2" NOSHADE COLOR=#FACD8A>
<H1><FONT FACE="Arial" COLOR="#6C000A" SIZE="7"><CENTER>Dave's Garden Shop & Nursery
</CENTER></FONT></H1>
<HR SIZE="2" NOSHADE COLOR=#FACD8A>

<BR>

<CENTER><IMG SRC="imagemap2.jpg" USEMAP="#imagemap"><CENTER>
<MAP NAME="imagemap">
<AREA SHAPE="rect" COORDS="1,2,142,80"          ⑦

<H3><FONT FACE="Arial">Click a link above to visit a particular page on our site</FONT></H3>

</BODY>

</HTML>
```

```
<HTML>
<HEAD>
<TITLE>Dave's Garden Shop & Nursery</TITLE>
<LINK REL="stylesheet" TYPE="text/css" HREF="Dave's_Garden_Shop_&_Nursery_StyleSheet1.css">
</HEAD>
<BODY BGCOLOR="#CCFFCC">

<HR SIZE="2" NOSHADE COLOR=#FACD8A>
<H1><FONT FACE="Arial" COLOR="#6C000A" SIZE="7"><CENTER>Dave's Garden Shop & Nursery
</CENTER></FONT></H1>
<HR SIZE="2" NOSHADE COLOR=#FACD8A>

<BR>

<CENTER><IMG SRC="imagemap2.jpg" USEMAP="#imagemap"><CENTER>
<MAP NAME="imagemap">
<AREA SHAPE="rect" COORDS="1,2,142,80" HREF="Dave's_Garden_Shop_&_Nursery_Events.html">     ⑧

<H3><FONT FACE="Arial">Click a link above to visit a particular page on our site</FONT></H3>

</BODY>

</HTML>
```

⑨ Repeat steps **5** to **8** for each area of the image map.

⑩ Type **</MAP>**.

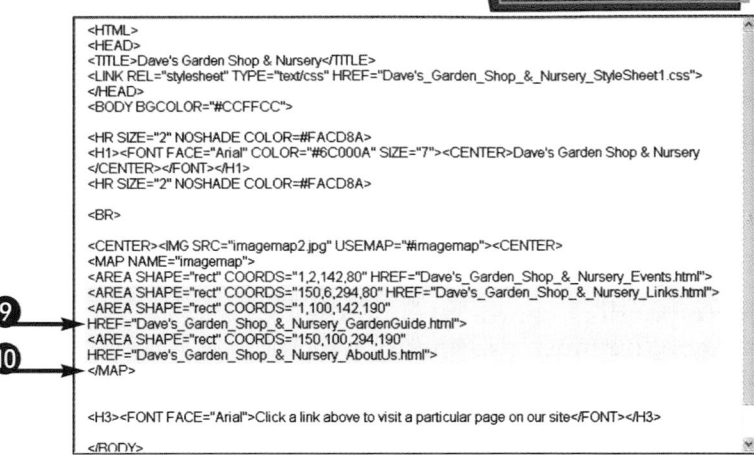

```
<HTML>
<HEAD>
<TITLE>Dave's Garden Shop & Nursery</TITLE>
<LINK REL="stylesheet" TYPE="text/css" HREF="Dave's_Garden_Shop_&_Nursery_StyleSheet1.css">
</HEAD>
<BODY BGCOLOR="#CCFFCC">

<HR SIZE="2" NOSHADE COLOR=#FACD8A>
<H1><FONT FACE="Arial" COLOR="#6C000A" SIZE="7"><CENTER>Dave's Garden Shop & Nursery
</CENTER></FONT></H1>
<HR SIZE="2" NOSHADE COLOR=#FACD8A>

<BR>

<CENTER><IMG SRC="imagemap2.jpg" USEMAP="#imagemap"><CENTER>
<MAP NAME="imagemap">
<AREA SHAPE="rect" COORDS="1,2,142,80" HREF="Dave's_Garden_Shop_&_Nursery_Events.html">
<AREA SHAPE="rect" COORDS="150,6,294,80" HREF="Dave's_Garden_Shop_&_Nursery_Links.html">
<AREA SHAPE="rect" COORDS="1,100,142,190"
HREF="Dave's_Garden_Shop_&_Nursery_GardenGuide.html">
<AREA SHAPE="rect" COORDS="150,100,294,190"
HREF="Dave's_Garden_Shop_&_Nursery_AboutUs.html">
</MAP>

<H3><FONT FACE="Arial">Click a link above to visit a particular page on our site</FONT></H3>

</BODY>
```

The Web browser displays the image map.

When a user clicks an area on the map, the corresponding Web page opens.

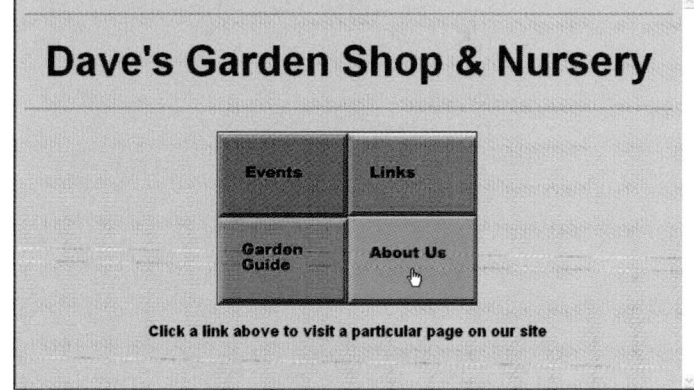

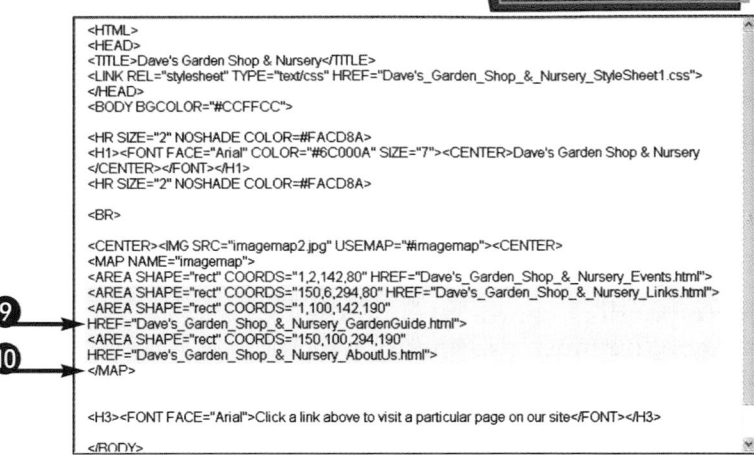

TIPS

How do I determine the coordinates for an area on my image map?

You can use an image map editor to help you create image maps. You can also use an image map editor to help you determine the coordinates necessary to define the clickable areas within the map. One of the most popular image map editors is Mapedit. You can find it at www.boutell.com/mapedit. You can also conduct a Web search for free image map editors. If your graphics editing program has a graph feature, you might use it to help you figure out the map coordinates as well.

What happens if my clickable areas overlap?

If you accidentally overlap two areas with your coordinates, the Web browser treats the second area as part of the first. If you enter coordinates that extend past the image area, the Web browser ignores the coordinates.

Create Thumbnail Images

Large image files can take a while to download. Rather than make the user wait, you can display a thumbnail of the image on the page. If the user wants to view the full image, he or she can click the thumbnail to open a window showing the full size image. To create this type of Web page, you need two image files, one showing the full-sized image, the other showing a thumbnail version.

Ideally, a thumbnail image should be 200 pixels wide or smaller. Most digital cameras produce original image sizes at a range of 1800–1600 pixels wide. By reducing the image size in width, you also reduce the overall file size.

Create Thumbnail Images

1 Click where you want to display a thumbnail image and type **<A HREF="?">**, replacing *?* with the location and name of the full-sized image.

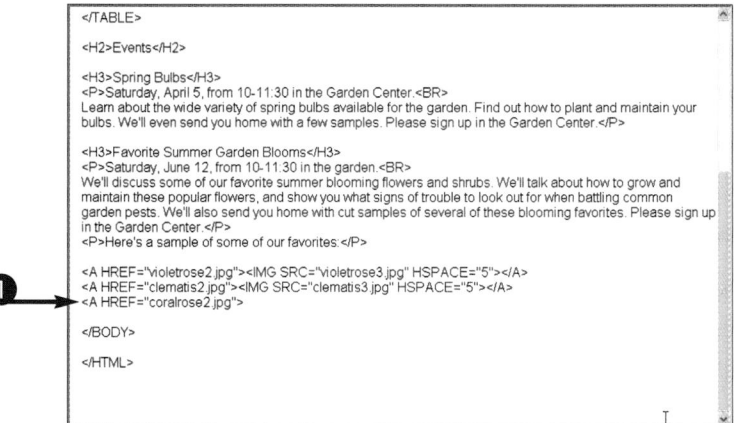

2 Type **<IMG SRC="?"**, replacing *?* with the name and location of the thumbnail version of the image.

● In this example, horizontal spacing is added to the image.

3 Type **</A>** after the <IMG> tag.

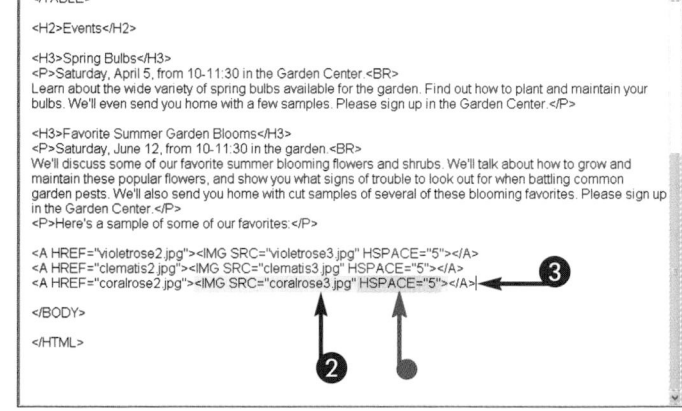

The browser displays the thumbnail image on the Web page.

● The user can click the thumbnail to view the full image.

The browser displays the full image.

Can I scale an image using HTML coding?
Yes. You can use the WIDTH and HEIGHT attributes within the <IMG> tag to set a width and height for an image. Here is an example of the code:

```
<IMG SRC="Leaves.jpg"
WIDTH="200" HEIGHT="180">
```

Keep in mind that assigning the WIDTH and HEIGHT in HTML does not subtract from the overall file size. In fact, the image takes longer to download than images truly sized smaller to fit. For best results, always use an image editor program to size your images for the Web. See Chapter 7 to learn more about working with images.

How do I find out the overall file size for an image on my Web page?
In the browser window, right-click (Windows) or control-click (Mac) the image on the Web page to display a menu. Click the **Properties** or **Get Image Info** command to open a box showing the dimensions and file size for the image.

Automatically Load Another Web Page

You can automatically load a Web page after a certain period of time has passed. You might use this technique to create a title page stating the Web page has moved.

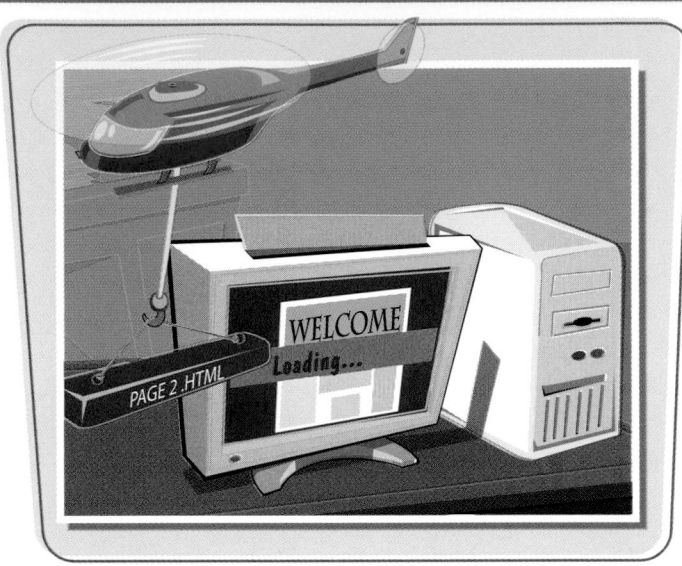

Automatically Load Another Web Page

1 Add a new line between the `<HEAD>` and `</HEAD>` tags.

2 Type **<META HTTP-EQUIV="Refresh"**.

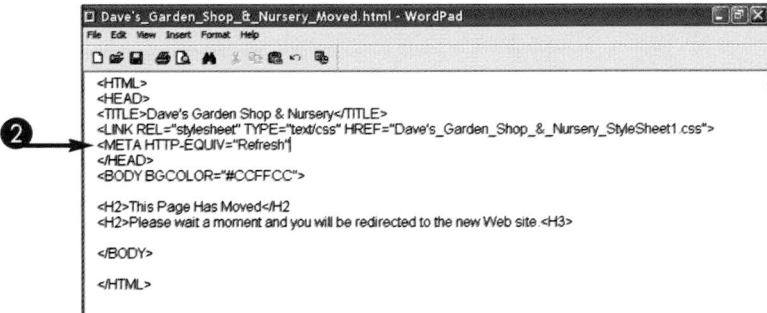

3 Type a blank space and **CONTENT="?;**, replacing *?* with the number of seconds you want to elapse before the new page appears.

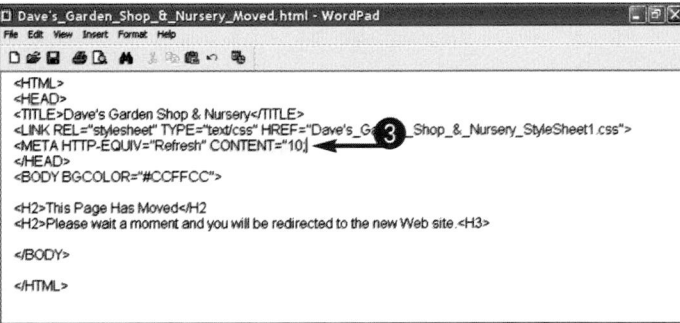

④ Type a blank space and **URL=?">**, replacing *?* with the location and name of the page you want to appear.

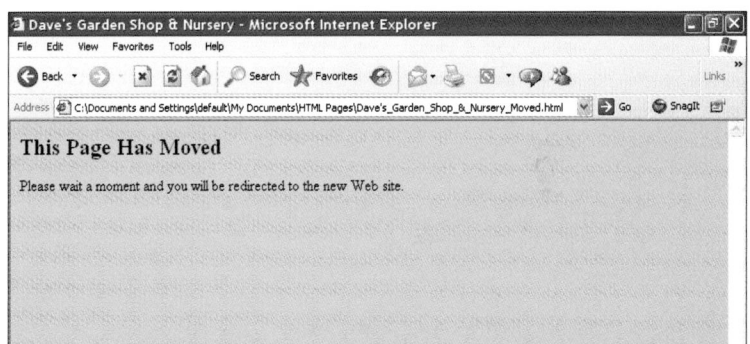

The Web browser displays the first page, and then after the allotted time period, the second page loads.

TIPS

Can I load one page right after another to create a slide show?

You can use the same <META> attribute for loading pages to set up an automatic Web slide show of your pages. The pages progress from one to another, each staying on-screen for a designated period of time. You might create a slide show of your favorite family photos, for example. Follow these steps:

① Add a new line between the <HEAD> and </HEAD> tags for the start page of your show.

② Type **<META HTTP-EQUIV="refresh" CONTENT="?";**, replacing *?* with the number of seconds you want the page to appear on-screen.

③ Type a space, and then **URL="?"/>**, replacing *?* with the URL of the next page you want to appear.

④ Repeat steps **2** and **3** for each page you want to appear in the slide show.

For the last page, be sure to reference the first page again so the show loops.

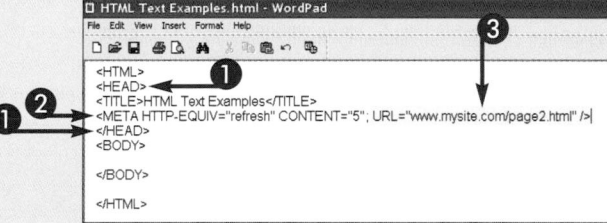

Publishing Your Web Pages

Are you ready to place your HTML document on the Web? This chapter shows you how to find a Web host and transfer your files to a server.

Understanding Web Page Publishing..........**280**

Transfer Files to a Web Server
with WS_FTP......................................**284**

Troubleshoot Your Web Pages **288**

Promote Your Web Site **290**

Understanding Web Page Publishing

The final phase of creating a Web site is publishing your page or pages. In the realm of HTML, the term *publishing* refers to all the necessary steps you must take to make your HTML documents available to others. This includes finding a Web host.

Web Hosts

To place your pages on the Web, you need a Web server — a computer specifically set up to store and manage Web pages. Commonly called *hosts*, Web servers allow you to transfer and store files, including HTML documents, images, and multimedia files. Unless you own your own Web server, you need to find a server to host your pages.

Determine Your Needs

Before you start looking for a Web host, first determine what features and services you need. For example, how much storage space do you anticipate using for your Web site? Does your site require e-commerce features, such as an online shopping cart, or a secure server for handling confidential information? Do you need to keep track of Web statistics, such as who visits your site and how often? Knowing your needs beforehand can help find the right hosting provider.

Web Hosting Scenarios

Numerous companies around the world provide Web site hosting. Some do so for free, in exchange for placing advertising on your site, while others charge a monthly fee. Many ISPs and commercial online services offer their members a certain amount of storage space for free. If you expect your site to generate a lot of traffic, you can use a dedicated Web presence provider — a company that specializes in helping others establish and maintain a presence on the Web. Web presence providers generally offer more features and support.

Search for a Web Host

The best place to start looking for a host is with your own ISP or commercial service. If it does not offer hosting services, you can look for Web hosting services on the Internet. For example, the Web Hosting Ratings site (www.webhostingratings.com/) can help you start your search. Also consider asking friends and family for recommendations, as well as searching through your local yellow pages.

Features to Consider

When considering a Web host, take time to compare what features and services are offered, as well as comparing fees. Find out how much disk space it allows. Although HTML documents are generally small in size, images and multimedia files included with Web pages can consume large amounts of space. Also find out the speed of its connection to the Internet and what advanced features and software it supports, such as CGI scripts. Ask whether it offers technical support, registers domain names, or provides Web hit statistics to track visitors to your site.

continued

After you find a host for your Web site and establish a domain name, if needed, the next step to publishing your Web page is to transfer the HTML documents from your computer to the Web server.

Ordinarily, when you publish your pages to a Web host, your Web address is the name of the host's domain followed by the path to your files. If you want a more unique address, you may want to obtain your own domain name. A domain name is a high-level address for a Web site, such as www.wiley.com (owned by the publisher of this book). To acquire a domain name, you must register and pay for the name.

Acquire Your Own Domain Name

You can register for a domain name through VeriSign (www.netsol.com), the keeper of domain names in the United States. Your Web hosting service may also offer a registration service for domain names, for a reduced fee. Once you acquire a domain name, you can ask your Web host to create a virtual domain for your site on their server. This allows you to use your unique domain name rather than the provider's server name in your URL.

Transfer Files

After you set up an account with a Web host, you can transfer your HTML files to the server and set up your Web site. When you transfer files from your computer to a Web server, the activity is called *uploading*. Depending on your server, you can transfer files using FTP (File Transfer Protocol) or a Web interface provided by your hosting service. More often than not, you use FTP to upload your files.

FTP Programs

FTP is the standard for file transfer on the Internet. In order to transfer files with FTP, you need an FTP program, also called a *client.* You can find free and shareware programs on the Internet. Many offer free trials. Popular FTP programs include WS_FTP for Windows (www.ipswitch.com/Products/WS_FTP/), CuteFTP (www.globalscape.com/products/cuteFTP), and Fetch for Mac (www.dartmouth.edu/pages/sofdev/fetch.html). You should also check your Web host to see what FTP clients or file upload tools they may offer. See the section, "Transfer Files to a Web Server with WS_FTP" for more information.

Maintain Your Site

After you upload your pages, you can view and test your site. One of your chores as a Web developer is to maintain your Web site. It is up to you to keep your information and links current. It is good practice to regularly test your site for broken links. See the section, "Troubleshoot Your Web Pages" to learn more about fixing page problems. Although some sites need more updating than others, it is also good practice to update your content on a regular basis or give it a fresh look or tweak from time to time. Stale data can keep visitors from returning to your site.

Publicize Your Site

Once you have published your Web site, you can look for ways to attract visitors. You can use keywords and useful page titles to gain the attention of search engines. You can also advertise your pages on other sites, through e-mails, and offline. See the section "Promote Your Web Site" for more information.

Transfer Files to a Web Server with WS_FTP

You can transfer your Web page files to a Web server using FTP software. In this section, you learn how to transfer files using Ipswitch WS_FTP, a program designed specially for transferring files on the Web. If you use another FTP program, your steps may differ.

Transfer Files to a Web Server with WS_FTP

SET UP YOUR CONNECTION

1 Open the WS_FTP program window.

The first time you use the program, the Connection Wizard appears to help you set up your server connection.

Note: If you have not downloaded and installed the program, visit www.ipswitch.com.

2 Type a name for your server or Web site.

3 Click **Next**.

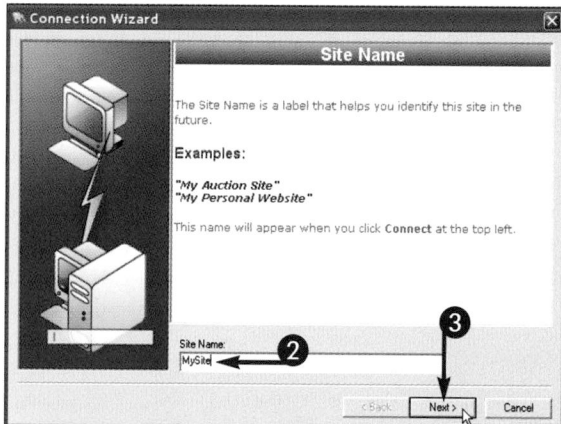

4 Type your server address.

If you do not know the server address, contact your Web host for more information.

Typically, you receive this information when you sign up for an account.

5 Click **Next**.

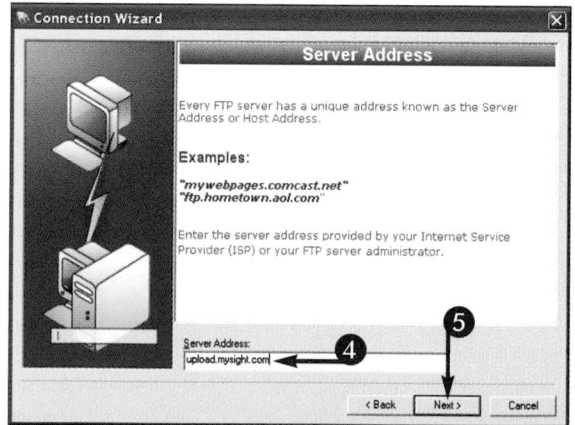

6 Type your user name.

7 Type your user password.

If you do not know your user ID or password, contact your Web host.

Typically, you receive this information when you sign up for an account.

8 Click **Next**.

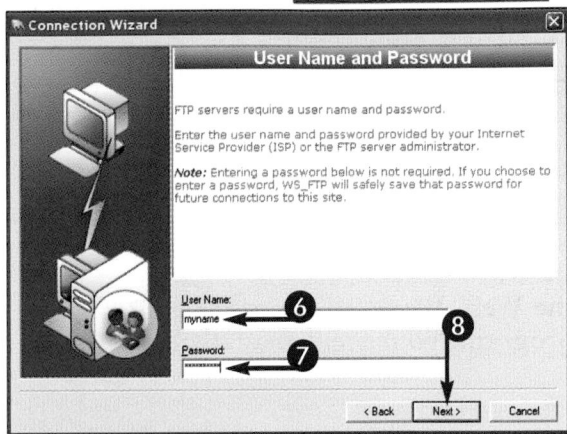

9 Select a connection type, if needed.

FTP is the default selection.

10 Click **Next**.

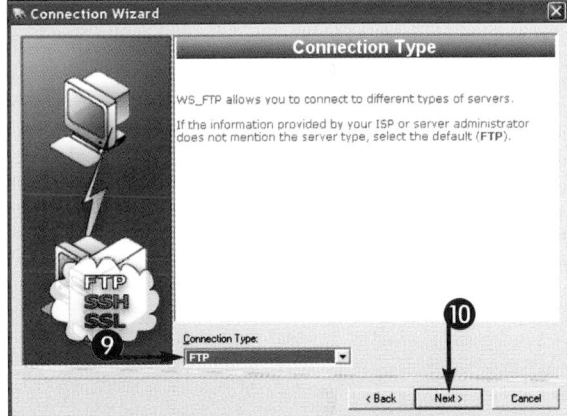

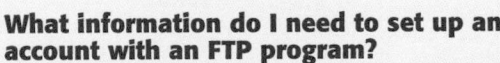

TIPS

Where can I find an FTP program?

You can find numerous FTP programs on the Internet, including freeware and shareware programs. Many programs offer a free trial version you can experiment with to see if you want to purchase the program. You can find a trial version of Ipswitch WS_FTP at www .ipswitch.com.

What information do I need to set up an account with an FTP program?

Most servers ask you for a server address, a user name, and a password. When you create an account with a Web host provider, you are assigned this information, including a destination folder on the server's directory. You can use this folder to store your HTML files, along with any image and multimedia files you include with your Web page. Be sure to contact your Web host for this information before attempting to upload files for the first time.

continued

After you establish your server connection, you can start transferring files. The WS_FTP program window shows two panes, one displaying the files on your computer, and the other for displaying files on your server. You can move files between the two using the Upload and Download buttons.

You can upload a single file or multiple files. Any time you need to update your site, you can transfer more files to the server.

Transfer Files to a Web Server with WS_FTP *(continued)*

● You can click this option if you immediately want to open your connection once you complete the Connection Wizard.

⑪ Click **Finish**.

Your connection information is saved and the program window remains open and ready for any file transfer activities you want to perform.

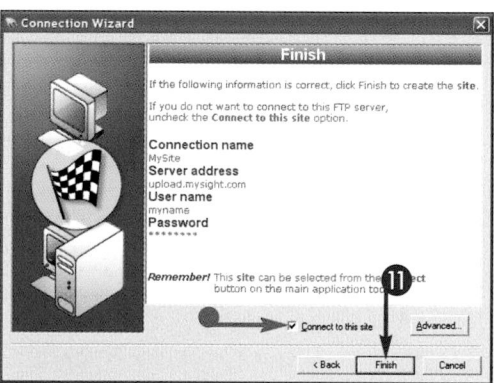

TRANSFER FILES

① If you have not connected to your server, click the **Connect** button (🖼️).

Note: You must connect to the Internet before transferring files.

② Click your connection name from the list.

WS_FTP connects your computer to the server.

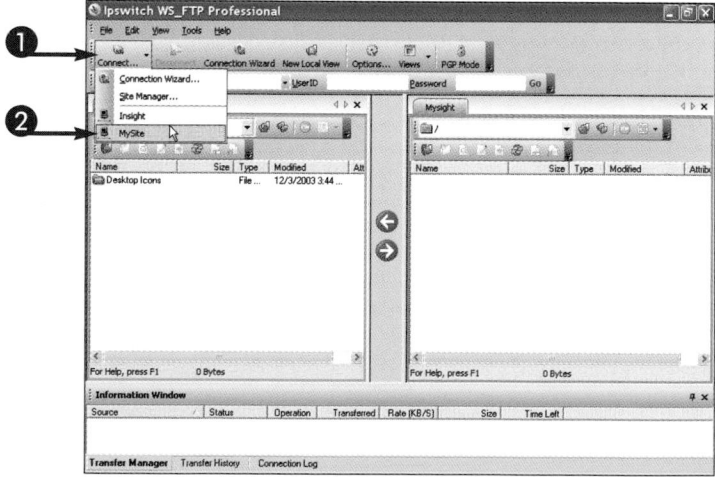

③ Click the files you want to transfer.

To select multiple files, press and hold Shift while clicking filenames.

④ Click the **Upload** button (→).

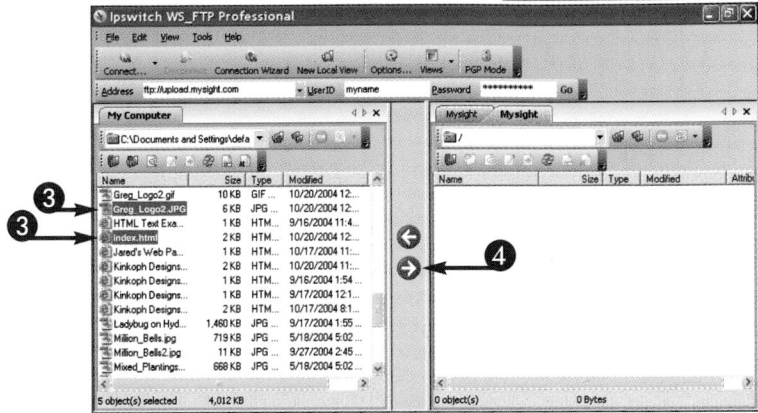

WS_FTP transfers the files.

Depending on the file size, the transfer may take several minutes.

● The transferred files appear listed on the server.

⑤ Click the **Close** button (✕) to exit the program when you have finished transferring files.

You can now use your browser to view the pages.

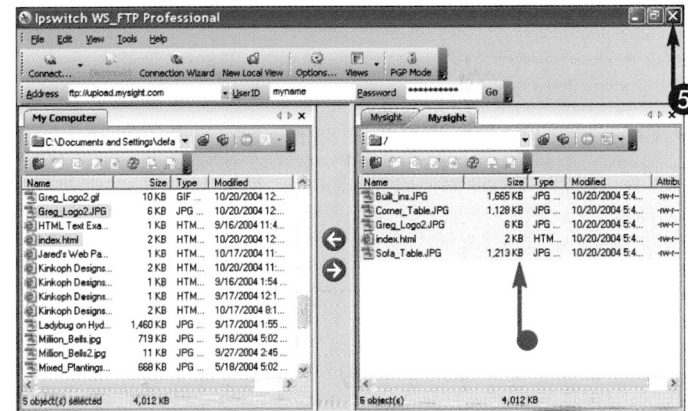

TIPS

How do I remove a file from my Web site?

Open your connection to the server, select the file you want to delete from the left pane and press the Delete button (🗑). A prompt box appears asking if you really want to remove the file. Click **Yes** to immediately remove your file from the server.

Can I transfer a new version of the same file already found on the server?

Yes. You can overwrite existing files. WS_FTP prompts you if the same file is found on the server. You then have the option of overwriting the file with the new file. Simply click **Overwrite** in the prompt box. If you prefer to wait and check the file later, click **Skip** and WS_FTP leaves the original file on the server intact.

Troubleshoot Your Web Pages

No matter how carefully you create your pages, errors can occur. If your Web page does not display properly in a browser, you must track down the problem. In most situations, you can track the problem to a common coding error. If, even after a thorough check, you still cannot find the error, share your document with another Web developer for feedback.

Typing Errors

Typing errors are the most common mistake in writing HTML documents. Web browsers ignore tags they do not recognize, so always start your troubleshooting process with a careful proofread of your document. Read each line in your document, paying close attention to tags and attributes. One mistyped character, quotation mark, or bracket can cause a problem in a browser window.

Invalid Paths

Typing the wrong path to a file can cause an error on your pages. If a server cannot locate a file, it cannot display the element. Double-check your text for the correct path to the element or link. If the Web browser cannot find your page, you may have entered the wrong directory path. It is also essential to use the correct file extensions when specifying files.

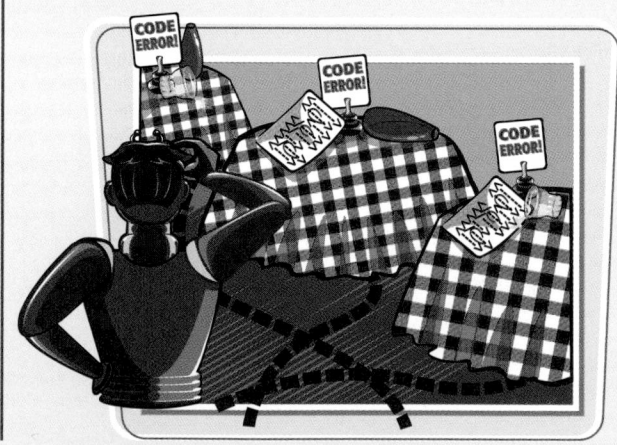

Broken Links

Nothing is more frustrating to Web page visitors than clicking a nonfunctioning link. Always make sure your links reference an active page. Checking links is an important part of maintaining your Web site. Pages come and go on the Web, so make it a regular practice to check your links.

Blank Display

If the Web browser fails to display your page at all, you may have a missing end tag. This can happen with larger elements in which lots of attributes are listed, such as tables, framesets, and styles. Make sure all of your page elements include the proper end tags.

Missing Image Files

If the Web browser cannot display your images, you may have entered the wrong filename. Verify your image name, making sure you typed the correct upper- and lowercase letters for the filename. It is also common to type the wrong file extension for an image file, such as typing GIF instead of JPG. Remember, not all browsers support all kinds of image files. Be sure to stick with formats commonly found on the Web. See Chapter 7 to learn more.

HTML Code Appears

If the browser displays your HTML code instead of the Web page, you probably saved the file as a TXT file instead of an HTML file. Also double-check to see if your <HTML> tag appears at the top of the page. If this tag is missing, the browser may not read your page as an HTML document.

Promote Your Web Site

After you publish your site, it is available for others to view on the Web. There are several ways you can bring attention to your Web site. You can advertise your site offline by adding your URL to business cards and stationery, or other products you distribute to others. You can advertise your site online by adding your URL to your e-mail message signature. You can also enlist the help of search engines to index your site.

Search Engines

Search engines are actually software designed to collect information about pages encountered on the Web. Search engines may work differently from one another, but the goal is the same — to gather information about HTML documents. Search engines do this by cataloging URLs, keywords, page titles, and text from HTML documents. When someone performs a search for keywords, the search engine compares the request with the information gathered in its database and displays matching results as links, listing the most relevant links first.

Submit Your Site

To help bring attention to your site, you can register with search engines. Most search engines offer an online form you can fill out to register your URL. It may take the search engine several weeks to index your site. Popular search engines to contact include Google (www.google.com/addurl.html), Yahoo (http:docs.yahoo .com/info/suggest/), and AltaVista (www.altavista.com/ sites/search/addurl/). You can also register your URL with search engines that specialize in a particular topic.

Add Keywords

When users look for Web sites, they type keywords into a search engine. You can add keywords to your page to help users find your site. You can add keywords to your metadata information, as well as use them in your title and headers. Keywords should honestly reflect your content. Take time to think about keywords other users might type to find your page, and then add them to your metadata tag. See Chapter 2 to learn how to insert metadata on your page.

Write Good Page Titles

Search engines also look through page titles for indexing information. Good page titles can help draw users to your site. Search engine results pages typically list page titles in the search results. A well-written title can tell a potential visitor whether your site is relevant or not. When writing titles, keep your text descriptive but concise. See Chapter 2 to learn how to add title text to your page.

Linking with Others

Another good way to publicize your site is through links. You can contact sites with similar content to see if they might link to your site. You can then link to their site in exchange. You can also join Web rings of similar sites. A Web ring is a group of sites focusing on a related topic, all linking to each other.

Advertising

You can advertise your Web site on other pages. Web sites such as LinkExchange (adnetwork.llnkexchange.com) can help you advertise your site free of charge. Other sites charge a fee. You can also solicit advertising from other Web sites and exchange ads.

HTML Tags

Basic Tags/Attributes

Tag/Attribute	Description
<!-->	Insert a comment
<!DOCTYPE>	Indicates what version of HTML is used
<BODY>	Identifies content on a Web page
 	Line break
<H1>, <H2>, <H3>, <H4>, <H5>, <H6>	Heading levels
<HEAD>	Contains information about a Web page title, style sheets, and search engine keywords
<HTML>	Identifies an HTML document
<META>	Contains extra information about the Web page itself
CONTENT	Specifies custom information about a page
NAME	Adds description or copyright information to a Web page
<P>	Starts a new paragraph
ALIGN	Aligns a paragraph
<TITLE>	Creates a title for a Web page

Text Formatting Tags/Attributes

Tag/Attribute	Description
<B>	Bold
<BASEFONT>	Specifies a default font for the entire page
COLOR	Specifies default text color
FACE	Specifies default font
SIZE	Specifies default text size
<BIG>	Makes text larger than surrounding text
<BLINK>	Makes text appear to blink
<BLOCKQUOTE>	Separates text from the main text for attention
<BODY>	
BGCOLOR	Sets a background color for a page
BOTTOMMARGIN	Changes the bottom margin
LEFTMARGIN	Changes the left margin
MARGINHEIGHT	Changes the top and bottom margins

Tag/Attribute	Description
MARGINWIDTH	Changes the left and right margins
RIGHTMARGIN	Changes the right margin
TEXT	Specifies a color for all the text on the page
TOPMARGIN	Changes the top margin
<CENTER>	Centers information on the page
<FONT>	Changes the appearance of text
COLOR	Changes the text color
FACE	Changes the font
SIZE	Changes the text size
<I>	Italicizes text
<NOBR>	Keeps all the text on one line, without breaks
<PRE>	Retains preformatted spacing for text
<Q>	For quoting short passages of text
<SMALL>	Makes the text smaller than surrounding text
<STRIKE>	Adds a strikethrough line through text
<SUB>	Places text slightly below the baseline
<SUP>	Places text slightly above the baseline
<TT>	Creates typewriter text
<U>	Underlines text

List Tags/Attributes

Tag/Attribute	Description
<DD>	Identifies a definition list
<DL>	Creates a definition list of terms
<DT>	Identifies a term in a definition list
<LI>	Identifies an item in an ordered or unordered list
<OL>	Creates an ordered list
START	Specifies a start number for an ordered list
TYPE	Specifies a number style for an ordered list
<UL>	Creates an unordered list
TYPE	Specifies a bullet style for an unordered list

Table Tags/Attributes

Tag/Attribute	Description
<CAPTION>	Adds a caption to a table
<CENTER>	Center aligns a table on a page
<COL>	Joins columns in a table for formatting as a nonstructural group
ALIGN	Aligns columns in a column group
SPAN	Specifies the number of columns in a column group
WIDTH	Specifies the default width for columns in a column group
<COLGROUP>	Joins columns in a table for formatting as a structural group
ALIGN	Aligns columns in a column group
SPAN	Specifies the number of columns in a column group
WIDTH	Specifies the default width for columns in a column group
<TABLE>	Creates a table
ALIGN	Controls table alignment
BACKGROUND	Inserts a background image to a table
BGCOLOR	Changes the table background color
BORDER	Adds a border to a table
CELLPADDING	Changes the amount of space around cell contents
CELLSPACING	Changes the amount of space between cells
HEIGHT	Controls the height of a table
WIDTH	Controls the width of a table
<TD>	Creates a data cell in a table
BGCOLOR	Changes the cell background color
COLSPAN	Combines two or more cells across columns
HEIGHT	Controls the height of a table cell
NOWRAP	Keeps text in a cell on one line
ROWSPAN	Combines two or more cells down rows
WIDTH	Controls the width of a table cell
<TH>	Creates a header cell
ALIGN	Aligns data in a header
BGCOLOR	Adds background color to a header cell
HEIGHT	Controls the height of a header cell

Tag/Attribute	Description
COLSPAN	Combines two or more header cells across columns
NOWRAP	Keeps text in a header cell on one line
ROWSPAN	Combines two or more header cells down rows
WIDTH	Controls the width of a header cell
<TR>	Creates a new row in a table
ALIGN	Aligns data horizontally in a table
BGCOLOR	Changes the background color of a row
VALIGN	Aligns data vertically in a table

Image Tags/Attributes	
Tag/Attribute	Description
<BODY>	
BACKGROUND	Inserts a background image on the page
CLEAR	Stops text from wrapping around an image
<CENTER>	Center aligns an image
<HR>	Adds a horizontal rule
ALIGN	Aligns a horizontal rule
NOSHADE	Displays rule without shading
SIZE	Changes the thickness of a horizontal rule
WIDTH	Changes the width of a horizontal rule
<IMG>	Inserts an image on a page
ALIGN	Aligns an image on the page
ALT	Displays alternative text when an image does not download
BORDER	Adds a border to an image
HEIGHT	Controls the height of an image
HSPACE	Adds space to the left and right sides of an image
SRC	Specifies the image location or path
VSPACE	Adds space above and below an image
WIDTH	Controls the width of an image

HTML Tags

Links Tags/Attributes

Tag/Attribute	Description
<A>	Creates a link
HREF	Specifies the location of a Web page and other resources
NAME	Names a Web page area displayed by selecting a link
TARGET	Specifies where linked information appears
<BODY>	
ALINK	Changes the color of a link as the user rolls over it
LINK	Changes the color of an unvisited link
VLINK	Changes the color of a visited link

Image Map Tags/Attributes

Tag/Attribute	Description
<AREA>	Specifies an image area
COORDS	Specifies all the coordinates for an image area
HREF	Specifies the location of a Web page linked to an image area
NOREF	Makes a clip in an image map have no effect
SHAPE	Controls the shape of an image area
TARGET	Specifies a window or frame that a link should display in
<IMG>	Adds an image to a page
USEMAP	Identifies an image map for an image
<MAP>	Creates an image map
NAME	Names an image map

Multimedia Tags/Attributes

Tag/Attribute	Description
<A>	
HREF	Specifies the location of a linked sound or video
<BGSOUND>	Specifies a background audio clip for a Web page
LOOP	Controls how often an audio clip plays
SRC	Specifies the path or location of the audio clip

Tag/Attribute	Description
<EMBED>	Adds an audio or video clip to a Web page
AUTOSTART	Plays a multimedia clip automatically
CONTROLS	Adds control buttons for the multimedia element
HEIGHT	Controls the height of a video clip
LOOP	Plays a multimedia clip continuously
SRC	Specifies the location or path of a multimedia clip
WIDTH	Specifies the width of a video
<OBJECT>	Embeds multimedia objects in Web pages
ALIGN	Aligns objects
BORDER	Adds a border to an object
CLASSID	Identifies the kind of object being embedded
CODEBASE	Defines the base URL of the source object
DATA	Identifies the source of the multimedia file
HEIGHT	Controls the height dimensions of the object
HSPACE	Adds space to the sides of the object
NAME	Identifies the object
STANDBY	Displays a message as the object is loading
TYPE	Identifies the object's MIME type
VSPACE	Adds space to the top and bottom of the object
WIDTH	Controls the width dimensions of the object

Java and JavaScript Tags/Attributes	
Tag/Attribute	**Description**
<APPLET>	Adds a Java applet to a Web page
CODE	Specifies the location of a Java applet
HEIGHT	Specifies the height of a Java applet
WIDTH	Specifies the width of a Java applet
<NOSCRIPT>	Displays alternative text when a JavaScript does not run
<SCRIPT>	Adds a JavaScript to a Web page
SRC	Specifies the location or path to a JavaScript
TYPE	Identifies the script as JavaScript

HTML Tags

Frame Tags/Attributes

Tag/Attribute	Description
<A>	
HREF	Specifies the location of a linked Web page to appear in a frame
TARGET	Specifies the frame where a linked Web page will appear
<BASE>	Specifies the information about links on a page
TARGET	Specifies the frame where linked Web pages appear
<FRAME>	Specifies information for a frame
MARGINHEIGHT	Changes the top and bottom margins of a frame
MARGINWIDTH	Changes the left and right margins of a frame
NAME	Names a frame
NORESIZE	Prevents users from resizing a frame
SCROLLING	Hides or displays scroll bars for a frame
SRC	Specifies the location of a Web page to appear in a frame
<FRAMESET>	Specifies a structure for frames
BORDER	Specifies a border thickness for a frame
COLS	Creates frames in columns
ROWS	Creates frames in rows
<NOFRAMES>	Displays alternative text to frames that do not appear

Form Tags/Attributes

Tag/Attribute	Description
<FORM>	Creates a form
ACTION	Specifies the location of a CGI script for a form
METHOD	Specifies how form information transfers to a Web server
<INPUT>	Creates an input item on a form
CHECKED	Automatically selects a radio button or check box
ENCTYPE	Specifies file transfer for form data over the Internet

Tag/Attribute	Description
MAXLENGTH	Specifies the maximum number of characters for a form entry
NAME	Identifies a form item for a server
SIZE	Specifies the form item size
TYPE	Specifies the form item type
VALUE	Identifies a form item
<LABEL>	For labeling form elements
FOR	Specifies which form element the label belongs to
<OPTION>	Creates a menu option for a form
SELECTED	Automatically selects a menu option
VALUE	Identifies a form item for a server
<SELECT>	Creates a menu item on a form
NAME	Identifies a form menu for a server
SIZE	Specifies the number of menu options
<TEXTAREA>	Creates a large text area on a form
COLS	Specifies a width for a large text area
NAME	Identifies a form text area for a server
ROWS	Specifies a height for a large text area
WRAP	Wraps text within a large text area

Style Sheet Tags/Attributes	
Tag/Attribute	**Description**
CLASS	Formats tags as groups
ID	Identifies particular tags for styles
STYLE	Applies a style to a single element
<DIV>	Applies a style to specific areas of a page
CLASS	Identifies a style

continued

Style Sheet Tags/Attributes *(continued)*

Tag/Attribute	Description
<LINK>	Links a Web page to an external style sheet
HREF	Specifies the location of an external style sheet
REL	Specifies a link to a style sheet, whether the sheet is primary or alternative
TYPE	Specifies the format of a style sheet
<STYLE>	Creates a style sheet

Style Sheet Characteristics

Characteristic	Description
background	Specifies a background color or image
background-color	Specifies a background color of an element
border	Specifies a border
border-color	Specifies a border color
border-spacing	Controls the amount of space between borders in a table
border-style	Specifies a border style
border-width	Specifies a line thickness for a border
color	Specifies a color
float	Wraps text
font-family	Specifies a font
font-size	Specifies a font size
font-style	Italicizes text
font-weight	Bolds text
height	Specifies a height
line-height	Specifies line spacing
list-style	Specifies a bullet or number style for lists
margin	Sets a margin
padding	Specifies the space between content and borders
text-align	Aligns text
text-decoration	Adds underlining to text
text-indent	Indents the first line
text-transform	Specifies a text case
width	Specifies a width

Style Sheet Syntax

To construct a style rule:

1 Type a selector, which identifies the element you want to format.

2 Type an opening curly bracket.

3 Type the declaration, which is the formatting property and value.

● If applying more than one declaration, separate the declarations with a semicolon.

4 Type a closing curly bracket.

Note: *For more color names, see the tear-out card at the front of the book.*

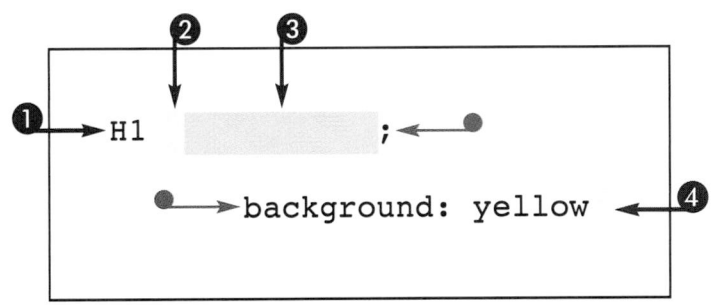

Sixteen Named Colors	
Color	*Name*
Insert black swatch	Black (#000000)
Insert silver swatch	Silver (#C0C0C0)
Insert gray swatch	Gray (#808080)
Insert white swatch	White (#FFFFFF)
Insert maroon swatch	Maroon (#800000)
Insert red swatch	Red (#FF0000)
Insert purple swatch	Purple (#800080)
Insert fuchsia swatch	Fuchsia (#FF00FF)
Insert green swatch	Green (#008000)
Insert lime swatch	Lime (#00FF00)
Insert olive swatch	Olive (#808000)
Insert yellow swatch	Yellow (#FFFF00)
Insert navy swatch	Navy (#000080)
Insert blue swatch	Blue (#0000FF)
Insert teal swatch	Teal (#008080)
Insert aqua swatch	Aqua (#00FFFF)

Index

A

absolute links, 135
active labels, forms, 224
adding
>   alternative text, 253
>   block quotes, 40
>   column labels, 162
>   document declaration, 28–29
>   file upload element, 226–227
>   Java applets, 267
>   keywords, 291
>   line breaks, 36
>   paragraphs, 34
>   scrolling marquee, 268–269
>   tables, 154–155
>   ToolTips, 265
>   to Web pages, 250

adding text
>   about, 32–33
>   change paragraph alignment, 35
>   create bulleted lists, 44–45
>   create definition list, 47
>   create nested lists, 46
>   create numbered lists, 42–43
>   insert blank spaces, 37
>   insert comments, 41
>   insert headings, 39
>   insert preformatted text, 38
>   insert special characters, 48–49

adjusting
>   cell padding and spacing, 158–159
>   cell width and height, 160–161
>   margins, 60

advertising, Web page publishing, 291
alert message box, JavaScript, 255
alignment
>   tables, 182–183
>   text, 89
>   vertical, 101

alternative text
>   adding, 253
>   frames, 195
>   images, 115, 120
>   JavaScript, 253

anchor element, links, 135
area on same page, links, 142–143
attributes, HTML, 11
audio, background, 243
automatically load another Web page, 276–277

B

background audio, 243
background color
>   to cells, 178–179
>   to elements, 103
>   text, 95

background images, 104–105, 130
banner images, 131
blank display, Web page publishing, 289
blank spaces, inserting, 37
block quotes, adding, 40

body, HTML pages, 19
bold text, 52, 82
borders
>   color frames, 192–193
>   formatting text, style sheets, 96–97
>   frames, 192–193
>   images, 128
>   tables, 166–167

broken links, Web page publishing, 289
browsers
>   about, 5, 8
>   create image rollover effect, 258–259
>   view HTML code in browser, 12–13
>   viewing HTML pages, 27

bullet styles, 108–109
bulleted lists, 44–45

C

cable modems, 4
captions, tables, 165
cascading style sheets, 29, 66
case-sensitivity of tags, 21
cells
>   alignment, 170–171
>   padding and spacing, 158–159
>   spanning, 152
>   width and height, 160–161

centering images, 125
CGI scripts, 208–209
check boxes, 206, 216–217
client-side image map, 271
client-side scripts, 247
coding HTML, 6
colors
>   background, 95, 103, 178–179
>   horizontal lines, 63
>   links, 106–107, 148–149
>   text, 58–59, 94

column groups, tables, 174–177
column labels, 162
comments, 41
compression images, 115
confirmation forms, 205
copy source code from another page, 13
copyright text images, 122
CSS file extension, 29, 66

D

data entry forms, 205
data forms, 208
date, JavaScript, 254
declarations, 66
definition list, 47
delivering media files, 232
design, forms, 205
directory path, URLs, 137
display alert message box, JavaScript, 255
display scroll bars, frames, 197
document declaration
>   adding, 28–29
>   HTML pages, 28–29

document header, HTML pages, 19
document type declaration, HTML pages, 18
domain name, Web page publishing, 282
downloadable files, links, 145
downloading images, 113
DSL service, 4

E

editing programs, images, 114
elements
 formatting text, style sheets, 98–99
 forms, 206–207
 HTML, 10
 HTML pages, 18
 tables, 153
e-mail addresses
 links, 146–147
 sending data, 209, 211
embedded files, 233
embedding
 with ActiveX controls, 235
 audio files, 238–239
 Flash movie, 242
 video file, 240–241
entities, HTML, 11
event handlers, 248, 249
extensible style language (XSL), 69
external media files, 233
external style sheets, 67–69

F

file formats, images, 112–113
file upload element, 226–227
filenames, URLs, 137
files
 audio or video links, 236–237
 embedded, 233
 JavaScript, 251
 links to another type, 144–145
 overwrite, Web page publishing, 287
 removing files from Web site, 287
 transfer, 282, 284–286
first HTML pages, 16–31
fonts
 about, 55
 size, 56–57, 85
 style sheets, 86–87
form data, validating, 260–261
formatting text
 about, 50–51, 80–81
 adjust margins, 60
 background color to elements, 103
 background images to elements, 104–105
 bold text, 52, 82
 borders, 96–97
 bullet or number styles, 108–109
 change font size, 56–57, 85
 change fonts, 55, 86–87
 change text color, 58–59
 color to text, 94
 elements, 98–99

horizontal lines, 62–63
indent text, 84
italicize text, 53, 83
kerning, 91
letter spacing, 91
line spacing, 90
link colors, 106–107
margins, 92
padding, 93
page background color, 61
scrolling, 99
text alignment, 89
text background color, 95
text case, 88
underlining text, 54
vertical alignment, 101
width and height of element, 102
wrap text around elements, 100
formatting text, style sheets
 about, 80–81
 background color to elements, 103
 background images to elements, 104–105
 bold text, 82
 borders, 96–97
 bullet or number styles, 108–109
 change font, 86–87
 change font size, 85
 color to text, 94
 elements, 98–99
 indent text, 84
 italicize text, 83
 kerning, 91
 letter spacing, 91
 line spacing, 90
 link colors, 106–107
 margins, 92
 padding, 93
 scrolling, 99
 text alignment, 89
 text background color, 95
 text case, 88
 vertical alignment, 101
 width and height of element, 102
 wrap text around elements, 100
forms
 about, 202–204
 active labels, 224
 add file upload element, 226–227
 CGI scripts, 208–209
 change tab order, 225
 check boxes, 206, 216–217
 confirmation, 205
 creating, 210
 data, 208
 data entry, 205
 design, 205
 elements, 206–207
 group form elements, 228–229
 how they work, 204
 HTML for, 204
 large text area, 214–215

Index

menu list, 220–221
menus, 207
radio buttons, 207, 218–219
reset button, 207, 223
sending data in databases, 209
sending data to e-mail address, 209, 211
submit button, 207, 222
text boxes, 206, 212–213
types, 205
Web servers, 209
frames
about, 186–188
advantages, 189
alternative text, 195
borders, 192–193
creating, 190–191
disadvantages, 189
display scroll bars, 197
framesets, 189
hide scroll bars, 197
inline, 189, 201
margins, 194
nesting, 189
nesting frameset, 200
resizing, 196
target links, 198–199
use, 188
framesets, 189
FTP, 136, 283

G

generic class, 75
GIF file format, 112, 113
group form elements, 228–229

H

headers, tables, 164
headings, 39
height of element, 102
hiding
JavaScript, 252
scroll bars, 197
hierarchical Web sites, 15
home pages, 14
horizontal images, 123
horizontal lines, 62–63
host name, URLs, 137
HTM file extension, 24–25
HTML
about, 6
attributes, 11
code appears, 289
coding, 6
editors, 9
elements, 10
entities, 11
errors, 11
forms, 204
standards, 6
syntax, 10–11
tags, 10, 292–301

values, 11
versions, 7
view code in browser, 12–13
writing, 10
HTML file extension, 24–25
HTML pages
body, 19
creating first, 16–31
document declaration, 28–29
document header, 19
document type declaration, 18
elements, 18
metadata, 19, 30–31
saving, 24–25
starting, 19–23
text wrapping, 23
title, 19
viewing, 26–27
HTML Strict, 29
HTML Transitional, 29
hyperlinks, 5, 134
HyperText Markup Language. *See* HTML

I

ID attribute, style sheets, 79
image map
client-side, 271
create, 270–273
server-side, 271
image rollover effect, JavaScript, 258–259
images
about, 110–111
alternative text, 115, 120
background, 130
background images, adding to elements, 104–105
banner, 131
borders, 128
for bullets, 109
centering, 125
compression, 115
copyright text, 122
downloading, 113
editing programs, 114
file formats, 112–113
horizontally, 123
inserting, 116–117
labels, 121
optimizing, 113
reducing, 114, 117
resolution, 115
space around images, 129
specify size, 118–119
stop text wrap, 127
vertically, 124
wrapping text between, 126
indent text, 84
inheritance, style sheets, 67, 75
inline frames, 189, 201
inserting
background images, 181
blank spaces, 37

comments, 41
date and time, 254
headings, 39
images, 116–117
images in cells, 180
preformatted text, 38
text over image, 264–265
internal style sheets, 67, 72–73
Internet
about, 4
connections, 4
speeds, 4
Internet service provider (ISP), 4
invalid paths, Web page publishing, 288
ISDN connections, 4
italicize text, 53, 83

J

Java applets, 267
JavaScript
about, 244, 246
adding alternative text, 253
adding to Web pages, 250
client-side scripts, 247
create image rollover effect, 258–259
creating file, 251
customize status bar message for links, 257
display alert message box, 255
display pop-up window, 256
event handlers, 248, 249
hiding, 252
how scripts work, 246
insert current date and time, 254
prewritten scripts, 247
script events, 248
scriptable events, 249
server-side scripts, 247
tips, 247
tools, 247
validate form data, 260–261
JPEG file format, 112
JPG file format, 112
JS file extension, 251

K

kerning, 91
keywords, 291

L

labels
columns, 162
images, 121
large text area, forms, 214–215
letter spacing, 91
line breaks, 36
line spacing, 90
linear Web sites, 15
links
about, 5, 132–133
absolute, 135

anchor element, 135
to another file type, 144–145
area on same page, 142–143
to audio or video files, 236–237
change colors, 148–149
colors, 106–107
downloadable files, 145
e-mail addresses, 146–147
to new window, 140–141
other areas on same page, 135
to other site pages, 135, 138–139
to other sites, 291
to other Web pages, 134
preset subjects for e-mail messages, 147
relative, 135
types, 134
underlines, 149
URLs, 136–137
loading Web pages, 276–277
local pages, 8
local style sheets, 78

M

maintain Web site, 283
margins
adjusting, 60
formatting text, style sheets, 92
frames, 194
media files, delivering, 232
media players, 234
menu list, forms, 220–221
menus, forms, 207
metadata
adding, 30–31
HTML pages, 19, 30–31
viewing, 31
missing image files, Web page publishing, 289
modem connections, 4
multimedia elements
about, 232
background audio, 243
delivering media files, 232
embed audio file, 238–239
embed Flash movie, 242
embed video file, 240–241
embed with ActiveX controls, 235
embedded files, 233
external media files, 233
link to audio or video files, 236–237
media players, 234
plug-ins, 234
streaming media files, 233
uses, 232

N

navigation bar, 265
nest table within table, 185
nested lists, 46
nesting frames, 189
nesting frameset, 200
newspaper-style columns, tables, 163

Index

number styles, 108–109
numbered lists, 42–43

O

other areas on same page links, 135
overwrite files, Web page publishing, 287

P

padding, formatting text, 93
page background color, 61
page titles, 291
paragraphs
    adding, 34
    alignment, 35
    style sheets, 77
passwords, text boxes, 212–213
plain-text editors, 9
planning Web sites, 14–15
plug-ins, 234
PNG file format, 112, 113
preformatted text, 38
presentation tables, 153
preset subjects for e-mail messages links, 147
prewritten scripts, 247
publicizing Web sites, 283, 290–291
publishing Web pages, 278–280

R

radio buttons, 207, 218–219
reducing images, 114, 117
relative links, 135
removing files from Web site, 287
reset button, 207, 223
resizing frames, 196
resolution, images, 115
row groups, tables, 174–177

S

saving
    HTML documents, 13
    HTML pages, 24–25
script events, 248
scriptable events, 249
scrolling, 99
scrolling marquee, 268–269
search engines, Web page publishing, 290
sending
    data in databases, 209
    data to e-mail address, 209, 211
server-side image map, 271
server-side scripts, 247
simple text editors, 9
size, tables, 168–169
sounds, 230–231
space around images, 129
span cells across columns and rows, 172–173
special characters, 48–49
specify size, images, 118–119
spider web layout Web sites, 15

standards, HTML, 6
starting HTML pages, 19–23
stop text wrap images, 127
streaming media files, 233
style classes, 67
style sheets
    about, 64–66, 80–81
    background color to elements, 103
    background images to elements, 104–105
    bold text, 82
    borders, 96–97
    bullet or number styles, 108–109
    change font, 86–87
    change font size, 85
    classes, 74–75
    color to text, 94
    comments, 71
    DIV tag, 76–77
    elements, 98–99
    external, 67–69
    ID attribute, 79
    indent text, 84
    inheritance, 67, 75
    internal, 67, 72–73
    italicize text, 83
    kerning, 91
    letter spacing, 91
    line spacing, 90
    link colors, 106–107
    links, 70
    local, 78
    margins, 92
    padding, 93
    paragraphs, 77
    scrolling, 99
    style classes, 67
    text alignment, 89
    text background color, 95
    text case, 88
    vertical alignment, 101
    width and height of element, 102
    wrap text around elements, 100
    writing syntax, 67
submit button, forms, 207, 222
submit sites, Web page publishing, 290
syntax
    errors, 11
    HTML, 10–11
    style sheets, 66

T

tab order, 225
tables
    about, 150–151
    add column labels, 162
    adding, 154–155
    adjust cell padding and spacing, 158–159
    adjust cell width and height, 160–161
    alignment, 182–183
    assign borders, 156–157

background color to cells, 178–179
borders, 166–167
captions, 165
cell alignment, 170–171
cell spanning, 152
column and row groups, 174–177
elements, 153
headers, 164
insert background images, 181
insert images in cells, 180
nest table within table, 185
newspaper-style columns, 163
preparing, 153
presentation, 153
size, 168–169
span cells across columns and rows, 172–173
structure, 152
traditional, 153
wrapping in cells, 184
tags
case-sensitivity, 21
HTML, 10
target links, frames, 198–199
TCP/IP connection, 5
text. *See also* adding text; formatting text
alignment, 89
background color, 95
case, 88
color, 58–59
over image, 264–265
wrapping, 23
text boxes, 206, 212–213
thumbnail images, 274–275
time, JavaScript, 254
title, HTML pages, 19
ToolTips, 265
traditional tables, 153
transfer files
Web page publishing, 282
with WS_FTP, 284–286
troubleshooting, Web page publishing, 288–289
typing errors, 288

U

underlining
links, 149
text, 54
URLs (Uniform Resource Locators), 5, 136–137

V

validate form data, JavaScript, 260–261
values, HTML, 11
vertical alignment, 101
vertical images, 124
videos, 230–231
view code in browser, HTML, 12–13
viewing
HTML pages, 26–27
metadata, 31

W

watermark, 265
Web hosts, 280–281
Web page publishing
about, 278–280
add keywords, 291
advertising, 291
blank display, 289
broken links, 289
domain name, 282
FTP, 283
HTML code appears, 289
invalid paths, 288
linking with other sites, 291
maintain site, 283
missing image files, 289
needs, 280
overwrite files, 287
page titles, 291
publicize site, 283, 290–291
remove files from Web site, 287
search engines, 290
submit sites, 290
transfer files, 282, 284–286
troubleshooting, 288–289
typing errors, 288
Web hosts, 280–281
Web pages
adding to, 250
links, 134, 135, 138–139
loading, 276–277
Web servers, forms, 209
Web sites
design options, 14
hierarchical, 15
linear, 15
planning, 14–15
spider web layout, 15
Web surfing, 5
width of element, 102
windows, links, 140–141
word processing programs, 9
WordPad, text wrapping, 23
World Wide Web, 5
World Wide Web Consortium (W3C), 6
wrapping
in cells, 184
text, 23
text around elements, 100
text between images, 126
writing
HTML, 10
syntax style sheets, 67

X

XHTML, 7, 10
XML (Extensible Markup Language), 7
XSL file extension, 69

Want instruction in other topics?

Check out these

All designed for visual learners—just like you!

Read Less—Learn More®
Visual

Teach Yourself VISUALLY

Teach Yourself VISUALLY

Yoga

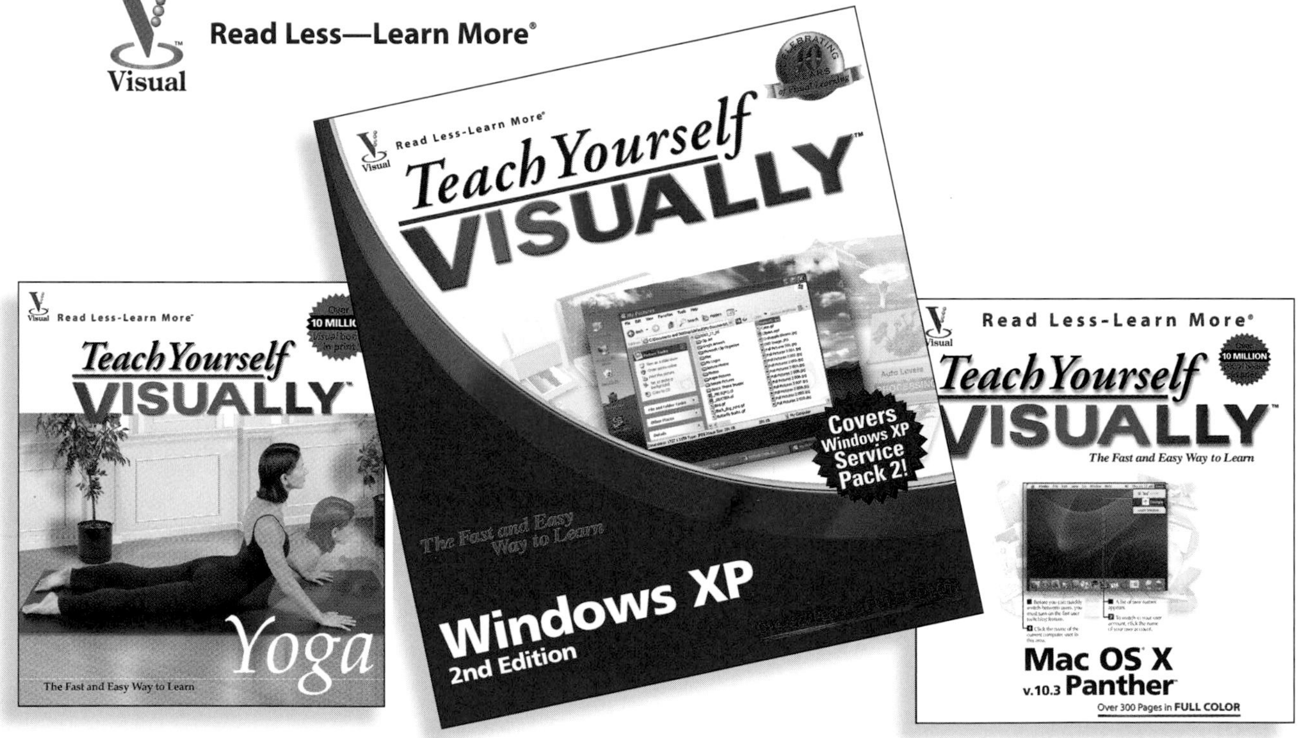

0-7645-2580-8

Covers Windows XP Service Pack 2!

Windows XP
2nd Edition

0-7645-7927-4

Teach Yourself VISUALLY
The Fast and Easy Way to Learn

Mac OS X
v.10.3 Panther
Over 300 Pages in FULL COLOR

0-7645-4393-8

For a complete listing of *Teach Yourself VISUALLY*™ titles and other Visual books, go to wiley.com/go/visualtech

Wiley, the Wiley logo, the Visual logo, Read Less-Learn More, and Teach Yourself Visually are trademarks or registered trademarks of John Wiley & Sons, Inc. and/or its affiliates. All other trademarks are the property of their respective owners.

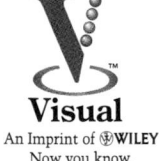

Visual
An Imprint of WILEY
Now you know.